Library of
Davidson College

FINANCIAL RATIO ANALYSIS
An Historical Perspective

This is a volume in the Arno Press collection

THE DEVELOPMENT OF CONTEMPORARY ACCOUNTING THOUGHT

Advisory Editor
Richard P. Brief

Editorial Board
Gary John Previts
Basil S. Yamey
Stephen A. Zeff

*See last pages of this volume
for a complete list of titles.*

FINANCIAL RATIO ANALYSIS
An Historical Perspective

Edited by
James O. Horrigan

With An Introduction

ARNO PRESS
A New York Times Company
New York • 1978

658.15
F491

Publisher's Note: This book has been reproduced from the best available copy.

Editorial Supervision: LUCILLE MAIORCA

Reprint Edition 1978 by Arno Press Inc.

Arrangement and compilation copyright © 1978 by Arno Press Inc.

THE DEVELOPMENT OF CONTEMPORARY ACCOUNTING THOUGHT
ISBN for complete set: 0-405-10891-5
See last pages of this volume for titles.

Manufactured in the United States of America

Library of Congress Cataloging in Publication Data

Main entry under title:

Financial ratio analysis.

   (The Development of contemporary accounting thought)
   Includes bibliographical references.
   1. Ratio analysis--Addresses, essays, lectures.
I. Horrigan, James O. II. Series.
HF5681.R25F56   658.1'513   77-87314
ISBN 0-405-10927-X 80-7576

ACKNOWLEDGMENTS

"The Historical Development of the Use of Ratio in Financial Statement Analysis to 1933" by Isadore Brown was reprinted by permission of The Catholic University of America Press.

"A Short History of Financial Ratio Analysis" by James O. Horrigan, "Limitations of Financial and Operating Ratios" by William Paton, "Appraising the Defensive Position of a Firm" by George H. Sorter and George Benston and "LIFO and Ratio Analysis" by George C. Holdren, from *The Accounting Review*, were reprinted by permission of the American Accounting Association.

"Capitalizing Leases—The Effect on Financial Ratios" by A. Tom Nelson, copyright July 1963 by the American Institute of Certified Public Accountants, Inc., was reprinted by permission of the American Institute of Certified Public Accountants.

"An Examination of the Working Capital Ratio" by F. K. Wright was reprinted by permission of *The Australian Accountant* and the author.

"Accounting Ratios" was reprinted by permission of *Accountancy*.

INTRODUCTION

Financial ratios are a fascinating part of accounting history because they were the first analytical devices used by external readers of accounting statements. Accounting is not an end in itself, and it continues to exist only if the readers of its statements find them useful for some purpose. In that regard, financial ratios were an extremely important artifact because they were the first tools used for making predictions about the future directions of firms.

In a fundamental sense, the development of financial ratios was probably inevitable. Accounting statements themselves report absolute numbers and those numbers only convey information about the size of firms. Big firms have big numbers and small firms have small numbers. Some kind of relative numbers had to be developed if analysts were to make any sense out of accounting data. Therefore, financial ratios really represented the first attempt to measure various underlying relationships that would reveal the true essence of firms.

This anthology presents articles selected from the literature during the initial evolutionary phases of financial ratio analyis, stopping short of the current quantitative era. Ratios emerged in the early part of the 20th century, but their first formal expositions occured during the 1920's. After that initial decade of formal development, the first serious empirical tests of financial ratios were conducted during the 1930's. Those tests, while crude by today's standards, did convincingly establish that financial ratios were very useful for predicting the future conditions of firms. But, oddly enough, those studies seem to have been overlooked for almost two decades. During the post World War II period, financial ratios were either severely criticized or just plain ignored. However, by the early 1960's, a few seminal articles appeared which suggested that we were about to take a renewed look at financial ratios. The stage was being set for an awesome quantitative and theoretical revolution in finance and accounting, and these simple historical artifacts, financial ratios, would play an important role in various sophisticated tests of accounting data. But that is another story for some other time. This anthology samples a long intellectual struggle to make accounting data useful in the absence of rigorous theory and sophisticated mathematical tools.

CONTENTS

I OVERVIEW OF GENERAL HISTORY

Brown, Sister Isadore
THE HISTORICAL DEVELOPMENT OF THE USE OF RATIO IN FINANCIAL STATEMENT ANALYSIS TO 1933 (Reprinted from *The Catholic University of America, Studies in Economics, Abstract Studies,* Vol. No. II) Washington, D. C., 1955

Horrigan, James O.
A SHORT HISTORY OF FINANCIAL RATIO ANALYSIS (Reprinted from *The Accounting Review,* Vol. XLIII, No. 2) Menasha, Wisconsin, April, 1968

II EARLY PROPONENTS OF FINANCIAL RATIO ANALYSIS

Wall, Alexander
STUDY OF CREDIT BAROMETRICS (Reprinted from *Federal Reserve Bulletin,* Vol. 5, No. 3) Washington, D. C., March 1, 1919

Foulke, Roy A.
THREE IMPORTANT BALANCE SHEET RATIOS (Reprinted from *Dun and Bradstreet Monthly Review,* Vol. XLI) New York, August, 1933

Foulke, Roy A.
THREE IMPORTANT INVENTORY RATIOS (Reprinted from *Dun and Bradstreet Monthly Review,* Vol. XLI) New York, December, 1933

Foulke, Roy A.
THREE IMPORTANT SALES RATIOS (Reprinted from *Dun and Bradstreet Monthly Review,* Vol. XLII) New York, May, 1934

Foulke, Roy A.
THREE IMPORTANT NET PROFIT RATIOS (Reprinted from *Dun and Bradstreet Monthly Review,* Vol. XLII) New York, November, 1934

Andersen, Arthur
OPERATING AND BALANCE SHEET RATIOS (Reprinted from *Manufacturing Industries,* Vol. XI, No. 5) New York, May, 1926

Andersen, Arthur
OPERATING AND TURNOVER RATIOS (Reprinted from *Manufacturing Industries,* Vol. XI, No. 6) New York, June, 1926

Bliss, J. H.
THE STORY TOLD BY THE FINANCIAL AND OPERATION STATEMENTS (Reprinted from *Management and Administration,* Vol. VII, No. 1) New York, January, 1924

Bliss, J. H.
THE OPERATING AND FINANCIAL RATIOS CHARACTERISTIC OF INDUSTRIES (Reprinted from *Management and Administration,* Vol. VII, No. 2) New York, February, 1924

III EARLY CRITICS OF FINANCIAL RATIOS

Paton, W[illiam] A.
LIMITATIONS OF FINANCIAL AND OPERATING RATIOS (Reprinted from *The Accounting Review*, Vol. III) Menasha, Wisconsin, September, 1928

Strain, Myron M.
BIBLIOGRAPHY AND ACKNOWLEDGMENTS FOR CHAPTERS IV AND V (Reprinted from *Industrial Balance Sheets: A Study in Business Analysis*) New York, 1929

IV EARLY EMPIRICAL STUDIES OF FINANCIAL RATIOS

Smith, Raymond F. and Arthur H. Winakor
CHANGES IN THE FINANCIAL STRUCTURE OF UNSUCCESSFUL INDUSTRIAL CORPORATIONS (Reprinted from *Bureau of Business Research*, Bulletin No. 51) Urbana, Illinois, 1935

Fitzpatrick, Paul J.
A COMPARISON OF THE RATIOS OF SUCCESSFUL INDUSTRIAL ENTERPRISES WITH THOSE OF FAILED COMPANIES, Washington, D. C., 1932

Merwin, Charles Lewis
PORTENTS OF DISCONTINUANCE (Reprinted from *Financing Small Corporations in Five Manufacturing Industries, 1926-36*) New York, 1942

V ANALYSES OF THE PROBLEMS AND SHORTCOMINGS OF RATIOS

Jackendoff, Nathaniel
THE MULTIPLICITY OF FINANCIAL RATIOS (Reprinted from *A Study of Published Industry Financial and Operating Ratios, Economic and Business Bulletin of the School of Business and Public Administration*, Temple University, Vol. 14, No. 3) Philadelphia, March, 1962

Nelson, A. Tom
CAPITALIZING LEASES—THE EFFECT ON FINANCIAL RATIOS (Reprinted from *The Journal of Accountancy*, Vol. CXVI) New York, July, 1963

Holdren, George C.
LIFO AND RATIO ANALYSIS (Reprinted from *The Accounting Review*, Vol. XXXIX, No. 1) January, 1964

Wright, F. K.
AN EXAMINATION OF THE WORKING CAPITAL RATIO (Reprinted from *The Australian Accountant*, Vol. 26) Melbourne, March, 1956

VI FUTURE THRUSTS: NEW RATIOS AND SYSTEMATIC MODELS

Sorter, G[eorge] H. and George Benston
APPRAISING THE DEFENSIVE POSITION OF A FIRM: The Interval Measure (Reprinted from *The Accounting Review*, Vol. XXXV) October, 1960

ACCOUNTING RATIOS (Reprinted from *Accountancy*, Vol. LXVII) London, July, 1956

OVERVIEW OF GENERAL HISTORY

THE HISTORICAL DEVELOPMENT
OF THE USE OF RATIOS
IN FINANCIAL STATEMENT ANALYSIS
TO 1933

Sister Isadore Brown

THE CATHOLIC UNIVERSITY OF AMERICA
STUDIES IN ECONOMICS
Abstract Studies
Vol. No. 11

The Historical Development of the Use of Ratios in Financial Statement Analysis to 1933

AN ABSTRACT OF A DISSERTATION
SUBMITTED TO THE FACULTY OF THE SCHOOL OF SOCIAL SCIENCE
OF THE CATHOLIC UNIVERSITY OF AMERICA IN PARTIAL
FULFILLMENT OF THE REQUIREMENTS FOR THE
DEGREE OF DOCTOR OF PHILOSOPHY

BY

SISTER ISADORE BROWN, O. S. U., M. A.

Mount Saint Joseph Ursuline Motherhouse
Maple Mount, Kentucky

THE CATHOLIC UNIVERSITY OF AMERICA PRESS
WASHINGTON, D. C.
1955

COPYRIGHT, 1955, BY
THE CATHOLIC UNIVERSITY OF AMERICA PRESS, INC.

PRINTED IN THE UNITED STATES OF AMERICA
BY J. H. FURST COMPANY, BALTIMORE, MARYLAND

PREFACE

Records and accounts were kept originally for purposes of the individual owners of business firms but with the growth of large-scale industry, other groups have become interested in the results of management and the financial status of the enterprise. The collection of adequate information requires not only the receipt of true financial statements but also competent methods of analyzing and interpreting these statements. Various tools have come into existence to fulfill this need during the past seventy years, prominent among them being financial ratios.

The purpose of this study is to trace the historical development of the use of financial ratios in financial statement analysis in the United States in order to ascertain the significance of these tools up to 1933. This year presents a logical point of termination. The deflation of credit, the banking holiday, the Securities Act, and various other factors of national importance led to a reorganization of business, a major readjustment of credit policies, and re-evaluation of accounting practices which well may be considered the beginning of a new era in analysis. Since no previous treatise has been published tracing the origin and development of the use of ratios, the present study will be advantageous because of its historical interest.

To prevent the study's growing beyond proportion, it is restricted to the history of the development of those ratios used by two main groups, namely, industrial and commercial enterprises, and commercial banks. This of necessity eliminates a few interesting facets of ratio history such as that related to the development of financial ratios for public utilities, railroads, mining, investment, and insurance. The study is not intended to be a list of all the individual ratios previously or currently used; neither is it an attempt to make explanatory comments upon the theory underlying each ratio. It is a report of the historical development of the use of ratios, in general, during the early period of financial statement analysis.

The work is organized in six chapters. As sound ratio analysis requires the presentation of reliable statements and scientific analysis was not possible until such time as bookkeepers and accountants furnished the necessary data, the first chapter presents a brief outline of the evolution and construction of financial statements. The second chapter furnishes a résumé of the theory of ratio analysis and stresses the simplicity of ratios and, at the same time, depicts their importance as statistical devices for the intelligent interpretation of financial statements.

The third and fourth chapters show that the history of financial ratios in industry and commercial banking is based on certain features of the credit system peculiar to the early American economy. As the economy progressed, more specific knowledge of a creditor's ability-to-pay was necessary. This led to improved accounting procedures, more informative financial statements, and advanced methods of analyzing these statements. These methods began with comparison of items on the balance sheet, developed into arithmetical computations of proportions between the items, and culminated in the scientific techniques of Alexander Wall, the leading exponent of ratio analysis.

The fifth chapter is an examination of the development of ratio analysis as employed by management and of representative studies applying the principles suggested by the authorities in this field. The last chapter consists of conclusions drawn from the research.

The writer wishes to express her sincere gratitude to her religious superiors for the opportunity of pursuing graduate studies at the Catholic University of America, and to her major professor, Paul J. FitzPatrick, Ph. D., for his expert guidance and gracious encouragement. She also thanks the readers, Henry W. Spiegel, J. U. D., Ph. D., and William J. Ryan, C. P. A., for their careful reading and constructive criticism. It is with wholehearted appreciation that she acknowledges her indebtedness to these and numerous other persons who have assisted her in so many ways.

TABLE OF CONTENTS

	PAGE
PREFACE	v

CHAPTER

I. EVOLUTION OF FINANCIAL STATEMENTS 1
    Early Use of Records
    The Balance Sheet
    The Income Statement
    Retained Income Statement and Supplementary Statements
    The Importance of Financial Statements
    Reliability and Limitations of Financial Statements

II. THE NATURE AND CONCEPT OF RATIOS 5
    Definition and Purpose of Ratio Analysis
    Classification of Ratios
    Characteristic Attributes of Ratios
    Standard Ratios

III. THE EVOLUTION OF RATIO ANALYSIS 8
    Mercantile Credit
    Origin of the Credit Agencies
    Bank Credit
    Bank Statements of Condition
    Borrowers' Statements
    Signed Uniform Statement Blanks
    Credit Departments
    Early Financial Statement Analysis
    Era of Scientific Credit Granting

IV. SCIENTIFIC RATIO ANALYSIS 13
    Recognition of the Need for Certified Statements
    The Current Ratio and the Quick Ratio
    Development of Analytical Analysis
    Credit Barometrics
    Inadequacy of Bank Statements of Condition
    Development of Significant Ratios in Bank Supervision
    Application of Ratios to Interbank Borrowing
    Ratios Employed for Better Bank Management

		PAGE
V.	SCIENTIFIC RATIO ANALYSIS APPLIED TO INDUSTRIAL MANAGEMENT	21

    Expansion of Managerial Activity
    Statistical Data Vital to Better Management
    Wholesale and Retail Trade Studies
    The Establishment of Principles for the Use of Ratios in Management
    The Application of Standard Ratios
    Practical Credit Analysis

VI.	CONCLUSION	26

CHAPTER I

Evolution of Financial Statements

Since the fundamental purpose of the business enterprise is to make a profit, the need for the determination of the results of business ventures has brought about the adoption of various methods of recording data relative to the income and expenses of the enterprise, the assets owned, and the liabilities owed. This necessity for accounting data has been intensified as the business unit developed from the individual household, through feudalism with the manorial system, followed by simple forms of industrialism with private enterprise consisting mainly of the single proprietorship and the partnership, into capitalism where the growth of the corporation has brought about the concentration of capital into colossal consolidations.

Early Use of Records

The first simple business units required no records other than a memorandum entry of receipts and payments but as commerce developed and the wandering merchant began to obtain a more stable position in society, it became necessary to have more adequate records of account. Historians do not set a definite date for the origin of double-entry bookkeeping. It was the result of a slow development through the centuries. Likewise, the development of financial statements has not been easy to trace. There is evidence of the balance sheet as early as the fourteenth century but these early statements were for the proprietor's information only. This private evaluation of ownership remained the predominant purpose for statements well into the twentieth century.

The Balance Sheet

For many years the balance sheet was the primary financial statement. The form, which includes both the arrangement and the classification of the various items, has not been uniform throughout the years. The account form and the report form are both in use in the United States. The classification of the balance-sheet items has developed from a variety of accounting ideas. The early balance sheet in the United States was, of necessity, the result of much personal opinion on the part of the accountants. This led to varied subdivisions and dissimilar classifications of items. Classification has become more uniform since the 1930's, however.

The content of the balance sheet was in the beginning, and still is, one of the major accounting problems. This comprises not only the inclusion of all relevant items, but the more perplexing aspect of valuation of the assets and liabilities included in the balance sheet. The valuation of the liabilities does not present such a difficult problem as the valuation of the assets. The inventory and fixed assets, due to fluctuation of the price level, are two important areas of difficulty.

The Income Statement

The income statement, although developed much earlier, was not generally submitted for public interpretation until the twentieth century. With this statement, as with the early balance sheet, the individual accountant's ideas brought about a difference in form and content. Even in the present era, the content of the income statement depends to a great extent upon the choice of form. Likewise, the form and arrangement may vary in accordance with the purpose of the statement and the nature of the business.

Retained Income Statement and Supplementary Statements

The use of the retained income statement and supplementary statements is of more recent origin. The form and content of the retained income statement is dependent upon the accountant's acceptance of the clean surplus theory or the current operating concept of net income. The supplementary statements have been developed to support the financial statements or for some specific purpose. As each is designed for a definite purpose, its importance depends upon the extent to which it fulfills that purpose. These statements, because of their later development, played no part in the early history of financial statement analysis.

The Importance of Financial Statements

The importance of financial statements can be estimated from the effort and study devoted to the subject during the past fifty years. Leading associations in the business world, professional educators, regulatory bodies, and corporate management have united to bring about improvement in the construction and usefulness of financial statements. An attempt has been made to educate business men, the government, and the public to a proper attitude toward, and interpretation of the figures each presents in his statement, as well as, to a method of understanding and interpreting the statements of those with whom each deals.

The shift of emphasis from the balance sheet to the income statement has been one of the notable changes of recent years. This transfer of importance was the result of increased attention to earning power due to the growth of corporations and stockholders' interest. A knowledge of the net worth was no longer considered adequate information for forming intelligent judgments.

Reliability and Limitations of Financial Statements

The extent to which financial statements may be relied upon is an important factor in their analysis. In a bulletin prepared in 1936, *Examination of Financial Statements by Independent Public Accountants*, the American Institute of Accountants pointed out that financial statements reflect a combination of recorded facts, accounting conventions, and personal judgments. As the judgments and conventions applied affect them materially, the reliability of financial statements depends upon the competence and integrity of the persons responsible for these important decisions.

Most statements are those of a " going concern." therefore, they are interim reports requiring accounting estimates in some instances where exact amounts are not available. In many cases the extent of the accuracy of these estimates will be the degree to which a careful analysis will prove correct. As the assets reflect historical costs rather than current values, the statements may not serve for comparative purposes without adjustment. Here, again, estimates and personal opinion play a part and will often obstruct accuracy.

There are some factors which affect the financial conditions and the operating results of business that cannot be expressed in dollar values. They will not be evident on the statement but they will have a definite effect on the financial condition of the firm. Ability of management, technological changes, shifting taxes, as well as other social and economic circumstances, are such factors and must be taken into consideration in the analysis of the financial statements submitted by an enterprise.

CHAPTER II

The Nature and Concept of Ratios

Definition and Purpose of Ratio Analysis

The analysis of financial statements is the compilation and study of relationships and trends. The statements are separated into component parts and each part is studied in relation to relevant items and in relation to the whole. Ratios, as tools of analysis, are measures of these relations. These measures, expressed as ratios, rates, or percentages, expedite comparison and reduce groups of figures to a form more readily comprehended and more easily retained.

Thus ratio analysis facilitates the determination of the financial position and the results of operations of the firm. Such information is essential for stockholders, investors, management, credit grantors, and the government.

Classification of Ratios

Various classifications of ratios have been advocated. Probably the most widely used classification is the division of ratios into two groups, financial and operating. The financial ratios are devised to reflect the efficiency with which capital needs are financed. The operating ratios are planned to manifest the efficiency with which the capital has been used. A second classification; static, velocity, and efficiency ratios, is also used and is similar to the plan of grouping the ratios into those calculated from balance-sheet items, those computed from income-statement items, and those derived from figures involving both statements. Another division is that of horizontal and vertical. The former being ratios of items in a series of statements to similar items in a base period statement, and the latter, the ratios of items in a statement to each other.

An examination of the various categories into which ratios have been separated discloses adequate similarity to warrant the opinion that elaborate classification appears to serve no definite purpose.

Characteristic Attributes of Ratios

A ratio, to be a logical instrument for measuring numerical relation, must be a fraction containing, as numerator and denominator, items which have an inherent and comparable relationship to each other. Ratios are statistical tools which, like other statistical devices, must be used within the range of their efficiency to prevent misuse. These tools aid the focusing of judgments in the interpretation of the dynamic aspects of financial activity. Because ratios are summary statistical data, it is expedient that the analyst take into consideration the possible changes that may be concealed in summarized data and the resultant change in computation due to the alteration of two summarized economic variables. A knowledge of the original data will aid in overcoming this limitation and in making a correct interpretation.

The calculation of a few basic ratios usually is sufficient to focus attention on the specific relationships which need to be investigated. One ratio cannot satisfy as an inflexible criterion and the use of a long list of ratios, many of which will have little if any significance, serve to promote obscurity rather than clarity. It is the responsibility of the analyst to study the purpose of the analysis and the type of industry and then determine the logical ratios to be used to obtain the information necessary for the desired level of performance.

Standard Ratios

To determine the satisfactory or unsatisfactory condition of an enterprise, a standard of comparison must be available. The best standard ratio comparison is the ratios of carefully selected competitors whose operations and economic conditions are similar. Complete comparability between firms is impossible but the standard ratio is not intended as an ideal condition that must be paralleled. The standard ratio is rather an average showing proportions existing in various industries at a given time, or during a specific period of time, which can be used to show a similarity or dissimilarity in standards of performance. This serves to set the analyst upon a trend of mental processes which should terminate in detailed investigation of differences in his firm that vary too widely from the average.

The comparison of ratios for successive periods is useful for measuring the trend of the enterprise and it supplies objective evidence of any disturbance of the financial structure or operations that deviate from the average. The ratio of itself, however, does not supply the solution to a problem. It can only be considered a symptom and this symptom is only as accurate as the figures from which it has been drawn. For this reason business had to meet the demand for more accurate financial statements before an effective ratio method of financial statement analysis could come into existence.

A counter method resulting from criticism of ratios was the trend percentage method presented by Stephen Gilman in 1925. This method applies statistical index numbers to various items of successive financial statements to establish a trend. Thus increases or decreases may be detected and related trends may be compared and interpreted for favorable or unfavorable tendencies.

CHAPTER III

The Evolution of Ratio Analysis

Mercantile Credit

The vast geographical territory and the lack of transportation and communication facilities in the early period of the commercial history of the United States made the use of long-term credit imperative. Letters of reference and personal acquaintance had formed the basis for granting credit at the beginning of this economic growth but soon neither of these methods was adequate. The severity of the panic of 1837 was thought to be due in part to this inability to secure prompt and accurate credit information.

The realization of this situation gave credit investigation a new importance and credit policies were revised. The credit period was reduced from twelve months to six months or less and business men in the East began to cooperate in the dissemination of credit information. This brought the period of the traveling agents who were employed to obtain and to forward to their employers information regarding the solvency and business characteristics of the merchants in the distant settlements.

Origin of the Credit Agencies

The unique system of the credit agency grew up to meet the distinctive needs of the American economy. The first credit agency was begun by Lewis Tappan in 1841 when he began selling the credit information he had gathered through the years previous to the failure of his firm. This was the beginning of the credit agency now known as Dun & Bradstreet, Inc.

This agency was followed within a relatively short period by similar ones established in the commercial centers throughout the country. Their purpose was to provide more adequate financial information for mercantile creditors.

Bank Credit

In the early colonial settlements the wealthy merchants or local capitalists performed the banking functions for the community. Credit was granted on personal knowledge of the debtor's ability-to-pay. After the organization of the early banks, merchants began to settle their merchandise accounts with notes and these notes were discounted at the banks. Thus mercantile credit transactions gave rise to the great bulk of banking credit while banking credit made possible increased mercantile credit.

Bank Statements of Condition

The requirement of statements of condition is as old as the first national bank. The actual beginning of the use of statements of condition for the control of national banks, however, may be considered as dating from the National Currency Act of 1863.

The first statements did not fulfill the purpose for which they were intended as window dressing was the general practice. This difficulty was remedied by a revision of the law through which the Comptroller was permitted to call for a statement as of a previous date with no notice of the date to be used before the Comptroller made the call.

A revision of the Act in 1869 required that specific returns be made of the dividends and net earnings of the national banks after the declaration of each dividend. It was in the analysis of these returns that John J. Knox, then Comptroller of the Currency, first used ratios in his annual report to Congress in 1872.

Borrowers' Statements

The growth of credit, due largely to the industrial expansion following the Civil War, continued until the panic of 1873 rocked the financial structure of the Nation. The reconstruction of credit policies which followed this period led to a wider use of borrowers' statements. The New York City banks began to discount single-name paper and the practice grew because selling commercial paper became an effective means of supplying credit by drawing idle funds from sections where funds were plentiful and at the same time equalizing the interest rates.

Sometime within the 1870's the Mercantile Agency prepared a property statement and asked business firms to submit property statement data to be used in the Agency's distribution of credit information. After the note brokers began buying paper outright in 1879, they too began a more extensive investigation of credit rating which led to their asking for sellers' statements.

Signed Uniform Statement Blanks

The growth of the economy and the organization of associations by bankers, professional men, and business men were accompanied by a further tendency toward improvement of credit methods. Under the stimulating influence of James Graham Cannon, the New York State Bankers Association adopted a uniform statement blank in 1895. These were to be written statements of assets and liabilities signed by the borrowers. A similar uniform statement was adopted three years later by the American Bankers Association. The statements were prepared but competition and fear of offending customers proved an obstruction to their efficient use.

Some groups opposed the uniform statement but advocated the signed statement. This use of signed statements was an innovation in credit methods which was not to become general practice for many years.

Credit Departments

The use and analysis of financial statements were accentuated by the organization of systematic credit departments. These credit departments were set up by the larger mercantile houses before they were adopted by banks and brokerage firms. James Graham Cannon, who was considered the leader in the development of commercial credits and who later became president of the Fourth National Bank of New York, was instrumental in the establishment of the first bank credit departments in the early 1890's.

It was the analysts in these credit departments who began to tabulate statements in columns in order to make comparisons of dollar figures over a period of years. The use of comparative statements was practiced more generally by bank credit departments than by the mercantile credit departments.

Early Financial Statement Analysis

The use of financial statements was in an embryonic stage prior to 1900 and the literature on the subject was proportionately meager. Peter R. Earling, a credit man of Chicago, may well be regarded as the pioneer in financial statement analysis literature. Earling's treatise, *Whom to Trust: A Practical Treatise on Mercantile Credits,* was an outgrowth of requests from business friends for an account of his methods of credit granting. The author claimed no new system but simply gave his experiences and his conclusions.

Prior to, and concurrent with, Earling's ideas. the amount of credit to be granted was estimated from the statement submitted by the borrower but the analysis of the statement appears to have gone no further than a careful reading of the figures and an investigation as to their accuracy. Earling's work illustrates the approach to a more analytical method. He determined asset valuation; he recognized the variation in the financial data of diverse industries; and he expressed relationship, or proportion, between the assets, the liabilities, and the net worth.

Era of Scientific Credit Granting

The science of credit granting was summaried and set forth by James Graham Cannon in a paper presented to the New Jersey Bankers Association in 1905. The cornerstone of credit science, according to Cannon, was the borrower's statement. The superstructure of credit science was the credit department. The most important feature, however, was the interpretation of the statement. An unanalyzed statement to Cannon was worse than no statement and skill in reading between the lines was a necessary part of the credit man's training.

Cannon summarized the following principles for credit science: the reduction of losses, the elimination of disproportionate risks, the conservation of worthy interests, and the combating of dishonesty and incompetence. The mechanism for carrying out the principles was made up of the statement and the credit department. The guiding rules were: quick assets should be the only basis for loans, fixed assets should be considered only an unknown support to the quick assets, and the debt limit was not to exceed fifty per cent of the borrowers' quick assets.

After presenting the principles and rules for scientific credit granting, Cannon made a prediction regarding future credit development. He said it would be in the direction of accuracy. He also predicted the requirement of joint certification of financial statements by a certified public accountant and an engineer. This would be followed by a searching analysis of the statement with a study of each individual concern taking the place of the hard and fast fifty per cent rule.

The most interesting section of Cannon's paper was his presentation of a study of business based on bank credits in 1905. The author averaged and analyzed a set of "typical balance sheets" for four groups of borrowers. In this analysis quick and fixed assets were expressed in percentages of total assets. The liabilities and net worth were given in percentages of total assets. The liabilities also were expressed as a percentage of quick assets. The relative proportion of quick assets to total assets and net worth to total assets were compared for each group of borrowers. Likewise, the gross sales per $1 of quick assets and gross sales per $1 of total assets were computed and the results compared for the four groups of borrowers.

To prove that a uniform credit test would fail even when applied to branches of the same line of business, Cannon chose fourteen manufacturing industries from the Census Report of 1900 and computed an average proportion of working capital to total capital for all concerns listed under the fourteen headings. These averages fluctuated from 37 to 76 per cent.

Cannon's study opened a wide field for use of percentages and proportion in the analysis of financial statements. Some credit men began to study the idea of a more scientific method for eliminating credit loss through financial statement analysis but, as the submission of financial statements was not yet the generally accepted custom, the practice of analysis by the ratio method was restricted.

CHAPTER IV

Scientific Ratio Analysis

Recognition of the Need for Certified Statements

The more far-sighted business men began to realize the exactions being made upon the credit system of the Nation and in the first ten years of the present century they became more disposed toward the presentation of financial statements. The statements prepared were not always proof of the true financial condition of the firm, however, and this fact brought about a demand for statements certified by reputable public accountants. The recommendation came in 1908 from the Committee on Credit Information of the American Bankers Association. A survey made by the American Association of Public Accountants in 1913 showed a representative number of bankers favored the idea but fear of offending customers and losing business was still too strong to permit effective enforcement of such a regulation.

The Current Ratio and the Quick Ratio

Quantitative analysis developed slowly during the years prior to World War I. The current ratio, or fifty per cent credit rule, was often refined by the credit analysts to the quick ratio, or the percentage of current liabilities to current assets not including inventories. These men's opinions were indefinite regarding the acceptable proportion between the items of both the current ratio and the quick ratio for the separate industries. Despite this diversity of opinion, credit men for a number of years based the decision for granting credit almost entirely on this test of ability-to-pay. Because of the limitations of these two ratios, analysts gradually developed other ratios, such as net worth to debt, sales to merchandise, etc., in order to obtain a more comprehensive picture of the financial operations of the enterprise.

Development of Analytical Analysis

An important improvement in early financial statement analysis was the recognition of the "going concern" value of the business. Assets were no longer scaled down to liquidation values. The new idea was to be more concerned with the continuance of the business and how it would perform in the future. The older method of granting credit on the personal qualifications of the borrower having been replaced by the analysis of the borrower's statement, the theory was carried to the extreme by a few credit men who wished to eliminate completely all elements from analysis except a cold, critical judgment of the statement figures. Most analysts, however, favored basing their credit estimate on the "three C's," character, capacity, and capital.

An item-by-item study of the financial statement remained the customary method of analysis up to the end of the first two decades of the twentieth century. Nevertheless, numerous individuals advocated the use of percentages in statement analysis. Some analysts pointed out the advantages of certain relationships in which the proportion of sales and operating data were used to determine earning power. A few even indicated the necessity for determining a standard for the various industries. This latter idea was impeded by the recognition that a general knowledge of terms of sale, customs, and economic conditions would be necessary to develop such a measure of efficiency.

Thus as the economy developed, financial statement analysis developed, but the progressive analysts were the relatively few who were able to obtain the necessary financial statements to make such computations. The earlier advocates of ratios did not attempt to present them as a systematic method of analysis. It was not until 1919 when Alexander Wall, Secretary-Treasurer of the Robert Morris Associates, prepared a study for the Board of Governors of the Federal Reserve System, that anyone presented a plan for crystallizing the use of ratios into a scientific method of financial statement analysis.

Credit Barometrics.

Alexander Wall began his study of the ratio method of statement analysis in 1912 and over a period of years determined the eight ratios he desired to utilize in his interpretation of financial statements. By applying these ratios to a large number of comparable cases, Wall established the norm or standard for each ratio in particular groups of firms. This "credit barometric" represented, under the theory of the law of averages, a normal point of concentration for the various ratios. This could not be considered an *ideal* figure, however.

Continuing his study, Wall realized that the financial statement data would not be sufficiently significant unless it were divided according to industry and then further broken down into geographical sections for the various industries. The first study of this type, "Study of Credit Barometrics," was made for the Board of Governors of the Federal Reserve System and published in the *Federal Reserve Bulletin* for March, 1919. The article outlined the author's ratio method of analysis and exhibited thirty charts prepared from 981 statements obtained from commercial paper brokers.

In 1921 Wall began his preparation of the weighted ratio index. This energetic analyst devised an ingenious method for reducing the various movements of the several ratios so that the net results of the movements could be expressed in a single index number, influenced but not controlled by any figure. The ratios, arbitrarily weighted to express their relative importance, were related, one set of data to another, expressed in percentages, added together, and divided by the number of values.

The Robert Morris Associates supported Wall's dynamic efforts to spread the principles of scientific ratio analysis. Proof of their success is evident from the volume of discussion in the accounting, banking administration, and credits literature of the 1920's. The method was widely accepted, even to the point of exaggeration in some instances.

The method was not without its critics, however. The principal objections raised by these critics were: the complexity of the method, the variability of the factors involved, and the difficulty of obtaining a sufficient number of comparable financial statements for calculating a meaningful mode or average.

Inadequacy of Bank Statements of Condition

The amount of data available and the manner in which they are presented control the facility and thoroughness of a financial statement analysis. For years the financial statements published by banks were not adequate for extensive analysis because of a lack of significant classification and clarity of expression. The early form of statement required by the Comptroller of the Currency remained the accepted form. This form, while considered adequate for supervisory purposes, was far from a classification of items or disclosure of facts that would permit interpretation of the status of the bank. The influence of tradition and custom gave impetus to the retention of obsolete arrangement and terminology in bank statements of condition.

Development of Significant Ratios in Bank Supervision

The primary application of percentages to bank statements appears to have been made by the Comptrollers of the Currency in their annual reports to Congress on the financial condition of national banks. They utilize these statistical devices to prepare parts of the data in a more concise form.

John J. Knox presented in his annual report to Congress in 1872 the returns of dividends and earnings of national banks in the form of statistical tables in which he showed the ratios of dividends to capital, dividends to capital and surplus, and earnings to capital and surplus from March 1, 1869 to September 1, 1872.

William B. Ridgely added to the number of percentages used in the annual reports by including in 1901 percentages of loans and discounts, United States bonds, and lawful money to aggregate resources, also capital, surplus and profits, and individual deposits to total liabilities. In 1906 he began computing capital to individual deposits, capital to loans, capital and surplus and other profits to individual deposits, and lawful money held to individual deposits.

John Skelton Williams, in a general résumé of bank conditions from 1903 to 1914 increased the list of ratios by adding lawful money to all deposits and lawful money to loans and discounts, and the percentage of gross earnings to total investments.

Pierre Jay, Chairman and Federal Reserve Agent for District No. 2, New York, in his report of the first year of operation of the Federal Reserve Bank of New York, made an interesting statistical analysis. He computed the relations of deposits, receipts from exchange, net earnings, dividends paid, and eligible paper held to total capital and total resources of the investments. He calculated the percentage of the total resources invested in loans and discounts, in bonds and securities other than United States bonds, and in eligible paper. He also separated demand and time deposits and computed the percentage of total deposits to demand deposits and total deposits to time deposits, as well as, the percentage of capital, surplus, and undivided profits to demand and time deposits. In addition the Agent presented gross receipts from exchange, net earnings, and dividends in relation to both total capital and total resources.

Application of Ratios to Interbank Borrowing

Banking literature prior to 1924 provides scant proof of ratios having been used extensively in bank statement analysis for interbank borrowing. Bankers were analyzing bank statements of condition but simply as an item-by-item process with special attention to legal reserves and loan restrictions.

A paying teller of one national bank, J. B. Newton, gave an explanation of the method of analyzing a bank statement of condition in 1908. His explanation was an item-by-item analysis of the various accounts on the statement. The only reference to proportion of items was in connection with surplus and loans. The larger the surplus in proportion to the capital the stronger the bank was considered. Loans were too varied to analyze except they were to be examined to make certain there was not too large a volume in proportion to capital, surplus, and deposits.

Harold G. Moulton gave no intimation of the use of quantitative tests for judging the financial standing of the bank in his explanation of bank statement analysis in 1917. His analysis was a qualitative examination of the nature and inherent soundness of the items of the statement of condition.

Henry Parker Willis and George William Edwards set out the

tests that were applied in analyzing the bank statement of condition by 1922. The first or primary test was to consider the ratio of deposits to the capital, surplus, and undivided profits. This was to be supplemented by the ratio of loans to deposits. In studying the character of the assets, attention was to be given to the amount of fixed assets in proportion to the volume of the bank's business and its capital.

In 1924 the credit editor of *The Bankers Magazine* prepared a pamphlet, *How to Analyze a Bank's Statement*, in which he applied ratios, already in use for supervisory purposes, to the bank statement of condition for the purpose of establishing standards to evaluate the financial strength of the bank. The choice of nine ratios pointed out the author's idea of the items of the statement that should be compared and the essential features that would normally indicate sound or unsound conditions. The pamphlet was often quoted and served as an inspiration for further study along this line.

In 1929 James B. Trant prepared a study of the 7,676 national banks reporting to the Comptroller of the Currency for October 3, 1928 from which he developed standards by which the national banks could be judged. The author grouped the statements according to the developed and undeveloped sections of the country, as well as, the agricultural, industrial, and financial centers. Trant carried the analysis beyond the balance sheet items and used the net earnings to net worth ratio which he interpreted by means of ratios of fluctuations in gross earnings, operating expenses, net income from operations, recoveries, losses and depreciation, and net income to net worth, to total deposits, and to total investment.

Ratios Employed for Better Bank Management

The great losses sustained in 1920-1921 caused bankers and their associations to become more interested in banking costs and better banking practices. H. N. Stronck and Company began to study the trend of earning power of banks from the analysis of income and expense items of banks. The company translated the income and expense figures of the national banks into percentages of gross income. These percentages were arranged according to amount of loans and investments; thus showing the trend of the disposition of each income dollar in the various size banks. This information was published in chart form along with the ratios of net profit and dividends paid to capital, surplus, and undivided profits for each category. These charts were published yearly and distributed to thousands of banks.

The Federal Reserve Bank of Boston was the first Federal Reserve Bank to submit an annual compilation of operating ratios for their member banks to the Board of Governors of the Federal Reserve System. The summary, covering the calendar year 1921, contained the operating ratio and the ratios of eight expense items to net loans and investments, giving the high, low, and average for 433 member banks. The Federal Reserve Bank of New York was the second to take up the practice of submitting this annual report of operating ratios of member banks. It first reported for the year 1923.

The Board of Governors of the Federal Reserve System manifested its interest in ratios in 1924 by publishing a series of articles in the *Federal Reserve Bulletin* in which they made use of ratios to analyze member bank earnings, expenses, and dividends. Although the *Bulletin* made no further mention of ratios until 1926, an article in the June issue of that year leads to the conclusion that they were being prepared regularly for member banks' costs and earnings.

Educators also made their contribution. In 1928 Horace Secrist prepared a study to discover, measure, and compare the nature and degree of consistency of ratios from time to time and from district to district. It was an analysis of the variability of a selected number of ratios. His *Banking Ratios*, published two year later, was a study of the national banks, particularly in the Twelfth Federal Reserve District, to determine and to measure the outcome of bank operations by means of ratios, and thus to supply standards by which bankers could judge their past policies and determine those of the future.

An extensive survey of bank operating ratios was carried out in 1929 by a Committee on Bank Budgets of the Clearing House Section of the American Bankers Association. This study resulted in the presentation of a group of comparative operating ratios based on capital and deposits rather than on gross income. Thus the size of the banks, as well as the composition of deposits, had to be taken into consideration. The survey revealed that one difficulty with the use of comparative ratios at this time was the lack of uniformity in accounting systems within banking institutions. The survey presented sources of profit, amount of interest paid, cost of deposits, range of salaries, and other operating data which heretofore had never been made public by banking authorities.

CHAPTER V

SCIENTIFIC RATIO ANALYSIS APPLIED TO INDUSTRIAL MANAGEMENT

Expansion of Managerial Activity

In the first decade of the twentieth century industry increased its interest in things scientific. Out of this influence grew scientific research, scientific management, cost accounting, and improved accounting systems. In conjunction with other developments, accountants and engineers recognized the need for a study of the relationship between income and expenses. Those enterprises which kept records of income and expenses found it advantageous to determine the relation of the individual expense items to total expense and to compare the per cent of profit over a period of years.

Rent was considered an important item of expense and was the topic of much discussion. Opinion varied as to the ratio rent should have to the total expense. Most business men determined the ratio arbitrarily. One business man, F. H. McAdow of Chicago, arrived at an average ratio of four per cent by means of an analysis of certain financial statements in his credit files. A second business man of Chicago, Samuel J. Kline, advocated a ratio of rent to gross profits.

Not all firms gathered sufficient data to form an intelligent estimate but cost accounting was being introduced into the larger firms, therefore, these were equipped to compare expense of operation with earnings and to study the percentage maintained between the two. In general, however, the smaller firms, and even a number of the larger ones, kept inadequate records.

Statistical Data Vital to Better Management

Prior to World War I, the demand for statistical data was practically nonexistent except in the field of governmental research. Economists and statisticians were awakening to the lack of essential economic statistics but it was not until immediately following the war that statistical data become an essential factor to so many business men. During these months of readjustment it became evident that business men would have to know the results of their activity in each period if they were to compete successfully in the future. What methods and forms would be required to meet the need was of interest to both individual managers and business associations.

The Illinois Manufacturers' Costs Association made a study of such requirements in 1921. Along with other recommendations, the committee suggested the form of statements to be used. It also presented fourteen factors to be considered in analyzing the financial statements. These fourteen points dealt with the interrelationships of balance-sheet and profit-and-loss items and made use of percentages and ratios in several points.

The Boston Chamber of Commerce organized a Bureau of Commercial and Industrial Affairs to promote better management methods in the Boston industries and in the anticipation of bringing additional industries to Boston. This Bureau set up a Committee on Industrial Accounting and Executive Reports which issued, in 1922, a report on analyzing and defining financial statements. The Committee presented the ratios which they regarded as an index of the financial condition and the general financial policy of a company. Four balance sheet ratios were chosen as the index of the financial condition and five operating ratios were selected as the index of the general financial policy of a company.

Wholesale and Retail Trade Studies

Trade associations, retail groups, and bureaus of business research, such as Harvard, Northwestern, and others, engaged in the study of financial statements of wholesale and retail firms for the purpose of determining percentages which might be used for a more efficient analysis of wholesale and retail operations. This resulted in the compilation of the data in the form known as "trade studies."

Some of these studies were ratio studies utilizing the ratios of balance-sheet items, income-statement items, or a combination of both. These trade studies were instrumental in bringing about a realization of the need for scientific analysis of financial statement data in these areas.

The Establishment of Principles for the Use of Ratios in Management

James Harris Bliss established his position as pioneer in the declaration of principles for the use of ratios in management with the first of his two books *Financial and Operating Ratios in Management*. Bliss made no claims to the originating of any ratios. His major objectives were to emphasize the importance of the use of financial statistics to management and to illustrate methods for deriving information and value out of this use.

Bliss divided his book into two parts. Part One contains the measures of efficiency, which the author uses for judging the status of the business, the method of computation, and the effect of each ratio on the general problem. These ratios, or yardsticks, include measures of earnings, measures of costs and expenses, turnovers, and financial relationships. Bliss maintains that there are more or less normal relations which must exist within a business if it is to be profitable. By applying the measures of efficiency the manager can determine what relations are out of proportion and corrective executive action can be taken.

Part Two of Bliss' book is the development of a survey to illustrate the author's principles and to determine standard ratios and turnovers for the mining, oil, merchandising, and manufacturing industries. The construction of the standard ratios was based on such a small number of firms the author's standards proved to be of less value than his illustration of the principles. Critics, on the whole, consider Bliss' contribution to the literature of analysis of genuine value.

The Application of Standard Ratios

Accountants, generally, did not devote much effort to the analysis and interpretation of data as early as the 1920's. The business men, however, began to be seriously interested in analyzing their industry or firm. Attempts were made to ascertain at what degree of normalcy the concern was operating, and in which phase of activity the firm was above or below normal. W. H. Justin and Henry Post Dutton were two advocates of Bliss' method of analysis who conducted such surveys. Justin surveyed the flour-milling industry and Dutton added data of the postwar years to the study Bliss had presented in his book in 1923.

Roy Anderson Foulke, working independently of Bliss and Wall's methods, made a study of the financial statements of commercial paper brokers in 1925 that resulted in his computation of thirteen financial ratios for twenty-nine different industries, each industry being represented by a number of firms ranging from twenty to two hundred sixteen. This series of thirteen ratios formed the basis for the author's fourteen ratios which are at present compiled annually in a series designated the " fourteen important ratios."

Practical Credit Analysis

Along with the theoretical method of ratio analysis there arose a movement for a more practical approach to the application of ratios. A study made by the School of Commerce and Business Administration of the University of Southern California was for the purpose, in part, of determining if a ratio analysis based on Bliss and Wall's methods was practical from the point of view of credit men, investors, and business executives. The study brought out the difficulty in securing adequate information to conduct a ratio analysis and the fact that an unequivocal study of the various ratios necessitated a study in conjunction with the business cycle.

The Manager of the Statistical Department of a trust company in Providence, Rhode Island won second prize in *The Bankers Magazine* contest in 1927 with the presentation of his system of practical application of the ratio method. The author claimed to have been using the method for three years and that it had been developed in a New York City trust company's credit department.

Eugene S. Benjamin, a business man who had served a number of years as credit consultant and trade adviser with the Irving Trust Company of New York, presented his practical method in 1933. Benjamin's book *Practical Credit Analysis* was intended to supply credit men, already well-grounded in credit fundamentals, with a technique of analysis which would serve as a practical adjunct to their knowledge. The author emphasized that statement analysis and credit analysis are not synonymous. He claimed that the statement analysis ratios had too limited a coverage to supply the necessary information for a proper conclusion.

Benjamin advocated a series of ratios, six primary and six supplementary, for testing the ability of the debtor to meet his payments out of the current assets of the business. He gave explicit directions for the preparation of the statement before making the analysis and presented graphic examples of how to compile and use the trade standards. As he intended his system to be practical and to assist the business man to evaluate his own statements, he wrote with this goal in mind.

Benjamin's *Practical Credit Analysis* was really the last ratio method to be presented because by 1933 the drastic readjustments necessary after the economic collapse of the early 1930's were heralding a new era in record keeping and in financial statement structure. This improvement in the form and content of financial statements resulted in a new prospect for ratios and standards.

CHAPTER VI

CONCLUSION

Ratios as tools of analysis are measures of the relation between two relevant items. When used as tools of financial statement analysis, ratios are effective only if the items on the financial statements are accurate and if the analyst has the ability to choose the appropriate ratio to fulfill the purpose for which the analysis is being conducted. The development of the use of ratios in financial statement analysis parallels the increased demand for statements.

As the national economy expanded, increased demands were made upon accountants for improved records and more intelligible presentation of financial and operating data. The early period of individual proprietorships yielded to the rise of the corporation. The result of operations was then no longer a matter of individual interest. Stockholders were entitled to the knowledge of how successfully their capital was being utilized.

Every major event, such as the National Bank Act of 1863, the Civil War, the increased network of railroads, the improved methods of communication, the depressions of 1873, 1893, and 1907, left its imprint upon the credit system of the country. When the business man no longer had personal contact with the individuals who sought his merchandise, credit rating firms sprang up to fill the need. With the rapid growth of trade and the general use of credit, it was expedient that a quicker method of analyzing credit risks be formulated. The result was the development of the credit department in large business firms and commercial banks. These credit departments requested information from borrowers in the form of property statements, or balance sheets, but many firms were unwilling to supply the information and many more were unable to supply the statement because of insufficient data. The information presented in the first decade of the twentieth century often proved a gross over- or under-statement. This inaccuracy led to a demand for the certification of statements by public accountants.

The inconsistencies of early balance sheets were not easily remedied. Government organizations combined efforts with professional and trade associations to obtain more satisfactory statements. But only comparative success was acquired up to 1933. Although sales figures had been requested by credit men since before the turn of the century, and some few credit analysts asked for operating data, income statements were neither in general demand nor arbitrarily submitted during this period.

Bank statements of condition proved no more enlightening than statements of industrial and commercial enterprises. The form was deceivingly simple and the reader could draw his own conclusions regarding the content of the items included in the statement. This was not conducive to uniform interpretation. Likewise, the practice of publishing statements on a determined date, for example, December 31, made window dressing possible. Of course, this weakness was overcome by a plan whereby the Comptroller of the Currency called for statements as of some previous date without any notice of the date before the moment of the call.

The evolution of analysis was an outgrowth of improved financial statements. The first simple property statements were read and destroyed or filed away until a new one was acquired. The idea of comparison came with the development of the bank credit departments. This in turn was the root of comparison of related items on the same statements. Proper proportion of assets and liabilities was advocated by a few analysts prior to 1900 despite the inadequacy of financial statement form and classification before the turn of the century.

The earliest use of ratios for the interpretation of statements in the field of banking, commerce and industry was in the field of bank supervision. Evidence of this is found in the annual reports of the Comptrollers of the Currency. The development of commercial and bank credit, in which James Graham Cannon was a recognized leader, led to the use of ratios in financial statement analysis by credit grantors. Alexander Wall has been acknowledged the pioneer in ratio work, not because he was the first to use ratios, but because he was the first to present a ratio method of analysis.

The acceptance or rejection of his method were predominant features of financial statement analysis in the 1920's.

The acceptance of the ratio method of analysis was slower in regard to bank statements of condition. This was most probably due to the retention of the unintelligible form of statement which banking tradition had kept in use. Ratio analysis as an aid to better bank management received its impetus from the credit losses of 1920-1921. This resulted in a number of successful surveys for establishing standards in bank management.

James Harris Bliss is lauded as the pioneer of ratio analysis applied to industrial management. Here again, the pioneer was not the first to use the ratios but the first to draw up principles by which standards could be established.

Opposition to the theoretical methods of ratio analysis resulted in the presentation of what was called a practical ratio analysis method. Eugene S. Benjamin's method was intended as a practical aid to both credit analysts and business managers. A comparison of the ratio methods presented during this era simply reveals different ideas as to which relationships have the greatest significance and as to the manner of expressing these relationships.

Industrial progress and credit development were the foundation upon which ratio analysis of financial statements had been built. The obstruction of this foundation in the early 1930's brought about a re-evaluation of the economic structure of the nation and a new era for financial statement development and analysis.

A SHORT HISTORY OF FINANCIAL RATIO ANALYSIS

James O. Horrigan

A Short History of Financial Ratio Analysis

James O. Horrigan

THE utility of accounting data seems to be assumed axiomatically by most accountants, but it is interesting to trace how accounting data have actually been used. In this article, the historical development of one particular usage, financial ratio analysis, will be followed from its early origins to the present time. Only the broad outline of this development will be presented;[1] and as seems appropriate, the discussions will be centered upon general analytical approaches or individuals. The presentation will follow the following chronological scheme: (1) Origins, (2) 1900–1919, (3) 1920–1929, (4) 1930–1939, (5) 1940–1945, and (6) 1946–to date. These demarcations in time are somewhat arbitrary, but they do encompass fairly well the important developments in ratio analysis. It must be borne in mind, however, that the discussion will relate mainly to the beginnings of developments within those periods. It is safe to say that virtually everything that has been started in ratio analysis is still going on today somewhere. Thus, a history of the development of ratio analysis is at the same time a fairly accurate description of its present practice.

Origins

The primary cause of the evolution of ratio analysis in general was Euclid's rigorous analysis of the properties of ratios in Book V of his *Elements* in about 300 B.C. However, the adoption of ratios as a tool of financial statement analysis is a relatively recent development.

The first causes of financial statement analysis can be traced back to the last stages of America's drive to industrial maturity in the last half of the Nineteenth Century. As the management of enterprises in the various industrial sectors transferred from the enterprising capitalists to the professional manager and as the financial sector became a more predominate force in the economy, the need for financial statements increased accordingly. Both of these changes were primary causes of financial statement analysis, but the shift in power to the financial institution was especially important.

Although there was much overlap, the development paths of ratio analysis for creditor purposes and for managerial purposes were different. Credit analysis emphasized measures of ability to pay

---

[1] For the reader interested in a more detailed history of ratio analysis, the early periods of development are covered in the following work: Sister Isadore Brown, "The Historical Development of the Use of Ratios in Financial Statement Analysis to 1933" (unpublished Ph.D. dissertation, School of Social Science, Catholic University of America, 1955). This is also available in a condensed, published version in Volume II of the "Catholic University of America: Studies in Economics."

James O. Horrigan is Assistant Professor of Business Administration at the University of New Hampshire.

whereas managerial analysis emphasized profitability measures. Both of these paths were followed in the United States and their proponents freely borrowed from each other; but the credit analysis approach dominated the general development of ratio analysis, especially in the early years. Therefore, one must look primarily to credit analysis to gain an understanding of how ratio analysis evolved.

Concomitantly with the introduction of single-name paper loans, commercial banks began to request financial statements for lending purposes as early as the 1870's; but this did not become a widespread practice until the 1890's.[2] During the 1890's, the volume and flow of financial information increased greatly.[3] This flow of data was initially analyzed on a casual item-by-item basis; next a comparative columnar basis of analysis was developed; at about the same time, the segregation of current from non-current items was begun; and finally, the relationships between different items began to come under scrutiny.[4] Sometime in the last few years of the 1890's there arose the practice of comparing current assets of an enterprise to its current liabilities.[5] Other ratios were developed in the 1890's;[6] but this ratio, the current ratio, was to have a more significant and longlasting impact upon financial statement analysis than any other ratio. Truly, the usage of ratios in financial statement analysis can be said to have begun with the advent of the current ratio.

1900–1919

After the turn of the century, some important developments in ratio analysis occurred during the period prior to and during World War I. Three of these developments were endogenous. First, a fairly large variety of ratios was conceived.[7] Second, absolute ratio criteria began to appear, the most famous being the 2 to 1 current ratio criterion.[8] Third, some analysts began to recognize the need for inter-firm analysis and, consequently, the need for relative ratio criteria.[9] Despite these developments, few analysts actually used ratios during this period; and those who were inclined to use ratios tended to use only one, the current ratio.[10]

There were also two exogenous developments in this period which were very important. These were the passage of the first Federal income tax code in 1913 and the establishment of the Federal Reserve System in 1914. Both of these developments increased the demand for financial statements and led to improvements in their content.

The events in the ante World War I period provided the ferment for a study which became the "catalyst" of ratio analysis development. In 1912 Alexander Wall reacted to the apparent needs for more types of ratios and for relative ratio criteria by beginning a compilation of a large sample of financial statements from the files of commercial paper brokers. This analysis was culminated in his classic report of 1919, "Study of Credit Barometrics."[11] In this study, Wall compiled

---

[2] Roy A. Foulke, *Practical Financial Statement Analysis*, 5th edition (McGraw-Hill Book Company, 1961), pp. 13–19.
[3] *Ibid.*, pp. 19–25; and John N. Myer, *Financial Statement Analysis*, 3rd edition (Prentice-Hall Inc., 1961), pp. 6–7.
[4] Alexander Wall, *How to Evaluate Financial Statements* (Harper and Brothers, 1936), p. 68.
[5] Foulke, *op. cit.*, p. 178. His research on the usage of the current classification in the balance sheet indicates that 1891 was the earliest possible year the current ratio could have emerged; see p. 181.
[6] For a few examples, see Brown, *op. cit.*, pp. 61–62.
[7] For example, James Cannon, a pioneer of financial statement analysis, used ten different ratios as early as 1905 in a study of business borrowers.
[8] For an example of an early attempt to supply criteria for a variety of ratios, see William H. Lough, *Business Finance* (The Ronald Press Company, 1917), pp. 500–24.
[9] *Ibid.*
[10] Foulke, *op. cit.*, p. 178; and Wall, *op. cit.*
[11] Alexander Wall, *Study of Credit Barometrics*, Federal Reserve Bulletin (March, 1919), 229–43.

seven different ratios of 981 firms, for an unspecified time period. He stratified these firms by industry and by geographical location, with nine sub-divisions in each of those strata. Although he did not subject this data to any further analysis, he believed he found great ratio variation between geographical areas and between types of businesses. His results would be vulnerable to criticism by today's standards; but his study was historically significant because it was a widely-read, overt departure from the customary usage of a single ratio with an absolute criterion. Wall had, in effect, popularized the ideas of using many ratios and using empirically determined relative ratio criteria.

Another important development was taking place at approximately the same time as Wall's study, but in the area of managerial usage of ratios. In retail managerial analyses, the notion of using profit margins and turnovers, which are basically ratio concepts, was already well-developed.[12] However, a manufacturing concern began the most comprehensive usage of those types of ratios. In about 1919, the du Pont Company began to use a ratio "triangle" system in evaluations of its operating results.[13] The top of the triangle was a return on investment ratio (profits/total assets) and the base consisted of profit margin ratio (profits/sales) and a capital turnover ratio (sales/total assets). This system held promise for providing a framework wherein ratios could be developed in a logical fashion. The idea behind this development would appear occasionally in the literature; but in contrast to Wall's study, it went largely unnoticed until recent times.

1920–1929

During the next decade, the 1920's, interest in ratios increased remarkably. A virtual explosion of publications on the subject of ratio analysis occurred.[14] At the same time, many compilations of industry ratio data were begun by trade associations, universities, credit agencies, and individual analysts.[15] This process of collecting industry ratio data and computing averages therefrom was called "scientific ratio analysis,"[16] but the label "scientific" appears to have been a misnomer because there is no evidence that hypothesis formulation and testing were carried out.

These developments of ratio analysis in the early 1920's can be viewed largely as reactions to Wall's 1919 study. From that viewpoint, perhaps the real legacy of his study comes from the other notion he introduced: the usage of many types of ratios in analysis. A rapid, prolific development of different types of ratios took place during the 1920's;[17] and this proliferation has persisted up to the present time.

Wall, himself, attempted to mitigate the effects of ratio proliferation by developing a ratio index. This index was essentially a weighted average of different ratios with the weights being the relative value as-

---

[12] For example, see: Henry C. Magee, "Department Store Accounts," *The Journal of Accountancy* (April, 1915), 268–91. It is interesting to compare Magee's article, which contains an extensive discussion of ratio concepts, to a credit analysis article which contained only a few obtuse references to ratio concepts: J. Edward Masters, "Financial Statements as a Basis of Credit," *ibid.*, May, 1915, pp. 334–43.

[13] C. A. Kline, Jr., and Howard L. Hessler, "The du Pont Chart System for Appraising Operating Performance," *Readings in Cost Accounting, Budgeting, and Control*, ed. William E. Thomas, Jr. (South-Western Publishing Co., 1955), p. 752. The original ideas underlying such a system appear to have come from Alfred Marshall; see his *Elements of Economics of Industry* (Macmillan and Co., Ltd., 1892), pp. 310–11.

[14] Much of the literature of this time dealt directly with the acceptance or rejection of Wall's approach; Sister Isadore Brown made this observation in the condensed, published version of her study (*op. cit.*, p. 28; see n. 1).

[15] The earliest surviving compilers of annual ratio data appear to have been the following: (1) trade association: United Typothetae of America, 1922; (2) university: Harvard Business School, 1923; (3) credit agency: Robert Morris Associates, 1923.

[16] W. H. Justin, "Operating Control Through Scientific Analysis," *The Journal of Accountancy* (September, 1924), pp. 183–95.

[17] Lincoln may hold the record here; he discussed and illustrated forty different ratios. Edmond E. Lincoln, *Applied Business Finance*, 3rd revised edition (A. W. Shaw Company, 1925), pp. 339–58.

signed to each ratio by the analyst.[18] This effort was much derided,[19] but he appears to have been engaged in a praiseworthy attempt to develop a naive linear discriminate function.

Other analysts were also attempting to bring some sophistication to ratio analysis during the 1920's. Bliss presented the first coherent system of ratios which were tied in together in a logical *a priori* fashion. He considered ratios to be "indicators of the status of fundamental relationships within the business;"[20] and furthermore, he believed standard relationships would be set by competitive conditions. From these premises he developed a model of the firm which consisted entirely of ratios. He continuously interwove the relationships of ratios which measured cost and expense, turnover, and financial relationships to ratios which measured earnings. Bliss' model and the few hypotheses which he generated from it were naive, but his work represented a very promising beginning for the development of a theory of ratio analysis.[21]

The decade of the 1920's was a period of great enthusiasm for the possibilities of using ratios as tools of analysis, and it is perhaps fitting that the first real critic of ratios emerged during this same period. In 1925 Gilman listed the following objections to ratios: (1) their changes over time cannot be interpreted because the numerator and denominator both vary; (2) they are "artificial" measures; (3) they divert the analyst's attention from a comprehensive view of the firm; and (4) their reliability as indicators varies widely between ratios.[22] Considering the first three criticisms, Gilman clearly did not believe that ratios portray "fundamental relationships within the business;"[23] indeed, he appears to have been diametrically opposed to Bliss, and any other ratio enthusiasts.

One would expect that "schools" of ratio analysis would have developed around these two opposite points—i.e., ratios are fundamental measures *vs.* ratios are artificial measures; but little happened. The contributions of Bliss and Gilman were acknowledged, but they were not expanded upon. Thus, the value of their contributions, for activating the development of a theory of ratio analysis, was largely lost.

1930–1939

In the next decade, the 1930's, the literary discussion of ratios and compilation of industry average ratios[24] continued unabated. The salient feature of this decade was the increased attention given to the empirical bases of ratio analysis.

A particularly important exogenous development was the formation of the Securities and Exchange Commission. This external influence, similar to those

---

[18] Alexander Wall and Raymond W. Duning, *Ratio Analysis of Financial Statements* (Harper and Brothers, 1928), pp. 152–79.

[19] One particularly caustic critic described Wall as the "... incurably optimistic theorist futilely and absurdly chasing the ratio absolute." Myron M. Strain, *Industrial Balance Sheets* (Harper and Brothers, 1929), pp. 169–70.

[20] James H. Bliss, *Financial and Operating Ratios in Management* (The Ronald Press Company, 1923), pp. 34–38.

[21] Bliss also attempted to demonstrate that normal ratio relationships could be determined by computing average industry ratios, but his attempt was unsuccessful; *ibid.*, pp. 225–387. Unfortunately, he is remembered mainly for that; see Myer, *op. cit.*, p. 12.

[22] Stephen Gilman, *Analyzing Financial Statements* (The Ronald Press Company, 1925), pp. 111–12. He also criticized the computation of industry average ratios, but he was really attacking the limitations of the underlying absolute accounting data, especially their lack of comparability and consistency. Statement analysts are still concerned about this problem, of course.

[23] Given the paucity of empirical studies at that time, it is not clear what basis Gilman could have used to develop his fourth criticism.

[24] This began to change somewhat in that attempts were made to stratify the ratio data beyond merely the firms' industry; e.g., George T. Bristol used such strata as product mix and credit policy in "Merchandising Problems of Grocery and Candy Wholesalers," *Dun's Review* (October, 1937), pp. 21–24, 46–47. Also, statistical information such as variances and graphic frequency distributions were sometimes being provided in addition to averages; e.g., A. H. Winakor, *Balance Sheet Structure of Automobile Manufacturing Companies* ("Studies in Financial Structure," Bulletin No. 29; Urbana, Ill.: Bureau of Business Research, The University of Illinois, 1930). However, neither of these changes proved to be generally enduring.

mentioned previously, also increased the supply of financial statements and influenced their content.[25]

There were two significant developments in this decade relating directly to ratio analysis. The first of these was embodied in a discussion in the literature pertaining to the determination of the most efficacious *group* of ratios. In this respect, the most successful promoter of his own particular group of ratios was, by far, Roy A. Foulke. He was successful largely because he could supply annual industry data for his group of ratios.[26] Foulke actually began to develop this group of ratios, which would eventually number fourteen, during the late 1920's while he was employed at the National Credit Office;[27] but they were not widely promulgated until the 1930's under the auspices of his next employer, Dun & Bradstreet. The publication of his ratios was begun in 1933,[28] and this collection of ratios quickly became the most influential and well-known industry average ratios series.

Foulke was a particularly important figure in the development of ratio analysis because his efforts brought to fruition the approach which became the essential "modus operandi" of ratio analysis in this country. In this approach, *a priori* analysis and/or empirical evidence were rarely provided to substantiate an author's claim that his particular selection of ratios represented an efficient collection of ratios for analyzing financial statements. Rather, the author's group of selected ratios—and sometimes accompanying absolute and relative criteria—were promulgated solely on the authority of his experience in statement analysis.[29] This approach, which might be called "pragmatical empiricism," probably sufficed for the needs of ratio analysis practitioners; but it left the subject of ratio analysis devoid of any well-developed, testable theory.

However, the second significant development in this decade can be viewed as a counter-balancing movement. In the early 1930's, studies were made of the efficiency of ratios as predictors of business financial difficulties. Winakor and Smith began this movement in their analysis of a sample of firms which had experienced financial difficulties during the period 1923–1931.[30] They analyzed the prior ten years' trends of the means of twenty-one ratios;[31] and they concluded that the ratio of net work-

---

[25] This was partially an endogenous development because the Commission began to publish ratio data itself. It sponsored a WPA project begun in 1936 in which a variety of ratio data of individual firms in various industries were compiled; see the "Industry Reports" of the *Survey of American Listed Corporations* (Securities and Exchange Commission). It has published aggregate ratio data since the 1940's with the Federal Trade Commission in their *Quarterly Financial Report for Manufacturing Corporations* (U. S. Government Printing Office).

[26] Cf., Eugene S. Benjamin, *Practical Credit Analysis*, revised 3rd edition (Eugene S. Benjamin, 1939). Benjamin argued very persuasively during the 1930's for the usage of his six primary and six secondary ratios in conjunction with industry average ratios. However, his groups of ratios were never compiled and published; and there is no evidence that any vestige of his ratio system survived to present times.

[27] Roy A. Foulke, *The Commercial Paper Market* (The Bankers Publishing Co., 1931), pp. 120–32.

[28] They were published in the following series of articles in the *Dun & Bradstreet Monthly Review*: "Three Important Balance Sheet Ratios," (August, 1933), pp. 7–11; "Three Important Inventory Ratios" (December 1933), pp. 6–11; "Three Important Sales Ratios" (May, 1934), pp. 6–11; "Three Important Net Profit Ratios" (November, 1934), pp. 2–7.

[29] Foulke justified his fourteen ratios and their accompanying criteria by citing his many years of experience with them; *Practical Financial...*, pp. 176, 229, 275, 352–54, 386. He explicitly rejected elsewhere the notion of *a priori* theorizing in regard to ratios and argued that only empirically obtained knowledge—especially ratio criteria—is possible for ratios; Roy A. Foulke, "Financial Ratios Become of Age," *The Journal of Accountancy* (September, 1937), pp. 209–10.

[30] They initially analyzed a sample of twenty-nine firms: Raymond F. Smith and Arthur H. Winakor, *A Test Analysis of Unsuccessful Industrial Companies* (Bulletin No. 31; Urbana, Ill.: University of Illinois, Bureau of Business Research, 1930); and they later analyzed 183 firms in the following work: Raymond F. Smith and Arthur H. Winakor, *Changes in the Financial Structure of Unsuccessful Industrial Corporations* (Bulletin No. 51; Urbana, Ill.: University of Illinois, Bureau of Business Research, 1935).

[31] They actually used a modified mean ratio which was computed from the inner half of their data—i.e., $(Q_2 - Q_1)/\tfrac{1}{2}N$.

ing capital to total assets was the most accurate and steady indicator of failure, with its decline beginning ten years before the occurrence of financial difficulty. However, their study suffered the shortcoming of lacking a contrasting control group of successful firms; this was a serious shortcoming because of the time period covered in the study.

Two other studies concerning the predictive power of ratios were also carried out in the early 1930's, and control groups were used in these. Fitzpatrick, using a case-by-case method of analysis, studied the prior three to five years' trends of thirteen types of ratios for twenty firms which had failed during the period 1920–1929.[32] Following this up with a comparative analysis of a matched sample of nineteen successful firms,[33] he concluded that all his ratios predicted failure to some degree but the net profit to net worth, net worth to debt, and net worth to fixed assets[34] ratios were generally the best indicators. Ramser and Foster analyzed eleven types of ratios of 173 firms with securities registered in the State of Illinois.[35] They found that firms which turned out to be less successful and those which failed tended to have ratios which were lower than the more successful firms. However, two turnover ratios, sales to net worth and sales to total assets, exhibited an opposite tendency. These studies also suffered some shortcomings. Fitzpatrick's sample was small and too selective, and many of the differences between the average ratios in Ramser and Foster's study were more apparent than real.

In general, the shortcomings of these three studies were outweighed by the essential importance of their contribution. They represented an extremely significant event in the development of ratio analysis because they were the first carefully developed attempts to utilize the scientific method for determining the utility of ratios.

1940–1945

In the early 1940's, the development of the empirical base of ratio analysis continued in both a direct and an indirect fashion. In a direct fashion, the ratio prediction studies described above were, in a sense, culminated in Merwin's study.[36] Merwin analyzed the prior six years' trends of a large, unspecified number of ratios of "continuing" and "discontinuing" firms. Comparing industry mean ratios of "discontinuing" firms against "estimated normal" ratios,[37] he concluded that three ratios were very sensitive predictors of discontinuance, up to as early as four to five years in some instances. These three ratios were the following: (1) net working capital to total assets;[38] (2) net worth to debt;[39] and (3) the current ratio. Merwin's study was the first really sophisticated analysis of ratio predictive power, and the findings of the study still appear to be credible. Thus, after approximately a half-century of existence, the

---

[32] Paul J. Fitzpatrick, *Symptoms of Industrial Failures* (Catholic University of America Press, 1931).

[33] Paul J. Fitzpatrick, *A Comparison of the Ratios of Successful Industrial Enterprises with Those of Failed Companies* (The Accountants Publishing Company, 1932).

[34] Cf. Smith and Winakor, *Changes in the Financial*.... Although they did not emphasize this point, their data demonstrate that the net worth to fixed assets ratio was also one of their best indicators.

[35] J. R. Ramser and Louis O. Foster, *A Demonstration of Ratio Analysis* (Bulletin No. 40; Urbana, Ill.: University of Illinois, Bureau of Business Research, 1931). They computed the first and third quartiles, but their analysis centered mainly upon the median ratios at time of registration.

[36] Charles L. Merwin, *Financing Small Corporations: In Five Manufacturing Industries, 1926–36* (National Bureau of Economic Research, 1942).

[37] The "estimated normal" ratios are estimates of what the discontinuing firms' ratios would have been if they had maintained the same average ratios as the surviving firms. This procedure was necessary because each year of discontinuance represented an assortment of calendar years. *Ibid.*, pp. 134–139.

[38] Cf, Smith and Winakor, *Changes in the Financial*....

[39] Cf., Fitzpatrick, *A Comparison of the Ratios*....

usage of some ratios was vindicated formally.

An important type of indirect development of the empirical base of ratio analysis accelerated noticeably in the early 1940's. During this period, ratios were increasingly used as independent and descriptive variables in aggregate economic studies. The idea of using single ratios for these purposes was not new, especially the profits to investment ratio;[40] but the practice of using a number of ratios to describe a wide variety of the firms' characteristics came into fruition during this period.[41] Although their center of attention was not the ratios as such, these studies did provide abundant information about the behavior of ratios over time and the variation of ratios between different groupings of firms; and a few of these studies did touch upon some questions relating directly to the possible usefulness of ratios in the analysis of financial statements.

These direct and indirect empirical studies were an important phase in the evolution of ratio analysis because they supplied materials which could be used for the formulation of hypotheses, as a preliminary step in the development of a formal theory of ratio analysis. However, the studies were not translated into the field of ratio analysis.[42]

1946-to date

Since the early 1940's, the development of ratio analysis in this country has continued along various paths. First, there was a flurry of excitement during the 1950's about the utility of a ratio breakdown of return on investment for purposes of managerial analysis.[43] The notion of breaking down return on investment into a profit margin and a capital turnover ratio was not a new idea,[44] but it had not received widespread attention before this period. This was a promising development because the possibility existed that the return on investment measure could serve as an apex in the development of an integrated ratio analysis system containing a variety of ratios.[45] However, the development along these lines in this country has generally not gone beyond the two secondary ratios of profit margin and capital turnover;[46] indeed, there is still ambivalence concerning the usefulness of even those two ratios.[47]

[40] This ratio, in various forms, was used earlier in the Federal Trade Commission's industry studies in the 1920's (e.g., U. S., Federal Trade Commission, *Report of the Federal Trade Commission on the War-Time Profits and Costs of the Steel Industry* (Government Printing Office, 1925)) and in the extensive research in the 1930's on the relationship of profits to the size of firms (e.g., William Leonard Crum, *Corporate Size and Earning Power* (Harvard University Press, 1939)).

[41] For example, Charles L. Merwin, *Financial Characteristics of American Manufacturing Corporations* "Temporary National Economic Committee: Investigation of Concentration of Economic Power," No. 15; (Washington: U.S. Government Printing Office, 1940); and Walter A. Chudson, *The Pattern of Corporate Financial Structure: A Cross-Section of Manufacturing, Mining, Trade, and Construction, 1937* (National Bureau of Economic Research, 1945). The "Financial Research Program" of the National Bureau of Economic Research is a particularly rich source of materials on ratios.

[42] As far as I can determine, the direct studies, as well as the indirect, have not been incorporated into the general ratio analysis literature. For example, a search by me of more than thirty books dealing with ratio analysis revealed that only two sources considered the ratio which was the best predictor in these studies—i.e., net working capital to total assets. Nathaniel Jackendoff reported a similar finding in "A Study of Published Industry Financial and Operating Ratios" *Economics and Business Bulletin*, Temple University (March 1962), p. 13.

[43] "Bibliography on Return on Investment," *N.A.A. Bulletin*, XLI (June, 1960), p. 91.

[44] Bliss appears to have been the first writer to introduce this idea into the field of ratio analysis; *op cit.*, pp. 91–93.

[45] One author has developed a system wherein return on net worth, rather than the return on total capital, serves as the apex; Kenneth R. Rickey, "How Accountants Can Help Management Manage," *N.A.A. Bulletin*, (July, 1963), pp. 25–36.

[46] An isolated example of a development beyond those two ratios is one writer's incorporation of inventory turnover and accounts receivable turnover as subcategories of total asset turnover; George Moller, "Try Budgeting for Return on Capital Employed," *The Controller*, (March, 1958), pp. 107–12, 128–36. An extensive ratio model of return on investment has been developed by Bela Gold in his *Foundations of Productivity Analysis* (University of Pittsburgh Press, 1955), pp. 272–77; but he used mainly productivity ratios, which require physical output and productive capacity data, rather than financial ratios.

[47] *Experience with Return on Capital to Appraise Management Performance* ("Accounting Practice Report,"

Another important aspect of this period has been the increased emphasis given to the role of ratios in the operations of small businesses. The Small Business Administration, in particular, has generated much interest in the utility of ratios as a managerial tool. It has published or financed a number of studies relevant to ratio analysis. There have been "how-to-do-it" booklets,[48] an evaluation of the reliability of industry average ratios,[49] analyses of the actual usage of ratios by small businesses,[50] and studies in which ratios were used as variables for examining and describing the operations of small business.[51]

Ratios were also being used as variables for examining and describing economic activity, thus further widening the empirical base of ratio analysis. First, additional evaluations of the predictive power of ratios were made. Hickman found that the times-interest-earned ratio and the net profits to sales ratio were useful predictors of the default experience of corporate bond issues during 1900–43,[52] and Saulnier and others found suggestive evidence from RFC lending experience during 1934–51 that borrowing firms with poorer current ratios and net worth to debt ratios were more prone to loan defaults.[53] Second, ratios were being used as independent variables in a series of studies dealing with the quality of credit under various cyclical conditions.[54] Among other things, these studies have established that certain financial ratios[55]—combined with some other ex-ante measures—were inversely correlated to an index of trade credit difficulties,[56] that loan criticisms made by bank examiners were consistently related to financial ratios,[57] and that the ability to obtain credit is associated directly with some financial ratios.[58] This series of studies should prove to be a rich source of materials for formulating ratio analysis hypotheses.

A recent direct study of the predictive power of ratios warrants separate attention here. Beaver has analyzed the ability of ratios to predict the failure of firms during 1954–64; and similar to Merwin, he has found that some ratios predict failure up to five years in advance.[59] Beaver's study differs from Merwin's in two important respects: his statistical techniques were more powerful and some of his ratios were computed from funds statement data. This study will undoubtedly become a landmark for future research in ratio analysis.

Another interesting development of this period was some empirical research begun

---

No. 14; National Association of Accountants, 1962), p. 4.

[48] Richard Sanzo, *Ratio Analysis for Small Business* ("Small Business Management Series," No. 20; 2nd edition; Small Business Administration, 1960).

[49] Jackendoff, *loc. cit.*

[50] Nathaniel Jackendoff, *The Use of Financial Ratios and Other Financial Techniques and Services by Small Business* (Temple University, Bureau of Economic and Business Research, 1961).

[51] For example, Joseph C. Schabacker, *Cash Planning in Small Manufacturing Companies* ("Small Business Research Series," No. 1; Small Business Administration, 1960), pp. 127–31, 226–56; and J. L. McKeever, *A Study of the Problems of Small Retailers in Wyoming* (University of Wyoming, Division of Business and Economic Research, 1960), pp. 23–30, 59–73.

[52] W. Braddock Hickman, *Corporate Bond Quality and Investor Experience* (Princeton University Press, 1958), pp. 390–421.

[53] Raymond J. Saulnier, Harold G. Halcrow, and Neil H. Jacoby, *Federal Lending and Loan Insurance* (Princeton University Press, 1958), pp. 456–81.

[54] Geoffrey H. Moore, "The Quality of Credit in Booms and Depressions," *Financial Research and Problems of the Day*, Thirty-Seventh Annual Report (National Bureau of Economic Research, 1957), p. 44.

[55] Three ratios used in all these studies were the current ratio, the net working capital to total assets ratio, and the net worth to debt ratio.

[56] Martin H. Seiden, "Trade Credit: A Quantitative and Qualitative Analysis," *Tested Knowledge of Business Cycles*, Forty-Second Annual Report (National Bureau of Economic Research, 1962), pp. 86–88.

[57] Albert M. Wojinlower, *The Quality of Bank Loans: A Study of Bank Examination Records* ("Occasional Paper," No. 82; National Bureau of Economic Research, 1962), pp. 9–12.

[58] Geoffrey H. Moore and Thomas R. Atkinson, "Risks and Returns in Small-Business Financing," *Towards a Firmer Basis of Economic Policy*, Forty-First Annual Report (National Bureau of Economic Research, 1961), pp. 66–67.

[59] William H. Beaver, "Financial Ratios as Predictors of Failure," *Empirical Research in Accounting: Selected Studies, 1966* (University of Chicago, 1967), pp. 71–111.

on the predictive power of ratios in regard to psychological characteristics of firms. Sorter and Becker have examined the relationships of financial ratios to a psychological model of "Corporate Personality" and have found that conservative corporations maintain higher liquidity and solvency ratios.[60] This research should also prove to be an extremely valuable addition to the empirical base of ratio analysis.

One more important empirical development of this period was the beginning of a more rigorous scrutiny of the nature of financial ratios as such. First, the effects on ratios of different accounting procedures were examined. For example, Holdren found that LIFO inventory valuation, as opposed to FIFO valuation, changed the inventory turnover ratios of a sample of firms significantly but did not change some other ratios;[61] and Nelson found that capitalizing leases changed a large number of ratios.[62] Second, the behavior of a variety of ratios purporting to measure the same thing, the "defensive position of the firm," was examined and quite different patterns were found.[63]

Finally, the post-war surge of interest in the funds statement has been accompanied by the emergence of a new type of ratio, the funds statement ratio—i.e., a ratio in which funds statement items are used as its components. Walter laid the foundation for this development very carefully,[64] and suggestions of specific ratios followed quickly.[65] This development, which is still in a relatively embryonic stage, has been characterized by careful and well-constructed a priori analyses in contrast to the senseless proliferation of ratios which characterized the early development of ratio analysis.[66]

The period since the early 1940's is also significant because interest in ratio analysis began to increase noticeably in other countries.[67] In Australia, ratios—especially the current ratio—have been subjected to rigorous scrutiny in order to determine their logicality and utility;[68] and they have been used as the basic ingredients of an application of the scientific method to financial management.[69] There is evidence that ratios similar to those used in this country are used in Australia, but the

---

[60] George Sorter and Selwyn Becker, "Accounting and Financial Decisions and 'Corporate Personality'—Some Preliminary Findings," *Journal of Accounting Research*, (Autumn, 1964), pp. 183–96. Also, George H. Sorter, Selwyn W. Becker, T. Ross Archibald, and William H. Beaver, "Accounting and Financial Measures as Indicators of Corporate Personality—Some Empirical Findings," in Robert K. Jaedicke *et al.*, (eds.) *Research in Accounting Measurement* (American Accounting Association, 1960), pp. 200–10.

[61] George C. Holdren, "Lifo and Ratio Analysis," THE ACCOUNTING REVIEW, (January, 1964), pp. 70–85.

[62] A. Tom Nelson, "Capitalizing Leases; The Effect on Financial Ratios," *The Journal of Accountancy*, (July, 1963), pp. 49–58.

[63] Sidney Davidson, George H. Sorter, and Hemu Kalle, "Measuring the Defensive Position of a Firm," *Financial Analysts Journal*, (January-February, 1964), pp. 23–29.

[64] James E. Walter, "Determination of Technical Solvency," *The Journal of Business*, (January, 1957), pp. 30–43. A few earlier usages of what were essentially individual funds statement ratios can be found (e.g., Bion B. Howard and Miller Upton, *Introduction to Business Finance* (McGraw-Hill Book Company, Inc., 1953)), pp. 135–38, but Walter was the first to specifically incorporate the funds statement into ratio analysis.

[65] Harold Bierman, Jr., "Measuring Financial Liquidity," THE ACCOUNTING REVIEW, (October, 1960), pp. 628–32; G. H. Sorter and George Benston, "Appraising the Defensive Position of a Firm: The Interval Measure," *ibid.*, pp. 633–40; and George Staubus, *A Theory of Accounting to Investors* (University of California Press, 1961), pp. 140–45.

[66] The general proliferation of ratios has certainly not ceased entirely; a contemporary writer, Tucker, recommended fifty-six ratios which could be computed from generally available financial statement data and, including other types of data, recommended a total of 429 ratios! Spencer A. Tucker, *Successful Managerial Control by Ratio-Analysis* (McGraw-Hill Book Company, 1961).

[67] Two authors of general works on this subject describe ratio analysis as a very recent development in two countries given the most attention here, Australia and England. Alexander Fitzgerald, *Analysis and Interpretation of Financial and Operating Statements*, 2nd edition (Butterworths & Company, Ltd., 1956), pp. 60–61; and Bradbury B. Parkinson, *Accountancy Ratios in Theory and Practice* (Gee and Company Limited, 1951), pp. 5, 12–13.

[68] F. K. Wright, "An Examination of the Working Capital Ratio," *The Australian Accountant*, (March, 1956), 101–07; V. L. Gole, "The Management of Working Capital," *The Australian Accountant*, (June, 1959), pp. 319–29.

[69] R. J. Chambers, "Business Finance and the Analysis of Financial Statements," *The Australian Accountant* (August, 1948), pp. 253–65.

listings are not as proliferated.[70] There is also evidence that some authors were anxious to obtain industry average ratios,[71] hinting that Australia lacks a developed empirical base for ratio analysis. In general, a "common thread" or a school of thought on ratio analysis does not appear to have emerged yet in the Australian literature.

In England, on the other hand, a very distinct "common thread" in ratio analysis has developed. The British Institute of Management has generated interest in ratios as devices for making inter-firm comparisons in order to help management to appraise its efficiency and to make policy decisions for the future.[72] It has adopted the essential premise that return on investment is the primary ratio to which all other ratios would be related— i.e., ratio analysis should be a process whereby changes or differences in return on investment are analyzed.[73] This premise has provided an implicit framework within which elaborate listings of ratios have been developed.[74]

An interesting outcome of this activity in England was the installation of the Centre for Interfirm Comparison, which provides industry ratio data to British management. The Centre collects a pool of confidential data from participating firms and publishes these data as a "pyramid" ratio system. Return on investment —i.e., net operating profits to total assets employed—sits at the top of this series and various profit and expense margins descend on one side and various asset and equity turnovers on the other side.[75] This British system is a logical outgrowth of the framework developed by Bliss and applied so long ago by the du Pont Company, and ironically it is now receiving attention in the United States.[76]

In general, ratio analysis in England is developing within a management orientation[77]—as opposed to a creditor orientation—to a greater extent than was true in the United States. To be sure, one can find recent examples of ratio listings in England which appear to be essentially the same as those found in this country;[78] but the British development does appear generally to be a more coherent one. It will be interesting to observe if this management oriented approach will lead to developments which are significantly different from those which took place in this country.

Ratio analysis was also being developed in various respects in some other countries. I did not evaluate the developments in these countries in detail, but the following bits of information were noted. There is interest in France in the British idea of exchanging information between firms within some systematic ratio framework, but their ratio lists do not reflect the return on investment ratio "pyramid" notion.[79] In India, there appears to have been ex-

[70] For example, see the ratio listings of the following: A. A. Fitzgerald, "Financial and Operating Ratios," *The Accountant's Journal*, (May, 1945), pp. 251–56; A. J. Cruikshank, "The Interpretation of Ratios," *The Australian Accountant*, (March, 1948), pp. 80–83; and V. L. Gole, "Financial Ratios and Credit Implications," *The Federal Accountant*, (January, 1951), pp. 7–10.

[71] Cruikshank, *loc. cit.*, Gole, "Financial Ratios and Credit Implications," *loc. cit.*, p. 10.

[72] "Accounting Ratios," *Accountancy*, (July, 1956), p. 267.

[73] *Ibid.*, pp. 268–69. Cf., with pp. 16–17 *supra*; This premise was not adopted in the United States despite the extensive attention given to the return on investment breakdown.

[74] *Ibid.*, pp. 269–71; and R. G. H. Nelson, "The Use of Ratios in Financial and Cost Accounting," *The Accountant*, (February 13, 1960), pp. 188–91.

[75] "Interfirm Comparison of Management Ratios" (Centre for Interfirm Comparison), pp. 1–3. Mimeographed.

[76] "To Diagnose Ills, Consult a 'Pyramid,'" *Business Week* November 24, 1962, pp. 128–30.

[77] Parkinson, *op. cit.*, pp. 12–13.

[78] For example, Harold C. Edey, *Introduction to Accounting* (Hutchinson University Library, 1963), pp. 142–59; and Bertram Nelson, "The Interpretation of Accounts," in W. T. Baxter and Sidney Davidson (eds.), *Studies in Accounting Theory* (Richard D. Irwin, Inc., 1962), pp. 490–97.

[79] Jean Nataf, "A New View of Financial Ratios," in Organization for European Economic Co-operation, European Productivity Agency, *Inter-Firm Comparisons: An Incentive to Productivity* (Project No. 379; Paris, 1957), pp. 95–101; and Maurice Renard, "Possible Solutions to Problems Raised by the Comparison of Ratios" *ibid.*, pp. 107–14.

tensive borrowing from American sources of not only types of ratios but their criteria as well.[80] In Japan, aggregate statistics of a large number of financial ratios are available by broad industry groupings and by size-of-firm categories.[81] In Russia and Red China, working capital turnover and return on investment ratios are used as control measures.[82] Finally, as might be expected, Canadian ratio lists are essentially the same as those in this country.[83]

These more recent developments in this country and abroad actually cut into the edge of the present. Thus, the point has been reached where this narrative of the development of ratio analysis must be concluded. No summary of this narrative will be offered here; instead, the end results of this development—i.e., the present state of ratio analysis—will be briefly examined.

The Present State of Ratio Analysis

From a negative viewpoint, the most striking aspect of the present state of ratio analysis is the absence of an explicit theoretical structure. Under the dominant approach of "pragmatical empiricism," the user of ratios is required to rely upon the authority of an author's experience. As a result, the subject of ratio analysis is replete with untested assertions about which ratios should be used and what their proper levels should be; and, similarly, the expected relationships of the various ratios with a quantification of some desired, or undesired, end have generally not been formulated. Studies have been conducted on the efficiency of ratios in predicting financial difficulties; but these have not been incorporated into the literature. The bulk of the ratio analysis literature consists of instructions on how to compute ratios. All of these short-comings are unfortunate because a quantitative, utilitarian activity such as ratio analysis could lend itself very well to a rigorous development.

However, there is a positive side to ratios. A need does exist for analytical devices which will enable analysts to compare financial statements between firms and over time periods. The ratio fills that need as a simple, quick method of comparison. In addition, the available evidence suggests that ratios do have predictive value, at least in respect to financial difficulties. Thus, the ratio is certainly a very admirable device because it is simple and it has predictive value.

The Future Role of Ratio Analysis

Accordingly, it is desirable that the shortcomings of ratio analysis be remedied, insofar as possible. The future role of ratios may be an important one. Wherever there is a need for fairly simple analytical devices, ratios will be useful. Such a need will usually arise when human and non-human analytical resources are limited. This means that ratios should at least be useful to the small firm for internal analyses and to most external analysts for investment and credit evaluations. An Indian accountant even claims that ratios should be useful in the management of the economic activities of underdeveloped countries.[84] These areas of endeavor are certainly important enough to warrant a re-examination of ratio analysis towards making it more useful.

---

[80] R. K. Dalal, "Accountancy Ratios," *The Chartered Accountant* (India), (May, 1956), pp. 452–57; N. N. Pai, "Use of Accounting Ratios in Management Accounting," *ibid.*, Chowdhry, *Analysis of Company Financial Statements* (Asia Publishing House, 1964).

[81] *Economic Statistics of Japan: 1962* (Bank of Japan, Statistics Department, 1963), pp. 233–36.

[82] Ching-wen Kwang, "The Economic Accounting System of State Enterprise in Mainland China," *The International Journal of Accounting*, (Spring, 1966), pp. 87–95; and Barry M. Richman, *Soviet Management* (Prentice-Hall, Inc., 1965), pp. 53–76, 230–34.

[83] For example, C. B. Taylor, "The Industry-Wide Approach to Financial and Operating Ratios," *Cost and Management*, (May, 1956), pp. 181–89; and W. G. Leonard and Frank N. Beard, *Canadian Accounting Practice*, 2nd edition, (McGraw-Hill Company of Canada Limited, 1963), pp. 452–57.

[84] Pai, *loc. cit.*, p. 559.

EARLY PROPONENTS OF FINANCIAL RATIO ANALYSIS

STUDY OF CREDIT BAROMETRICS

Alexander Wall

Study of Credit Barometrics.

In the following pages are given the results of a study of "credit barometrics" prepared by Mr. Alexander Wall, of the National Bank of Commerce, Detroit, Mich., at the request of the Board, under the general supervision of the Division of Analysis and Research of the Federal Reserve Board. This report was first prepared for the use of the Federal Reserve Board and of the Federal Reserve Banks, but the general interest in credit conditions has led to its publication in the belief that it may attract comment and discussion relative to the principles presented in it. The methods pursued were originated by Mr. Wall and have been carried out by him along his own lines, subject only to general criticism and suggestion.

To the Federal Reserve Board, Washington, D. C.:

This report on credit barometrics will consist of several main divisions, the first treating the theory involved; the second the method of compilation in the examination just made; the third displaying the results of the examination.

THE THEORY.

The theories lying behind the credit barometric work about to be outlined developed from a desire to establish some sort of indicator in credit work. Common practice has (as far as has been made public) developed only one general theory, which has become accepted as more or less standard. This theory is known as "the two-for-one rule" and consists of the principle that, in order to establish a good credit proportion, the subject statement must show at least two dollars of current assets for every dollar of current liability. The reason for this measure is basicly sound, because from a credit standpoint companies must be looked at partially, at least, as a liquidating proposition in which there is bound to be a shrinkage of assets, in that some accounts will be slow and bad and some merchandise out of season and antequated, whereas the corresponding debt is not subject to shrinkage. These proportions have become accepted only by common practice, and there is a question as to whether the two-for-one or the 200 per cent ratio is right, too large, or too little. It provides a substantial margin, and has on that account become rather generally acknowledged as safe. The establishment of any such ratio is not a matter of theory, but has been a matter of experimentation.

While the establishment of such a ratio can not be a matter of pure mathematics, there is a mathematical principle which can be evoked in the experimentation so as to arrive at a fairly definite standardization. This is the law of averages, and it has been applied by insurance actuaries in different kinds of insurance, so that the extent of an individual's life, the probability of fire or accident, etc., which are not mathematical problems, have been reduced to an almost exact science. All of this has been done by using the law of averages as a mathematical principle upon which to base the experimentation. The present study is based on the adaptation of the law of averages in the establishing of certain measures to be used with intelligence by bank-credit men, manufacturers, and merchants in their attempts to disclose weaknesses in the financial structure.

It can not be definitely determined what proportion of the final decision in any credit risk rests entirely upon an analysis of the property statement. Different bank-credit men who have been interviewed in this connection estimate the percentage of the entire decision that rests on the statement at between 40 and 60 per cent, leaving in contra 60 to 40 per cent of the final decision resting upon the so-called moral risk, the knowledge of the credit grantor of the ability of the management to produce economically, the moral fiber of the managers, the condition of the plant, general business conditions, localized business conditions, and other matters of this kind. Even if only 40 per cent of the decision rests upon an analysis of the statement, it still behooves the credit man and the financial system of the country to develop this 40 per cent to a 100 per cent efficiency within itself, if possible, and it is with this in mind primarily that the theories in this report are advanced. However, as the study develops it will be seen that by comparison the barometrics compiled will do a great deal toward uncovering sectional and type trade conditions that may be unsound or top-heavy.

The adoption of the current ratio theory is in itself purely a quantative proposition, in which the current assets in bulk are measured against the current liabilities in bulk. It is quite as important, however, that a qualitative analysis of the current assets be made, and for that reason other ratios have been developed in this study, which it seems wise to explain, perhaps, in detail at this point.

It has become custom to insist that merchandise inventory, both finished product, merchandise in process, and raw material, be entered on the property statement at cost, unless market conditions are such that the market value of the commodities has fallen below cost, when a reduction in the valuation is called for. This is done to prevent the inflation of the assets by the taking of profits before they have been actually realized, as no profit is actually sure until the merchandise has been sold and the actual cash or equivalent received. This is sound business sense. When we consider, however, the next economic step in manufacture and distribution, the book account, or the bills receivable, we do not find that this cost proposition exists. We do not hear it argued that the accounts and bills receivable should be carried on the statement at cost; and there is a large question as to whether or not such a plan would be feasible, equitable, or even possible. We are then confronted with the fact that, in the current assets, we have merchandise figured at cost, and receivable at cost plus. It seems very evident that if at any time any manufacturer or merchant billed out his entire inventory, transforming it into receivables, there would be a considerable increase in the total amount of the current assets, which would not make necessary any increase in the current debt, as has the cost of manufacture. It might be a mere bookkeeping transaction, accomplished easily and injecting into the current assets an amount equivalent at the very least to the entire expected profits on the transaction.

The effect of such a transformation would unquestionably be to raise the current ratio. In an explanation of the result of this action, I have used the following example in a number of instances, and have used figures which, at the start, showed a 200 per cent ratio, simply because that has been the more generally advertised proper current ratio. We start with the following presumption that a merchant has 50 units of merchandise against which he owes 25 units of debt—thus establishing the 200 per cent ratio. We then presume that this merchandise is turned into receivables, and that, in so doing, the merchant adds 25 units for profit, etc., giving 75 units of assets against 25 units of debt, producing a 300 per cent current ratio by the mere transformation from physical merchandise into receivables. It is not a question as to whether the receivables are more desirable than the merchandise, as there are arguments pro and con in this connection. It is, however, unquestionaly a fact that the transfer tends to raise the current ratio.

Therefore it becomes interesting in the study of successive statements of any company to determine the proportions that have existed from year to year between the receivables and the merchandise. If we find that the percentage of the receivables to the merchandise is increasing we may be certain that there is a larger percentage of profit included in the current assets, and logically we should expect to see an increase in the current ratio itself. If this is not the case, it makes it possible for us to inquire from the customer how this change or proportion has been affected, and why the current ratio has not risen. This is the first qualitative analysis of the current ratio, in that it gives us some comparative idea as to the value of the receivables at cost plus, as compared to the value of the merchandise at cost.

The liquidity of the receivables is a most important qualitative consideration in studying the current ratio. It is manifestly evidenced that if we were positive that the receivables of subject A were collectible with greater certainty, or more rapidly, than the receivables of subject B, we ought to be content to allow A to operate with a lower current ratio because of the better quality. This liquidity can, in a certain measure, be determined by establishing a ratio between the net sales for the year and the receivables. If subject A discloses a percentage of this kind amounting to 600 per cent, we have the indication that his receivables are being collected six times a year, or that the average length of sale approximates 60 days. Whereas, if an analysis of the statement of subject B discloses the fact that this ratio is only 400 per cent, we see that subject B is collecting his receivables only four times a year, or that the average life of the receivables is 90 days. Everything else being equal, the receivables of subject A are more liquid, and hence of greater value.

Very much the same reasoning may be applied as between the sales and the merchandise, indicating the liquidity of the merchandise.

These two tests of integral parts of the current assets are a further analysis of the current ratio from the qualitative sense, and, if properly used, may offset a decrease in the quantitative measure of the current ratio.

While the nonliquid or fixed assets of a company under credit analysis are often not seriously considered as of much value, they may be used to good effect if a proper analysis of them is made. The net worth of a partnership or corporation is distributed over all the assets, divided between the current and noncurrent. It is a well-defined credit axiom that the noncurrent assets should be provided for by the invested funds of the owners of the business. It has been recognized in the Federal Reserve act that paper is only rediscountable when the proceeds from its issue have been used for commercial purposes and not for plant development. If we were to establish a ratio relationship between the net worth of any credit subject, and its plant investment, we would determine what amount over and above that required for plant the stockholders or owners of the business had provided. If the net worth of a company is 50 units and the plant is 25 units, the owners of the business have supplied all of the money necessary for the plant and 25 units additional active commercial working capital, which may be used to purchase raw materials, pay for the cost of manufacture, carry their customers, etc. Therefore, whereas the noncurrent or fixed assets are not very generally used in determining the credit risk, the relationship between the invested funds and the noncurrent assets discloses an interesting condition of how much the owners have put into the current part of the business. If this ratio is studied from year to year it makes an interesting check on net worth. A mere increase in net worth, as shown by comparative analysis is interesting, of course, but the distribution of this increase is far more interesting. If the percentage between net worth and fixed assets is a falling one, it is pretty certainly disclosed that the subject company is expanding its plant more rapidly than the net worth of the company in proportion. It is tying up a greater fraction of its invested funds in nonliquid assets and its capitalization is becoming more and more fixed capital. It is an indication of transformation of active into semimoribund capital and is a very decided mark of a condition which when it exists on a broad scale is conducive to tightness of commercial credit, and this is one of the first steps toward a condition of crisis. It is often brought about by an optimism due to rising prices and the hope of great profits through increased production. It is a check on building operations that may leave the subject company plant topheavy.

Whereas we have already considered sales in their relationship to receivables, and merchandise, in order to determine the liquidity of certain of the current assets, we may also use them in order to determine the activity in the invested funds by establishing a ratio between sales and net worth. This may disclose any one of three conditions. First, the proportion between sales and net worth may be such that it appears to be normal. Second, this ratio may show a too rapid turnover, which may indicate undercapitalization and a feverish condition of the business. Third, this ratio may show a too low turnover, indicating dry rot or nonproductivity of the invested funds.

There is also an additional study of the statement that is of considerable value. As we have considered the net investment in its comparison of the fixed assets and sales, it is also well to consider it in proportion to that part of the funds used in the production which have been supplied by outside interests. This is the commercial or floating capital of the country, and is represented in the individual statement by the total debt. If we establish, therefore, a ratio between the total debt, as disclosed upon the property statement, and the net worth of the company, we disclose the proportion of the total capital used that is being supplied by creditors and by the owners of the business.

The seven ratios, briefly outlined, are those which the writer has adopted under the caption of internal analysis, in an attempt to analyze the current ratio, the capitalization plans, and the vitality of the business. Taken year after year in comparison they bring out interesting phases that there mere quantitative analysis or the current ratio, in the old comparative analysis of statements would not disclose.

The internal analysis theory, while interesting and instructive, is only part of the business study which could be made, and for the making of which this report is an argument. There can be no question but that different proportions should and do exist between the assets and liabilities of different types of business. It would hardly be logical or fair to compare the current ratio of a hardware concern with the current ratio of a millinery company, although, when we admit the two for one theory this is largely what is done, with purely inspirational mental reservations. Type is a certain factor in credit analysis, and the establishment of type is what should be attempted upon a large scale. This would consist first of all in assembling the property statements of as many businesses as possible, sorting or segregating them into types, and accumulating them into a typical type statement, made up of the totals of the different items of all of the individual statements. The proportions that were then found to exist upon this type statement would be a decided advance, if used in the measurement of the individual statements, over the hard-boiled two-for-one theory. These would vary from year to year with changing conditions and would create a flexible barometric measure.

However, the mere segregation into types is not by any means sufficient or scientific, as the different customs, economic and social requirements of different parts of the country would affect companies even in the same line of business. It is hardly to be supposed that a dry-goods company operating in New England would operate under the same economic laws, or be able to maintain the same proportions as one operating in California. Therefore it seems advisable in the type study to separate the types on some sectional plan, and to establish typical figures by economic sections, so that within any one section any type of business may be measured up against the typical ratios for that kind of business within that section.

Before leaving this section of the argument and taking up the method by which this was done, I can not but call attention to the fact that the sales of a company are a most important matter in the proper analysis of the property statement. The scope of the present examination would have been at least doubled, and probably trebled, if for every statement examined the sales were forthcoming. The number of statements upon which the figures of this report are based is 981. In order to secure these 981 statements in which complete figures were available, it was necessary to examine between 2,000 and 2,500 property statements. I would urge upon the Federal Reserve Board that, if possible, they develop a policy that rediscounting eligibility be dependent upon the supplying of sales, and possibly operating memoranda, in addition to the property statement. This in some lines of business would be radical, and in some lines of business not necessary, but by and large the principle is one that should unquestionably be put forth without fear or favor, and insisted upon, excepting where good cause can be advanced why the information should not be forthcoming. The principal argument has been that customers do not wish to disclose their sales for fear that their competitors will gain an intimate knowledge of the business to which they are not entitled. This seems to be a very weak-kneed position, and I would strongly urge that the Federal Reserve Board take this particular thing under very serious consideration.

THE METHOD.

Through consultation and otherwise, on the basis of establishing sections of the country which could be considered in analyzing on the type basis, a number of sections were laid out, which have been used in the statistical work of this report. These sections were indicated on an accompanying skeleton map. They are, of course, subject to adjustment, and may not meet the approval of other credit students. They, however, follow general economic lines, and have served in this particular compilation.

The commercial paper brokers were used as the source of information, and almost without exception they have forwarded to the writer complete sets of the statements of their commercial paper names, totaling something in the neighborhood of 2,500 names. These statements were first segregated according to sections, and the essential items of each statement transcribed to a form for ready compilation herewith attached.

The figures on these forms were then totaled by sections, and the following mixed type table developed, indicating the scope of the examination. In this table, which has been labeled No. 1, the first column represents the number of statements within the section that have been found available for use. The second column indicates the number of the section in which the name originated, and the following columns indicate the amounts of the various items. In order to condense and simplify the work, three ciphers have been omitted, and in reading the tables this must be remembered. (See table marked "No. 1" attached hereto.)

These figures were later sorted according to types of business within sections, listed in the same manner, and the results are indicated on the tables marked "Nos. 2 to 10," both inclusive, attached hereto and made a part hereof.

The next process was to establish the seven ratios, which have been discussed on a national basis, taking all of the statements as disclosed on Chart No. 1. These figures establish the seven ratios for mixed figures in the nine different sections, and also for the total mixed figures over the country as a whole. (Chart No. 11.)

Following this Charts Nos. 12 to 20, inclusive, were perpared, taking up several principal lines of business in which the statements received seem to provide enough statistics so that an analysis as between sections would be possible.

Following this the ratio Charts Nos. 21 to 29, inclusive, were developed, carrying out the development of the seven-point analysis for these lines of business in the varying sections, establishing the type sectional barometric figures. Charts Nos. 11 and 30 were also developed to indicate mixed type ratios and total national ratios and also the ratios for the several types of business taken as examples.

RESULTS.

A proper understanding of the results of this analysis is, of course, best disclosed by a careful comparison of figures, in detail. This, perhaps, would not be within the province of this report, other than to call attention to the more salient features, because deductions from the figures will vary with the individual knowledge and inspiration of the person making the analysis. It may be interesting however, to indicate, briefly, some of the more evident thoughts that are brought to the surface.

At the beginning of this examination, mention was made of the current ratio theory of two for one, or 200 per cent. If we turn to Chart 11, and investigate the current ratio, it will be found that the lowest point in the mixed types is displayed in section 1, and registers 233.43 per cent. The highest ratio is found in section 8 and registers 305.55 per cent, a considerable fluctuation, and the minimum being substantially above 200 per cent. The proportion of the ratio of receivables to merchandise varies from the low point in section 9 of 56.11 per cent, to the high point in section 4 of 82.43 per cent. The worth to fixed assets ratio varies from the low point in section 3 of 165.15 per cent to a high point in section 7 of 345.43 per cent. The liquidity of the receivables ratio varies from a low point of 515.08 per cent in section 5, to a high point of 890.14 per cent in section 3. The liquidity of the merchandise varies from a low point of 360.82 per cent in section 5 to a high point of 544.55 per cent in section 3. The activity of the invested funds varies from a low point of 142.52 per cent in section 8 to a high point of 297.60 per cent in section 6. The ratio of debt to net worth ranges from a low point of 22.16 per cent in section 8 to a high point of 52.46 per cent in section 3. If we are to consider these ratios in their relationship to types of business, we will find a, perhaps, even more interesting variation. In this particular phase, I have eliminated from the consideration the types of business in sections where less than five statements have been considered. The highest current ratio found is in the hardware type in section 6, based on 13 names, and runs to 381.05 per cent. The lowest ratio in this type is 253.97, based on 16 names in section 7. The lowest current ratio for type by sections is 157.98 per cent, being a somewhat peculiar ratio, in that it is one taken between the current assets and the total liabilities, because of the fact that in this particular section, in this particular line of business, a large part of the debt has been funded in several instances, but still from a liquidating standpoint is still largely current. This ratio is found as a result of 10 packers' statements in section 3. The highest packers' ratio is found in section 2, being made up of only one statement, which shows a current ratio of 640 per cent, and is probably not typical. The national figures, using the current assets and current liabilities only for packers, is 235.49 per cent, and the ratio between the current assets and the total liabilities, thereby taking account of the bonded or deferred debt, is 160.65 per cent. A fair credit current ratio is probably something in the neighborhood of 185 per cent.

An analysis of Chart No. 30, made up of the national ratios of various types of business, discloses the fact that type No. 7, or farm implements, registers the highest current ratio. It amounts to 355.78 per cent, based on the composite figures of 20 statements, representing in bulk a net worth of $61,328,000 and sales of $63,074,000. Taken on the purely quantitative two-for-one theory, this would seem like a very high average. When taken however, from the qualitative angle, this extremely high ratio does not appear so prominently supersatisfactory. While the final mixed current ratio taken from the whole 981 statements is only 241.56 per cent, giving type 7 an apparent margin of betterment of 114.22 points, the qualitative ratios of sales to receivables, and sales to merchandise, do not show to as good advantage. These by comparison are as follows:

	Mixed national figures.	Type 7.
	Per cent.	Per cent.
Current ratio	241.56	355.78
Sales—Receivables	734.61	329.62
Sales—Merchandise	473.44	209.33

The greater slowness of turnover, both of receivables and merchandise, evidences much less liquidity of receivables, and slower merchandising.

The ratio of sales to worth of 102.84 per cent, as compared to the mixed ratio of 249.34 per cent, indicates a very much slower than the average turnover, or a more torpid investment.

In contra to this type study it will be interesting to analyze the typical indications of type 12, or the packer group. Here we find a current ratio of 235.08 per cent, some 6 points below the mixed type. When we substitute for this ratio between current assets and total debt, 160.65 per cent, or an estimate true ratio of say 175–180 per cent, we find the current ratio from 60 to 70 points below national mixed current ratio. Here again, however, we find the qualitative ratios supporting the lower ratio in the same manner in which they tended to level the higher ratio. The same kind of comparative summary is interesting.

	Mixed national figures.	Type 12.
	Per cent.	Per cent.
Current ratio	241.56	160–170
Sales—Receivables	734.61	1,027.30
Sales—Merchandise	473.44	829.57

The very much faster turnover of receivables and merchandise indicates clearly greater liquidity in the current assets, and hence a greater potential liquidating strength in the current ratio, even if quantitatively lower.

The ratio of sales to worth, 483.27 per cent, as compared to the mixed ratio of 249.34 per cent, also indicates a much more active investment. This is somewhat offset by the fact of the higher debt ratio of 80.36 per cent compared to the mixed ratio of only 47.19 per cent.

This shows how the internal 7-point ratio analysis expands ordinary analysis by checking and explanatory studies. This same comparison between the ratios of an individual statement and the type and national mixed figures shows weaknesses of collection methods, poor or good merchandising, etc.

The two types used in detail were selected because they formed radical extremes, but typical variations occur in the other types, and within any type sectional variations of a similar nature are so very apparent that a detailed explanation in this report is omitted other than to call attention to the charts on which they are indicated.

In order to eliminate unnecessary details and still to disclose the principle, I have compiled Chart No. 30, indicating a comparison between nine types of business, using the national ratios. These businesses are as follows:

Dry goods, wholesale	1
Hardware, wholesale	2
Grocers, wholesale	3
Milling	4
Tanners	5
Drugs	6
Farm implements, etc	7
Furniture	8
Lumber	9
Packers, fruits, etc	10
Department stores	11
Packers	12
Boots and shoes	13
Paper	14
Iron and steel	15
Oils	16
Hats, caps, men's clothing, etc	17
Seeds, etc	18
Knitting mills, etc	19
Building materials, etc	20
Machinery	21
Household supplies	22
Foodstuffs, miscellaneous	23
Rubber goods	24
Auto accessories, etc	25
Cotton mills	26
Fuel	27
Woolen	28
Automobiles	29
Miscellaneous	30

An examination of this chart indicates that the current ratio in the packing business is lowest of that of any of the types. With the old-fashioned 200 per cent current ratio theory this might lead the analyst to believe that the packing business was weak, because of the lowness of its current ratio, although inspirational analysis has made indefinite allowances. If, however, we apply to the condition the qualitative analysis, we find that the receivables in the packing business display a very much greater liquidity, as does also the merchandise, the sales to receivable ratio and the sales to merchandise ratio being very much higher than in any of the other types of business. This substantiates the general belief that a packing company can operate safely on a very much lower current ratio than can the other types of business. We also find that the activity of the investment in the packing business is very much higher than that of other lines of business. The ratio of worth to fixed assets indicates that the packers rely very largely upon outside investment for the carrying of their current assets, because it displays a very low ratio. This is substantiated also by the ratio of debt to net worth, and it is considerably higher than any of the other types under discussion.

This national chart, taken as a first guide in comparison with an individual statement, would indicate whether or not the figures of the individual statement were approximately in line with the type of business into which they fall. This being generally established, we may progress to the analysis of the figures by comparing them with the section within which the type operates and get a further viewpoint as to the nearness of the approach to the actual condition in the line of business.

Chart No. 1.—*Mixed national figures.*

Statements.	Section.	Current assets.	Current liabilities.	Debt.	Receivables.	Merchandise.	Fixed.	Worth.	Sales.
91	1	$199,451	$85,443	$91,177	$75,184	$101,774	$110,008	$210,651	$440,701
138	2	273,596	116,508	124,321	87,423	145,813	155,780	286,737	576,535
165	3	774,845	328,285	419,068	252,652	412,997	483,659	798,773	2,248,963
107	4	66,278	25,374	26,514	27,224	33,026	21,079	61,119	152,147
72	5	167,817	61,958	78,428	62,364	89,025	85,228	170,007	321,225
144	6	195,008	82,273	83,276	70,094	106,046	96,615	180,478	537,104
127	7	101,250	40,110	40,802	38,902	54,113	24,113	83,295	244,267
36	8	33,330	10,908	10,971	12,416	17,860	27,673	49,491	70,538
41	9	68,461	26,668	26,786	22,026	39,253	28,953	69,421	170,932
981		1,880,036	777,517	901,343	648,285	1,005,907	1,033,108	1,909,972	4,762,412

CHART NO. 2.—Section No. 1.

Statements.	Type.	Current assets.	Current liabilities.	Debt.	Receivables.	Merchandise.	Fixed.	Worth.	Sales.
6	1	$11,215	$4,646	$5,067	$5,039	$5,674	$2,037	$8,191	$29,749
2	2	788	352	352	319	325	193	833	1,974
5	3	3,207	1,578	1,643	1,470	1,470	451	2,027	10,037
1	4	587	150	150	122	411	87	524	7,165
6	5	22,709	10,847	10,847	8,332	12,790	1,870	12,554	45,226
2	6	18,427	6,749	6,749	3,913	13,611	35,461	42,532	44,711
1	8	640	230	230	219	349	398	809	1,459
4	9	3,522	1,312	1,359	1,654	1,612	2,220	4,391	8,056
1	10	2,548	941	941	1,685	717	232	1,840	10,000
1	11	694	226	226	263	411	559	812	2,199
1	12	641	430	430	290	282	688	797	2,629
20	13	51,265	23,669	24,083	23,200	23,871	13,678	41,616	109,817
2	14	1,040	501	575	236	714	2,144	2,069	2,502
2	15	2,445	836	998	601	1,742	2,014	3,661	4,628
4	17	2,751	1,371	1,423	749	1,786	722	2,039	4,503
2	19	953	353	353	303	595	597	1,139	1,942
5	20	6,224	2,741	3,782	3,121	2,395	6,489	8,863	16,328
5	21	5,028	1,968	2,267	1,543	2,342	5,921	8,069	9,709
3	23	1,587	305	305	1,002	316	635	1,871	6,562
4	24	18,424	8,123	8,127	7,166	9,246	11,128	21,425	35,800
14	28	44,776	18,115	21,270	13,958	27,715	22,484	44,589	85,705
91	....	199,451	85,443	91,177	75,184	107,774	110,008	210,651	440,701

CHART NO. 3.—Section No. 2.

Statements.	Type.	Current assets.	Current liabilities.	Debt.	Receivables.	Merchandise.	Fixed.	Worth.	Sales.
7	1	$11,690	$5,436	$6,048	$5,500	$5,400	$2,026	$7,659	$25,266
10	2	6,428	2,410	2,791	1,706	4,155	1,372	4,949	13,760
24	3	17,858	7,794	10,707	6,835	9,213	9,326	16,568	59,123
7	5	9,051	3,452	3,731	3,028	4,717	2,632	7,889	14,474
3	6	5,755	2,154	2,154	1,640	3,430	3,892	7,050	12,234
2	7	2,798	1,360	1,360	1,070	1,453	1,886	3,323	6,618
2	8	4,406	2,384	2,384	2,334	1,735	6,092	8,120	5,944
3	9	2,533	1,059	1,059	1,175	802	948	2,410	6,300
1	10	228	69	69	51	143	802	961	1,038
10	11	34,515	12,617	12,727	11,980	19,102	29,711	52,286	83,707
1	12	1,120	175	175	278	751	2,189	2,685	2,652
14	13	43,765	20,216	20,241	12,860	24,570	1,503	24,473	53,080
3	14	2,606	759	2,855	880	917	7,361	5,999	7,135
1	15	661	300	300	139	507	1,023	662	1,905
7	16	27,126	13,743	13,743	7,839	17,058	14,897	28,740	100,552
18	17	45,383	20,723	20,770	14,759	27,792	33,830	57,222	78,057
2	18	1,767	453	453	308	1,311	519	1,833	1,897
8	19	6,762	3,293	3,435	2,075	4,050	5,697	8,385	19,604
2	20	1,783	367	587	406	1,272	1,144	2,339	3,422
4	21	6,333	2,413	2,413	2,179	3,539	2,652	6,275	17,599
2	22	4,313	1,852	2,950	1,187	1,757	6,358	7,495	12,062
3	23	9,447	5,476	5,476	3,456	4,975	13,398	17,504	33,264
2	24	26,518	7,462	7,462	5,508	6,727	6,226	11,304	15,787
2	28	740	431	431	230	437	296	606	1,950
138	....	273,596	116,598	124,321	87,423	145,813	155,780	286,737	576,535

CHART No. 4.—Section No. 3.

Statements.	Type.	Current assets.	Current liabilities.	Debt.	Receivables.	Merchandise.	Fixed.	Worth.	Sales.
12	1	$12,680	$5,093	$5,125	$4,831	$7,209	$2,623	$10,184	$23,783
14	2	8,898	2,253	2,693	3,318	5,234	3,446	9,578	18,192
29	3	24,420	10,038	10,095	7,423	15,601	6,477	20,642	80,095
1	4	820	76	76	43	97	454	1,049	5,869
8	5	17,443	5,561	6,989	4,517	11,894	7,195	16,857	33,697
3	6	1,908	939		806	970	554	1,078	4,211
5	7	7,806	2,983	4,483	1,141	5,093	9,758	12,818	11,475
10	8	6,585	2,269	2,458	2,088	4,364	5,793	9,838	12,935
6	9	12,309	4,432	4,607	3,199	7,656	14,970	20,690	23,148
1	10	1,045	606	606	564	373	278	717	1,775
2	11	1,143	653	1,059	280	820	1,200	1,256	2,767
10	12	397,286	169,890	251,470	146,215	176,792	157,932	297,443	1,490,928
9	13	6,258	2,025	2,137	2,742	3,243	861	4,922	13,438
4	14	1,900	682	682	656	1,134	2,688	3,788	5,514
7	16	11,510	5,290	5,846	3,138	7,254	8,818	13,225	32,009
4	17	5,578	2,679	2,679	2,266	2,714	497	3,024	8,759
4	18	5,060	3,153	5,837	806	3,888	5,294	4,957	6,009
4	19	2,848	949	949	704	1,919	1,272	3,058	3,779
3	20	3,330	765	2,003	1,116	2,041	9,877	10,727	4,996
8	21	12,963	4,731	5,111	3,957	7,688	6,781	13,940	16,347
4	22	9,458	4,211	4,273	1,586	7,250	16,896	21,698	18,450
2	23	5,676	3,116	3,116	2,539	1,483	8,882	11,313	42,966
6	24	155,008	71,858	71,901	41,308	100,052	142,477	211,522	274,343
1	25	9,796	3,924	3,924	2,318	6,300	16,354	22,048	24,103
1	27	1,869	1,092	1,092	1,621	1	601	1,294	9,262
2	28	2,730	1,555	1,555	779	1,216	731	1,432	5,456
5	29	48,511	17,462	17,462	12,691	30,711	50,950	68,885	72,577
165		774,845	328,285	419,068	252,652	412,997	483,659	798,773	2,248,963

CHART No. 5.—Section No. 4.

Statements.	Type.	Current assets.	Current liabilities.	Debt.	Receivables.	Merchandise.	Fixed.	Worth.	Sales.
6	1	$4,287	$1,497	$1,497	$1,920	$2,340	$472	$3,494	$7,817
25	2	19,791	7,281	7,327	8,077	10,655	2,693	15,530	36,303
47	3	20,139	7,574	7,646	9,242	9,526	3,623	16,387	64,049
4	4	1,890	166	166	629	322	895	2,515	8,264
1	5	203	99	99	61	128	15	119	479
4	6	2,405	794	996	944	1,368	556	1,962	4,743
1	7	764	280	280	361	390	152	636	941
2	8	1,715	564	564	983	669	324	1,501	2,652
2	9	1,437	664	664	675	897	562	1,339	2,566
6	11	6,205	3,074	3,644	1,709	3,255	5,935	8,453	10,712
1	13	815	216	216	470	324	71	669	914
5	19	5,263	2,352	2,602	1,665	2,648	4,082	6,170	10,626
1	20	846	530	530	314	470	1,068	1,362	1,005
2	22	518	283	283	174	334	621	952	1,086
107		66,278	25,374	26,514	27,224	33,026	21,079	61,119	152,147

CHART No. 6.—Section No. 5.

Statements.	Type.	Current assets.	Current liabilities.	Debt.	Receivables.	Merchandise.	Fixed.	Worth.	Sales.
4	1	$9,203	$4,216	$4,446	$4,104	$4,055	$1,551	$6,290	$13,598
8	2	21,262	8,074	8,108	8,487	11,805	5,810	18,765	41,161
15	3	20,638	8,683	10,319	8,812	10,455	4,067	13,957	60,143
2	5	20,241	8,635	8,635	4,978	14,255	9,302	20,880	31,983
3	7	31,971	5,858	11,871	12,376	15,776	14,910	31,413	22,176
3	8	1,236	448	448	376	818	555	1,325	1,773
11	9	13,273	5,516	6,220	6,595	5,953	4,154	11,163	22,210
3	12	6,087	2,950	2,950	1,754	3,505	4,059	7,155	33,864
7	13	9,082	3,930	3,930	3,847	4,417	1,695	6,722	16,125
2	14	4,902	2,347	9,273	1,346	1,158	16,079	11,707	9,651
3	16	3,360	1,450	1,526	922	2,166	2,590	4,425	24,035
3	17	7,712	3,562	4,357	2,986	4,419	3,449	6,679	12,173
1	18	349	148	148	97	237	140	338	634
2	19	4,109	2,204	2,204	1,250	2,537	2,486	4,300	6,459
1	20	269	63	63	75	186	783	987	404
2	21	5,510	2,163	2,163	1,980	3,116	4,296	7,643	8,356
1	22	8,252	1,445	1,445	2,349	3,846	8,798	15,605	15,000
1	24	361	266	302	30	321	504	563	1,479
72		167,817	61,958	78,428	62,264	89,025	85,228	170,007	321,225

CHART No. 7.—*Section No. 6.*

Statements.	Type.	Current assets.	Current liabilities.	Debt.	Receivables.	Merchandise.	Fixed.	Worth.	Sales.
12	1	$42,364	$21,648	$21,648	$19,137	$20,442	$9,654	$26,546	$82,025
13	2	8,989	2,359	2,434	2,309	5,944	1,182	7,536	18,290
27	3	24,384	10,228	10,348	8,499	14,443	5,079	18,968	75,238
25	4	17,093	6,853	6,853	3,786	7,615	15,674	25,105	134,939
1	5	435	167	167	147	273	73	341	371
4	6	2,401	412	412	844	1,471	535	2,503	5,265
6	7	4,491	1,597	1,669	1,876	2,334	2,103	4,693	6,239
1	8	262	133	133	99	158	72	201	454
15	9	8,984	3,551	3,552	3,556	4,555	3,702	9,315	13,495
4	11	15,571	5,568	5,718	4,256	8,654	22,311	32,177	42,201
1	12	220	118	118	20	195	155	257	916
10	13	52,600	22,904	23,084	19,374	29,979	26,212	33,822	121,073
2	14	576	129	129	170	394	310	697	2,226
2	16	663	280	280	286	341	256	648	1,645
4	17	4,920	2,632	2,632	1,817	2,806	540	3,230	7,402
2	18	915	259	259	274	538	358	1,014	3,055
1	19	1,056	355	355	530	515	182	683	1,413
4	20	3,422	1,400	1,685	1,108	2,185	4,116	5,320	8,048
5	21	3,998	1,394	1,514	1,274	2,432	2,168	4,528	8,688
3	22	791	245	245	310	424	654	1,184	1,526
2	23	873	41	41	422	348	879	1,710	2,095
144	......	195,008	82,275	83,276	70,094	106,046	96,615	180,478	537,104

CHART No. 8.—*Section No. 7.*

Statements.	Type.	Current assets.	Current liabilities.	Debt.	Receivables.	Merchandise.	Fixed.	Worth.	Sales.
27	1	$31,834	$13,118	$13,128	$12,106	$16,392	$7,020	$25,752	$61,409
16	2	10,865	4,278	4,359	3,734	6,306	1,466	7,642	19,856
46	3	34,425	15,383	15,658	14,013	18,134	4,373	22,898	96,495
9	4	2,906	918	918	777	1,616	1,965	3,901	25,241
1	5	1,526	226	226	883	454	339	1,645	5,632
1	6	806	213	238	291	482	168	739	2,156
1	7	208	53	53	75	103	86	242	502
4	8	2,248	998	998	946	1,261	662	1,917	3,112
4	9	2,030	412	412	938	968	2,612	4,232	2,188
6	11	4,102	1,381	1,396	1,286	2,594	2,385	5,091	7,923
2	13	2,179	673	673	798	1,237	222	1,729	3,290
1	14	395	128	128	238	151	100	367	666
2	15	3,741	919	1,080	1,433	2,092	1,120	3,720	7,949
2	16	622	279	279	323	214	537	841	2,799
1	17	337	47	47	136	160	13	303	608
2	20	1,074	273	273	153	830	507	1,308	1,610
2	21	1,937	811	936	772	1,119	538	968	2,831
127	......	101,250	40,110	40,802	38,902	54,113	24,113	83,295	244,267

CHART No. 9.—*Section No. 8.*

Statements.	Type.	Current assets.	Current liabilities.	Debt.	Receivables.	Merchandise.	Fixed.	Worth.	Sales.
4	1	$1,849	$698	$698	$743	$1,058	$837	$1,987	$4,027
4	2	4,851	1,899	1,899	1,732	2,977	1,741	4,651	9,949
5	3	1,811	562	562	761	977	195	1,429	4,790
1	4	796	126	126	276	305	538	1,008	6,751
1	6	512	73	73	149	347	33	467	1,122
7	9	5,315	2,116	2,116	2,550	2,467	2,295	5,416	11,430
1	10	422	......	......	122	268	672	1,043	1,231
3	11	1,353	427	427	324	878	1,031	1,926	3,158
1	12	1,776	1,046	1,046	591	1,108	1,272	2,003	4,987
1	13	211	118	118	98	80	156	249	401
1	17	533	152	152	165	367	......	381	716
1	21	1,790	968	1,031	570	1,165	1,024	1,801	1,466
1	22	905	415	415	394	464	83	554	2,043
4	23	10,780	2,096	2,096	3,759	5,175	17,579	26,148	17,301
1	25	426	212	212	182	224	217	431	1,166
36	......	33,330	10,908	10,971	12,416	17,860	27,673	49,494	70,538

CHART No. 10.—Section No. 9.

Statements.	Type.	Current assets.	Current liabilities.	Debt.	Receivables.	Merchandise.	Fixed.	Worth.	Sales.
5	1	$7,854	$3,178	$3,178	$2,956	$4,006	$546	$5,525	$12,659
7	2	10,417	3,595	3,655	3,006	6,808	1,887	8,512	18,175
7	3	5,591	2,229	2,262	2,292	3,067	872	4,200	17,727
4	4	8,533	2,414	2,414	2,626	2,935	6,112	12,233	50,560
2	5	4,263	1,761	1,787	1,368	2,521	1,099	3,576	5,848
3	6	2,812	1,006	1,006	852	1,823	336	2,106	5,597
2	7	8,888	3,869	3,869	2,256	5,681	3,185	8,203	13,123
3	8	4,846	2,028	2,023	2,317	2,421	1,285	4,103	6,911
2	9	1,789	697	697	696	922	3,550	4,675	4,264
2	11	3,700	1,530	1,530	574	2,814	821	2,990	9,866
2	12	10,330	3,663	3,663	2,584	5,368	9,114	12,212	22,805
2	13	1,638	698	698	519	987	146	1,086	3,397
41		68,461	26,668	26,786	22,026	39,253	28,953	69,421	170,932

CHART No. 11.—National mixed type ratios.

Sections	1	2	3	4	5	6	7	8	9	Nat.
Number of statements	91	138	165	107	72	144	127	36	41	981
	Per ct.	Per ct.	Per ct.	Per ct.	Per ct.	Per ct.	Per ct.	Per ct.	Per ct.	Per ct.
Current ratio	233.43	234.65	236.02	261.20	270.85	237.02	252.40	305.55	256.81	241.24
Receivable merchandise	69.76	59.95	61.17	82.43	70.05	66.09	71.89	69.51	56.11	64.64
Worth—fixed assets	191.48	184.06	165.15	289.95	199.47	186.80	345.43	178.84	239.77	184.47
Sales—receivable	586.16	659.48	890.14	558.87	515.08	766.26	627.90	598.12	775.04	734.61
Sales—merchandise	408.91	395.39	544.55	460.68	360.82	506.48	451.53	394.94	435.46	473.44
Sales—worth	209.21	200.71	281.55	248.97	188.94	297.60	293.25	142.52	246.22	249.34
Debt—worth	43.28	43.35	52.46	43.38	46.13	46.14	48.98	22.16	38.58	47.19

CHART No. 12.—Wholesale dry goods—Type 1.

Statements.	Section.	Current assets.	Current liabilities.	Debt.	Receivables.	Merchandise.	Fixed.	Worth.	Sales.
6	1	$11,215	$4,646	$5,067	$5,039	$5,674	$2,037	$8,191	$29,749
7	2	11,690	5,436	6,048	5,500	5,400	2,026	7,659	25,266
12	3	12,680	5,093	5,125	4,831	7,209	2,623	10,184	23,783
6	4	4,287	1,497	1,497	1,920	2,340	472	3,494	7,817
4	5	9,203	4,216	4,466	4,104	4,055	1,551	6,290	13,598
12	6	42,364	21,648	21,648	19,137	20,442	9,654	26,546	82,025
27	7	31,834	13,118	13,128	12,106	16,392	7,020	25,752	61,409
4	8	1,849	698	638	743	1,053	837	1,987	4,027
5	9	7,854	3,178	3,178	2,956	4,006	546	5,525	12,659
83		132,976	59,530	60,855	56,236	66,576	26,766	95,628	260,333

CHART No. 13.—Wholesale hardware—Type 2.

Statements.	Section.	Current assets.	Current liabilities.	Debt.	Receivables.	Merchandise.	Fixed.	Worth.	Sales.
2	1	$788	$352	$352	$319	$325	$193	$833	$1,974
10	2	6,428	2,410	2,791	1,706	4,155	1,372	4,949	13,760
14	3	8,898	2,253	2,603	3,318	5,234	3,446	9,578	18,192
25	4	19,791	7,281	7,327	8,077	10,655	2,693	15,530	36,303
8	5	21,262	8,074	8,108	8,487	11,805	5,810	18,785	41,151
13	6	8,989	2,359	2,434	2,309	5,904	1,182	7,536	18,290
16	7	10,865	4,278	4,359	3,734	6,306	1,466	7,642	19,856
4	8	4,851	1,899	1,899	1,732	2,977	1,741	4,651	9,949
7	9	10,417	3,595	3,655	3,006	6,808	1,887	8,512	18,175
99		92,289	32,501	33,528	32,688	54,209	19,790	77,996	177,660

CHART No. 14.—*Wholesale grocer—Type 3.*

Statements.	Section.	Current assets.	Current liabilities.	Debt.	Receivables.	Merchandise.	Fixed.	Worth.	Sales.
5	1	$3,207	$1,578	$1,643	$1,470	$1,470	$451	$2,027	$10,037
24	2	17,858	7,794	10,707	6,835	9,213	9,326	16,568	59,128
29	3	24,420	10,038	10,095	7,423	15,601	6,477	20,642	80,095
47	4	20,139	7,574	7,646	9,242	9,526	3,623	16,387	64,039
15	5	20,638	8,653	10,319	8,812	10,455	4,067	13,957	60,143
27	6	24,384	10,228	10,348	8,499	14,443	5,079	18,968	75,238
46	7	34,425	15,383	15,658	14,013	18,134	4,373	22,898	96,495
5	8	1,811	562	562	761	977	195	1,429	4,790
7	9	5,591	2,229	2,262	2,292	3,067	872	4,200	17,727
205	....	152,473	64,069	69,240	59,247	82,886	34,463	117,076	467,692

CHART No. 15.—*Tanners—Type 5.*

Statements.	Section.	Current assets.	Current liabilities.	Debt.	Receivables.	Merchandise.	Fixed.	Worth.	Sales.
6	1	$22,709	$10,847	$10,847	$8,332	$12,790	$1,870	$12,554	$45,226
7	2	9,051	3,452	3,721	3,028	4,717	2,632	7,889	14,474
8	3	17,443	5,561	6,989	4,517	11,894	7,195	16,857	33,697
1	4	203	99	99	61	128	15	119	479
2	5	20,241	8,635	8,635	4,978	14,255	9,302	20,880	31,983
1	6	435	167	167	147	273	73	341	871
1	7	1,536	226	226	883	454	339	1,645	5,632
2	9	4,263	1,761	1,787	1,368	2,521	1,099	3,576	5,848
28	....	75,881	30,738	32,481	23,314	47,032	22,525	63,861	138,210

CHART No. 16.—*Drugs—Type 6.*

Statements.	Section.	Current assets.	Current liabilities.	Debt.	Receivables.	Merchandise.	Fixed.	Worth.	Sales.
2	1	$18,427	$6,749	$6,749	$3,913	$13,011	$35,461	$42,532	$44,711
3	2	5,755	2,154	2,154	1,640	3,430	3,892	7,050	12,234
3	3	1,906	939	939	806	970	554	1,478	4,211
4	4	2,405	794	996	944	1,368	556	1,962	4,743
4	6	2,401	412	412	844	1,471	535	2,503	5,265
1	7	806	213	238	291	482	168	739	2,156
1	8	512	73	73	149	347	33	467	1,122
3	9	2,812	1,006	1,006	852	1,823	336	2,106	5,597
21	....	35,024	12,340	12,567	9,439	22,902	41,535	58,837	80,039

CHART No. 17.—*Farm implements—Type 7.*

Statements.	Section.	Current assets.	Current liabilities.	Debt.	Receivables.	Merchandise.	Fixed.	Worth.	Sales.
2	2	$2,798	$1,360	$1,360	$1,070	$1,453	$1,886	$3,323	$6,618
5	3	7,806	2,983	4,483	1,141	5,093	9,758	12,818	13,475
1	4	764	280	280	361	390	152	636	941
3	5	31,971	5,858	11,871	12,376	15,776	14,910	31,413	22,176
6	6	4,491	1,597	1,669	1,876	2,334	2,103	4,693	6,239
1	7	208	53	53	75	103	86	242	502
2	9	8,888	3,869	3,869	2,236	5,681	3,185	8,203	13,123
20	....	56,926	16,000	23,585	19,135	30,830	32,080	61,328	63,074

CHART No. 18.—*Lumber—Type 9.*

Statements.	Section.	Current assets.	Current liabilities.	Debt.	Receivables.	Merchandise.	Fixed.	Worth.	Sales.
4	1	$3,522	$1,312	$1,359	$1,654	$1,612	$2,220	$4,391	$8,056
3	2	2,533	1,059	1,059	1,175	802	948	2,410	6,300
6	3	12,309	4,432	4,607	3,199	7,656	14,970	20,690	23,148
2	4	1,437	664	664	675	597	562	1,339	2,566
11	5	13,273	5,546	6,220	6,595	5,953	4,154	11,163	22,210
15	6	8,934	3,551	3,552	3,556	4,551	3,702	9,315	13,495
4	7	2,030	412	412	938	938	2,612	4,232	2,188
7	8	5,315	2,116	2,116	2,550	2,467	2,295	5,416	11,430
2	9	1,789	697	697	696	922	3,550	4,675	4,264
54		51,192	19,759	20,686	21,038	25,528	35,013	63,631	93,657

CHART No. 19.—*Packers—Type 12.*

Statements.	Section.	Current assets.	Current liabilities.	Debt.	Receivables.	Merchandise.	Fixed.	Worth.	Sales.
1	1	$641	$430	$430	$290	$282	$688	$797	$2,629
1	2	1,120	175	175	278	751	2,189	2,685	2,652
10	3	397,286	169,890	252,470	146,215	176,792	157,932	297,443	1,490,928
3	5	6,087	2,950	2,950	1,754	3,505	4,059	7,155	33,864
1	6	220	118	118	20	195	155	257	916
1	8	1,776	1,046	1,046	591	1,108	1,272	2,003	4,987
2	9	10,330	3,663	3,663	2,584	5,268	9,114	12,212	22,805
19		417,460	177,272	259,851	151,732	187,901	175,409	322,552	1,558,781

CHART No. 20.—*Boots and shoes—Type 13.*

Statements.	Section.	Current assets.	Current liabilities.	Debt.	Receivables.	Merchandise.	Fixed.	Worth.	Sales.
20	1	$51,265	$23,669	$24,083	$23,200	$23,871	$13,678	$41,616	$109,817
14	2	43,765	20,216	20,241	12,860	24,570	1,503	24,473	53,080
9	3	6,258	2,025	2,137	2,742	3,243	816	4,922	13,438
1	4	815	216	216	470	324	71	669	914
7	5	9,082	3,930	3,930	3,847	4,417	1,695	6,722	16,126
10	6	52,600	22,904	23,084	19,374	29,979	26,212	33,822	121,073
2	7	2,179	673	673	798	1,237	222	1,729	3,290
1	8	211	118	118	98	80	156	249	401
2	9	1,638	698	698	519	987	146	1,086	3,397
66		167,813	74,449	75,180	63,908	88,707	44,499	115,288	321,536

CHART No. 21.—*Dry goods—Type 1.*

Sections	1	2	3	4	5	6	7	8	9	Nat.
Number of statements	6	7	12	6	4	12	27	4	5	83
	Per cent.	Per cent.	Per cent.	Per ct.	Per cent.	Per cent.	Per cent.	Per cent.	Per cent.	Per cent.
Current ratio	241.39	215.04	248.96	288.37	218.28	195.69	242.67	264.89	247.13	223.33
Receivable merchandise	90.41	101.85	67.01	82.05	101.21	93.61	73.85	70.22	73.48	84.61
Worth—fixed	402.11	378.03	388.29	740.25	405.54	274.97	366.83	237.39	1,011.90	357.27
Sales—receivable	590.37	459.38	492.29	407.13	331.33	428.16	507.26	541.49	428.24	462.10
Sales—merchandise	524.30	467.88	329.90	334.05	335.33	401.25	374.62	380.62	316.00	391.03
Sales—worth	363.19	329.88	233.53	223.72	216.18	308.99	238.46	202.66	229.12	272.23
Debt—worth	61.86	78.96	50.32	42.84	71.00	36.36	50.97	35.12	57.52	63.66

CHART No. 22.—*Hardware—Type 2.*

Sections	1	2	3	4	5	6	7	8	9	Nat.
Number of statements	2	10	14	25	8	13	16	4	7	99
	Per cent.	Per cent.	Per cent.	Per ct.	Per cent.	Per cent.	Per cent.	Per cent.	Per cent.	Per cent.
Current ratio	223.22	266.72	394.94	271.82	263.33	381.05	253.97	255.45	289.76	283.95
Receivable merchandise	98.15	41.06	63.39	75.80	71.89	38.84	59.21	58.17	44.15	60.29
Worth—fixed	431.60	260.70	277.94	576.68	322.97	637.56	521.28	267.14	457.00	394.11
Sales—receivable	618.80	806.58	548.28	449.46	484.98	792.11	531.76	574.42	604.62	543.50
Sales—merchandise	607.38	331.16	347.57	340.71	348.67	207.70	314.87	334.19	266.96	327.78
Sales—worth	236.97	278.03	189.93	233.76	219.34	242.70	259.83	213.91	213.52	227.78
Debt—worth	42.25	56.39	27.17	47.15	43.20	32.29	48.86	40.82	42.93	42.98

CHART No. 23.—*Grocers—Type 3.*

Sections	1	2	3	4	5	6	7	8	9	Nat.
Number of statements	5	24	29	47	15	27	46	5	7	205
	Per cent.	Per cent.	Per cent.	Per ct.	Per cent.	Per cent.	Per cent.	Per cent.	Per cent.	Per cent.
Current ratio	203.26	229.12	243.27	265.89	237.68	233.42	223.78	322.22	250.82	237.98
Receivable merchandise	100.00	74.18	47.58	97.56	84.26	58.84	77.27	77.89	74.73	71.60
Worth—fixed	499.41	177.66	318.69	452.58	343.17	373.45	523.62	732.82	481.65	339.71
Sales—receivable	682.78	865.07	1,079.03	692.91	682.51	585.25	688.61	629.43	773.42	788.06
Sales—merchandise	682.78	641.77	413.39	672.25	575.25	520.93	532.12	490.29	577.89	564.25
Sales—worth	495.16	356.87	338.01	390.79	430.91	396.65	421.41	335.19	422.07	399.47
Debt—wotrh	81.05	64.61	48.90	46.65	73.93	54.55	68.38	39.32	53.85	59.14

CHART No. 24.—*Tanners—Type 5.*

Sections	1	2	3	4	5	6	7	8	9	Nat.
Number of statements	6	7	8	1	2	1	1		2	28
	Per cent.	Per cent.	Per cent.	Per ct.	Per cent.	Per cent.	Per cent.	Per cent.	Per cent.	Per cent.
Current ratio	209.35	262.19	313.66	205.05	234.40	260.47	379.64		241.28	246.86
Receivable merchandise	65.14	64.19	37.97	47.65	34.92	53.84	25.59		54.26	49.57
Worth—fixed	671.33	299.73	234.28	793.33	224.46	467.12	487.90		325.37	283.51
Sales—receivable	542.79	359.33	746.00	785.24	642.98	592.51	637.82		427.48	592.81
Sales—merchandise	353.60	306.84	283.31	374.21	224.36	319.04	1,240.52		231.97	293.86
Sales—worth	360.25	183.47	199.89	402.53	153.17	255.42	342.37		166.53	216.42
Debt—worth	86.40	47.29	41.46	43.35	41.35	48.97	13.37		49.97	50.86

CHART No. 25.—*Drugs—Type 6.*

Sections	1	2	3	4	5	6	7	8	9	Nat.
Number of statements	2	3	3	4	0	4	1	1	3	21
	Per cent.	Per cent.	Per cent.	Per ct.	Per cent.	Per cent.	Per cent.	Per cent.	Per cent.	Per cent.
Current ratio	273.03	267.17	202.98	302.89		582.75	378.40	701.36	279.52	283.83
Receivable merchandise	30.07	47.81	83.09	69.00		57.37	60.37	42.94	46.73	41.21
Worth—fixed	111.94	181.14	266.78	352.87		467.85	439.88	1,415.15	626.78	141.85
Sales—receivable	1,142.62	745.97	522.45	502.43		623.81	740.89	753.02	656.92	847.96
Sales—merchandise	343.64	356.66	434.12	316.71		357.91	347.30	333.33	307.02	349.48
Sales—worth	105.12	173.53	284.91	241.74		210.34	291.74	240.25	265.76	136.05
Debt—worth	15.86	30.55	63.53	50.76		16.46	32.20	15.63	47.76	21.35

106597—19——8

CHART No. 26.—*Farm implements—Type 7.*

Sections	1	2	3	4	5	6	7	8	9	Nat.
Number of statements..	....	2	5	1	3	6	1	....	2	20
	Per cent.	Per cent.	Per cent.	Per ct.	Per cent.	Per cent.	Per cent.	Per cent.	Per cent.	Per cent.
Current ratio	....	205.73	261.68	272.85	545.78	281.21	483.61	....	329.72	355.78
Receivable merchandise	....	73.64	22.40	92.56	78.45	80.37	72.81	....	39.35	63.50
Worth—fixed	....	176.19	131.35	418.42	210.88	223.15	281.39	....	257.56	191.17
Sales—receivable	....	618.50	1,180.98	260.66	179.18	232.56	569.32	....	586.86	329.62
Sales—merchandise	....	455.47	264.57	241.28	140.56	267.30	487.37	....	230.99	209.33
Sales—worth	....	199.15	105.12	147.95	70.59	132.94	207.43	....	150.97	102.84
Debt—worth	....	40.92	34.97	44.02	37.79	35.56	21.90	....	47.16	38.45

CHART No. 27.—*Lumber—Type 9.*

Sections	1	2	3	4	5	6	7	8	9	Nat.
Number of statements..	4	3	6	2	11	15	4	7	2	54
	Per cent.	Per cent.	Per cent.	Per cent.	Per cent.	Per cent.	Per cent.	Per cent.	Per cent.	Per cent.
Current ratio	268.44	239.18	277.72	216.41	240.62	252.99	492.71	251.18	256.67	259.08
Receivable merchandise	102.60	146.50	41.78	113.06	110.78	78.13	96.90	103.36	75.58	82.37
Worth—Fixed	97.79	254.21	138.20	238.25	268.92	251.62	162.02	186.43	131.68	181.73
Sales—Receivable	487.06	536.17	723.60	380.14	336.77	379.49	233.26	448.23	612.64	445.18
Sales—Merchandise	499.75	785.53	302.35	429.81	373.08	296.52	226.03	463.31	462.47	366.87
Sales—Worth	184.46	261.41	111.87	191.63	198.96	144.87	51.70	211.04	91.20	147.18
Debt—Worth	30.94	43.94	22.25	49.58	55.71	38.13	43.92	39.06	17.90	32.50

CHART No. 28.—*Packers—Type 12.*

Sections	1	2	3	4	5	6	7	8	9	Nat.
Number of statements..	1	1	10	....	3	1	....	1	2	19
	Per cent.	Per cent.	Per cent.	Per cent.	Per cent.	Per cent.	Per cent.	Per cent.	Per cent.	Per cent.
Special current ratio	149.06	640.00	157.98	....	206.33	186.44	....	169.79	282.00	160.65
Current ratio			233.84	....			....			235.49
Receivable merchandise	102.83	37.02	82.70	....	50.04	10.25	....	53.33	49.05	80.75
Worth—Fixed	110.02	122.65	188.33	....	176.27	165.80	....	157.46	133.99	183.88
Sales—Receivable	906.55	953.95	1,019.68	....	1,093.67	4,580.00	....	843.82	882.54	1,027.30
Sales—Merchandise	932.36	353.12	813.32	....	766.16	469.74	....	450.00	432.89	829.57
Sales—Worth	329.86	98.77	501.24	....	473.06	356.42	....	248.97	186.74	483.27
Debt—Worth	53.95	6.50	84.54	....	41.22	45.91	....	58.22	29.98	80.56

CHART No. 29.—*Boots and shoes—Type 13.*

Sections	1	2	3	4	5	6	7	8	9	Nat.
Number of statements..	20	14	9	1	7	10	2	1	2	66
	Per cent.	Per cent.	Per cent.	Per cent.	Per cent.	Per cent.	Per cent.	Per cent.	Per cent.	Per cent.
Current ratio	216.59	216.48	309.03	377.31	231.09	229.65	323.77	178.81	234.67	225.40
Receivable merchandise	97.18	52.34	84.55	145.06	87.09	64.62	64.51	122.50	52.58	72.04
Worth—Fixed	204.25	1,628.27	513.18	942.25	396.57	129.05	778.82	159.61	743.85	259.07
Sales—Receivable	473.34	412.75	490.08	194.46	419.18	624.92	412.28	409.18	654.52	503.12
Sales—Merchandise	460.04	216.03	414.36	282.09	365.08	403.85	255.96	501.25	344.17	362.46
Sales—Worth	263.88	216.89	273.01	136.62	239.89	357.97	190.28	161.04	312.79	278.89
Debt—Worth	57.86	82.70	43.41	32.28	58.46	68.25	38.92	29.82	64.27	65.21

CHART No. 30.—*National type ratios.*

Types	1	2	3	5	6	7	9	12	13	
Number of statements	83	99	205	28	21	20	54	19	66	
	Per cent.	Per cent.	Per cent.	Per cent.	Per cent.	Per cent.	Per cent.	Per cent.	Per cent.	
Current ratio	223.38	283.95	237.98	246.86	269.35	355.78	259.08	235.49	225.40	
Special current ratio								160.65		
Receivable merchandise	84.61	60.29	71.60	49.57	41.21	63.50	82.37	80.75	72.04	
Worth—Fixed	357.27	394.11	339.71	283.51	141.65	191.17	181.73	183.88	259.07	
Sales—Receivable	462.10	543.50	788.06	592.81	847.96	329.62	445.18	1,027.30	503.12	
Sales—Merchandise	391.03	327.73	564.25	293.86	349.48	209.33	366.87	829.57	362.46	
Sales—Worth	272.23	227.78	390.47	216.42	136.05	102.84	147.18	483.27	278.89	
Debt—Worth	63.66	42.98	59.14	50.86	21.35	38.45	32.50	80.56	65.21	

NOTE.—These tables are of course not complete, but are indicative of what may be accomplished by coordinated barometric research.

DEVELOPMENT OF THE COLLECTION SYSTEM.

The New York Clearing House Association has adopted a new set of rules and regulations relating to the method of making collections for members of the association or for others clearing through such members, as well as the rate to be charged for the collections in question. Simultaneous with the transmission of these regulations, effective March 1, the Federal Reserve Bank of New York has sent out under date of February 26 a schedule showing when the proceeds of acceptances will be available if collected through the Federal Reserve Bank of New York. There is herewith reprinted the circular sent out by the clearing house, as follows:

NEW YORK CLEARING HOUSE—RULES AND REGULATIONS REGARDING COLLECTIONS OUTSIDE OF THE CITY OF NEW YORK.

(Effective Aug. 12, 1918; amended Sept. 3, 1918; Feb. 10, 1919, effective Mar. 1, 1919.)

Pursuant to authority conferred upon it by the constitution of the New York Clearing House Association, the clearing house committee of said association establishes the following rules and regulations regarding collections outside of the City of New York (except as to items on clearing nonmembers), by members of the association, or banks, trust companies, or others clearing through such members, and the rates to be charged for such collections, and also regarding enforcement of the provisions hereof:

SECTION 1. These rules and regulations shall apply to all members of the association, and to all banks, trust companies, or others clearing through such members, but not to branches in foreign countries of member banks. The parties to which the same so apply are hereinafter described as collecting banks.

SEC. 2. For all items deposited by or collected for the account of the Governments of the United States, the State of New York, or the City of New York, from whatever source received (but not checks, warrants, etc., issued by said Governments and deposited by or collected for the account of the bank's other customers), the charge shall be discretionary with the collecting banks.

SEC. 3. For checks or drafts drawn on banks, bankers, and trust companies, and for all other items, the charges shall be not less than those prescribed for the respective points in the following schedule, subject to the provisions of sections 4, 5 and 6:

States.	Checks or drafts drawn on banks, bankers, and trust companies.	All other items.
Alabama	One-tenth of 1 per cent.	One-tenth of 1 per cent.
Arizona	do	Do.
Arkansas	do	Do.
California	do	Do.
San Francisco	One-twentieth of 1 per cent.	
Colorado	One-tenth of 1 per cent.	Do.
Denver	One-twentieth of 1 per cent.	Do.
Connecticut	Discretionary	Do.
Delaware	do	Do.
District of Columbia	do	Do.
Florida	One-eighth of 1 per cent.	One-eighth of 1 per cent.
Georgia	One-tenth of 1 per cent.	One-tenth of 1 per cent.
Atlanta	One-fortieth of 1 per cent.	Do.
Idaho	One-tenth of 1 per cent.	Do.
Illinois	One-twentieth of 1 per cent.	Do.
Chicago	One-fortieth of 1 per cent	Do.
Indiana	One-twentieth of 1 per cent.	Do.
Iowa	One-tenth of 1 per cent.	Do.
Kansas	do	Do.
Kansas City	One-fortieth of 1 per cent	Do.
Kentucky	One-tenth of 1 per cent.	Do.
Louisville	One-fortieth of 1 per cent	Do.
Louisiana	One-eighth of 1 per cent.	One-eighth of 1 per cent.
New Orleans	One-twentieth of 1 per cent.	One-eighth of 1 per cent.
Maine	Discretionary	Do.
Maryland	do	Do.
Baltimore	do	Do.
Massachusetts	do	Do.
Boston	do	Discretionary.[1]

[1] See section 6.

THREE IMPORTANT BALANCE SHEET RATIOS

Roy A. Foulke

THREE IMPORTANT BALANCE SHEET RATIOS

by ROY A. FOULKE

Manager, Analytical Report Department, Dun & Bradstreet, Inc.

THE Treasurer of a business enterprise of quite substantial proportions sat down beside my desk about twelve months ago to discuss the financial condition of his business with me. He had been the Treasurer for eight years, those eight consequential years which covered the latter part of the inflation period when the investment security market was flourishing, when corporate funds were readily available and no questions asked regarding their use; during the period when sales began to stumble and commodity prices began to droop; through the months that business failures and liabilities steadily expanded, when hope was the strongest national conscious force, and then along through the current fluctuating course of the depression. He had carefully studied his intricate job of handling thousands of trade creditors, keeping in touch with his banks, preparing sound budgets, keeping expenses fairly well into line, and had the reputation of handling his division of the business with practical everyday simplicity and efficiency.

The business had been started in a very small way with a few thousand dollars in 1884—the year Cleveland was elected to his first term as President—and was now after a lapse of forty-eight years operating on a capital of $18,000,000 and surplus of $5,000,000, a sizable enterprise. Through a group of subsidiaries it operated an extensive chain of 276 retail stores located largely in the Eastern, Southern, and Middle Western States. Its annual sales which amounted to $48,000,000 were entirely on a cash basis. The chain had grown steadily year by year, the expansion having been carried on by funds raised by the sale of preferred stock, the sale of debentures and the issuance of "rights" to common stockholders, and also to an extent by the retention of part of the profits in the business.

The yearly purchases of merchandise approximated $32,000,000 to care for the discriminating requirements of $48,000,000 sales. For a year or so, I had been wondering how the equity of the stockholders could be protected under the management's existing operating policies in a depression, but as we examined the financial condition of the business together, I began to wonder whether the business was even responsible for its current bank and merchandise credit.

The outward indications of normal credit stability in this enterprise appeared evident to the Treasurer. Trade obligations for the purchase of merchandise were being discounted on discount terms and paid promptly on the prompt terms. Substantial credit aggregating $2,000,000 was being extended by its banks on its own unendorsed notes.

Fixed Assets Unduly High

My friend, the Treasurer, pointed out a loss of $2,200,000 in his profit and loss account for 1931, but a loss, under existing conditions, even though certain competitors were operating successfully, was nothing to be ashamed about. And besides it was the first red figure in its 48 years. But then as we began to examine the individual items in the balance sheet, their relationships to each other, and their changes when compared with corresponding items in the immediately preceding balance sheets, my heart began to sink. How could this concern work out of its morass? A fundamental conception of the weakening condition of his business seemed to be lacking and when I pointed out to him that the balance sheet disclosed fixed assets, that is, real estate, buildings, furniture, fixtures and leasehold improvements which amounted to 110 per cent of the tangible net worth on December 31, 1931, 98 per cent on December 31, 1930, and 90 per cent on December 31, 1929, the significance of this trend was totally lacking. The Treasurer who believed his business was in satisfactory condition because it was currently able to pay its bills, obtain bank credit, and had raised substantial capital in the securities market, simply replied, "Well, isn't that a normal trend and a normal condition during these times?"

Today that business is bankrupt.

Asset and Debt Ratios Significant

Balance sheets and profit and loss accounts in the past fifteen years have become open books to an increasingly large percentage of bankers, economists, investment analysts, business officials, and creditmen. Annual corporate reports have improved somewhat in the quantity of information but there is a real question if there has been any noticeable improvement in the quality. Wide, clear logical deductions can be made by one who is experienced in the interpretation of these figures.

There are at least fourteen ratios made with sales, profits and balance sheet items which are of great significance but of these, two which were of particular importance in this case had not been recognized by the management. These two are (1) the size of the fixed assets relative to the capital funds invested in the business and (2) the size of mortgage and funded debts relative to the current assets in excess of the current liabilities, i. e., working capital. Notice in the second item, I say relative to the excess current assets, and not to the underlying security which is real estate and buildings. Department stores or chain stores show a normal condition when the depreciated book value of their fixed assets ranges between 50 and 75 per cent of the capital and surplus; and if there are mortgage or funded liabilities, those liabilities should be equivalent to not more than 75 per cent of the excess current assets. Percentages greater than these indicate a weakened condition.

During the past eight months I have had numerous conversations with the acting Treasurer of another concern which operates a chain of important stores. This enterprise had a net investment of about $26,000,000 on its last fiscal balance sheet. The aggregate book value of the fixed assets was almost identical. The excess current assets amounted to approximately $9,000,000, while the funded indebtedness was $9,800,000. The proportions were entirely out of balance. The enterprise represented a merger of established units but it had been put together in the boom days on "boom valuations." The volume of annual business, however, had dropped 45 per cent from the peak in three years and the decreased sales were unable to support the operating overhead assumed during better times.

I explained one day that the depreciation charges on such a large proportion of fixed assets plus the interest charges on a funded debt which was larger than the excess current assets, were excessive and could only be carried with extreme difficulty. There are only thirty-six inches in the yard. "But," I was told, "these charges virtually represent rent. Together these two charges would no more than cover rental charges if the properties were all being leased and were not owned." This statement of reasoning was, of course, a generality. Its accuracy could only be tested by the current appraisals of outside authorities. Obviously, however, if the space had all been under lease, there would have been an excellent case for a revision of the terms of the leases with a 45 per cent drop in sales, and a substantial operating loss. With the property owned in fee, the story was different.

That business has been operated by receivers for several months.

First Speculation in Land

In the years of reconstruction and rehabilitation following the speculative panic of 1873—and they were long lean years—there appeared a remarkable volume of English literature from the pen of an economist, a philosopher, and social thinker, a volume which was destined to be translated into almost every language of the world. The power and inherent strength of its thoughtful, restrained persuasion has placed it on a plane which has been reached by few economic treatises. That volume is *Progress and Poverty*, by Henry George.

After one of the most painstaking, broad studies of primary economic theories covering the fundamental problems of wages and capital, of want amid plenty, population and subsistence based upon the Malthusian theory, laws of distribution, of labor condemned to involuntary idleness, the effect of progress upon the distribution of wealth, the author arrived at the consideration of the bottom cause of the ever-recurring paroxysms of industrial depression. That fundamental cause he believed to be the speculative advance in land values. In every progressive community, population gradually increases, and improvements succeed one another, bringing about an increase in the value of land. That steady increase leads to speculative activity in which future increases are anticipated. In this manner, land values are carried beyond the point at which, under existing conditions, the accustomed return is expected by wages and capital, an increasing proportion of income going to rent. Production begins to decline at some point and this cessation is communicated to an ever-widening circle of industrial activity. There are other proximate causes such as the growing complexity and interdependence of the machinery of production, defects of currency and credit, protective tariffs and artificial barriers to the interplay of productive forces, the pursuit of monetary profit, but beneath all factors, according to Henry George, lies the fundamental initiatory cause in the speculative advance of land values.

In 1795 the Georgia "Yazoo" land frauds, the most notorious and widespread of the early American land gambles, took place—approximately 30,000,000 acres comprising most of the present States of Alabama and Mississippi were sold to four separate land companies, for the aggregate of $500,000 or about a cent a half an acre. Shares or scrip in the early land companies, representing a pro rata equity in the trusted property were generously offered to the public. Philadelphia, New York, Hartford and Boston were the principal centers, each city having its own "deals" and selling its shares throughout a wide area. Their purchases of land extended from Lake Erie to the Gulf of Mexico and from Maine to the Mississippi. The size of their operations is not to be despised even from present day extensive speculative operations.

With the early consolidation of railroads, headed by the New York Central and the Hudson River lines in 1869 by Commodore Vanderbilt there was slowly ushered in that period of large scale production and commerce under the corporate enterprise which provided a medium of wealth in the form of corporate securities, stocks and evidences of debts, which together with government securities of all classes, gradually appeared more important to the layman than real estate.

While stocks and bonds became the favored medium for investment and speculation, land naturally continued to play a most important part. It was not so many years ago that real estate development companies were giving prospective purchasers free trips to Florida and to Muscle Shoals. The Florida real estate boom while antedating the stock market crash of 1929 is too recent an occurrence to be easily forgotten. The skyscrapers of New York in many cases with a small or moderate percentage of their space leased, the precipitate drop in rental values in all parts of the country, the failure of chain stores because of excessive rentals, the inability of mortgage guaranteeing companies to meet their obligations, the uniform extensions granted by insurance companies to mortgagors, all of these developments of the past few months and years are indications of the nation-wide interest in farm lands, suburban real estate and city properties. In all economic reasoning up to the time of Henry George, land value was a preeminent factor in the consideration of speculation, investment and wealth. Today that factor has been joined and probably superseded in importance by a second factor, corporate and government securities.

Speculative Trend to Securities

In the development of accounting and credit technique by accountants, bankers, and creditmen, a certain group of items in the financial statement have come to be known as fixed assets. Those fixed assets are primarily real estate and buildings but also cover broadly rolling stocks, pipe lines, furniture, fixtures, machinery, tools, and leasehold improvements. These items represent a very substantial part of the net worth of railroads, public utilities, pipe lines, and mining concerns, a smaller percentage but still a substantial part in the case of manufacturers, generally a somewhat smaller percentage in the case of retailers, then followed by decreasing percentages in the case of jobbers, wholesalers and banking institutions.

The widespread policy of investing in land in the early years of our national life now came to be represented by the broader investment in corporate securities and the corporations in turn invested in fixed assets with the broad connotation of that term. The toll of these topheavy holdings in fixed assets during depressed conditions has come to be recognized by the repossession of real estate and buildings by mortgagees, by the widespread losses of corporate enterprises brought about in no small degree by the depreciation charges on excess fixed assets in times of relative inactivity, by the payment of interest on mortgages, bonds, debentures, and long term notes issued to cover the cost of wide expansion programs. This is not new, strange, or only theory. It is elemental. It is business today. In 1904 Veblen made this idea the crux of his theory of depression and in more recent years that theory has received most careful attention by outstanding students of the business cycle.

The financial embarrassment of the Insull group of utilities entailing an estimated loss to investors of $700,000,000, of the International Match Co., Paramount Publix Corporation, McLellan Stores, F. & W. Grand-Silver Stores, General Theaters Equipment, Inc. (which controls Fox Film Corporation) and Warner Bros. Pictures, Inc., are generally laid to over-expansion, or the result of the economic depression. These causes, one and all are blended together into the one fundamental weakness of over-investment in fixed assets, land, theater buildings, stores, leasehold improvements, and fixtures, with concurrent, heavy, outstanding funded liabilities. The Missouri Pacific Railroad, the Chicago & Eastern Illinois, Southern Railroad, Atlantic Coast Line, these and so many other railroads operating with defaulted funded debts are likewise the result of too heavy funded liabilities to carry immense valuations of properties and rolling stock.

Three Fundamental Ratios Evolved

About 1900, James G. Cannon who became President of the Fourth National Bank of New York and who was one of the early, orginal students of credit and credit problems instituted the practice of setting successive balance sheets in parallel columns. By this simple, improved mechanical arrangement the first great intensive step was taken in creating a method of analyzing financial statements. It early became the practice of comparing current assets with current liabilities and of expecting at least two dollars of current assets to be shown, to every dollar of current liabilities as a margin of protection. For years this "two for one" current rate was the alpha and omega of analyses and even today the business men are legion who believe in this one ratio as the infallible guide to credit interpretation.

When creditmen began to question the complete efficacy of the current ratio as a credit guide, a second, simple, supplemental comparison came into existence; the comparison of the sum of cash and receivables with the current debt. If the current ratio was "two for one" or better and the cash and receivables equalled or exceeded the current liabilities, an account was said to give double assurance of credit stability. Where the cash and receivables were less than the current debt, some doubt was thrown on the inherent current credit strength of the balance sheet no matter what the current ratio happened to be. This second comparison gave added prestige to receivables as a realizable asset and less to merchandise.

No one ratio, no one comparison, can possibly give a clear picture of the credit capacity of a financial statement and profit and loss account. There are at least fourteen important ratios, all of vital significance. Each one in its turn tells a story and each one in conjunction with some other ratio and other facts then tells a supplemental story but these stories are all relative depending for their full significance on an understanding of industrial and commercial seasons and variations. A current ratio of two to one on a fiscal balance taken at the low point of a season is of little value unless it is known that in the normal operations of that business the ratio might shortly drop to 1.30 at the peak of a season.

There are three ratios which are of such fundamental significance that their full value should be realized by every important manufacturer, jobber, wholesaler and retailer in business. These three ratios are:

(1) Fixed Assets compared to the Tangible Net Worth.
(2) Current Debt compared to the Tangible Net Worth.
(3) Funded Debt compared to the Excess Current Assets (Working Capital).

Fixed Assets comprise the depreciated values of real estate, buildings, furniture, fixtures, machinery, tools, leasehold improvements and such similar items. The *Tangible Net Worth* is the sum of capital and surplus less any intangible items in the assets such as goodwill, trade-marks, copyrights, treasury stock, mailing lists and organization expenses. The *Current Debt* is the sum of liabilities due and payable within a year. *Funded Debt* is a liability due more than a year away.

Excess Current Assets (Working Capital) is the difference between the current assets and the current liabilities.

In each of the years from 1925 to 1929 the National Credit Office which is now a division of the Dun & Bradstreet organization determined the fourteen important average ratios on every concern which sold its commercial paper in the open market. These concerns operated in the important line of industrial and commercial activity in every State. They represented the better credit risks among the group of the larger enterprises as their tangible net worth ranged between $250,000 and $350,000,000. The number varied from 2,754 in 1925 to 1,623 in 1929. As a result of the uniform healthy condition of these enterprises, the ratios represented by these studies were undoubtedly of a somewhat superior type.

Widely Different Lines Studied

The averaged ratios for each line of business varied. Wholesale grocers and wholesalers of drugs naturally invested a smaller percentage of their capital in fixed assets than manufacturers of hosiery; lumber manufacturers obtained a much smaller yearly turnover of their net worth than the meat packers; the average collection period of wool dealers was much less than retailers of furniture. The significant points brought out by this five-year study of important national enterprises were (a) cotton cloth manufacturers, both New England and Southern gave the highest average percentage of net worth invested in fixed assets ranging around 65 to 70 per cent and (b) cotton goods converters gave the highest average ratio of current debt to the tangible net worth, ranging around 55 per cent. These two percentages are most important and undoubtedly are much lower than those realized by the average businessman.

Last year, the Dun & Bradstreet organization made a further ratio study based on a larger sample of typical cases. The balance sheets and profit and loss accounts were studied on 5,754 average cases divided into refined industrial or commercial groups located in all parts of the country but with a Tangible Net Worth which occasionally went a little below $50,000. Typical ratios naturally vary, in some cases greatly and in others very moderately, from one line of business endeavor to another, and also to a smaller degree, in certain lines of business in different sections of the country. Ratios in the same industrial and commercial groupings show some variation from year to year, but the important yearly variations are those in which sales or profit figures are one part of the fraction. Ratios between balance sheet items, and particularly the three I have already outlined fluctuate relatively little from year to year in the same divisions of an industry. These three ratios are of outstanding fundamental importance. If correct proportions are maintained in these automatic controls of safety, profits will be earned more steadily, more profits will be earned, and many of the financial embarrassments, particularly of larger enterprises would be forestalled.

Representative Averages Compiled

A business enterprise is surely operated for a monetary profit. Too many business men, however, are like the ancient philosopher who fell into the gully because he gazed too intently at the stars. Sustained profits are earned more by giving constant attention to the minute details of a business and to broad economic knowledge, than by having the "will to profit." Excessive inventories might give a temporary increase in profits by having immediately available all of the possible demands of customers, but excessive inventories will bring losses because of depreciation and change in styles, in most lines of business, just as surely as one day follows another. Heavy investments in fixed properties, large current liabilities, and substantial funded liabilities are the nemesis of American businessmen. These attributes would have no material unfavorable effect in an endless economic Springtime but there always comes a day of reckoning.

The following schedule gives the averages for two of these three important ratios in twenty of the more important divisions of business activity throughout the country:

Number of Concerns	Line of Business	Average Ratios	
		Fixed Assets with Tangible Net Worth Per Cent	Current Debt with Tangible Net Worth Per Cent
	Manufacture		
163	Cloaks and Suits	7.7	36.3
41	Converters' Silks	1.7	48.8
175	Dresses	9.2	54.3
130	Furriers	4.6	23.4
76	Knit Goods	23.7	26.6
126	Men's Clothing	8.7	34.4
50	Men's Shirts	12.7	43.0
45	Men's Shoes	19.6	28.2
75	Printers	58.2	27.9
179	Women's Shoes	32.7	44.6
	Wholesale		
51	Cotton Goods	1.7	40.3
47	Furs	2.3	33.8
40	Grocers	25.9	39.5
52	Hosiery	2.5	34.2
52	Men's and Women's Shoes	5.0	50.5
42	Paper	12.0	51.7
	Retail		
99	Department Stores	57.4	34.3
56	Furniture	14.4	26.6
40	Men's and Women's Shoes	34.5	35.2
79	Women's Specialty Shops	37.5	36.1

Too Heavy Debt to be Avoided

It is somewhat difficult to generalize but then generalizations are always easily remembered. If you have a business which has a tangible net worth in excess of $50,000, stop and take stock of your program if (1) *your fixed assets are equivalent to more than two-thirds or three-quarters of the tangible net worth of your business*, if (2) *the current debt is greater than two-thirds or three-quarters of the tangible net worth* or if (3) *the funded debt is as large as the working capital*. These three ratios are outstanding signposts of financial strength, credit stability, business health.

Only two important lines of industrial and commercial activity in the above schedule, 75 printers with an average ratio of 58.2 per cent and 99 department stores with an average ratio of 57.4 per cent, showed more than half of their tangible net worth in fixed assets. A ratio of 66⅔ per cent to 75 per cent allows a fair leeway. Most wholesalers and manufacturers in the needle industries naturally invest lightly in fixed properties. Larger manufacturers and retailers have substantial properties and equipment. As a concern increases in size, the tendency to place more and more funds in real estate, buildings, improvements, equipment and expansion programs, becomes stronger so the smaller ratio, 66⅔ per cent, applies more to concerns in the brackets from $50,000 to about $250,000, increasing to 75 per cent as an outside limit in concerns above that size.

The variation in the average ratios of current liabilities to tangible net worth is by no means as broad as the ratio of fixed assets to the tangible net worth. The range is from a low of 23.4 per cent in the case of 130 manufacturing furriers to a high of 54.3 per cent in the case of 175 manufacturers of women's dresses. In only one instance does the average ratio exceed one-half of the tangible net worth, namely, the manufacturers of women's dresses. Here again extreme care should be exercised when current liabilities go above the range of 66 2/3 to 75 per cent of the tangible net worth.

Beware of top-heavy liabilities. Don't owe too much.

Adequate ratios are not available to show a proper relationship statistically at this time between working capital and funded debt. The examination of thousands of balance sheets in all lines of activity in good times and poor have lead to the one conclusion that rarely, if ever, should the aggregate of funded debts exceed working capital. Such a relationship is top-heavy. With all of its own capital tied up in non-liquid assets, the business is then being currently operated from day to day on borrowed capital. Interest and amortization becomes a burden often too great to be carried. The importance of this fact, which relates almost exclusively to the larger concerns cannot be overestimated.

There are 1,950,000 business enterprises in all lines of business in existence in the United States. About 180,000 are manufacturers, 60,000 wholesalers and jobbers, 1,600,000 retailers, and 110,000 theaters, hotels and similar non-commercial or industrial units. The principles I have outlined here are particularly applicable to the larger industrial and commercial concerns with a net investment of $50,000 or more. The same principles apply to the immense group of the smaller concerns, most of which are local retail enterprises but with somewhat greater variation as smaller concerns generally have a smaller percentage of their net worth in fixed assets and often a somewhat larger percentage of current liabilities.

The average businessman examines his profit and loss account to ascertain how he can make more profits or reduce his losses, but rarely does he make an analytical study of his balance sheet as a most important supplemental or prior guide to the same end. An intelligent comparison of the distribution of assets and liabilities, or of average ratios, of the more successful concerns in any industry or territory, should be of inestimable value to executives, bringing out how the financial picture of their business could be modified or rebuilt to permit improved operating results.

THREE IMPORTANT INVENTORY RATIOS

Roy A. Foulke

THREE IMPORTANT INVENTORY RATIOS

by ROY A. FOULKE

Manager, Analytical Report Department, Dun & Bradstreet, Inc.

IN 1910 a small business was started quietly and inconspicuously in New York City by two young men who had formerly been employed by a concern engaged in the jobbing of silk piece goods. The business, like hundreds of thousands of others, began operations on a side street where rents were low, just about providing means of livelihood to the officers and the few employees.

The years went by, and then came the War and the Armistice followed by heavy speculation in commodities, prominent among them being sugar and raw silk. In 1919, a year without precedent in the annals of the raw silk market, the price of Japanese Filature No. 1 Shinshiu at New York had made the spectacular rise under speculative influences both here and in Japan from $5.90 per pound on February 1 to $12.60 on December 1, continuing its upward climb to $16.85 on February 1, 1920 when the demand which had been almost limitless, suddenly and tragically collapsed. The downward course of the market then reversed the upward climb, and the year ended with a price of $5.75 after a demoralization in the raw silk market lasting several months and when support was given to the Japanese market only with governmental assistance in the form of a buying syndicate.

All of these varied difficulties were encountered and gradually surmounted, the business grew, new ambitious young men were taken in, profits were earned steadily, and a substantial portion of the profits retained in the business as capital. As business conditions changed and styling became more important, the concern had gone into converting operations but these changed operations had been entered into thoughtfully and conservatively as no dyeing, printing or finishing plants were acquired, all processes being carried on in outside mills.

By December 31, 1929—nineteen years of conscientious operations —the capital and surplus had grown in excess of $1,000,000. The business had become a very important factor in the converting silk industry and as very little of its funds were represented by miscellaneous assets, the working capital amounted to around $950,000. One feature of this December 31, 1929 balance sheet was strikingly unusual, an enormous inventory of $2,800,000 which compared with previous year-end balance sheet inventories of around $1,200,000. Such a sudden spectacular increase would indicate that something was palpably out-of-line. An investigation verified the fact that the inventory was admittedly large but prices had been very low in the last quarter of the year, and the management carefully explained that heavy purchases had been made in anticipation of an early upward trend.

The speculative instinct had erred. Silk prices failed to react upwards. All through 1930 until November, prices declined, month after month, month by month. The business depression which started in the Fall of 1929, gathered momentum at the turn of the year, stocks of raw silk in New York had mounted to an unprecedented total. Japan was experimenting unsuccessfully with silk stabilization plans, and warehouses at Yokohama and Kobe were accumulating heavy stocks in spite of restrictive influences such as the sealing of 20 per cent of the reeling basins in the filatures early in the year.

When December 31, 1930 came around the inventory was $50,000 higher than the preceding year and this increase was accompanied by a loss of $400,000 in working capital. More greige goods had been bought at each drop in price, hoping to catch the bottom and make that initially hoped for inventory profit. But fate was unkind as it often is in business. It is the unexpected, the worse, which must be anticipated in the business world, and the really successful enterprise is the one which has a stalemate prepared for every economic move, every step of competition, every accident of nature. The really successful mangement follows changes in the business world, particular indexes and prices, and often anticipates fluctuations in the price of a primary commodity but only to a limited degree and not unrestricted, unhampered, hazardous speculation.

The President of this company came in to see me early in 1931 with his December 31, 1930 balance sheet and together we discussed the problem of this heavy inventory. Still optimistic he was most convinced that prices would turn upward and that a handsome profit would shortly be recorded, and that anyway his styling had been unusually successful and if necessary finished goods could readily be disposed of. Apparently it was a case of reasoning to justify a policy instead of what was needed, operating efficiency with preparations for any unexpected emergency, especially in a division of industry noted for extreme competition.

Downtrend Continues In 1931

Silk prices continued downward during the first six months of 1931. The combination of continued falling prices and the necessity of forced liquidation proved to be the death-knell of a business which a year and half previously had been a model of successful operations and which had a liquid capital of $1,000,000.

One year and a half! Economic facts grind inexorably.

The June 30, 1931 figures showed a reduction in the inventory to $1,200,000, a reduction of 58 per cent but the accomplishment of this feat had involved heavy operating losses bringing the working capital down to $150,000. In one and a half years the working capital had been reduced 83.5 per cent. Nineteen years to build a business by hard conscientious work and progressive business practices, and a year and a half to lose it by inventory speculation. Operations continued until December when a creditors' meeting was held and the following month the concern was out-of-business.

A few weeks ago I had occasion to examine a somewhat unusual 1933 midyear balance sheet of one of the larger business enterprises in a division of the New York cutting-up textile trade. The concern has been in active operation almost fifty years and during that continuous period of time it has always been under watchful experienced eyes, first of the assiduous founder of the business and then of his competent son. On an initial investment of a few thousand dollars, profits have been earned with rare exceptions, year after year, until today that business represents a net investment, that is, a combined capital and surplus in the neighborhood of $2,000,000. Its salesmen and its well-made fashioned products are known in every State in the Union. The intimate life story of this business would make a saga of American industry and commerce during the period in our expanding national horizon when the bonds of youth were burst asunder and the mechanism of manufacture and exchange, transportation and communication, grew to maturity under a system of orthodox economics and competition.

The particular line of business in which this enterprise operates had become extensively known prior to the formulation and adoption of its National Recovery Code for its extreme unhealthy, stubborn competition; the inordinately low level wages paid to its operators, and the long hours its employees were forced to labor to retain their jobs during a depression, particularly in plants located in small outlying country towns

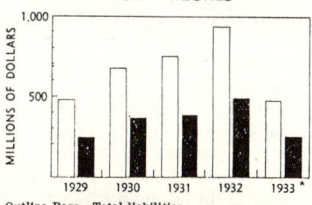

LARGE FAILURES

Outline Bars—Total liabilities.
Solid Bars—Liabilities of large failures.
In this period, large failures (those involving over $100,000 in liabilities) averaged only 4 per cent of the total number. Their liabilities averaged 51 per cent of the total.

and villages. As a result of the uncommon amount of competition, the profit and loss accounts throughout this division of the textile industry have been almost uniform in reflecting operating losses for the past four years. Losses have been the rule and not the anomalous exception. The successful establishment which had come to my attention, had been one of the singular exceptions. Under the same capable management, profits had been recorded in three out of the last four years notwithstanding steadily decreasing sales. Those results would seem to merit high commendation.

Inventory Gain Shown

This 1933 mid-year balance sheet was unusual insofar as it disclosed an aggregate inventory of piece goods merchandise, in process, and manufactured goods amounting to approximately $2,250,000. For the preceding fiscal year the annual sales had amounted to around $3,000,000. No previous balance sheet on June 30 had ever shown an inventory in excess of $1,000,000. A most unparalleled contrast! This contrast was particularly unusual as it represented the condition of a concern which had regularly kept its affairs in well-balanced financial shape for many, many years. Suddenly the inventory has taken a jump to an amount which appeared, on the basis of the existing operating record, out of all reasonable proportion to its legitimate business merchandise requirements. Such a striking change in the dollar amount of the same item in two successive balance sheets, like the unusual happenings, the clues, in a detective mystery, would appear to need enlightenment and rather thorough explanation.

Translated into merchandising terms, these figures indicated that the aggregate inventory on hand, if normally balanced, would produce sales somewhat in excess of $3,000,000. That is, the cost of labor, overhead administrative and selling expenses plus the profit, when added to the raw material, merchandise in process, and finished merchandise on hand, would produce total sales, if there were no material fluctuation in wholesale prices, somewhat larger than the volume that had been transacted during the entire preceding fiscal year. This condition was anything but healthy from the viewpoint of efficient operations as the normal concern in this line of business turns its inventory between three and four times yearly. From the viewpoint of a speculator this situation would have been more attractive, but from the viewpoint of a business executive, the condition was one which needed immediate considerate attention.

On July 17, the National Recovery Administration cotton mill code became effective and on August 14 the woolen mill code became effective. Both codes provided for increased costs throughout the various divisions of their industries by the payment of higher wages, shorter working hours, and the complete elimination of child labor on the part of all spinning and weaving mills. On August 1, the cotton processing tax of 4.2 cents per pound on raw cotton became effective making a further increase in the cost of producing cotton threads, yarns, piece goods, and knit goods. These multiple increased manufacturing expenses have in turn, all been passed on to the cutters-up and they in turn to the wholesalers of dry goods, chain stores, mail order houses, department stores, the general retail trade, and then to you and to me, the ultimate consumers.

Service Idea Basic

The fundamental theory of the business enterprise is based upon the conception and performance of a service. In cases of monopolies, trusts, cartels, price-fixing agreements, holding companies, interlocking directorates and such other variations of combinations which have evolved in economic organization largely since the turn of the century, greater emphasis is placed upon the practical working out of the profit motive. These modifications of competition, which have evolved from the tremendous accumulation of capital for large scale production, do cut across the freedom of the market and destroy the normal price determining mechanism.

When a manufacturer in our closely knit economic fabric sells his product, he receives payment for (a) turning a raw material into a finished product, (b) for taking a risk in judging the need and style which will be demanded, when the product is finished, by the market, and (c) for keeping a stock of merchandise with a wide range of sizes and colors available until such time as particular products are needed by its customers; a wholesaler receives payment for distributing its products between the manufacturer and retailer, which also involves keeping merchandise on hand and judging future demands; and the retailer for having merchandise available and distributing it to the ultimate consumer which also involves the risk of keeping the correct merchandise on the shelves. The net profit for the performance of a service, and by service we include the risk of anticipating style and demand, is rarely large or abnormal. The profit from a single speculative transaction or a series of speculative transactions is, however, sometimes immense.

Superior Performance Essential

The business enterprise which is unusually successful year after year is the one which performs its fundamental service in a manner superior to competition in its field but where the management at the same time is able to some extent to discern general economic trends, anticipate the changing needs of its customers, understand to a degree the forces which affect the market value of its primary commodity, and is able to take advantage of any unusual variation in price of the products which go into its manufacturing process somewhat earlier than others. These are legitimate business functions and are qualifications only of management of the highest order. It does not follow that indiscriminate speculation, that is, the purchase of an excessive amount of raw material in expectation of higher prices and consequently bringing about a strained financial condition characterized by exorbitant liabilities, should be indulged in as the risk involved in such a policy is outside of the legitimate field of the business enterprise.

So we are led by a chain of cause and effect to the theory that the profit of a business enterprise in a capitalistic system based upon free competition is earned both by the performance of a series of service operations plus a profit in the increased market value of its inventory or less a loss in the value of its inventory as its inventory fluctuates in market value, except in cases of monopoly, regulation or association. The nearer the commodity handled is to the raw product the more important does the fluctuation in market value become. It is of primal concern to a copper mine, silver mine, cotton mill, silk weaver or a flour mill; less importance to manufacturers of automobiles, radios, picture frames, mechanical refrigerators, furniture and still less to the department store and the general retail distributor of merchandise which is the farthest away from industrial or commercial processes.

The cutter-up, the manufacturer of garments, with merchandise in the neighborhood of $2,250,000 on June 30, 1933, had an obvious excess of inventory. There was every indication of an attempt at an old style jamboree of 1927-1929. Cloth currently valued at many hundreds of thousands of dollars had been purchased in the second quarter of the year in anticipation of a rise in the selling price of mills due to the higher manufacturing costs under the wide-reaching N.R.A. program and also in the case of cotton, to the further addition of a processing tax. If prices remained high while that merchandise was being disposed of, the management would show an abnormally high profit—not on the service it had performed in judging accurately the future style demand for its products, not in taking a manufacturing risk in anticipation of orders, not in keeping certain stocks of finished merchandise on hand for immediate delivery to customers, but on its "unearned increment" of profits from speculation.

Failures Extremely High in 1932

There were 31,822 business failures in 1932, by far the greatest number that has ever occurred in any one year in our entire economic history. It is in itself a striking indication of the severe depth of the current depression. The number of business embarrassments has increased each year since 1923. Moreover, this record was unusual in its severity relatively as in 1932 there were 153.2

failures for each 10,000 active business establishments and only once in our history—way back in 1878—had this relationship been exceeded when there had been 155 failures for each 10,000 business concerns.

The failure records for 1930 and 1931 were also indicative of the difficulties business enterprises were having in adjusting their operations to rapidly changing price levels, markets, competition and overhead expenses, as in those two years the failures had amounted to 120.7 and 133.4 respectively per 10,000 concerns which were record figures since 1900 with the one exception of the year 1915.

I am bringing out the immensity and intensity of this failure record during these three dramatic years because it so clearly emphasizes the widespread tragic importance of an evolution which has been going on in business operations. Failures are said to be due to business incompetence, the lack of working capital, the undue extension of credit to poor risks, unusual competition, physical disasters such as floods, fires and unseasonable weather, over-trading and under-trading, personal extravagance of partners and officers, speculation, and even that most abused of all intangible, impersonal reasons, "general business conditions."

Poor Management Ultimate Cause

It is generally reported that the largest percentage of failures is directly chargeable to poor management closely followed by the lack of capital. It is quite likely, however, that most of the failures attributed to other causes such as competition, over-trading, speculation, general business conditions, and even unseasonable weather would have been anticipated under more capable, far-seeing, conscientious management. Does not the very excuse of "lack of capital" point to lack of foresight, to poor management? Is it good judgment in the first place to begin operations in any line of business with inadequate capital, and in the second place, if losses are assumed to such an extent that the remaining invested funds are then insufficient for continued sound operations, then cannot those losses invariably be laid to the door of poor management?

Poor or misguided management is brought to light by a great variety of factors. Of these, the one which is of outstanding importance is the wholesale price level of commodities. Failures increased absolutely and relatively in 1930, 1931 and 1932 partly because of the steadily downward trend in the market value of practically all commodities, manufactured or semi-manufactured articles as well as primary products.

In other words, the number of failures and the movements of wholesale commodity prices, have moved in some direct sympathy with each other, emphasizing the extreme importance of inventory to business management. When liabilities and inventory are both heavy, a material drop in the price of products comprising the inventory often ends in a business embarrassment; where liabilities are light or only moderate, a loss is invariably assumed. These factors emphasize the paramount importance which the correct amount of inventory assumes in business success and failure in a refined economic organization where price and competition play so great a part in the life of the typical enterprise.

Enterprise Dependent upon Income

The daily, weekly, and monthly income, that is, the collectibility of its sales, is the very life blood of the business enterprise. "As in

Comparative Yearly Average Inventory Ratios

Number of Concerns 1931 / 1932	Line of Business	Net Sales to Inventory (Times)	Inventory to Working Capital (Per Cent)	Current Debt to Inventory (Per Cent)
163 / 135	**Manufacturers** Cloaks and Suits	22.8 / 26.7	38.7 / 32.0	107.0 / 90.2
126 / 167	Clothing, Men's and Boys'	9.9 / 9.6	56.6 / 56.6	78.5 / 72.2
41 / 43	Converters of Silk	14.8 / 12.0	54.5 / 54.5	93.0 / 84.5
175 / 187	Dresses	28.2 / 27.6	38.6 / 40.5	152.4 / 137.6
35 / 46	Furniture	4.7 / 4.8	87.4 / 78.0	79.2 / 76.3
130 / 102	Furriers	13.8 / 13.0	40.1 / 47.9	65.0 / 62.7
76 / 89	Knit Goods	17.0 / 17.1	46.0 / 48.8	77.2 / 67.7
44 / 64	Paints and Varnishes	9.0 / 8.5	48.0 / 54.5	102.6 / 100.0
50 / 66	Shirts, Underwear and Pajamas	6.9 / 7.4	64.5 / 65.9	92.4 / 80.2
179 / 78	Shoes, Women's and Children's	16.8 / 16.8	67.2 / 51.8	107.3 / 86.8
36 / 92	Underwear, Silk	14.4 / 14.6	52.2 / 48.5	122.9 / 112.6
33 / 74	**Wholesalers** Automobile Parts and Accessories	5.4 / 4.5	87.6 / 94.4	71.8 / 53.9
97 / 113	Dry Goods	8.5 / 7.0	53.3 / 51.8	98.3 / 74.3
47 / 30	Furs, Hides and Skins	13.5 / 12.8	42.3 / 41.7	88.8 / 64.0
40 / 85	Grocers	8.1 / 8.9	78.5 / 81.3	68.4 / 51.0
39 / 66	Hardware	3.6 / 3.3	69.2 / 76.5	51.6 / 43.0
52 / 47	Hosiery	12.5 / 10.2	48.3 / 47.8	84.2 / 65.7
30 / 54	Lumber	4.2 / 3.1	78.0 / 69.0	70.0 / 79.1
42 / 73	Paper	10.5 / 9.0	70.1 / 60.0	90.1 / 81.3
22 / 53	**Retailers** Clothing, Men's and Boys'	3.3 / 3.6	116.7 / 98.3	48.7 / 59.7
99 / 151	Department Stores	6.2 / 6.0	96.7 / 88.8	70.2 / 74.5
56 / 95	Furniture, Installment	5.1 / 4.8	36.5 / 47.0	92.9 / 100.4
40 / 35	Shoes, Men's and Women's	4.6 / 5.1	136.4 / 116.6	56.4 / 45.8
79 / 87	Women's Specialty Shops	10.9 / 9.5	82.4 / 75.9	91.4 / 90.7

natural life, the quality, quantity, and above all, the regularity of the flow govern the physical appearance" of the balance sheet and the internal condition of a concern. The business income flows first from merchandise into receivables, then from receivables into cash, and finally from cash back into merchandise, labor, and overhead expenses. "Merchandise is accumulated in keeping with an expected sales demand, receivables rise and fall with the flow of sales, and cash fluctuates with the income from sales and the disbursements made to create or replenish the merchandise."

The income of a manufacturing business may be divided into three parts, each portraying a broad use (1) to purchase raw material, (2) to pay labor in the manufacturing process and (3) to care for all other expenses such as selling, administrative, taxes, interest, rent, insurance. The first two of these elements, the cost of raw material, and the cost of labor, are the principal elements which go to make up the final cost of the finished product which is then carried on the books of the company at "cost or market, whichever is lower."

When that finished merchandise is sold, an additional sum, a mark-up is added to the value at which it is carried on the books to cover all other expenses and under more normal conditions, a profit. That mark-up generally amounts to 15 per cent to 25 per cent of the selling price in the case of a manufacturer, 10 per cent to 25 per cent in the case of a wholesaler and 20 per cent to 50 per cent in the case of a retailer. That is, an article valued at $90 in the inventory, when sold on credit terms, is now carried at $100 to $145 in the receivables, depending upon the article, competitive conditions, and whether the seller was a manufacturer, wholesaler or retailer.

To obtain the actual merchandise turnover of a business enterprise, it is necessary to have a detailed profit and loss account from which it is possible to compute accurately the average percentage mark-up. If the annual sales volume is reduced to the extent of this percentage, it is then possible to obtain an average figure representing the physical turnover of the merchandise, by dividing this sum, representing the cost of the merchandise going into the annual sales, by the actual cost of merchandise on hand.

The very explanation of this process indicates the difficulties in carrying out a plan broadly to obtain reliable indexes of merchandise turnovers in widely varied lines of business activity, the lack of a sufficient number of complete profit and loss statements of moderate or large business enterprises. As a result there has been gradually developed in credit circles, the realization of the importance of the simple arithmetical ratio obtained by dividing annual sales by the inventory on the fiscal date. Such a ratio fills the need created by the difficulty in obtaining accurate merchandise turnover figures as long as the business executive, banker, accountant, creditman, statistician, and student realizes that the resultant figure is a simple arithmetical ratio.

Statement Analysis Made in 1933

During 1933, the balance sheets and operating schedules for the year 1932 were studied on 6,111 business enterprises in widely varied lines of industrial and commercial activity in all parts of the country. By far the greater percentage of these cases had a Tangible Net Worth in excess of $50,000. The average ratios of sales to inventory in 24 important divisions of industry for the entire country covering the years 1931 and 1932 are contained in the schedule found on the preceding page. Manufacturers of shoes, wearing apparel, underwear, and furriers, all show a relatively high ratio of sales to inventory as inventories are invariably at the low point when the balance sheets are drawn off. Wholesalers of hardware and retailers of men's clothing show relatively low ratios indicating the low volume generally handled by these two lines of activity in 1931 and 932.

There are two other ratios in which the inventory is one part of the fraction, which are both of real interest and deep significance. These two ratios are (1) the percentage of working capital represented by the inventory and (2) the percentage of the inventory represented by the current liabilities. These two ratios are relatively stable.

The figure which gives the percentage of working capital represented by the inventory is obtained by dividing the inventory (raw material, merchandise in process, and finished goods in the case of the manufacturer) by the excess of current assets over current liabilities (i. e., Working Capital). A particular concern might be transacting a very large volume of business, have an inventory of proportionate size, and show a most satisfactory relationship between sales and inventory. In many lines of business activity it is necessary to place forward orders or contracts to be assured of the necessary raw material to carry on a substantial volume. If for any unanticipated reason, orders suddenly drop off or certain orders on the books are cancelled and for business reasons the cancellations accepted, or if expected orders fail to materialize, the inventory just accumulates. There is a real fundamental question as to whether it is good business or poor business to overtrade, that is, to handle a greatly excessive volume of business when based on the working capital because of this reason. The one ratio which will give an indication as to whether an inventory is heavy or not, irrespective of the volume of business is this ratio. It is an important, pertinent ratio and one which is gradually receiving increased deserved recognition.

Heavy Inventory to be Avoided

Heavy or excessive inventories are to be avoided just as much as over-investments in fixed assets and large liabilities. These three items are crucial in the successful operations of a business enterprise. The same yearly depreciation charges must be taken when a plant is operating at 25% capacity as on 100% capacity and the same interest charges must be paid on mortgages or funded obligations in a depression as in good times. Heavy or excessive inventories likewise are a drag on a business and result in depreciation losses due to changes in style, perishability, and constant price fluctuations.

If you have a manufacturing or jobbing business which is operating on a tangible net worth greater than $50,000, be careful even if your ratio of sales to inventory seems in satisfactory proportion, if your inventory is greater than two-thirds or three-quarters of your working capital, and a retail business if your inventory is greater than your working capital. The smaller ratio of 66 2/3 per cent applies to concerns with tangible net worths ranging from $50,000 to $250,000 and 75 per cent to concerns above that size.

Only one manufacturing group included in this study, 179 concerns engaged in manufacturing both women's and children's shoes in 1931, shows a ratio of inventory to working capital above the 66 2/3 per cent and that only fractionally to 67.2 per cent. The average percentage for the 78 1932 balance sheets dropped to 51.8 per cent. Two wholesaling lines where selling terms are carefully restricted to 30 days and with 2 per cent discount allowed in 10 days are above this minimum guide, wholesale grocers with 78.5 per cent and 81.3 per cent for 1931 and 1932, respectively, and wholesale hardware with 69.2 per cent and 76.5 per cent for 1931 and 1932, respectively. Only one retail line where terms are largely cash, retailers of men's and women's shoes with 136.4 per cent and 116.6 per cent for 1931 and 1932 are above the 100% minimum guide.

The figure giving the percentage of inventory represented by the current liabilities is obtained by dividing the current liabilities by the inventory. Most balance sheets are taken from the books at a time of the year when seasonal fluctuations are at or near the low point and so it would be natural to expect that the liabilities would grow during seasonal upturns at other periods during the year. During the period 1926-1929 this one ratio was often the indication of the need of additional capital on the part of larger business enterprises which was corrected by the injection of additional cash into the business, obtained by the underwriting and public distribution of stocks and bonds. This ratio is often the indication of a top heavy debt which can be corrected only by adding capital or by following the policy of cutting down sales.

Seasonal Influences Important

The ratio of current liabilities to inventory can be high due to a small inventory as well as large liabilities. The lines of business activity in this study in which this ratio is high, are those where there is a seasonal liquidation of merchandise at the end of the year, manufacturers of cloaks and suits, dresses, silk underwear and wholesalers of furs, hides and skins. These lines of business activity are among those which have the smallest investment in fixed assets and so can keep their affairs in healthy shape even though liabilities at times seem a little out-of-line. For 1931 the spread ranges from a low of 51.6 per cent in case of 39 wholesalers of hardware to a high of 152.4 per cent in the case of 175 manufacturers of dresses. Liabilities were materially lower in all lines of business for 1932 and so this percentage is noticeably smaller when compared with 1931. For 1932 the spread ranges from a low of 43.0 per cent in the case of 66 wholesalers of hardware to a high of 137.6 per cent in the case of 187 manufacturers of dresses.

It is extremely difficult to place the full importance of a current act in its place, its respective niche, in history. Likewise it is extremely difficult to orient a business in the current movements and trend of economic activity. When prices are falling, the turnover of inventory is a matter of great importance in restricting losses. Since March of this year, wholesale prices have been generally upward, indexes up to December showing a 20 per cent to 25 per cent increase. When prices are rising, the turnover of inventory and its size, are of fundamental importance in keeping a business in healthy condition. A heavy or excessive inventory purchased for a speculative profit, decreases the turnover; changes in style, customs, needs, and competitive products result in hazardous complications particularly in those cases where inventories are excessive and liabilities comparatively heavy.

Watch your inventory. Keep it well balanced and in satisfactory proportions to your sales, your working capital and your current debt. Control your balance sheet, don't let the proportions of your balance sheet control you.

COMPARISON OF COMMERCIAL FAILURES AND PRICES

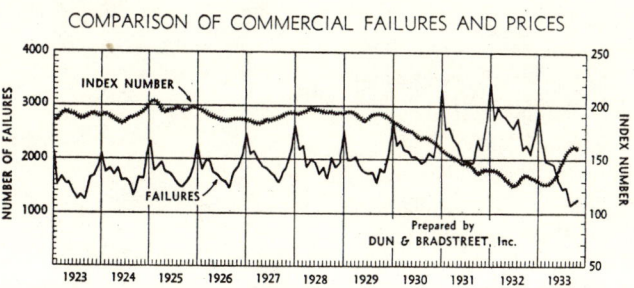

The comparison of failures and prices since 1923 shows a distinct relationship. As prices began to decline in 1930 failures started to increase. When the price decline ceased, failures became fewer.

THREE IMPORTANT SALES RATIOS

Roy A. Foulke

THREE IMPORTANT SALES RATIOS

by ROY A. FOULKE
Manager, Analytical Report Department, Dun & Bradstreet, Inc.

ABOUT ten months ago I called upon the president of a New York corporation at his request to examine, in a general way, the financial statement of his business with him. The corporation had been in active operation about six years and its successive profit and loss accounts had shown profitable operations every year. These results were most striking as the six years spanned the treacherous period of the depression. The combined capital and surplus was around $260,000, so the enterprise while it could not be classed among the large corporations, was by no means small.

During the third quarter of 1933, activities in most lines of business were gradually improving, sales were expanding, wages were being raised by an increasing number of concerns, wholesale prices were heading upward, profits were being reported, failures and liabilities were the lowest in several years, and the N.R.A. was giving evidence of historical business cooperation and eventful industrial revival.

This concern was manufacturing a product used in the building trade and the tragedy in this tale lies in the fact that the building trades even at this time have shown only a moderate recovery In some unusual manner, however, the net sales of this enterprise had dropped in no single year of the depression. Each year showed further progress as the volume increased from $410,000 to $500,000 and for the year ending June 30, 1933, to $960,000. In two years of continuous economic bob-sledding and in the one line of business activity which had the longest and steepest run, this concern had increased its sales 134 per cent. That looked almost like the millennium.

I sat in a deep leather upholstered chair in the president's office as I looked over the balance sheet and profit and loss schedule for the year ending June 30, 1933. To him the figures made an impressive showing and disclosed most satisfactory profits. To me, after I had studied the figures for a while, the picture seemed like London in a Spring fog, dark and dismal. In fact, the longer I examined the figures, the darker and more dismal they became. Here was the reason.

For the year ending June 30, 1933, the sales had amounted to $960,000 or at the average rate of $2,630 per day. The balance sheet disclosed combined notes and accounts receivables of $415,000. Mentally I divided the total receivables by the average sales per day and obtained an average collection period for the outstanding accounts of 158 days or approximately five months. Now, this concern sold its merchandise on terms of 30, 60 and 90 days and so it was obvious that at least half of the receivables were in a very archaic semi-conscious condition. Even if all sales were made on 90 day terms, something was wrong. A very substantial portion of those receivables had sleeping sickness.

A further cursory examination of the figures revealed a working capital (i. e., excess current assets) in the neighborhood of $200,000. If half of the receivables were worthless, the concern actually had no working capital and was ready either for a strenuous reorganization or for the ultimate resting place of second-hand automobiles when the final exchange value approximates the sum of twenty-five dollars.

After I had taken a period which my host apparently thought was sufficiently long to study the intricacies of his financial statement and operating figures, he interrupted my meditation by asking for my reaction. I explained to him as carefully as I could the condition which I have outlined here in the preceding paragraphs. His initial surprise was turned into a kind of medieval mystification. My reasoning seemed logical but somewhere there must be a misleading premise as the sum total of his intimate knowledge of the business emphasized to him how continuously profitable operations had been.

The fact that the annual sales had expanded so steadily and rapidly in the one line of business which had been outstandingly dormant, should have put him on his guard. It took no great imagination to realize that the sales had been increased by means of granting increasingly liberal credits and as a result accumulated losses had actually been covered up for two or three years in an expanding amount of uncollectible receivables.

Two weeks later we met together again. This time we examined a detailed aging of the receivables which he had had his accountant carefully make at my suggestion. That aging verified the more general analysis which I had made on the basis of the average sales per day. About 10 per cent of the receivables in dollars were in the hands of attorneys for collection. About 20 per cent were from 30 days to over 180 days past due and the company itself was naturally having extreme difficulty in making collections from this group. And finally, around 22 per cent had been renewed or extended on the original terms of sale or otherwise they would have been 30 to over 180 days past due. Fifty-two per cent of the entire receivables were off color (without giving any consideration to the condition of the receivables created by current sales) and that sum represented 58 per cent of the number of debtors. The situation was very involved. The patient was ill and the diagnosis had been delayed long past the critical period.

Poor Collections Cause Difficulty

One day late in 1920 a small unimpressive store was opened in western Pennsylvania on an initial capital of $15,000, to sell clothing to men and women on the installment plan. The background of the installment clothing business calling for an initial down payment of 10 per cent and the balance in twelve to twenty equal weekly payments goes back to the last quarter of the nineteenth century, but this division of retail trade developed most rapidly immediately prior to the depression. This enterprise which started in such a small way turned out to be one of the fastest moving streamlined band wagons in the commercial world. The story moves rapidly. By 1923 three stores were in operation. Then there followed a period of wholesale expansion as additional units in widely scattered States were opened and similar businesses and chains were purchased, merged, or absorbed into this growing nation-wide enterprise. Millions of dollars needed to finance these operations were obtained as successive issues of cumulative preferred stock and common stock were marketed to the hungry investing public. By January 31, 1931, seventy-six stores were in operation over a wide territory extending as far south as Texas and as far west as Wisconsin. The working capital and tangible net worth were measured by the millions amounting to $3,900,000 and $4,580,000, respectively. No such sums had ever been invested before in the installment clothing business.

When the financial statement and profit and loss account for the year ending January 31, 1931, were made available, I had a talk with the president. Those figures showed net sales for the year of $5,400,000 and the balance sheet carried receivables of almost the same identical amount. It took no oracle of Delphi to realize that at least four-fifths of the receivables were worthless, as the receivables should at the most have disclosed an average collection period based upon the sales, of ten weeks and here they were showing fifty-two weeks. I outlined the details of this reasoning to the president but here again his intimate knowledge of his business would not allow him to realize the full significance of a few easily recognizable vital facts.

In October a voluntary petition in bankruptcy was filed. No settlement has been made with the creditors up to this time. Receivables carried on the books slightly in excess of $5,000,000 were sold for the nominal sum of $44,000. The stockholders' investment of $4,580,000 has been entirely wiped out and it now appears as though creditors would be fortunate if they received five cents on the dollar in the final settlement. That condition was due largely, if not entirely, to the widespread unwise extension of credit. Heavy uncollectible receivables were rolled up like a snowball which then melted in time of need when funds were required to meet bank and trade obligations. That picture emphasizes the tremendous waste which can accumulate in the loose extension of credit.

On the other hand, credit when

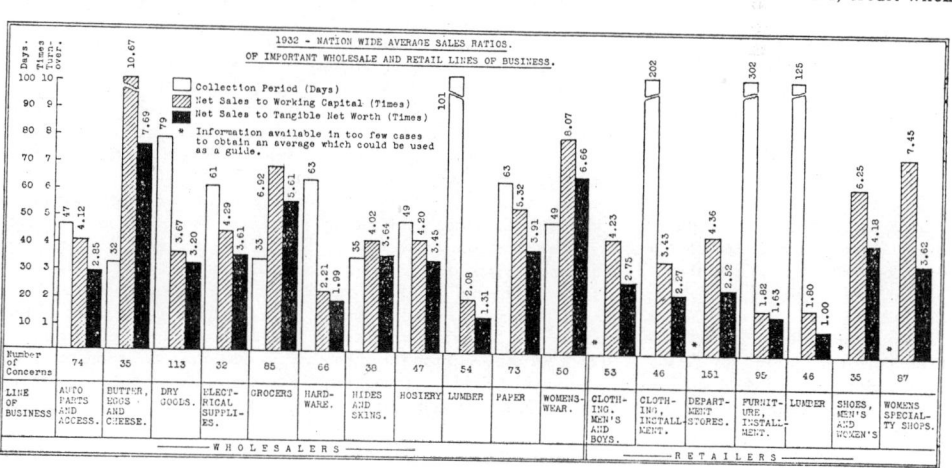

properly administered can and should be an outstanding constructive force in a recovery program. Credit terms can be expediently relaxed to assist temporarily heavy but sound buyers of merchandise in passing through a top-heavy or critical period. The ability to make exceptions, to change rules and terms to meet an unusual situation is, after all, the mark of the capable, experienced executive.

Depression Hardships Widespread

The years 1930, 1931, 1932, and 1933 comprised a period of overcast skies, and an almost continuously falling barometer with the exception of the last half of 1933 when there was some return of benignant confidence. For four years there had been a steady drop in the number of active business enterprises, manufacturers, jobbers, wholesalers, and retailers, in existence in our forty-eight States. From the all-time peak of 2,212,779 concerns on December 31, 1929, the number shrank to 1,980,700 on December 31, 1933, a decrease of 11.7 per cent. Since the turn of the century, in only one other year, 1918, had there been any falling off in the number of active business establishments when compared with the number for the previous year. The figures showing this steady decrease during these four years of sagging business activity are as follows:

Decrease in Number of Active Business Concerns 1930-1933

	No. in Business at End of Year	Decrease During Year	Per Cent of Decrease
1933	1,980,700	95,880	4.8
1932	2,076,580	48,708	2.3
1931	2,125,288	57,720	2.7
1930	2,183,008	29,771	1.4

Total decrease 1930-1933 232,079

From the latter part of 1929 until the early part of 1933, our national economic outlook was dominated by fear, hesitation, and a questioning faith in what had come to be accepted as the absolute laws of orthodox economics. Increasing unemployment, failing banks, restricted bank and trade credit, collapsing commodity and security prices, unhealthy competition, the banking moratorium, reduced wages, increasing fear of the unknown, undermined the morale of employers and employees. One shock followed another. Ambition was stifled by the first law of nature.

Failures and their liabilities increased by leaps and bounds, reaching in 1932 the immense record total of 31,822 embarrassments involving liabilities of $928,000,000. The limited number of new concerns was insufficient to offset the tremendous onslaught of failures and the far greater number of voluntary liquidations. In 1933 the number of failures dropped to 20,307, involving liabilities of $502,831,000, but the great increase in the number of voluntary liquidations brought about the greatest decrease in the number of active business concerns in our economic history.

The number of newly organized manufacturers which might have needed a substantial or even moderate investment in real estate, buildings, machinery and equipment, and of retail stores in which an investment in furniture and fixtures might have been required, dropped off because of the existing stress and strain, large failures, and the imposing array of operating losses in all lines of business. Men were more reluctant than ever before to part with their liquid resources to start new enterprises. And then no one knew from one day to another whether personal resources might or might not be needed for actual living expenses. Capital underwritings, except governmental notes and bonds and highly speculative stocks, almost disappeared from sight.

The New Deal has gone a long way along the routine of placing social consciousness on an honored pedestal. Jeremy Bentham condensed this political philosophy over 125 years ago in the phrase of "The greatest good for the greatest number." That apt phrase has received great popular currency during recent months. There is no doubt that the philosophy of the New Deal is based upon its implications. We are attempting by fluid experiments to apply that principle by industrial and commercial self-regulation and governmental action to the field of business where self-interest has been the underlying motive since the days of ancient trading.

N.R.A. Aids Operations

The New Deal is explained by its spokesmen as a measure of planned economy in contrast to the individual initiative which dominated our colonial aggressiveness, the winning of the West, and the high standard of living made possible by manufacturing ingenuity and compactness. But be that as it may, business activity in the United States is still the expression of individualism and so it undoubtedly will remain.

Competition, after all, remains today the most effective element in business activity. Under the N.R.A., competition has been relieved of certain abuses, such as underselling due to low wages as the primary element in cost, and unfair trade practices peculiar to respective industries. Every business organization, except trusts, monopolies, and combines, does and should face the possibility that more active competitors will obtain increased business, that more visionary far-looking competitors will invent new machinery and processes, that because of bad judgment plant assets might be large and depreciation charges too heavy, and that because of poor judgment an excessive or a poorly balanced inventory might be created. These are axioms of the business world.

Flexibility of wages above a minimum is socially and economically desirable, but business men should understand that no attempt has been made to belittle the desirable effects of competition and individual initiative. Marginal concerns must overcome their difficulties or fall over the precipice into the chasm of business embarrassments. Successful concerns must produce the products demanded and needed by their customers and the public or join the ranks of the past. The National Recovery Act did not abolish competition and monopolistic practices are still outlawed.

For four difficult years competition became keener and harder. Because of the very pressure on existence, prices were cut below production costs in order to obtain business. Wages were cut and then further reduced. Never had there been a similar period in our economic history and the story is told by the immense total of failures, their aggregate yearly liabilities and the drop of 232,079 concerns in active operation during 1930-1933. These facts belong to economic history. Profits are now being recorded, the number of failures is below the corresponding weeks of 1933, liabilities are down and wholesale prices are up. For about a year prices have been rising upward, with constant fluctuations, but still going up, and it is this price trend which more than any other single factor has put life and breath into trade and industry. No small part of current profits, however, are inventory profits and inventory profits are not healthy profits because they give a sense of security and confidence which is somewhat akin to self-hypnosis.

What is needed by business executives today as never before is a thorough fundamental understanding of the financial basis of successful business operations. In an economic society where the spread of wages within an industry is suddenly greatly narrowed and where flagrant unfair trade practices are outlawed, competition must of necessity become somewhat keener along the normal front of service. A greater premium is placed upon efficient operation, but efficient operation is predicated upon policies which are invariably reflected in healthy balance sheet proportions.

By this I mean that every official of an important business enterprise should realize the sheer folly and the inherent difficulties involved in carrying heavy fixed assets, substantial current liabilities, large mortgages and funded liabilities, excessive inventories, as one and all are indications of a weakened or a weakening financial condition. Heavy fixed assets drain the profit and loss account with heavy depreciation charges. Substantial current liabilities tax operating efficiency to meet trade and bank obligations when they become due. Large mortgages and funded liabilities make inroads upon operating figures in the form of interest charges. Excessive inventories involve unexpected losses by changes in style and in deterioration.

Along with these strategic balance sheet proportions which must be kept in line for sustained successful operations is the relationship of sales and receivables known as the aver-

Three Comparative Yearly Average Sales Ratios

Number of Concerns 1931 / 1932	Line of Business	Collection Period (Days)	Net Sales to Working Capital (Times)	Net Sales to Tangible Net Worth (Times)
	Manufacturers			
163 / 135	Cloaks and Suits	38 / 30	7.48 / 6.69	6.08 / 5.65
126 / 167	Clothing, Men's and Boys'	64 / 65	4.96 / 4.49	3.89 / 3.56
28 / 39	Converters of Cotton	59 / 47	5.35 / 6.38	5.05 / 5.82
41 / 43	Converters of Silk	43 / 43	7.62 / 6.20	7.35 / 6.27
175 / 187	Dresses	42 / 35	9.67 / 8.45	7.41 / 6.49
35 / 46	Furniture	75 / 92	3.85 / 2.78	2.31 / 1.50
130 / 102	Fur Garments	40 / 51	4.16 / 3.20	3.74 / 2.78
19 / 40	Fur Trimmings	43 / 38	3.69 / 3.37	3.50 / 2.96
76 / 89	Knit Goods	45 / 38	7.75 / 6.64	3.93 / 3.53
22 / 30	Luggage, Leather	58 / 69	4.87 / 3.66	3.22 / 3.03
44 / 64	Paints and Varnishes	77 / 86	3.71 / 3.68	2.06 / 1.53
75 / 72	Printers, Job	47 / 64	7.77 / 7.39	2.71 / 2.48
50 / 66	Shirts, Underwear and Pajamas	48 / 63	4.33 / 5.22	3.54 / 3.68
38 / 50	Silk Piece Goods	38 / 41	7.33 / 6.60	6.15 / 5.02
179 / 78	Shoes, Women's and Children's	40 / 37	9.50 / 8.06	3.85 / 3.71
36 / 92	Underwear, Silk	49 / 40	8.08 / 7.59	5.54 / 5.27
	Wholesalers			
33 / 74	Automobile Parts and Accessories	45 / 47	5.31 / 2.77	3.27 / 2.85
29 / 35	Butter, Eggs and Cheese	28 / 32	12.51 / 10.67	9.20 / 7.69
97 / 113	Dry Goods	77 / 79	4.40 / 3.67	4.00 / 3.20
24 / 32	Electrical Supplies	60 / 61	5.21 / 4.29	4.14 / 3.61
40 / 85	Grocers	34 / 33	7.51 / 6.92	6.18 / 5.61
39 / 66	Hardware	83 / 63	3.13 / 2.21	2.61 / 1.99
47 / 38	Hides and Skins	49 / 35	3.89 / 4.02	3.56 / 3.64
52 / 47	Hosiery	66 / 49	4.93 / 4.20	4.40 / 3.45
33 / 54	Lumber	84 / 101	3.56 / 2.08	2.68 / 1.31
42 / 73	Paper	55 / 63	6.74 / 5.32	4.60 / 3.91
27 / 50	Women'swear	43 / 49	8.79 / 8.07	6.94 / 6.66
	Retailers			
22 / 53	Clothing, Men's and Boys'	*	4.07 / 4.23	2.62 / 2.75
35 / 46	Clothing, Installment	172 / 202	3.57 / 3.43	2.37 / 2.27
99 / 151	Department Stores	*	4.45 / 4.36	2.82 / 2.52
50 / 95	Furniture, Installment	246 / 302	1.86 / 1.82	1.70 / 1.63
38 / 46	Lumber	126 / 125	2.59 / 1.80	1.23 / 1.00
40 / 35	Shoes, Men's and Women's	*	6.37 / 6.25	4.20 / 4.18
79 / 87	Women's Specialty Shops	*	8.40 / 7.45	3.88 / 3.62

(*) Part of the sales are for cash and part are on charge account. To obtain an average collection period it would be necessary to deduct the cash sales from the annual net sales and then determine an average collection period on the balance. This necessary information is available in too few cases to obtain an average figure which could be used as a broad guide.

age collection period. Each year many concerns fall by the wayside as a result of heavy losses from bad debts. During a depression this is particularly so.

Collection Period Must be Watched

When merchandise is sold, the gross profit is taken into the profit and loss account. This is so with every line of business with the exception of those very few installment furniture houses which make it a practice of setting up a sum equivalent to the mark-up as unrealized profit. Actually, the gross profit is not earned until the account is collected. The longer the terms of sale, the more important the collection becomes. "Distance lends enchantment" is no adage to describe sales terms. Chain stores early made this discovery.

Early in 1932 the Research Department of R. G. Dun & Co., in co-operation with several thousand representative business concerns throughout the United States, made a survey of bad debt losses for 1931 in primary divisions of industrial and commercial activity. From the results of this survey, a set of industrial and commercial credit loss averages were computed so that credit men might have a measure of the effectiveness of their own individual credit policies.

Bad debt losses were studied on aggregate sales of $4,010,726,000 from 122 different lines of businesses. The lowest percentage of loss was reported by 62 manufacturers of electric motors, dynamos, lamps and electric furnaces. On aggregate sales of $462,843,000 for 1931, bad debt losses to this group amounted to only $559,043, or .121 per cent. The other extreme was reflected by the reports received from dealers in builders' supplies, such as stone, brick, sand and cement. In this line the loss averaged 4.345 per cent of sales, or about four times the average of the 122 reporting lines of business. These are average percentages. Percentages for individual businesses in some cases ran materially higher.

No study was made of the bad debt losses of the installment clothing line, but known losses ran around 22 per cent on sales in the Southern States and 16 per cent to 18 per cent in the Northern States. The well-operated installment chains anticipated this loss ratio by a proportionate mark-up.

Bad debt losses are only interesting as a recapitulation; they are analogous to a text-book study of the battles of Waterloo, or Gettysburg. There is, however, one early analysis of business transactions which can invariably be used to indicate the comparative effectiveness of collections. That analysis gives the guide known as the average collection period based upon sales. It is obtained by dividing the annual sales by 365 days to secure the average sales per day and then dividing that result into the combined sum of accounts and notes receivable plus any assigned accounts and discounted notes.

The average collection period obtained in this way should be in fair proportion to the net selling terms of the business unless the receivables on hand are larger than usual due to recent seasonal sales, such as the receivables of a department store on December 31, of the cutting-up trades on March 31, or wholesalers of lumber on August 31.

The average collection period has been determined for both 1931 and 1932 operations on sixteen manufacturing lines of business, eleven wholesaling lines and three retailing lines for this study. The number of concerns whose balance sheets and operating schedules were examined ranged from 5,754 in 1931 to 6,111 in 1932. The terms of sales used by the concerns in the various divisions in these studies were quite uniform.

Sales Volume is Vital Factor

From the gross income, that is, the sales of a business, come the funds to repay bank loans, to pay merchandise invoices, salaries, wages, rent, light, heat, transportation, insurance and other expenses. Sales are to the business enterprise what oxygen is to the human being. They both support life. A very material increase in the volume of sales has the same effect upon the business organism as an increase in the quantity of oxygen has on the human organism.

I can best point out the practical value of these two important comparisons by describing the actual happenings of a concern which until a short time ago was recognized as one of the very successful leaders in the cutting-up trade, a manufacturer of popular-priced dresses ranging from $3.75 to $6.75. This enterprise had an operating history of six years, its progress had been rapid, the president had a national reputation for being able to anticipate the demands of the market consistently, and the business was quite generally looked upon as one of the outstanding profitable concerns in the cutting-up trade. From an initial investment of about $50,000 the capital and surplus gradually increased, after liberal salaries and dividends, to around $312,000 in its six years.

The figures of this concern, issued after the Easter shipments and consequently with large receivables on its books, came across my desk a little over a year ago. The liabilities were somewhat heavy but this fact was in general outweighed by the splendid record of the corporation and the uniformly high esteem with which the personnel was regarded. Two factors, however, indicated the existence of some undue strain and those two factors were the comparisons of net sales to working capital and net sales to the tangible net worth. Here is the contrast of these two guides as reflected by the figures of this particular enterprise, and the average for the industry.

Comparison	This Company	Average, 187 Concerns
Net Sales to Working Capital	20.00	8.45
Net Sales to Tangible Net Worth	16.00	6.49

For the fiscal year, this enterprise handled a volume of approximately $5,000,000 on a working capital of $250,000 and on a tangible net worth on the statement date of $312,000. The dominating policy was one of large volume and small profits, but comparatively heavy liabilities were necessarily involved in carrying out that policy. The turnovers of both working capital and tangible net worth were two and a half times the average of the industry; the disparity was so great that it was too much not to expect some developments.

Balanced Appraisal is Essential

I have mentioned that when a concern is transacting a very heavy volume of business, a strain is set up and continued operation can only be maintained under a delicate balance. What did I mean by "delicate balance?" Merely the relationship between the income and the outgo of funds. The lapse of time between the day funds are taken in and the day those same funds are disbursed is very short and nothing can disturb that balance without having a real effect upon the business.

The operation of a concern which is trading heavily is based upon an anticipated volume of business. Orders are placed for raw material to be manufactured into finished products to be available for shipment at some near future date. If anticipated orders suddenly drop off or collapse, if certain important orders already received and confirmed are cancelled and for business reasons the cancellations are accepted, if a strike occurs and raw materials continue to pile up; any one of these factors in a period of one to three months can and in the past have resulted in a still further increase in liabilities already heavy simultaneously with a drop in income to meet the larger obligations. That is an almost ideal combination for financial embarrassment. The ceiling falls and no landing place is discernible through the clouds. Funds to meet liabilities are missing.

This is what actually happened in this spectacular case. The result came fast and the record books now show a settlement of 70c. on the dollar with creditors.

In the business world, the two indications of the stress and strain from overtrading, from great speed, are these comparisons of net sales to working capital and tangible net worth. Watch them closely, particularly as sales climb upward.

Collection Periods Increase

This study gives the average collection period in days based upon sales of 30 divisions of industry and the average number of times the working capital and tangible net worth is turned over for 34 divisions. Moreover, this study gives these average results for both 1931 and 1932.

The year 1932 was a little further along toward the trough of the depression than 1931 and we would naturally expect comparative studies to show the effect of decreasing sales. In all except four of the 34 divisions of industry which make up this study, there is reflected a slower turnover of working capital and tangible net worth. When the 1933 figures are made available we shall find an upward tendency as a result of the material improvement in most of the lines of business activity in the last six months of last year.

The comparison of the average collection period for the two years shows a far different tendency. Of the 30 divisions of industry on which average collection periods could be obtained 17 show longer periods for 1932, 12 shorter periods, while one, the converters of silk piece goods, is identical for both years. The lines which disclose a shorter period are those which probably realized the full importance and need for cash and gave greater uniform attention to their collections notwithstanding the disturbed business outlook.

The highest average turnover of working capital is found in the case of the wholesalers of butter, eggs and cheese. Here we have a turnover of 10.67 times for 1932 and 12.51 for 1931. This line is followed by the cutting-up trade with the manufacturers of dresses well in the van. Then come manufacturers of shoes, wholesalers of women's wear, retail specialty shops, manufacturers of silk underwear, job printers, manufacturers of knit goods, manufacturers of silk piece goods, wholesale grocers, and converters of silks.

The turnovers of net worth generally vary among industries somewhat similar to the turnovers of working capital, except that this statement is qualified by those lines which have heavy fixed investments. Job printers, manufacturers of knit goods, and specialty shops have relatively low turnover of their tangible net worth, while wholesalers of butter, eggs and cheese, manufacturers of dresses, silk underwear, and wholesale grocers, continue with the turnovers of net worth only slightly below those of working capital.

Sales are Business Lifeblood

The operating personnel of every business wants increased sales as above a certain point sales bring into effect that natural law of increasing returns. Above that point the cost of producing a product per unit drops, the cost of wholesaling or retailing a quantity of merchandise is lowered, and profits increase at a more rapid rate. It might cost $50,000 to produce one automobile but 500,000 of the same model can be produced at $400 each.

Ever increasing sales will continue to be the alpha and omega of the business world as long as the profit motive and the institution of private ownership serve their broad fundamental purposes. But in the process of continued economic expansion, businesses to be successful must guide their policies with a clear understanding that increased sales must be constantly accompanied by a healthy collection period, sufficient working capital, and adequate net worth.

THREE IMPORTANT NET PROFIT RATIOS

Roy A. Foulke

THREE IMPORTANT
NET PROFIT RATIOS

by ROY A. FOULKE

IN a recently published volume, *Attending Marvels* by the paleontologist, George Gaylord Simpson, the extreme difficulty of making headway against a hundred mile wind in the bleak, cheerless, windy stretches of far off Patagonia, is described vividly. A plane took off from Comodoro for Deseado before dawn one morning as the pilot hoped to anticipate the wind which daily gained vigor with the sun. On this particular day, however, the wind also arrived a few hours before its accustomed schedule. As the plane gained altitude less and less progress was made. The pilot gradually realized his unusual predicament and decided to work back over the landing field but in the meantime the gale had reached such a force that a landing would have meant instant death. There was nothing left to do but to head again into the wind for Deseado.

Then began a duel which lasted four hours. "The powerful motor and the wind were almost evenly matched. Sometimes the plane would gain a few hundred yards, then the savage wind from the distant Cordillera would retaliate and drive the plane out over the open sea. For most of the time the two were so evenly balanced that the plane simply hung as if suspended in space. All this time it was never out of sight from the field from which it had risen."

In another spot Simpson writes, "It is probably not true that a man once inadvertently fired a rifle straight into the wind and was killed by his own bullet as it was blown back." But it is true, he swears by his own eyes, "that wild geese trying to fly into the wind are often rapidly carried backward and that it is sometimes impossible for a man to progress except on his hands and knees, clutching bushes for anchorage."

The strange naturalness of nature has ever been a fundamental if almost an unbelievable fact. And so also is the strange naturalness, the bare truths of economic laws which underlie the success of the business enterprise.

Have you ever heard about a business earning a net profit which was "too large"? Well, I have.

You say the millennium would be here if that should happen and there would be no further apprehension about unbalanced government expenditures. Net profits could never be "too" large. I have examined the operations and financial conditions of several concerns which have shown profits that I believe were relatively and objectively "too" large.

Abnormally high profits at times have been the ruination of sound business policies as the underlying basic reasons for such profits often are unrecognized and superficial credit for the spectacular results invariably is taken by the active managements. It seems to be a weakness of human nature to analyze superficially and to take full credit for accomplishments which we fail to realize are brought about by efforts other than our own. Have you never seen a halfback throw back his padded shoulders after making a touchdown, never realizing that the score would have been impossible if his tackle had not taken out the opponent's safety man so timely and effectively?

First Radio Profits Extremely High

That an occasional business concern discloses net profits which are "too" large is just as fundamental and unfortunate a fact as the ever blowing Patagonian wind.

For instance, take the case of a concern which only a few years ago was one of the larger well-known manufacturers of radio receiving sets. In 1928 and 1929 radio parts and radio tube manufacturers were almost delirious with profits. Tubes were selling at five dollars each and in those days of radio experimentation they did not wear quite so well as old friends. Battery sets had only begun to give way to the use of direct and alternating current, and battery manufacturers were still working overtime. For the year ending May 31, 1929, the net profits after all charges except dividends and management bonus, reached the magnificent sum of $5,110,000.

Net profits of this amount would not seem exceptionally large under more normal business conditions to a corporation with a tangible net investment in excess of one hundred million dollars but here was a concern which unblushingly showed net earnings of about five million dollars when the tangible net worth at the end of the fiscal year of May 31, 1929, was only $12,550,000. That was certainly phenomenal if anything in the business world ever was.

As a matter of fact these earnings would appear to be even more striking when it is realized that the corporation opened its fiscal year on May 31, 1928, with combined capital and surplus of only $2,358,500. An increase of $1,077,300 in the tangible net worth was brought about by the issuance of 14,175 shares of stock, to net the company $76 per share after underwriting fees in August of that year but the realization of the smaller capital in use at the beginning of the fiscal year makes the comparison of the earnings with the average net investment over the entire year appear even more gargantuan. Manufacturing radio sets at this stage of development was far more profitable than mining gold. Confidence was our strongest national force. Poverty was still being outlawed. The age of plenty was almost at hand.

With this background of economic exuberancy and with full confidence in their own ability to continue most profitable operations, the management decided to expand its enviable program and to enlarge its plant. The decision was not unusual under the circumstances but the manner and extent of putting that decision into effect was most unfortunate. In January, 1929, as well as in August of the previous year, stockholders were offered the privilege of subscribing to stock, this time to 72,840 shares at $80 per share (net to the company at $76) to raise $5,535,840 and in November, 1929, 249,737 additional shares were offered at $40 per share (net to the company at $36) to raise $8,990,532 additional. Those were the days when money could be had for the mere asking!

Plant Greatly Expanded

Five additional million dollars net were then put into plant facilities during the year ending May 31, 1930, and over seven million dollars more during the succeeding year. A legend has come down to us that construction costs, building materials, machinery and equipment were a trifle high during these particular years. Then skies began to cloud, *sales resistance* succeeded *conference* in our vocabulary, depreciation and amortization increased and a business which for one year had reported most phenomenal profits now began to report phenomenal losses. The rush of water over the dam could not be stopped.

On November 24, 1933, equity receivers were appointed. On February 20, 1934, a petition in bankruptcy was filed and in March the company was adjudicated bankrupt. Those spectacular profits for the single fiscal year ending May 31, 1929, had been "too" large. The strong light had blinded the eyes of the management and it became impossible to focus correctly on continued sound healthy policies in a developing industry in such a rapidly changing business world. There was no more economic justification of putting those twelve million dollars into fixed assets in two years because one year had been extraordinarily profitable than there was for the building boom from 1927 to 1929.

Another tale of all conquering ambition of about this same time, has to do with a much smaller and less widely known New York corporation in the same lively line of radio manufacturing activity. This tale is even more melodramatic. The enterprise had been manufacturing small electrical devices for several years in a most inconspicuous but successful manner when the radio field opened up. The wide awake management rapidly and naturally seized upon the profitable possibilities of producing certain small parts for receiving sets and went into the game with complete abandon. When the year December 31, 1929 ended, the figures disclosed a net profit of $765,000 compared with combined capital and surplus of $1,740,000 on

Trend of Three Average Net Profit Ratios (1931-1933)
MANUFACTURERS

Line of Business—Manufacturers	Number of Concerns 1931 1932 1933	Net Profits on Sales	Net Profits on Tangible Net Worth	Net Profits on Working Capital
Cloaks and Suits	163 / 135 / 170	0.76(L) / 1.45(L) / 0.24	4.60(L) / 8.81(L) / 1.62	5.69(L) / 9.75(L) / 1.79
Clothing, Men's and Boys'	126 / 167 / 238	1.42(L) / 3.30(L) / 1.70	5.64(L) / 11.45(L) / 7.18	7.12(L) / 14.85(L) / 8.40
Confectionery	22 / 23 / 26	2.04 / 0.78(L) / 0.20(L)	4.80 / 1.64(L) / 0.47(L)	10.88 / 3.28(L) / 1.01(L)
Converters of Cotton Goods	28 / 39 / 54	0.45(L) / 0.17 / 2.00	2.19(L) / 0.94 / 11.19	2.42(L) / 1.06 / 12.50
Converters of Silk	41 / 43 / 66	0.83 / 0.78(L) / 0.80	2.45 / 4.83(L) / 4.73	2.60 / 5.01(L) / 4.82
Dresses	175 / 187 / 186	0.47(L) / 0.77(L) / 0.92	3.42(L) / 4.83(L) / 6.44	4.56(L) / 6.31(L) / 7.95
Fruits and Vegetables, Canners	30 / 33 / 28	1.51(L) / 1.90(L) / 0.44	4.62(L) / 5.72(L) / 1.70	14.17(L) / 21.19(L) / 6.49
Furniture	35 / 46 / 52	2.40(L) / 11.10(L) / 1.76(L)	5.50(L) / 16.70(L) / 2.90(L)	9.28(L) / 31.08(L) / 5.38(L)
Fur Garments	130 / 102 / 87	1.28(L) / 4.07(L) / 2.56	4.80(L) / 10.50(L) / 7.59	5.35(L) / 12.99(L) / 8.65
Fur Trimmings	19 / 40 / 35	0.95 / 4.15(L) / 1.58	3.27 / 12.36(L) / 4.57	3.56 / 13.75(L) / 5.22
Knit Goods	76 / 89 / 106	0.43 / 1.12(L) / 0.53(L)	1.70 / 4.08(L) / 1.01(L)	3.38 / 6.86(L) / 1.85(L)
Luggage, Leather	22 / 30 / 27	3.20(L) / 3.00(L) / 0.99	8.72(L) / 9.05(L) / 3.07	12.50(L) / 10.46(L) / 3.64
Millinery	28 / 36 / 35	0.02(L) / 1.10(L) / 0.85(L)	0.08(L) / 6.10(L) / 3.38(L)	0.12(L) / 9.38(L) / 6.66(L)
Neckwear, Men's	28 / 48 / 50	0.48(L) / 2.20(L) / 0.23	1.65(L) / 7.32(L) / 0.72	2.11(L) / 9.76(L) / 0.90
Paints and Varnishes	44 / 64 / 85	0.17(L) / 5.20(L) / 0.12	0.54(L) / 7.81(L) / 1.96	0.63(L) / 19.74(L) / 4.35
Printers, Job	75 / 72 / 53	0.55(L) / 3.24(L) / 2.52(L)	0.91(L) / 8.15(L) / 5.14(L)	2.70(L) / 23.68(L) / 15.80(L)
Shirts, Underwear and Pajamas	50 / 66 / 82	0.26(L) / 1.70(L) / 1.98	0.96(L) / 6.27(L) / 7.45	1.14(L) / 8.84(L) / 9.29
Silk Piece Goods	38 / 50 / 48	1.30(L) / 0.56(L) / 0.22	8.10(L) / 2.34(L) / 0.99	9.62(L) / 3.05(L) / 1.20
Shoes, Women's and Children's	179 / 78 / 76	1.33 / 2.14(L) / 0.70(L)	4.75 / 9.35(L) / 2.65(L)	12.60 / 17.12(L) / 5.62(L)
Underwear, Women's Silk	36 / 92 / 120	1.91(L) / 0.48(L) / 0.89	1.81(L) / 2.57(L) / 4.71	2.65(L) / 3.65(L) / 5.01

the very same date. That is almost like pole-vaulting fifteen feet or running the hundred yards in eight seconds flat.

On July 31, 1928, seventeen months prior to the fiscal closing the combined capital and surplus had amounted to but $352,000. In November, 1928, fifteen thousand shares of capital stock had been offered to the stockholders at $20 per share and in September ten thousand shares had been offered to the public by a Chicago investment banking house at $21 per share. By these issues of stock around $408,000 additional capital was raised, after deducting estimated underwriting fees of 20 per cent which would probably have been a conservative charge for an underwriting of this type in the days of financial freedom.

If $408,000 had gone into the treasury from these sources a balance sheet as of December 31, 1928, if it had been issued, would have shown a tangible net worth around one million dollars and profits for the entire fiscal year beginning on that date, were more than three-quarters of this sum. Such a showing was only a little less than Arabian magic. It was too good to be true. Reaction set in before the management realized what was happening and it came with a vengeance. Losses were reported for 1930, 1931 and in June, 1932, the business was bankrupt.

The net profits had been "too" large for the good of the operating management.

Profit Causes Should Be Sought

If the net profits of a business enterprise for a particular year are materially greater than those of all competitors, that is the time an inventory should be taken of accounting methods, of policies, depreciation charges, valuation of merchandise, the use of hidden reserves, and the results of abnormal temporary prosperity. Occasionally a concern shows a large profit due to a speculation in merchandise, buying heavily and opportunely when prices are low. Heavy speculative purchases are rarely indulged in by experienced business executives as the chances for heavy losses are greater than those for substantial gains. The occasional time that this practice is successful, the sudden increase is really nothing more or less than a non-recurring profit in the income account, a spectacular flash in the pan which affects the figures for a single year.

When a business enterprise is the owner or licensee of a patent or a formula or process or a product which is in great demand, then the profits often mount temporarily and materially above the average for the industry. If the patent or formula or process is new and the demand is suddenly created, the combination of propitious factors leads to immediate profits. The same is true if a new industry is in process of creation. The early manufacturers in a virgin field charge a higher price, as the demand cannot be filled, with very profitable results. But rarely if ever can a full set of auspicious circumstances be capitalized upon for more than a year or two. Competition is a necessary antidote for the protection of the consumer.

The principle of operating on a low overhead, in order to increase profits, has been recognized by chain store operations for decades. The Great Atlantic and Pacific Tea Company was begun in 1859 and in 1900 had 225 stores. The Grand Union Company dates back to 1872. F. W. Woolworth Company was started in 1879. But this chain idea only occasionally wandered away from the retail grocery field until around 1910 or 1912 when it began to spread into the domain of slightly higher and then still higher priced merchandise. The profits of the early successful operated chains were large and the profits of some units have remained quite steady throughout this depression, but as one chain after another was organized, operating in the same localities, competition in the great majority of cases brought net profits to quite a reasonable figure and even losses to some.

Earnings Disproportionately High

A few months ago the officers of a moderate size chain handling sales of about two million dollars annually sent in their figures for the year ending December 31, 1933. Forty-five stores were operated and they were all located in the eastern part of the country, handling ladies' outerwear, hosiery and specialties. These figures showed a tangible net worth of $175,000 of which $85,000 represented net profits earned and retained in the business during the year. In other words, this concern earned practically one hundred per cent on its combined capital and surplus at the beginning of the year. The showing was so remarkable that it seemed to take on characteristics of the tale of the man who was killed when the bullet from his rifle was blown backwards by the Patagonian wind.

The President of the company came in one spring day and we examined the comparative figures of his business together but we made no appreciable headway toward a common understanding. The greater part of this increase in net worth was represented in the assets by materially larger receivables, increased inventory and several miscellaneous slow items. If these items were actually worth the full value at which they were carried on the balance sheet, the net profits were correct but there was no way of verifying the value of these assets outside of a full audit by a well known firm of accountants and the expense of such a sound undertaking proved to be a stumbling block. We could accept the figures or not just as we choose!

After weighing the human possibilities, it was conceivable that the balance sheet values of these assets could be correct and that under a peculiar set of most propitious circumstances, an abnormally high percentage of profit could be earned on the tangible net worth even in a line of business where competition is keen and operating costs do not vary greatly. If this were so, however, the liabilities had been liquidated to the very last cent to show a satisfactory fiscal balance sheet. The inventory only amounted to $65,000 and the current liabilities $70,000. If the figures disclosed the exact condition of the corporation, the concern was over-trading to the breaking point in handling annual sales of two million dollars as to do so the merchandise in season would have to expand to about $175,000 and the liabilities to approximately $200,000.

The President readily admitted that the window had been dressed for the fiscal statement and that in season the showing would approximate these figures. There were no non-recurring profits which might give a key to an explanation, no great increase in the inventory value, no credit from hidden reserves. The profit and loss account disclosed no information out of the ordinary except the large volume of business being handled on the limited invested capital. Every symptom pointed either to a case of complete and absolute delusion or a case of exaggerated over-trading.

Situations like this are not run across in the examination and study of one out of a thousand concerns. The fundamental problem after all in this day and age is not the threat to business health and well being as a result of a high percentage of net profits on the tangible net worth but the low percentage of profits and actual operating losses in the wide array of durable goods industries operating at a nominal percentage of capacity. It is quite possible, however, that here is another of those rare species where profits have been "too" large for the lasting good of the management.

Earnings Basic Under Profit System

Underlying any thoughtful consideration of profits or losses, whether "too" large or "too" small, and also the widespread current discussion of our economic plight, are the problems of the distribution or re-distribution of raw material, manufactured goods, farm products, wealth and income. These far reaching problems are based upon the conceptions of two fundamental economic realities, those of private property and the elusive profit motive.

The institution of private property is merely a concentrated way of saying that almost everything is owned by someone, some business enterprise or some governmental unit—that is, almost everything except air and fish, and if you are a deep-sea diver or a stratosphere explorer you must buy oxygen; and if you do not live near the ocean or the backwoods you must pay cash directly to the dealer for your fish or indirectly to the State through the agency of a fishing license.

People did not always live thus and in the great experiment which is being carried on in Russia today, they do not live entirely that way now. In primitive societies as with the Indians prior to their conflict with the colonists, land was not privately owned; most tribes moved from place to place as the seasons changed and the wild animals moved. Water was free and so also were the bounteous gifts of nature. But the institution of private property existed even with the Indians, as the warriors owned their own bows and arrows, tents and simple clothing, and wampum was the accepted medium of exchange.

The institution of the profit motive is merely another way of saying that business enterprises are in existence to earn a profit. The will to profit often is not strong or intelligent enough to overcome natural economic or highly competitive factors and if a business concern operates at a loss year after year it must end in only one place and that is the bankruptcy heap. The quest for wealth more than for a happier contented life has always existed. The treasures of the ages have successively appeared in the market places of the world, Alexandria, Rome, Venice, Amsterdam, Paris, London and New York. But with the gradual development of a higher and higher technique in manufacturing processes during the past one hundred and fifty

Trend of Three Average Net Profit Ratios (1931-1933)
WHOLESALERS

Line of Business — Wholesalers	Number of Concerns 1931 1932 1933	Net Profits on Sales	Net Profits on Tangible Net Worth	Net Profits on Working Capital
Auto Parts and Accessories	33 / 74 / 85	1.78(L) / 2.70(L) / 0.28	5.86(L) / 7.54(L) / 0.82	9.48(L) / 11.39(L) / 1.30
Butter, Eggs and Cheese	29 / 35 / 39	0.28 / 0.45 / 0.95	2.60 / 3.57 / 7.09	3.59 / 4.90 / 8.75
Dry Goods	97 / 113 / 128	0.80(L) / 2.18(L) / 1.90	3.22(L) / 6.92(L) / 6.14	5.59(L) / 8.06(L) / 7.34
Electrical Parts and Supplies	24 / 32 / 42	3.40(L) / 3.20(L) / 0.37	14.10(L) / 11.74(L) / 1.08	17.71(L) / 13.86(L) / 1.15
Fruits and Produce	10 / 19 / 27	0.48(L) / 0.59(L) / 0.59	3.48(L) / 5.70(L) / 5.00	6.80(L) / 10.67(L) / 10.05
Grocers	40 / 85 / 136	0.33 / 0.26 / 0.78	2.20 / 1.45 / 4.10	2.62 / 1.72 / 5.30
Hardware	39 / 66 / 72	2.44(L) / 4.28(L) / 1.30(L)	6.39(L) / 8.54(L) / 2.60(L)	7.20(L) / 9.91(L) / 3.15(L)
Hosiery	52 / 47 / 44	0.37(L) / 1.60(L) / 2.30	1.75(L) / 5.65(L) / 8.31	1.85(L) / 7.15(L) / 9.01
Lumber	33 / 54 / 55	1.52(L) / 12.67(L) / 0.60(L)	4.10(L) / 17.69(L) / 0.84(L)	5.45(L) / 24.14(L) / 1.37(L)
Paper	42 / 73 / 79	0.30 / 0.92(L) / 1.78	1.45 / 3.65(L) / 6.05	2.02 / 4.90(L) / 8.20
Wom'nsw'r, C'ts, S'ts and Dresses	27 / 50 / 34	1.05(L) / 0.80(L) / 1.71	7.80(L) / 5.28(L) / 11.90	9.36(L) / 6.39(L) / 14.59
Woolen and Worsted Piece Goods	20 / 29 / 44	1.51(L) / 1.27(L) / 2.20	6.15(L) / 3.98(L) / 11.52	6.63(L) / 4.27(L) / 12.64

years and the growing emphasis upon the freedom of the market, the profit motive has increased in world-wide intensity, and often at the expense of fair-dealing, justice, and humanity.

If Soviet Russia solves the problem of substituting a social consciousness for the profit motive of the individual, a miracle of the ages will have appeared on the pages of history. Even Henry George in his revolutionary philosophy of the single tax went no further than to advocate the total payment of ground-rent as a tax, predicating his full program of creating a more just, logical background for a happier, fuller life on the institution of private property in all but land, air, and water— and on the profit motive which gives varying degrees of wealth, "for" he writes with his ever careful discernment, "there are differences among men as to energy, skill, prudence, foresight and industry."

Profit System Adopted by Colonists

When the Pilgrims landed at Plymouth in the autumn of 1620, there was no immediate consideration of either private property or the profit motive. This was due to the fact that the whole body of colonists had found themselves together in a pact, the terms of which provided that for seven years they would work together, put their produce in a common warehouse and receive their subsistence out of the common store. At the end of the seven years there would be a settlement with the London merchants who had furnished funds to finance the Mayflower trip, purchase supplies, clothing, equipment and such sundry articles as were needed in making a settlement in a barren, new land.

There were other problems which were more pressing and immediate than the ones of owning property and obtaining credit for labor. The first and most important was of survival in a cold, unfriendly wilderness and that problem was not solved any too well. During the first winter more than half of those brave adventuring souls died and you will recall in your early readings of history that the graves were carefully covered over so that the Indians would be unaware of the depletion in numbers.

When the first spring apppeared the problems then became those of clearing land, planting crops, and building houses and without any hesitation the little group banded together and worked as one in the fields. The crops would be for all. The primitive attempts at farming were immediately supplemented by fur trading, fishing and lumbering, all of which furnished cargoes for the return voyages of visiting ships. On the lapse of the third year, the system of common tillage which even in those earliest of colonial days rewarded idleness and paralyzed industry was given up and each family was allotted land for its own cultivation. After chafing three years more under the bondage of the London merchants, the original contract was set aside and the colonists bought outright all claims of the original investors. So after six, instead of the original seven years, the colony became one in which the institution of private property was finally evolved and where private initiative dominated in economic if not in religious matters.

High Profit Common in Finance

Money, and the fields of activity which bring the greatest monetary return or profit, even to the extent of "too" great a profit, seem to have a close affinity for each other. That is an economic truism as old as orthodox English economic theories. The Mississippi Bubble of 1720, the Ponzi episode in Boston two hundred years later in 1920 and the equally disastrous if less known Clarke Bros. affair in New York in 1929 are logical if tragic extreme examples of this fateful affinity.

This early theory, however, is even more fundamental and broad than might be exemplified by isolated cases of forced credulity. Prior to the World War, London was the money center of the world as English investors for more than a hundred years had recognized the possibility of greater returns by investing funds in the Argentine, on the continent, in Canada, in Africa, India and in the United States than at home. At the opening of the War approximately five billion dollars of our securities were held abroad and a substantial portion of this immense sum was owned by investors in Great Britain.

In the years which followed the War, New York financiers began to compete with London for foreign loans and we were quite successful in obtaining our full measure of loans, too successful in fact! Our financial circles recognized the possibility of greater profits in loaning funds not only to the less developed portions of the world but even in highly industrialized Germany. And so today the foreign bond column of the daily financial page gives silent testimony to our youthful urge for experience, for easy profits, in the long list of defaulted bonds, Peru, Chile, Brazil, Colombia. And in addition there are the millions tied up in the stand-still agreement with Germany as well as the default in the payment of interest on the Dawes and Young loans.

Profits Attract Funds

As it was with national movements of funds in the "old days" so it was and is—to some extent—with industries today. Funds find their way into industries where profit possibilities are bright while industries and divisions of industries with excess investments are eaten into by operating losses, unwise dividend disbursements, voluntary liquidations and bankruptcies.

But this orthodox theory, with the weight of decades and a long line of classical scholars behind it, is not strictly or entirely true. We know only too well that very little money is seeking investment today either in the organization of new concerns, the flotation of stocks in established successful enterprises, or even in the distribution of funded securities for well-known business corporations. Something has affected that close affinity between money and profitable possibilities. We are going through one of those arid periods in our economic life when safety, security of principal, and not the possibility of profit or return is the effective broad motivating power.

Perhaps this aridness is due to the very widepread idea in the business world that for many months confidence in the future has been on a vacation. Business men, bankers, investors and the small promoter, the man who would like to invest in a small corner retail store, all have been wondering and still are wondering what affect national policies will have upon the pocketbook and profits. When will the budget be balanced? Will we run the printing presses? What new taxes will be necessary to finance the huge Federal expenditures? Will gold be revalued again? What will the next Congress do with the bonus?

Uncertainty Retards Funds

These are reported to be fundamental problems of the moment and there is no doubt that they have the prestige which comes from reiteration. Funds will not find their way into new investments of industrial, public utility or railroad stocks or bonds in any appreciable amount with uncertainty in the air; and businessmen, on their part, are reluctant to borrow additional long term funds to renovate or expand productive facilities when they have no idea with what kind of dollars long term loans in future years will have to be paid.

After all, is such a theory very healthy under existing conditions? I know one important chain which operates 450 units in all parts of the country which for twelve months has operated on the aggressive policy that now is the time to make all possible physical improvements in their stores. The reasoning is readily understood and appears to be far more logical than a watchful waiting policy which after all is often but an admission of indecision. They are securing increased business at the expense of less progressive competitors.

Here are the reasons. First, prices are relatively low. Second, labor is anxious to work and to give a full day's return for its pay. Third, improvements today when most competitors are standing still, are actually bringing business to the doors. Fourth, if inflation should come, and that is the primary worry of business, investments in the latest machinery, equipment, and improvements, will be far more valuable than dollars in the bank. If these facts were more generally recognized, that recognition itself would tend to breed confidence, speed up activity, put more men to work, and assist in locating the elusive profit.

Prices Affect Demand

Higher prices have reduced business failures, brought substantial net profits to certain larger business organizations during the past two years, placed a premium on adequate working capital to support larger inventories and higher receivables, given managements a breathing spell to stop, look, and listen. But higher prices have not assisted the flow of products from manufacturers to wholesalers to retailers and to consumers. In fact, if there is one generally accepted universal law of economics which is older than Confucius, it is the one which points out that higher prices tend to diminish sales and lower prices to increase sales. The automobile business industry felt the results of a price increase almost immediately early in the summer and as soon as the pulse slowed up, prices were reduced and orders immediately picked up. The lumber industry increased prices and orders fell off precipitately and have remained off.

Perhaps after all prices should not be raised to the 1926 level. A temporary stabilization or even a rise in prices is quite expedient in the early period of a depression but when business goes along with no materially increased consumer demand but even decrease in unit volume, it would not seem beyond the realm of probabilities that somewhat lower prices in certain industries might be essential to bring out the full demand. Sufficient demand at a lower price level has many times in the past given the basis for increased employment, a moderate net profit after paying reasonable wages, and the impetus to move forward out of the slough of a depression.

Trend of Three Average Net Profit Ratios (1931-1933)
RETAILERS

Line of Business — Retailers	Number of Concerns 1931 1932 1933	Net Profits on Sales	Net Profits on Tangible Net Worth	Net Profits on Working Capital
Clothing, Men's and Boys'	22 / 53 / 52	2.44(L) / 5.10(L) / 0.33	6.69(L) / 14.26(L) / 0.95	9.92(L) / 24.15(L) / 1.45
Clothing, Installment	35 / 46 / 50	2.22(L) / 2.82(L) / 3.85	5.02(L) / 6.62(L) / 6.43	7.55(L) / 9.58(L) / 6.94
Department Stores	99 / 151 / 173	1.46(L) / 3.72(L) / 0.70	4.08(L) / 9.73(L) / 1.82	6.52(L) / 16.21(L) / 3.35
Furniture, Installment	56 / 95 / 60	6.46(L) / 10.86(L) / 6.80(L)	10.91(L) / 18.07(L) / 6.98(L)	12.05(L) / 20.10(L) / 9.17(L)
Lumber	38 / 46 / 52	4.10(L) / 8.75(L) / 1.40(L)	5.22(L) / 8.75(L) / 1.59(L)	10.65(L) / 15.72(L) / 2.69(L)
Shoes, Men's and Women's	40 / 85 / 31	2.60(L) / 1.40(L) / 0.44	10.51(L) / 5.81(L) / 1.66	16.90(L) / 8.18(L) / 2.72
Women's Specialty Shops	79 / 87 / 122	0.22 / 3.89(L) / 0.10	0.85 / 8.62(L) / 0.36	1.90 / 18.20(L) / 0.72

OPERATING
AND
BALANCE SHEET RATIOS

Arthur Andersen

Operating and Balance Sheet Ratios

In the Financial and Industrial Investigation

By ARTHUR ANDERSEN

Arthur Andersen & Co.

SURVIVAL under conditions of modern competitive business necessitates a constant vigil over financial relationships and operating results. All businesses strive to obtain competitive advantages in industry and thereby secure an increased return on capital. This very effort tends to narrow the margins of profit and any business which is not alert to competitive progress soon finds itself facing elimination. Sales price levels are seldom within the control of a single business. They are set fundamentally by competition, so that the average concern will realize a reasonable return under average conditions over a period of time. The margin between sales and costs must pay operating expenses and costs of financing, and then yield a fair return on capital invested. The individual business must give its attention to those factors over which it has control, namely, costs of financing, rates of turnover and expenses.

One of the most significant indices to the condition of a business is that afforded through the use of ratios developed from balance sheet and operating statement figures. Some few ratios are commonly used, such as the ratio of net profits to sales, or to net worth, and the ratio of current assets to current liabilities. Other ratios of still greater significance may be only rarely used. The relationships of inventory to sales or cost of sales, of charge sales to receivables, of mortgage debt to assets pledged, of sales to total assets, all have a meaning if it be read.

Ratios as Indices to Operations

Ratios are valuable indices because they picture relationships uninfluenced. by changes in economic values. The economic law of supply and demand is constantly exerting its influence on the general level of prices. In periods of high prices, commodities are high and the purchasing power of money is low. In periods of low prices, commodities are cheap and the purchasing power of money is high. During times of general inflation, profits of business will naturally increase as the buying power of money will be diminished. During times of general deflation, profits will naturally decrease as the buying power of money will be enhanced. An enterprise may realize an increase in profits during a period of rising prices, but may

[1] Previous articles on "The Industrial and Financial Investigation" by Arthur Andersen appeared in this journal as follows: December 1925, page 325; January 1926, page 17; February 1926, page 113; March 1926, page 201; April 1926, page 277.

find that there is an actual decrease in ratio or margin on net sales.

The true measure of profits is not the amount of profits realized, but the ratio of those profits to net sales, ratios constituting a measure uninfluenced by changing values. Business should be so conducted that it will yield, as nearly as may be, the same ratio of net profits, all other factors being equal, in periods of inflation and deflation as in normal times, and that ratio should be complementary to a reasonable return on the current value of capital employed. The point to be kept in mind is that the expression of sales values and other current items keeps pace with current economic conditions, but the expression of capital does not. Yet an intelligent study of ratios will aid materially in determining whether a business has kept pace with or perhaps even anticipated changing conditions, especially during times of marked instability, such as were experienced from 1914 to 1921.

Types of Ratios

Profits are effected by management through three main sources, namely, low financing costs secured through balanced capital structure, rapidity of turnovers and profit margins which include control of expenses. Significant ratios concern the relationships in the same three sources: turnover ratios, operating ratios and balance sheet ratios. The more important ratios in each of these three groups are as follows:

Balance sheet ratios:
  Working capital ratio.
  Net worth to total capital employed.
  Mortgage debt to assets pledged.
  Common and preferred stock equities to net worth in cases of preferred stock financing.
  Earnings retained in business to total earnings.
Turnover ratios:
  Sales to total assets.
  Charge sales to receivables.
  Sales or cost of sales to inventories.
  Sales to plant.
  Net profits to net worth.
Operating ratios:
  Gross profits to sales.
  Selling and general expenses to sales.
  Operating profits to sales.
  Earnings available for financing to annual cost of financing.
  Surplus net profits to sales.

In the analysis of a business, these ratios are applied

further in detail to the various elements of financial condition and operating results to the extent warranted by relevant information desired in each particular case. Each of the typical ratios noted above has significance from an analytical viewpoint.

Significance of Ratio

Thus the working capital ratio is significant in the light of ability to pay current obligations. This influences credit standing and purchasing power. The company that can purchase at lowest prices has an initial competitive advantage. The ratio of net worth to total capital employed reveals the adequacy of capital investment as compared with borrowed capital and the policy of financing as to proprietary risk. There is a vast difference between a management that finances to acquire temporary borrowed funds and one that finances to have the public furnish most of the capital. The ratio of mortgage debt to assets pledged reflects a measure of the security and assurance that the borrowed capital will be repaid. The ratios of common and preferred stock equities to net worth show the segregation of proprietary risk and are of particular interest in cases of preferred stock financing. The ratio of earnings left in the business to total earnings has embodied in it the elements of conservatism, normal expansion and gradual liquidation of liabilities.

The ratio of sales to total assets embodies the general efficient use of total capital employed. The ratio of charge sales to receivables is the fruit of an efficient or lax credit and collection system. The ratio of sales or cost of sales to inventory is the result of a quick turnover or the carrying of surplus, unbalanced or obsolete stocks. The ratio of sales to plant may show conservative policy or over-expansion. The ratio of net profits to net worth involves the turnover of investment and shows the earning power of a business from the viewpoint of stockholders.

The ratio of gross profits to sales represents the spread between the cost of goods purchased and their selling price or between manufacturing costs and sales. It is the margin of profit between sale price and cost by purchase or manufacture. The ratio of selling and general expenses to sales shows the relative cost of marketing the products and administering the business. It is the proportion of sales expended in selling goods and in administrative conduct of the enterprise. The ratio of operating profits to sales is one of the chief factors in determining whether the business is measuring up to standard in obtaining a fair return on capital. Operating profits are profits before earnings from extraneous sources, cost of financing and income taxes. The ratio of earnings available for financing to annual cost of financing is one measure of the degree of protection to borrowed capital. The ratio of surplus net profits to sales has its significance in the light of rapidity of turnover of net worth to sales, the result of these two factors being the ratio of return on investment.

The working capital ratio is the one most frequently used, being the ratio of current assets to current liabilities, and sometimes known as the "bankers ratio." It reveals the proportion of working capital which is furnished by the business and the proportion which is obtained from creditors, and is thus of prime concern to ordinary trade creditors in the usual course of business and to those making short-time loans.

Factors affecting the working capital ratio are rapidity of turnover of receivables and inventory, amount of credit utilized from trade creditors and the amount of working capital furnished by the capital permanently invested in the business as compared with the amount obtained on short-time loans. Receivables and inventory are major items in the working capital of most enterprises. Conditions which result in favorable or unfavorable turnover of these assets have their effect upon the working capital ratio. Rapidity of turnover of receivables is affected by the terms of credit, business conditions affecting customers' ability to pay and stringency of enforcing collections. Turnover of inventory is influenced by the character and price of the unit of product, its balanced relationship in accordance with production demands, the accumulation of slow moving and obsolete stocks and the general volume of inventory carried in relation to sales.

Both receivables and inventory of a particular business will vary under the influence of changes in these underlying conditions. The working capital ratio is affected directly by the amount of credit utilized from trade creditors. When bills are paid promptly, outstanding accounts payable are less and the ratio is more favorable. When enterprises find it difficult to pay creditors, accounts payable increase and the ratio diminishes. The working capital ratio is affected by the extent to which the necessary working capital is furnished by capital invested in the business. When working capital requirements exceed that furnished by the capital in the business, the excess is ordinarily obtained on short time loans, usually through the medium of bank loans. As such short time loans increase, the working capital ratio diminishes; as they are liquidated, the ratio increases.

Temporary Financing for Fluctuations

Nearly every business has seasonal fluctuations to a greater or lesser degree. Seasons of production, of consumption, and of intense or lesser activity place varying demands upon the working capital requirements. The normal working capital should be furnished by the invested capital or net worth of a business, but peaks within the year occasioned by conditions or seasonal business may be financed by current bank loans. Fundamentally sound policy requires that current bank loans be virtually paid at least once each year in off-peak periods.

The working capital position and ratio is thus of vital significance and under constant scrutiny by commercial bankers. The ratio is likewise of importance in connection with bond and stock issues, for no business can be conducted successfully without a sound working capital position.

The range of working capital ratios as between industries depends somewhat upon the characteristics of the industry. In business involving turnover of receivables and inventory, rapidity of turnover and purchase credit terms of the trade are dominant factors having their effect upon the ratio. An industry handling low priced commodities and giving short terms of credit requires less working capital and usually shows a higher ratio than one dealing in higher priced articles and granting longer terms of credit. Ordinarily, a ratio of at least 2 to 1 is required. This ratio has its inception, no doubt, on the theory that the enterprise shall have equally as much at stake as the creditors if not more. Business not involving turnover of receivables and inventory does not require as high a ratio. Operators of office buildings, public utilities and professional lines frequently have ratios, but slightly in excess of 1 to 1. As between enterprises within the same industry, there are no definite characteristic ratios.

RATIO OF NET WORTH TO TOTAL CAPITAL EMPLOYED

The ratio of net worth to total capital employed reveals the relative proportions of invested capital and borrowed capital to the total capital employed in the business. Net worth includes earnings retained in the business, for those constitute a part of invested capital just as much as the original investment. Borrowed capital includes both long term debt and current liabilities. This ratio is a measure which assists in determining the adequacy of invested capital and the security of borrowed capital. Fundamentally, the more capital the borrowing enterprise has at stake, the safer the loans. Ordinarily, except in the case of public utilities and other enterprises whose earnings possess a higher degree of stability, invested capital should exceed borrowed capital. The function of borrowed capital is to finance reasonable requirements, either temporary or over a term of years. When borrowed capital exceeds invested capital, it is assuming the aspect of financing the enterprise, of sharing the element of proprietary risk and must take added precaution as to its security.

The ratio furnishes a basis for determining the policy of financing. Sound and conservative business will borrow capital only to finance reasonable requirements which may be either temporary or over a term of years. It gives borrowed capital every assurance that it will be repaid and does not expect it to assume the least semblance of proprietary risk. The ratio of net worth to total capital employed in such business is usually high. There is another type of management that has limited invested capital and has ambitions in business beyond that warranted by the capital structure. It will borrow capital to the maximum extent possible often without much conscience as to its security. The ratio of net worth to total capital employed under this type of management is usually low and creditors must exercise precaution as to the security of borrowed capital. An enterprise that borrows capital to finance reasonable requirements is ordinarily sound and successful. One that conducts business on maximum borrowed capital often contains the elements of speculation and evades the full responsibility of proprietary risk. The ratio of net worth to total capital employed over a period of time is the key to the financial policy of an enterprise and an index to the responsibility of its management.

ELIMINATING INFLUENCE OF DEPRECIATION

It is always well to ascertain the ratio of cash or properties actually invested in the business to the total actual capital employed, eliminating all appreciation of book values in excess of original cost. The ratio then reveals the actual capital contributed by invested capital as compared with borrowed capital. Irrespective of present appraisal value of properties, the investor and banker are privileged to know how much the enterprise has actually at stake as compared with capital borrowed. It has an influence on the amount which the banker is willing to loan and on the investor in selecting his investments. The ratio on this basis may be supplemented by a ratio based upon present value of properties as substantiated by acceptable appraisals. Consideration may then be given this supplemental ratio as conditions warrant. Fundamentally, the ratio on the cost basis has much the greater significance. This is particularly true when appraisals are not carefully and conservatively used.

This ratio concerns creditors in the order of their security. Unsecured creditors are concerned most, as they are the first to lose in case of liquidation. Secured creditors are primarily concerned with the margin of security pledged, but are also interested in the ratio of net worth to total capital employed from the standpoint of continuance of the enterprise as a going business. Few creditors covet foreclosures. Properties are of greatest value to a business as a going concern. The ratio of net worth to capital employed reveals to the secured creditor a measure of assurance that the enterprise will continue successfully as a going business and that borrowed capital will be repaid without encountering refinancings or foreclosures upon assets pledged. The ratio of a particular secured loan plus equal and underlying liens to total capital employed is likewise a measure of security of the particular secured loan. Junior liens and unsecured creditors would first absorb loss in event of financial difficulties.

RATIO OF MORTGAGE DEBT TO ASSETS PLEDGED

The ratio of mortgage debt to assets pledged reflects a measure of the security and assurance that the borrowed capital will be repaid. The function of mortgage debt is to furnish permanent capital for a term of years. At maturity it is either paid or refunded. This is in contrast to the function of commercial loans. While current loans are primarily for the purpose of financing and facilitating movement of commodities during peak periods and should be liquidated at least once each year in off-peak periods, mortgage debt furnishes part of the permanent capital of the business over a period of years. It supplements the capital furnished by investment. In a profitable enterprise where earnings are in excess of the interest rate on funded debt, it automatically increases the return on investment.

The ratio of mortgage debt to assets pledged is usually based on present fair values of the assets mortgaged. In the case of commercial properties, the usual maximum ratio is approximately 50 per cent. Public utility properties are bonded as a rule on the basis of a considerably higher ratio. The permanence and utility of properties have a bearing on the extent to which they may be mortgaged. By basing the ratio on present values, the owner of properties acquired in periods of low prices receives consideration on the same basis as one who has purchased more recently. Likewise, excessive considerations paid for properties are reduced to a safe bondable basis.

Ratios of Stock Equities to Net Worth

The ratios of common and preferred stock equities to net worth show the segregation of proprietary risk and are of particular concern in cases of preferred stock financing. This applies to any of the various classes of stock, both common and preferred, in accordance with their terms of priority. Stocks assume all proprietary risk. The particular business engaged in is its venture. Net profits or losses from the conduct of business are its reward. In case of reorganization or dissolution, it is the first to lose. The ratio of common stock to net worth and of preferred stock to net worth show the relative proportion of proprietary risk in the light of their respective provisions. The larger the common stock equity, the better the preferred stock. This is the same fundamental principle that underlies the safety of mortgage debt. The larger the junior equity, which loses first in case of loss, the sounder is the particular security.

Preferred stock financing is undertaken under varying conditions. It may be issued when it is not feasible to sell common stock, when it is not desirable to relinquish voting control, in place of mortgage issues with provisions restricting further liens on physical assets or as junior financing to mortgage issues when additional capital is required. When an enterprise is in its infancy with unproven earning power, or when the level of earnings of a business make it difficult to sell additional common stock, preferred stock financing is often resorted to as being more inviting to the conservative investor.

In the normal industrial or commercial enterprise the ratio of preferred stock to net worth should not exceed the ratio of common stock to net worth. When preferred stock equity exceeds common stock equity, the preferred stock is assuming the major proprietary risk and its value is correspondingly weakened. Occasionally one sees preferred stock issued in excess of common stock equity but, in most such instances, it is protected by personal guarantees or deposits.

To realize the significant value of this ratio, it becomes necessary to analyze the net worth. This includes ascertaining how the capital stock was paid for, and a segregation of surplus into its elements of earnings retained in the business and the various forms of capital surplus.

Importance of Earned Surplus

For purposes of comparative analysis various ratios may be drawn from the balance sheet figures giving the relations of retained earnings to the items of contributive capital, net worth, appreciation surplus, etc. The significance of these ratios is great, when considered from the viewpoint of judging management policies.

The retaining of earnings in business is essential to survival. Competition tends to result in a fair return to the average concern under average conditions over a period of time.

This fair return, which business must normally yield in accordance with its hazards, permits of adoption of the policy of distributing dividends representing normal interest return upon investment and retaining the balance of earnings in the business. Earnings retained in the business, constituting additional capital, are worthy of their hire and must earn a fair return the same as the original investment. Unless material financial reverses are encountered, these retained earnings accumulate with accelerating rapidity over a period of years upon the compound interest principle. Capital invested receives conservative dividends while, at the same time, the value of additional gradually increases. Of the three sources of additional capital—investments, loans and earnings—earnings are most significant. Favorable results attract the other two sources of capital; unfavorable results turn them to other channels.

When earnings are distributed through dividends, they become diffused, just as do the earnings of an individual who fails to conserve his income. A large portion of them are spent and thus lose their productiveness. Retained in the business, they are conserved as productive assets resulting in increased and cheaper production. The tendency of business today as indicated by the increasing number of mergers and consolidations, is toward larger business units. This increases competition and makes survival more and more difficult for the smaller business unit. The small business that does not conserve its earnings cannot hope to survive permanently in competition with the many financial advantages which larger business enjoys. The ratio of earnings retained in business to total earnings over a period of years is the greatest index of the general financial policy of an enterprise, as indicating a dissipating or conservative management and the sincerity with which it seeks to maintain a competitive position in the industry in the effort to insure a stable and relatively permanent existence.

OPERATING AND TURNOVER RATIOS

Arthur Andersen

Operating and Turnover Ratios

In the Financial and Industrial Investigation

By ARTHUR ANDERSEN

Arthur Andersen & Co.

IN a former article[1] the general use of ratios in financial analysis was shown, and some detailed discussion was given of the significance of various balance sheet ratios. But the most interesting type of analysis from a going business viewpoint is that given by a study of turnover ratios, which as a whole expresses the relationship between operating results and the capital employed. In other words, a comparison between profit-and-loss figures and balance-sheet figures.

Turnover ratios as related to current assets are affected little by inflation and deflation, unless these movements are violent. Both sales and inventories are directly affected by changes in price levels and the ratio is affected but slightly in enterprises which have reasonably rapid turnover. It is only in industries which have very low turnover, where the process of manufacture extends over a period of from six months to one year or more, and when inflation and deflation occur very suddenly, that the ratio is noticeably affected by this factor. Ordinarily the relationship between purchase and sales prices remains reasonably constant.

Turnover ratios over a period of time reflect improved or less effective use of capital resulting from management and business conditions. If an enterprise has been unsuccessful, it furnishes a basis for study to determine whether capital has been inefficiently employed or whether there is insufficient general demand for the product to enable operations upon a successful basis.

It is a self-evident condition that a capital of $1 turned twice will yield the same amount of profits as $2 turned once and the rate of return on investment will be twice as great. Under competitive conditions, $1 turned twice can do business upon one-half the margin of profit and yield the same rate of return on investment as $2 turned once. Ordinarily, operating ratios which deal with margins and control of expenses are given more attention in analyzing the trend, success or failure of an enterprise. Turnover ratios are equally vital in their effect on the relationship of profits to a reasonable return on investment and in the ability to reduce profit margins in times of keen competition. Effective turnover of capital and profits are each essential factors in the determination of a reasonable return on investment. Efficient or inefficient use of capital, which is reflected in turnover ratios, has equal influence in determining the return on investment as the percentage of profits realized.

TURNOVER OF TOTAL CAPITAL EMPLOYED

The ratio of sales to total assets used in producing sales reveals the turnover of total capital employed. Total capital employed is represented by the assets of an enterprise irrespective of the source from which the capital is obtained. The portions of capital obtained through credit, short and long term loans, and investment do not alter the amount of capital employed. The assets of an enterprise ordinarily include cash, receivables, inventory, deferred charges, plant and frequently intangibles. Receivables, inventory and plant are usually major items. Extraneous investments in securities or properties having no connection with the business should be eliminated in ascertaining turnover, as such assets yield income independently from income of the business.

Normal turnover, in accordance with the characteristics of each industry, fixes the relationship between turnover ratio and operating profit margin so that a reasonable return will be realized on capital employed. Operating profits as used in this sense are net profits from the business available to pay cost of financing and yield return on net worth. An enterprise, marketing large units or higher priced products, will have a lower turnover than one selling small units or lower priced products. A lower turnover must of necessity have a higher profit margin in order to realize a fair return on the investment.

TURNOVER OF RECEIVABLES

The fundamental relationship between turnover and profit margin constitutes the basis by which operating results are to be judged. It is the starting point for determining the weaknesses or strength of an enterprise. The extent to which weaknesses in turnover have contributed to an insufficient return may be ferreted out through a process of elimination, by applying the turnover ratio to the principal assets comprising capital employed. These ordinarily are receivables, inventory and plant.

Turnover of receivables is revealed by the ratio of charge sales to trade receivables. Cash sales and receivables other than from trade should be eliminated

---

[1] See MANUFACTURING INDUSTRIES, May 1926, page 351. For other articles on this subject see December 1925, page 325; January 1926, page 17; February 1926, page 113; March 1926, page 201; April 1926, page 277; May 1926, page 351.

as they are unrelated to credit extended on sales. In case of a seasonal business, the receivables must be averaged in order to obtain a more correct turnover for each of the periods under consideration. The turnover may be shown in the usual way in terms of sales times receivables as for example 5 to 1. Another form of expressing it is by showing the number of days' sales carried in receivables as, for instance, the receivables are equivalent to 45 days of charge sales. This is obtained by dividing the receivables by the average charge sales of one day's business.

The ratio of total charge sales to average trade receivables gives the composite turnover of all receivables. In a business making all sales upon uniform credit terms, and selling over limited territory, this composite ratio is often sufficient for general analysis of a business. When sales are made in many states and in different countries, and when varying credit terms are established in different territories and on different commodities or departments, the composite ratio is hardly sufficient in determining whether turnover has been favorable or unfavorable. The ratio must then be applied to groups of receivables arising under different credit terms and in different territories.

The turnover ratio of receivables is significant in determining the effectiveness of the credit and collection department. A comparison of the rate of turnover with the usual terms of credit gives an indication in normal times of how rigidly collections are enforced in accordance with terms of credit extended. During periods of changing business conditions and periods of depression, credit departments are always confronted with increasing problems. Over such periods, the ratio is indicative of the general policy of credits and collections. The degree of caution with which credit has been extended, and the enforcing of collections, wield their influence in molding the ratio. The movement of the ratio over a period of years furnishes the key to changes in credit policies, to the ease of collections as affected by business conditions and to the efficiency of the credit and collection department in periods of depression as well as in normal times.

Turnover of Inventory

The benefits of a high rate of turnover, in contrast to a low one, are less collection expense, less possibility of bad debt losses, and decreased cost of financing. The longer an account is carried, and the longer collection effort is applied, the greater the collection expense. The possibility of bad debt losses is increased because customers who do not pay promptly often drift into financial difficulties. Low turnover results in increased capital invested in receivables which increases the cost of financing. All of these factors converge into the final result of an increase or decrease in return on capital employed and in return on net worth.

Turnover of inventory may be stated on the basis of either sales or cost of sales. It is frequently shown in terms of sales as sales constitute the common basis for other turnovers, ratios, of expenses and margins of profits. The more correct basis, however, is cost of sales. The actual turnover is represented by the ratio of cost of sales to average inventory. The ratio on the basis of sales will usually show similar trends, but is less accurate because of the variations in profit margins. Under the retail method of accounting, the ratio of sales to inventory at sales prices gives the same turnover ratio as cost of sales to inventory at cost prices.

The composite ratio based on total inventory gives the turnover as a whole. More useful information is obtained by ascertaining turnover with respect to the various classes of inventory. The ratio of cost of sales to finished product gives the turnover of manufactured product or merchandise sold. The ratio of finished product to work-in-process gives the turnover of work-in-process. The ratio of total materials and supplies used to inventory of materials and supplies gives the turnover of raw materials and supplies. Ascertaining the ratio with respect to different kinds of products sold and principal classes of raw materials used leads to information on movement of stocks and the balance maintained in inventory in accordance with production and sales.

The turnover ratio of inventory over a period of years is of assistance in ascertaining the rapidity of realization, the policy with respect to advantageous purchasing, and alertness of the purchasing department in buying as warranted by current business conditions. Variations reflect primarily the efficiency in use of capital. By ascertaining the ratio by departments or on various classes of merchandise, information can be obtained on the extent of excessive stocks and on slow moving or obsolete goods. In a manufacturing enterprise, it assists in determining the degree of co-ordination between production and sales of the various products, and also the balance maintained in raw materials used in production. Very frequently, some materials used in manufacture are considerably over stocked while an insufficient quantity of others is carried. Surplus stock occasioned by advantageous purchasing is sometimes justified, but it has its dangers as well as advantages and can not form the basis of continuous policy. The foresight of a management is often revealed in the steadiness of turnover in periods of depression as well as in periods of advancing prices.

The advantages of rapid and efficient turnover are decreased cost in carrying inventories, less possibility of excess and obsolete stocks and minimum danger of loss from price declines.

Turnover of Property Investment

Turnover of property investment is reflected by the ratio of sales to plant. This relationship may be shown by the ratio of sales in dollars, or by the ratio of sales in units to plant. The ratio of sales in dollars is more frequently used. During periods of inflation and deflation, the ratio based on sales in units supplements the ratio based on sales in dollars in that it eliminates the effect of and is uninfluenced by changes in price levels. In this respect it expresses a more accurate relationship between sales and production and plant.

The ratio of sales to property investment over a period of years is of assistance in determining the general policy of plant expansion, the wisdom of plant expansion which has been made and the favorable or unfavorable competitive position of the enterprise. A study to ascertain the causes of fluctuations in the ratio will reveal whether plant expansion has been undertaken in order to supply permanent sales demands, or whether the construction expenditures were made in the ambition to expand relying upon ability to dispose of the added production. Expansion undertaken by the conservative management does not affect the ratio noticeably except perhaps for a very brief period during and following construction. Expansion based upon uncertain volume usually results in lowering the ratio for a considerable period following construction.

A period of several profitable years in succession is exceedingly tempting to the undertaking of expansion. This was well illustrated during the war period. The wisdom of such expansion is demonstrated in the ability to utilize subsequently the increased capacity and maintain the ratio of sales to plant investment. The ratio when compared with competitors will reveal a measure of competitive advantage or disadvantage which will have its effect in return on net worth.

Ratio of Surplus Net Profits to Net Worth

The ratio of surplus net profits to net worth, when placed on an annual basis, expresses the earning power of a business from the viewpoint of stockholders. Although this, in itself, is not strictly a turnover ratio, it constitutes the basis for the relationship between turnover of net worth and surplus net profit margin. Normal turnover of total capital employed fixes its relationship with the ratio of operating profits. Total capital employed in this sense is total assets; operating profits are profits available for financing. After deducting from operating profits the cost of borrowed capital and income taxes, a comparable relationship exists between turnover of net worth and surplus net profit margin. The ratio of final net profits to sales must generally be sufficient, on the basis of normal turnover, to yield a fair return on net worth. The ratio of final profits to net worth is the final summing up of all turnover and operating ratios and reveals the success obtained through management in financing, turnover and operating.

The ratio of final net profits to net worth varies according to business conditions, competitive conditions, character of business, risks involved and management. A business well established and having stable conditions will realize a more uniform return and attract capital more readily than one that is new and easily affected by disturbances. New industries, such as the radio industry of to-day, are more speculative in character and must yield a higher return in order to attract investment. A succession of profitable years encourages expansion. Periods of depression bring keener competition forcing lower returns and often eliminating the less efficient.

Ratio of Gross Profits to Sales

The ratio of gross profits to sales represents the spread between cost of goods sold and net sales. Fundamentally, this margin in competitive industry varies within a range which will yield to the average concern under average conditions a fair return on capital over a period of time. This is essential to the survival of a business. From the standpoint of the individual enterprise, the margin is set by competition. As competition becomes keener in proportion to demand, gross profit margins narrow. Increasing demand in proportion to supply tends to increase prices and profit margins. Each enterprise endeavors to dispose of the commodities at maximum prices consistent with volume and thus realize as high a gross margin as competition will permit. From the gross profits realized selling and general expenses and cost of financing must be paid. The balance remaining represents the return on investment.

The ratio in the case of merchandising or trading companies represents the spread between purchase cost and sales. It is the margin of the middleman as an agency in the handling of commodities from producer to consumer. Variations of the ratio in trading companies over a period of years are the result of business conditions, effectiveness of purchasing power and sales policies. Business conditions constitute undoubtedly the greatest factor in affecting demand for goods and thus influence gross profit margin continuously. Profit margins are under continuous surveillance by a management with the view of maintaining profitable turnover under existing business conditions. Purchasing power and changes in policies in purchasing and sales departments wield a lesser influence on the ratio of gross profits.

The ratio in the case of manufacturing companies represents the spread between manufacturing costs and sales. Cheaper production means lower competitive prices or larger profits. High production costs may mean competitive elimination.

In analyzing a manufacturing enterprise, some of the more important ratios concerning manufacturing costs are the ratio of total manufacturing cost to sales, ratios showing proportionate cost of materials, labor and factory expenses to total manufacturing cost, and the ratio of property expenses to property investment and to sales. Variations in the ratio of total manufacturing cost to sales are caused by conditions, competitive advantages or disadvantages, internal policies and disorders. The ratios showing proportionate cost of materials, labor and factory expenses often lead to information on material market and labor conditions. The factory expense ratio should ordinarily decrease with increased volume. Assuming approximately uniform general price levels, a reasonably normal relationship exists between property expenses, property investment and sales. Property expenses include depreciation, insurance, taxes and repairs. Variations in these ratios over a period of years furnish a basis for study of the very vital issue of whether a concern can manufacture its product and market it at a reasonable profit.

RATIO OF SELLING AND GENERAL EXPENSES TO SALES

The ratio of selling and general expenses to sales is significant of the control exercised over these expenses in relation to sales. Expenses constitute a first lien on gross profits and must be paid before arriving at earnings available for cost of financing and return on investment. Even in times of financial difficulties, expenses must be paid before bond interest, bond principal or stocks have any claim.

Fluctuations in the ratio over a period of years will reflect the change in relationship of expenses to sales as caused by business conditions. Sales are subject to continuous fluctuation by reason of changing demands and by the adoption of sales policies in accordance with changing conditions. Expenses, on the other hand, are reasonably fixed. When expenses are once increased in order to take care of sales expansion, they can not be so readily contracted when sales volume diminishes. The ratio of expenses to sales should ordinarily decrease with increased volume. If the expense ratio increases with increased volume, there is usually a lack of co-ordination of expenses with sales and an indication of weakness in management. The increase in expense ratio to sales during and since the deflation of 1920 and 1921 is the most outstanding illustration of the effect of business conditions.

RATIO OF OPERATING PROFITS TO NET SALES

Operating profits constitute net profits, exclusive of income from investments and non-operating sources, available for interest on borrowed capital and income taxes. Income from investments and non-operating sources are extraneous to the particular business under consideration and cannot be included in the relationship of operating profits to sales. Interest on trade receivables and purchase discounts are elements of operating profits. Because of usual concern in the ratio of profits to sales before interest received and purchase discounts, operating profits are generally shown both before and after these items. Federal and state income taxes are shown as deductions with interest paid for the reasons that extraneous income and interest paid are included in computing the tax and, in theory at least, income taxes constitute a sharing of profits.

The ratio of operating profits to net sales represents the operating margin realized on sales. It is complementary to the turnover ratio of total capital employed both borrowed and invested. The turnover of total capital employed fixes the relationship with operating profit margin so that a fair return is realized on capital employed. The higher the characteristic turnover of capital in an industry, the lower the characteristic profit margin. This ratio is not influenced by the manner of financing, except in-so-far as a certain ratio between borrowed capital and stockholders' equity is normal for a particular industry. The greater the average stability of earnings the greater will normally be the proportion of borrowed capital and the lower will be the average ratio of operating profits. From operating profits, the cost of borrowed capital is paid, leaving the remainder as a return on stockholders' investment.

RATIO OF SURPLUS NET PROFITS TO SALES

Surplus net profits represent the final net profits remaining as return on investment. Its ratio to sales shows the percentage realized as net profits and is the final result of all other operating ratios. This ratio is complementary to the turnover of net worth in relation to sales. Normal turnover of net worth in relation to sales determines the ratio of surplus net profits to sales necessary to yield a fair return on investment which is expressed by the ratio of net profits to net worth. This relationship is fundamental to the permanence of an enterprise.

Variations in the ratio of surplus net profits to net sales over a period of years result from the same causes as influence the ratio of operating profits which are business conditions, competitive conditions and management. It is also influenced by the additional factor of cost of borrowed capital. A strong financial structure can borrow money at less cost than one less favorably financed and thus increase its net profits.

It is evident that the analyses cited are just as applicable by the management in directing the course of its own business as they are by outside investigation in showing what the course of the business has been in the past.

With the movement of business cycles, an enterprise will experience normal times, periods of high earnings and periods of depression. During years of normal and high earnings, the management must conserve its resources, and keep a tight rein of control over operations and expenditures if it is to fortify itself to weather the trials of less favorable conditions. Careless financing and dissipation of earnings through dividends in successful years multiply the problems and usually result in financial difficulties in periods of depression. The managements of all sizable enterprises are constantly seeking improvements and greater efficiency which will enable marketing a better product or at less margin as compared with competitors. They cannot afford to overlook a single means of control. The enterprise that stands still and is content with itself soon finds itself in competitive disadvantages which result in eventual elimination. Business is characteristic of the individual. Survival, comparative position and success are the rewards of a definite constructive financial and operating policy, which reveals itself through intelligent analysis and the use of analytical findings to better the status of the business and the industry.

THE STORY TOLD BY
THE FINANCIAL AND
OPERATING STATEMENTS

J. H. Bliss

The Story Told by the Financial and Operating Statements

"Capital Requirements and Control"—Article Two

By J. H. BLISS
Controller, Libby, McNeill & Libby

	Index Number
Financial control	658.14
Factory accounting	657.524

FINANCIAL statements and operating statistics are the final product of accounting procedure and should tell the story of the business—the condition of its finances, and the efficiencies and results obtained in its operations. But as such statements are commonly presented this story has to be read out of them by careful study and analysis.

Following is a typical financial report, such as will be found in daily papers, financial magazines, manuals, etc. It is the report of a well-known and representative company, with its statements slightly changed in order to conceal its identity. Statements such as this are found in the reports presented to business men daily. It is true that not all published reports contain as much detail on operations as is shown here, as many companies do not publish figures for sales and gross earnings, but in other respects it may be considered typical.

A balance sheet is not the "cold statement" of assets and liabilities that it seems to so many readers of such statements. It is in fact a picture of the financial structure of an organization, stated in dollars and cents and indicating what the business owns, what it owes, and what it is worth net.

Consider the foregoing statement. Think of the items and the amounts given, not in sums of money, but look beyond the figures and see the quantities of goods, the investments represented, and the various sources from which capital is secured.

The balance sheet is presented as if in answer to the two leading questions which may be asked about the financial affairs of a business:

1. From what sources are funds drawn into the business?
2. How is such capital used or invested within the business?

The balance sheet shows on the one hand from which of the following sources the business draws its capital:

1. Stockholders' investments, which are represented by the original investment and the earnings left in the business.
2. Investments of bondholders; that is, capital secured on long-term loans.
3. Capital drawn from short-term borrowings, such as current notes and bills payable, accounts payable, sundry liabilities, etc.

The balance sheet indicates, on the other hand, how the organization has invested this capital in the business. That is, how much of it is tied up in:

1. Current assets, which are used in the daily transaction of business, such as cash, accounts receivable, inventories, etc.
2. Investments in plants and equipment, etc., which represent property in which business is carried on, and which are to be distinguished from the current assets turning over in the daily transactions of a business.
3. Investments in and advances to other companies—securities owned, such as stocks and bonds, etc.
4. Other types of fixed investments, such as deferred charges, intangible assets, good-will, trade-marks, etc.

It will be of very material assistance if the conception of the balance sheet as a picture of the financial structure of the business is kept in mind. One cannot read out of such a statement more than he sees in it. A complete analysis of any balance sheet requires the visualization of the various kinds of assets and investments which make up the financial presentation.

The asset side of the balance sheet should convey to the reader a picture of the financial conditions under which the business operates. He should visualize the stocks of goods moving through operations and on the way to market, and consider the turnover. He should measure the funds tied up in accounts receivable and

> "Of the financial statements read by the multitude of business men interested in and using such statistics, probably not one in a thousand tells the full story it should to its readers. Few business men are able fully to analyze and understand such a statement." With this in mind Mr. Bliss takes a typical financial statement and analyzes it so as to show the wide range of essential information that can be drawn from its figures.

judge them on the basis of terms of sales, character of business, and general business conditions. He should consider the proportion of capital tied up in fixed property investments, and inquire as to the volume of business handled therein, noting whether advantages or disadvantages arise therefrom.

THE BALANCE SHEET

	Last Year	This Year
Assets		
Cash	$2,628,000	$2,361,000
Accounts and Notes Receivable	1,665,000	2,314,000
Inventories	3,392,000	6,245,000
Investments and Securities	1,436,000	1,636,000
Fixed Property Investments	13,010,000	15,040,000
Deferred Charges	1,341,000	1,928,000
	$23,472,000	$29,524,000
Liabilities		
Notes Payable		$6,430,000
Accounts Payable	$323,000	1,210,000
Deposits and Advances Received	2,567,000	1,283,000
Bonds Outstanding	3,000,000	3,000,000
Reserves	1,101,000	1,005,000
Capital Stock	10,000,000	10,000,000
Surplus	6,481,000	6,596,000
	$23,472,000	$29,524,000

THE CONDENSED INCOME STATEMENT

	Last Year	This Year
Sales	$10,157,000	$10,380,000
Cost of Manufacture and Sales	7,889,000	7,550,000
Gross Margin	$2,268,000	$2,830,000
Expenses, Admin. and General	306,000	682,000
Operating Profits	$1,962,000	$2,148,000
Add Other Income	112,000	84,000
Deduct Interest Charges	180,000	180,000
Surplus Net Profits	$1,894,000	$2,052,000
Dividends Paid	1,987,000	1,937,000
Balance to Surplus Account	$93,000*	$115,000

* Decrease in Surplus.

On the other hand, the manner in which capital is drawn into a business should be noted from the liability and capital side of the balance sheet. The methods of financing a business may yield substantial advantages or disadvantages to its stockholders. The proportion of capital secured from each of the various sources should be noted in view of the character of the investments. The working capital position, though not emphasized in the form of statement usually presented, is of prime importance. The character of long-term borrowings and the proportion to stockholders' investments may yield substantial advantages to stockholders and should be carefully noted.

Balance Sheet Variations

It is of the greatest importance that a concern should adopt and conform to a conservative basis for preparing its balance sheet statements. This is not alone an accounting affair but is as well a matter of sound business practice. The integrity and value of all statistics and financial statements is dependent upon the continuous observance of sound principles and conservative policies in preparing them.

Varying bases for valuing accounts in the balance sheet and inconsistent or irregular practices in handling accounts from year to year, not only affect the balance sheet but impair the value of the income statement and supporting statistics. The policy of providing reserves out of good years, and omitting charges in bad years—a pitch-fork method of accounting—cannot possibly affect the facts in the case, but only impairs the value of the statistics and makes them unreliable for use in studying the trends of the fundamental relationships in the business. To provide double depreciation in a good year and omit the charge in a poor year, does not stay the actual depreciation of the assets. It only impairs the cost statistics, income statements, and all other statistics involved. To value inventories on a bed-rock basis after a good year, and on an optimistic basis after a poor one, does not change the facts as to the real profits or losses, but only changes the statistics and books.

The Income Statement

The income statement reports the operations and transactions of a business for a definite period of time, states the volume of business done, the cost of sales, expenses, and results. This statement, together with the balance sheet, at the close of the period, makes up the financial report of the business. Each contains significant information in itself, but the two must be taken together, in order to read the full story of the business.

The income statement, particularly, tells the story of operations and transactions. That is its function. It should be presented in a form that will clearly answer the questions which a business man asks about his transactions. In fact, each section of the income statement states a concrete fact as if in answer to a pertinent question.

The following are the salient points to be emphasized by the various sections of the income statement of the average business:

1. The volume of sales for the period.
2. The cost of goods sold.
3. The margin of gross profits realized.
4. The selling, general, and overhead expenses.
5. The net profits realized from operations.
6. The amount of non-operating income and expenses, including interest charges.
7. The surplus net profits available for distribution in dividends, or transfer to Surplus account.

These divisions of the income statements are basic. The relationships between these various items, as expressed in ratio of profits, costs, and expenses on sales, are fundamental. While the amounts stated for sales, expenses, results, or other items are interesting, it is the relationships between these various items, the ratios, and turnovers, which are important.

The Return Earned on Net Worth

The measure of the earning power of a business to be noted first is the relation of the surplus net profits to the net worth. This measure states the earning power of the business from the stockholders' point of view.

It is the amount of profits realized on their investment in the business.

For example, referring to the report presented—found by adding capital stock and surplus and deducting from the sum the amount of surplus earned during the year—the return earned on net worth at the beginning of the year by this company would be figured in the following way:

	Last Year	This Year
Net Worth at Beginning of Year	$16,574,000	$16,481,000
Surplus Net Profits for Year	1,894,000	2,052,000
Percentage on Net Worth	11.45	12.45

This indicates an improvement in return earned over the preceding year of 1/2 of 1 per cent. This measure should be distinguished from the ratio of profits earned to capital stock. It is proper to figure the return earned on net worth because the surplus represents a part of the stockholders' investment in the business. It represents accumulated earnings which stockholders have seen fit to leave in the business and on which the business should be expected to earn a return.

Margin of Surplus Net Profits Earned on Sales

The relationship between surplus net profits and the sales for a period is the measure of earning power based on turnover, or volume of business done, as distinguished from the preceding ratio, which indicates the return earned on the total investment. These two are the measures to be applied to surplus net profits of the business. The one, is the ratio of profits earned on investment; the other, the ratio of profits earned on volume of business done. Both are basic measures of results.

The ratio of surplus net profits to sales is commonly expressed as a percentage of profits on net sales. It indicates the number of cents out of each dollar of sales realized net—after the deduction of all costs, expenses, interest, and extraordinary charges, and is the amount which is available either for distribution to stockholders as dividends, or to be transferred to Surplus account, thereby increasing their equity in the business.

The following illustrates the method of figuring the ratio of surplus net profits on sales for the financial statement preceding:

	Last Year	This Year		
Sales	$10,157,000	$10,380,000	Increase	$223,000
			or	2.2%
Surplus Net Profits for Year	1,894,000	2,052,000	Increase	$158,000
			or	8.3%
Percentage on Sales	18.6	19.7	Better by	1.1%

Here is to be noted a slight increase in the volume of business—2.2 per cent—and a substantial increase in the amount of surplus net profits, with the result that the margin on sales increased from 18.6 to 19.7 per cent. That is, out of each dollar of sales the company realized 1.1 cents more final net profits than in the preceding year.

The Book Value of Capital Stock

The book value of capital stock is the measure commonly used for expressing the value per share of the stock outstanding, as shown by the accounts and report of the company. This value is to be distinguished from the market value and the par value of shares.

The book value means the value per share of the stockholders' equity in the business—the net assets of the company—based upon the valuation at which assets and liabilities are carried on its books.

The following table illustrates the manner of figuring the book value of capital stock from the foregoing report:

	Last Year	This Year
Net Worth at Close	$16,481,000	$16,596,000
Shares of Stock Outstanding	100,000	100,000
Book Value per Share	$164.81	$165.96

Operating Profits Earned on Total Capital

The real measure of the earning power of a business is the operating profits earned on the total capital used in such operations shown by the asset footing of the balance sheet. This measure is to be distinguished from the return earned on net worth discussed previously. This ratio is a sounder measure of the earning power of the operations, because it is based on the net results realized from operations and the full amount of capital used therefor. It is clearly a measure of operating earning power.

The following table indicates the method of figuring this ratio for the financial report presented:

	Last Year	This Year		
Total Capital Used	$23,472,000	$29,524,000	Increase	$6,052,000
			or	26 per cent
Operating Profits	1,962,000	2,148,000	Increase	$186,000
			or	9.5 per cent
Percentage on Capital Used	8.35	7.26	Poorer by	1.1 per cent

Note here the unusually large increase in the amount of capital used—$6,000,000 or 26 per cent more investment at the close of the year than at the beginning. While the operating profits show 9.5 per cent increase over the preceding year, the increase in the investment used is so much larger that the average return upon the investment is reduced from 8.35 to 7.26 per cent.

The matter of economy and efficiency in the use of capital is just as important in the final success of the business as the efficiency or effectiveness of operations, merchandising, or other affairs.

Operating Profits Earned on Sales

The ratio of operating profits to sales is the measure of operating profits on turnover or volume. It is related or complimentary to the ratio of operating profits earned on the total investment employed. Therefore the two measures should be applied to operating profits both for the business as a whole and for any separate department, plant, or unit of the organization. The following table indicates the method of figuring the ratio of operating profits on sales from the foregoing report:

	Last Year	This Year		
Sales	$10,157,000	$10,380,000	Increase	$223,000
			or	2.2 per cent
Operating Profits	1,962,000	2,148,000	Increase	$186,000
			or	9.5 per cent
Percentage on Sales	19.3	20.6	Better by	1.3 per cent

With a small increase in sales volume, 2.2 per cent, and a larger increase in the amount of operating profits, 9.5 per cent, the ratio is improved from 19.3 to 20.6

per cent on sales. But note that even with this wider margin of profits on sales the return on the total capital used was smaller, as indicated in the preceding calculation because of the unusually large increase in the amount of capital used. The significance of this point should not be overlooked.

As pointed out in the preceding section this report shows a smaller return of operating profits on total capital used in the latter year, in spite of a wider margin of operating profits on sales. The reason for this is the poorer turnover of total capital used. The turnover of total capital used expresses the relationship existing between the volume of business done and the total investment employed. Obviously, the larger the volume of business done on a given investment the more favorable will be the return produced by any given margin of profit on sales. Sales of $1,000 made at a margin of 10 per cent will yield a return of 10 per cent on an investment used of $1,000, whereas if the sales were of $2,000 at the same 10 per cent margin they would yield a 20 per cent return on the same investment of $1,000.

The same point may be illustrated from the report under consideration. The following table shows the method of figuring the turnover of total capital used:

	Last Year	This Year		
Total Capital Used	$23,472,000	$29,524,000	Increase or	$6,052,000 26 per cent
Sales for Year	10,157,000	10,380,000	Increase or	$223,000 2.2 per cent
Turnover on Total Capital Used Stated in Dollars of Sales per Dollar of Capital Used	0.433	0.352	Poorer by	8.1 cents

Relation of Expenses to Sales

The ratio of expenses to sales is effectively stated in the percentages of such expenses to net sales. This indicates the cents out of each dollar of sales which are absorbed in expenses. In some industries volume is commonly stated in physical units—tons, hundredweights, barrels, cases, etc.—and this ratio is customarily figured in per unit costs. The percentage ratio is the sounder measure and expresses more accurately the basic relationships.

The following table shows the ratio of expenses to sales, figured from the foregoing report:

	Last Year	This Year		
Sales	$10,157,000	$10,380,000	Increase or	$223,000 2.2 per cent
Expenses	306,000	682,000	Increase or	$376,000 120.0 per cent
Percentage on Sales	3.0	6.6	Increased	3.6 per cent

Here is an increase in sales of only 2.2 per cent, while expenses more than doubled, with the result that the ratio increased from 3.0 to 6.6 per cent. That is, in the earlier year 3 cents of each dollar of sales was absorbed in the selling and overhead expenses, while in the latter year they increased to 6.6 cents out of each dollar of sales.

The gross margin earned on sales is the difference between the net sales and the cost of goods sold. In manufacturing industries this gross margin is commonly figured as the spread between sales and factory cost of goods sold. As factory costs include material, labor, and factory expenses this measure combines both merchandising and operating elements. In merchandising businesses this gross margin is figured as a spread between the net sales and the purchase cost of the goods sold, with the result that it is expressive of only the merchandising transactions.

The following table shows this ratio applied to the foregoing report:

	Last Year	This Year		
Sales	$10,157,000	$10,380,000	Increase or	$223,000 2.2 per cent
Gross Margin	2,268,000	2,830,000	Increase or	$562,000 24.8 per cent
Percentage on Sales	22.3	27.2	Increased	4.9 per cent

Note here the increase in sales of only 2 per cent, whereas the amount of gross margin increased 24.8 per cent, with the result that the ratio increased from 22.3 to 27.2 per cent on sales. This large increase in gross margin is more than half absorbed by the heavy increase in expenses, with the result that the operating profits show a much smaller proportionate increase than does the gross margin.

	Per Cent on Sales
The Gross Margin Increased from	22.3 to 27.2 or 4.9
The Selling and General Expenses Increased from	3.0 to 6.6 or 3.6
Operating Profits Increased from	19.3 to 20.6 or 1.3

Turnover of Inventories

The turnover of inventories is one of the basic measures of merchandising transactions. It expresses the rapidity with which stocks of goods are bought and sold—the turnover of that investment. Obviously the more business that can be done on the capital tied up in inventories, the more favorable will be the return on the investment produced by any given margin of profit.

The following table illustrates this turnover applied to the preceding report:

	Last Year	This Year		
Cost of Goods Sold	$7,889,000	$7,550,000	Less by or	$339,000 4.3 per cent
Inventories	3,392,000	6,245,000	Increased or	$2,853,000 84 per cent
Turnover—Times	2.33	1.21	Poorer by	1.12 times

As already noted, the turnover of total capital used was substantially slower in the latter year. One of the principal reasons for this condition is the poorer turnover of inventories noted in the above table. The cost of goods sold in the latter year was 4.3 per cent less than in the earlier year, but the amount of inventories carried increased 84 per cent with the result that the turnover in the latter year was only one-half as rapid as in the earlier year. With this condition the latter year would require twice as wide a margin of profit on sales to produce a given return on this inventory investment as would be required by the earlier year.

Turnover of Accounts Receivable

The margin of profit on a sale is fixed at the time the transaction is made. It does not become any larger, regardless of how long the account remains uncollected. On the other hand, the older the account becomes, the heavier the carrying expenses are, the larger the possibility of losses, and the poorer the return on the investment. The turnover of accounts receivable indicates the economy and efficiency observed in handling capital tied up in accounts receivable. It may be effectively stated in the number of average days' sales outstanding in accounts receivable at the close of a period.

The following table shows this turnover applied to the report preceding:

	Last Year	This Year		
Sales	$10,157,000	$10,380,000	Increase or	$223,000 2.2 per cent
Accounts Receivable	1,665,000	2,314,000	Increase or	$649,000 39 per cent
Days of Average Sales Outstanding	44	67	Poorer by	23 days' sales

Note here that with an increase in volume of sales of only 2.2 per cent the amount of accounts receivable increases 39 per cent. At the beginning of the year there were outstanding in accounts receivable 44 days of average business, whereas at the end of the year the outstanding accounts amounted to 67 days of average business. This also is a factor in the slower turnover of total capital used, noted in an earlier paragraph.

Turnover on Fixed Property Investment

The turnover on fixed property investment is an effective method of stating the relation between the volume of business done and the amount of capital tied up in fixed plant and equipment investments. As fixed overhead expense burden—depreciation, insurance, taxes, etc.—bear quite a constant relationship to the amount of such property investments, it is obvious that the more business that can be done in a given period the more favorable will be the unit expenses and costs arising out of these fixed charges.

The following table shows this turnover applied to the report preceding:

	Last Year	This Year		
Sales	$10,157,000	$10,380,000	Increase or	$223,000 2.2 per cent
Fixed Property Investment	13,610,000	15,040,000	Increase or	$1,430,000 10.5 per cent
Turnover—Stated in Dollars of Sales per Dollar of Property Investment	0.75	0.69	Poorer by	6 cents

Here is an increase in volume of but 2.2 per cent, and an increase in plant investment of 10.5 per cent. The direct results are poorer turnover and heavier unit fixed expense burdens. The turnover here dropped from 75 cents to 69 cents of sales per dollar of plant investment. This also is a factor in the poorer turnover of total capital shown in an earlier calculation.

Working Capital and Ratio

The working capital position, that is, the relation between the current assets and the current liabilities of the business, is the point generally noted first in reading a balance sheet. It is probably more commonly understood than any other ratio or relationship to be read out of a balance sheet.

The net working capital is the difference between the total current, or liquid, assets in the business, i. e., its cash, accounts, and notes receivable, and the inventory, and its total current or quick liabilities, i. e., its notes and accounts payable, and its deposits and advances received. The ratio expressing the relationship between these is sometimes stated in percentage, or may be stated in dollars of current assets per dollar of current liabilities.

The following table shows the working capital position and ratio to be noted from the report preceding:

	Last Year	This Year		
Total Current Assets	$7,085,000	$10,920,000	Increase	$3,835,000
Total Current Liabilities	2,890,000	8,923,000	Increase	6,033,000
Net Working Capital	$4,195,000	$1,997,000	Decrease	$2,198,000
Ratio	2.45	1.23	Poorer by one-half	

This is a serious change: an increase in current assets of $3,835,000, an increase in current liabilities of $6,000,000, leaving a decrease in the net working capital of the business of $2,198,000, which is reflected in a ratio only one-half as good as at the beginning of the year. The several elements causing these changes are noted in later paragraphs.

Proportion of Earnings Left in the Business

Any going business finds it necessary, from time to time, to make additions and betterments to its properties and finds need for added working capital as volume increases. Except as these requirements may be financed by additional permanent investments in the business or long-time borrowing, the new capital necessarily must come from one of two sources—either current borrowings or profits left in the business.

In the case of the average concern, permanent financing does not occur every year, and its added capital requirements have to be cared for from earnings or current borrowings. But there is a limit to the amount which may be borrowed currently, and certainly it would not be conservative to invest funds borrowed on short terms in plants or other permanent investments. Hence, earnings left in the business are absolutely necessary to care for expansion and improvements.

The following table shows the disposition of surplus net profits indicated in the preceding report:

	Last Year	This Year
Surplus Net Profits	$1,894,000	$2,052,000
Dividends Paid	1,987,000	1,937,000
Balance to Surplus	93,000	115,000
Proportion of Earnings Left in Business	None	5.6 per cent

Note here that while two years of operations have produced quite satisfactory surplus net profits there has been left in the business out of almost $4,000,000 of profits, only $22,000 or less than 1 per cent.

From the published reports of 236 representative companies it appears that 43 per cent of the annual earnings of the war and post-war years were left in the business.[1]

The report discussed in the present article appears in substantially the form published in the daily newspapers. It is, as already stated, a typical published report. It is also about the form in which balance sheets and income statements are usually presented in auditors' reports and to business executives by industrial accountants.

How much more effective these reports would be if presented in analytical form! How much more the average business man would read out of them, and how

---

[1] "Financial and Operating Ratios in Management," J. H. Bliss, p. 183.

much more value they would prove to him if they carried the analysis of ratios and relationships which may be so readily supplied!

The following balance sheet and income statement shows the same report carrying analytical data:

THE BALANCE SHEET IN ANALYZED FORM

	Last Year		This Year		Increase or Decrease
	Dollars	Per Cent	Dollars	Per Cent	
Assets					
Cash	2,028,000	8.6	2,361,000	8.0	$333,000
Accounts and Notes Receivable	1,665,000	7.1	2,314,000	7.8	649,000
Inventories	3,392,000	14.5	6,245,000	21.1	2,853,000
Total Current Assets	7,085,000	30.2	10,920,000	36.9	$3,835,000
Investments and Securities	1,436,000	6.1	1,636,000	5.5	200,000
Fixed Property Investments	13,610,000	58.0	15,040,000	51.1	1,430,000
Deferred Charges	1,341,000	5.7	1,928,000	6.5	587,000
	23,472,000	100.0	29,524,000	100.0	$6,052,000
Liabilities					
Notes Payable			6,430,000	21.9	$6,430,000
Accounts Payable	323,000	1.4	1,210,000	4.1	887,000
Deposits and Advances Received	2,567,000	11.0	1,283,000	4.4	*1,284,000*
Total Current Liabilities	2,890,000	12.4	8,923,000	30.4	$6,033,000
Bonds Outstanding	3,000,000	12.7	3,000,000	10.0	
Reserves	1,101,000	4.7	1,005,000	3.4	*96,000*
Capital Stock	10,000,000	42.6	10,000,000	34.0	
Surplus	6,481,000	27.6	6,596,000	22.2	115,000
	23,472,000	100.0	29,524,000	100.0	$6,052,000

THE INCOME STATEMENT IN ANALYZED FORM

	Last Year		This Year		Increase or Decrease
	Dollars	Per Cent	Dollars	Per Cent	
Sales	10,157,000	100.0	10,380,000	100.0	$223,000
Cost of Manufacture and Sales	7,889,000	77.7	7,550,000	72.8	*339,000*
Gross Margin	2,268,000	22.3	2,830,000	27.2	562,000
Expense, Admin. and General	306,000	3.0	682,000	6.6	376,000
Operating Profits	1,962,000	19.3	2,148,000	20.6	186,000
Add Other Income	112,000	1.1	84,000	0.8	*28,000*
Deduct Interest Charges	180,000	1.8	180,000	1.7	
Surplus Net Profits	1,894,000	18.6	2,052,000	19.7	158,000
Dividends Paid	1,987,000	....	1,937,000	....	*50,000*
Balance to Surplus Account	*93,000*	....	115,000	....	208,000

Summarizing Changes in Financial Position

While the foregoing analyzed report emphasizes a great many of the points to be noted from such statements there are large advantages in summarizing these reports, by stating the changes in financial position, and the important changes in ratios. It is a very simple matter to summarize all of these changes and ratios in such a manner that they may be readily understood by anyone who should use the information in the conduct of a business.

The changes in financial position shown in the foregoing report may be stated in different ways. The following will emphasize some of the outstanding changes which should be noted by those who might make use of this particular statement. In preparing such a summary the points should be particularly emphasized which should come to the attention of those interested in the report.

The following will illustrate:

The current liabilities increased $6,033,000
The current assets increased 3,835,000

Resulting in a decrease in the net working capital of the business of $2,198,000
This amount of money has been withdrawn in some manner from the net working capital of the business.

In addition to the foregoing there were surplus net profits earned, which first became added net working capital. These amounted to $2,052,000

Together, these make the total of funds withdrawn from working capital, and disposed of outside of the business, or permanently tied up in fixed investments amounting to $4,250,000

These funds were disposed of as follows:

Dividends paid $1,937,000
Invested in Plant 1,430,000
Invested in additional securities 200,000
Tied up in increased deferred charges 587,000
Reserves liquidated 96,000

Total as above $4,250,000

The important changes in ratios and relationships occurring during the year were as follows:

1. A small increase in volume of sales, 2.2 per cent.
2. A wider gross margin earned on sales, 22.3 to 27.2 per cent—Increase 4.9 per cent.
3. Heavier selling and general overhead expense, 3.0 to 6.6 per cent—Increase 3.6 per cent.
4. Leaving a small increase of margin of operating profits, 19.3 to 20.6 per cent—Increase 1.3 per cent.
5. And a smaller increase in surplus net profits on sales, 18.6 to 19.7 per cent—Increase 1.1 per cent.
6. Which yielded a better return on stockholders' investment, 11.4 to 12.4 per cent—Increase 1.0 per cent.
7. But operating profits on the total capital used were poorer, 8.35 to 7.26 per cent—Decrease 1.1 per cent.
8. Because of poorer turnover of total capital used, 43.3 to 35.2 cents—Decrease 8.1 cents.
9. Which was the result of poorer turnovers of inventories, 2.33 to 1.21—Slower 1.1 times.
10. And poorer turnovers of accounts receivable, 44 da. to 67 da.—or 23 da. sales.
11. And poorer turnover on plant investment, 75 to 69 cents—Poorer by 6 cents.

In addition to the foregoing the following conditions should be noted:

1. The volume of sales increased 2.2 per cent.
2. The inventories carried increased 84.0 per cent.
3. The accounts receivable outstanding increased 39.0 per cent.
4. The plant investment increased 10.5 per cent.
5. Ninety-five per cent of the profits were paid out in dividends.
6. The net working capital was cut in two.
7. The ratio dropped from 2.45 to 1.23.

Can it be doubted that such analyses of financial statements placed before the average business man would be welcome and also prove useful in the better management of business affairs?

THE OPERATING
AND
FINANCIAL RATIOS CHARACTERISTIC
OF INDUSTRIES

J. H. Bliss

The Operating and Financial Ratios Characteristic of Industries

"Capital Requirements and Control"—Article Three

By J. H. BLISS
Controller of Libby, McNeill and Libby

Index Number
658.14 Financial control
338 Production

IN a general way most business activities other than those of an agricultural nature may be classified into groups along the following distinct lines:

Manufacturing
Merchandising
Transportation
Public utilities
Mining
Banking and financial
Fiduciaries
Institutional
Professional
Miscellaneous
Insurance
Agencies and commission

Considering these general divisions of industries it is at once apparent that great differences exist in the types of operations performed and services rendered, and that these various industries must of necessity have different individual characteristics. Beyond that, within manufacturing industries, there are many and various lines of business — the Census Report, for instance, specifies more than 350 distinct manufacturing industries. Among these are widely varying operations and processes and material differences in the character of the services performed.

The viewpoint maintained in this article is that of the manufacturing and merchandising industries. However, many of the principles stated herein, for manufacturing and merchandising businesses, are quite applicable to others of the industries mentioned.

There is less uniformity and standardization of accounting practices in manufacturing and merchandising industries than there is in railroads, public utilities, banks, and insurance companies, and there is less possibility of uniformity. This emphasizes the necessity for recognizing sound accounting and business principles in handling accounts and preparing reports for manufacturing and merchandising concerns. The field for accounting services in these industries is broader than in others and the possibilities for development far greater.

The gross margin, the relation between manufacturing or buying costs and selling prices, is highly characteristic of the different lines of business. The margin which an industry has to work on tends to such a figure as will cover the costs and expenses of the average organization engaged in that line of business and leave a fair return on the capital used.

The relation of expenses to the volume of business done, indicated by expense ratios, is likewise highly characteristic of various industries. These relationships depend entirely upon the character of the operations performed, and the services rendered. The ratios of labor costs, factory expenses, selling, advertising, and administrative expenses are distinctive characteristics of different lines of business. Some industries have expensive factory operations, others have relatively inexpensive processes; some businesses carry heavy selling and general expenses, while others characteristically have much lighter general overhead expenses. In some industries the value added by manufacture is as low as from 8 to 12 per cent of the sales value of products; in others it is as high as from 70 to 80 per cent of the sales value of the products. When a man buys a cash register, upwards of 80 per cent of his payment is disbursed for manufacturing and distributing services. Of the sum he would pay for a pound of butter or meat, only 10 or 15 per cent is required for manufacturing and distributing services.

Characteristic Ratios of Operating Results

With highly characteristic gross margins and expense ratios it follows that there are characteristic ratios of operating results in different lines of business. The margin of operating results on sales is of necessity wider in those lines which have slow turnover and may be much narrower in other lines with rapid turnover and still permit both types of industries to earn about the same average return on invest-

> Referring to the distinctive differences between the various industries, Mr. Bliss says: "Differences in operations performed and services rendered are necessarily reflected in differences in organization, differences in financial structure, and differences in accounting procedure. These result directly in differing relationships, ratios, and turnovers. The ratios, turnovers, and relationships common in any line should be considered as the personal characteristics of that particular industry." The present article gives these "personal characteristics" for some of the more important lines of industry and shows their importance as indicia of trend and condition.

ment used. In some businesses the annual sales average is as low as ¼ of the total investment used, and a very wide margin of operating profits is necessary to yield a fair return on such investment. In other lines of business the annual sales may be as much as three or four times the amount of capital used, with the result that a narrow margin of operating profits on sales would yield a satisfactory return on the investment used. Different industries, therefore, have characteristic margins of operating profits, which are the direct result of the types of operations and business conducted. Of course, these margins are affected by changing general business and competitive conditions from time to time.

Each industry has characteristic turnovers of capital tied up in accounts receivable, in inventories, and in plant investment. The terms of sale vary widely in different lines; some businesses sell on a cash basis, others extend credit for long periods. These terms affect the amount of capital necessary to carry customers' accounts and are, therefore, reflected in the turnover of accounts receivable. In some lines of business it is necessary to carry stocks of goods for longer periods than in others; in some industries the manufacturing processes require very short periods of time, while in others many months may be consumed. The function of certain businesses is to render a storage service, carrying seasonable products from times of production and plenty, to times of scarcity and demand. At the other extreme would be merchandising industries with very rapid turnover of stocks of goods.

Some industries require only relatively small investments in production facilities, while others because of the type of the operations performed have to maintain extensive and costly plants. No one would think of trying to manufacture steel products in a packing house, nor make butter in a foundry. Obviously the type of operations or services rendered by a business requires a certain type of plant and equipment. These are highly characteristic of different industries. It follows naturally that the investment tied up in plants in different industries bears a characteristic relationship to the volume of business done, as well as to the total amount of capital used in the conduct of a business. These relationships are expressed in the turnover on plant investment and in the relation of plant investment to total capital employed.

Characteristics Within Industries

Within an industry different concerns will naturally have somewhat different characteristics, though as a whole their operations and transactions must measure up to competitive standards if an average return is to be earned on the investment used. Of course variations will occur in individual ratios and turnovers. Some companies will enjoy a better gross margin than others, perhaps because of better merchandising, quality of product, method of distribution, or services rendered. Some may have more economical and efficient operations than others. Some may enjoy better turnovers of accounts and inventories than others. Some may have more advantageous turnovers on plant investment than others. A going concern will seldom be found best in every relationship, and certainly not the poorest in every one, but, far and wide, the various companies in an industry necessarily have to average out to competitive standards as a whole, if they are to realize the competitive average return on the investment used.

Statistics on Volume Costs and Margins

Some idea of the characteristics of various industries and the wide variation between different lines of business may be obtained from the following table of statistics prepared from the 1914 and 1919 abstracts of the Census of Manufactures. The columns of this table show for the more important industries of the country:

1. The value of the products.
2. The cost of materials used, including fuel.
3. The value added by manufacture, which would include all expenses and profits.
4. The total wage and salary payment.
5. The percentage of value added by manufacture to the value of the product, which indicates clearly the wide variation in gross margins on sales.
6. The ratio of wages to the sales value of the product, stated in percentages, which indicates the widely varying amounts of labor necessary in different lines of business.
7. The percentage of all other expenses and profits to sales value of products.

After deducting the wages from the value added by manufacture the balance remaining has to cover all other expenses and profits. It is impossible to separate these elements from the statistics available, but the figures will serve to indicate the wide variation between industries in the amount of expenses and the possible margins of profit. They also indicate the widely varying relationships between prices, costs, and wages in the various industries.

Table 1 gives statistics on about 40 of the more important industries of the country. The Census Report classifies the industries covered in 342 separate kinds of manufacturing establishments in 1914, and 356 in 1919. The total number of establishments covered by the Census survey was 275,791 in 1914 and 290,105 in 1919.

The expansion of industrial activities over the war period with surprisingly stable relationships is worthy of note. Table 2 shows the figures for all manufacturing industries covered by the census statistics.

The increase in the value of products from 24 billions to 62 billions is tremendous. Of course, the larger part of this increase is due to higher prices. Wholesale price indices indicate that the 1919 price levels were about double those of 1914, but after allowing for this there is apparent a substantial increase in the physical volume of production of these manufacturing industries.

Similar relative increases in costs of material, gross margins, wages and salaries are particularly noteworthy. One of the striking features of the period of expansion was that prices, wages, and profits increased in about the same proportion. The figures for each sepa-

TABLE 1. STATEMENT COMPARING, FOR DIFFERENT INDUSTRIES, THE VALUE OF PRODUCTS, COST OF MATERIALS, WAGES, ETC.

Data from Abstract of Census of Manufacturers, 1914 and 1919—(000's Omitted)

INDUSTRIES	(1) VALUE OF PRODUCTS 1914	(2) COST OF MATERIALS 1914	(3) VALUE ADDED BY MFG. 1914	(4) ALL WAGES AND SALARIES 1914	(1) VALUE OF PRODUCTS 1919	(2) COST OF MATERIALS 1919	(3) VALUE ADDED BY MFG. 1919	(4) ALL WAGES AND SALARIES 1919	(5) PER CENT VALUE ADDED BY MFG. 1914	(5) 1919	(6) WAGES PER CENT TO VALUE OF PRODUCTS 1914	(6) 1919	(7) PER CENT OTHER EXP. AND PROFITS TO VALUE OF PRODUCTS 1914	(7) 1919
All Industries in Total	$24,246,435M	$14,368,089M	$9,878,346M	$5,306,240M	$62,418,079M	$37,376,390M	$25,041,699M	$13,423,972M	40.7	40.1	22.1	21.5	18.6	18.6
Agricultural implements	$164,086M	$73,508M	$90,578M	$47,604M	$304,961M	$144,573M	$160,389M	$88,630M	55.2	52.6	29.0	29.1	26.2	23.5
Auto bodies and parts	129,601	63,610	65,990	54,552	692,171	362,027	330,144	213,924	50.9	47.7	42.1	30.9	8.8	16.8
Automobiles	503,230	292,597	210,632	84,901	2,387,903	1,578,652	809,251	379,382	41.9	33.9	16.9	15.9	25.0	18.0
Boots and shoes	501,760	310,356	191,403	128,623	1,155,041	715,269	439,772	269,860	38.1	38.1	25.6	23.3	12.5	14.8
Bread and other bakery prod.	491,893	274,257	217,635	96,634	1,151,896	713,239	438,657	207,057	44.2	38.1	19.6	18.0	24.6	20.1
Brick and tile, terra-cotta.	135,921	42,723	93,198	65,454	208,423	67,488	140,935	94,037	68.6	67.7	43.2	45.2	20.4	22.5
Butter	243,379	212,546	30,532	14,000	583,163	514,346	68,817	28,575	12.7	11.8	5.8	4.9	6.9	6.9
Canning fruits and vegetables	149,175	103,293	45,882	22,412	402,243	265,629	136,614	54,944	30.7	34.0	15.0	14.0	54.3	10.9
Cars & shop cons. & rep. stm. R. R.	514,041	243,528	270,213	258,549	1,279,235	515,803	763,422	754,563	52.6	59.7	50.3	59.0	2.3	.7
Cash registers	30,520	3,992	26,528	11,592	83,539	10,890	72,649	26,520	87.0	87.0	38.0	31.7	49.0	55.3
Cement	101,756	51,986	49,770	24,258	175,265	79,510	95,755	42,631	48.9	54.6	23.8	24.4	25.1	30.2
Chemicals	153,054	89,451	63,603	31,087	439,610	216,301	222,338	97,189	48.4	50.6	19.7	22.1	23.7	28.5
Clothing, men's	458,211	230,032	223,179	113,800	1,162,986	605,752	557,234	250,165	49.8	47.9	24.8	22.3	25.0	25.6
Clothing, women's	473,588	252,345	221,543	118,697	1,208,543	680,407	528,136	254,332	46.7	43.7	25.0	21.0	21.7	22.7
Cotton goods	676,569	431,603	244,967	161,680	2,125,272	1,277,786	847,486	392,839	36.2	39.8	23.9	18.4	12.3	21.4
Electrical machinery	335,170	154,728	180,442	109,098	997,968	425,098	572,870	330,369	54.9	57.4	32.6	33.7	22.3	23.7
Fertilizers	153,196	107,955	45,242	17,774	281,144	185,041	96,103	30,935	29.5	34.2	11.6	13.1	21.9	21.1
Flour and grist-mill products	877,680	752,270	125,410	40,963	2,052,434	1,799,181	253,253	82,901	14.3	12.4	4.7		9.6	8.4
Foundry and machine-shop prod.	866,545	358,122	508,423	328,550	2,289,251	948,069	1,341,182	804,346	58.6	58.6	37.9	35.1	20.7	23.5
Glass	123,085	46,017	77,069	55,205	261,884	90,780	171,104	100,691	62.6	65.3	44.9	38.7	17.7	26.6
Knit goods and hosiery	238,913	146,687	112,225	71,039	713,140	427,096	286,044	157,526	43.3	40.1	27.5	22.1	15.8	18.0
Iron and steel, blast furnace	317,654	264,580	53,074	29,805	794,467	621,286	173,181	57,204	16.7	21.8	9.1	11.0	7.6	10.8
Iron & steel, st. wks. & roll. mills	918,663	590,828	327,839	225,638	2,828,902	1,630,576	1,148,326	737,518	35.7	40.6	24.6	26.1	11.1	14.5
Leather	367,202	284,245	82,956	39,291	928,592	646,522	282,070	109,384	22.6	30.4	10.7	11.7	11.9	18.7
Lumber and timber products	715,310	281,952	433,358	272,634	1,387,471	470,060	915,511	545,347	60.6	66.1	38.0	29.3	22.6	26.8
Lumber, planing mills products	307,672	184,227	123,445	79,945	500,438	299,266	201,172	120,313	40.1	40.2	26.0	24.1	13.1	16.1
Oil, cottonseed and cake	212,127	180,976	31,151	14,400	581,245	495,192	86,053	30,551	14.7	14.8	6.8	5.3	7.9	9.5
Paper and wood pulp.	332,147	213,181	118,966	66,164	788,059	467,483	320,576	165,643	35.8	40.7	19.9	21.0	15.9	19.7
Petroleum, refining	300,381	229,296	71,977	27,290	1,632,533	1,247,908	354,625	116,360	18.0	23.6	6.9	7.1	11.1	16.5
Printing & publ., book and job	307,331	96,453	210,878	113,419	597,603	211,067	386,596	207,197	68.7	64.6	36.9	34.7	31.8	29.9
Printing & publ., newspaper	495,906	129,082	366,824	179,581	924,153	300,385	623,768	288,199	74.0	67.5	36.3	31.2	37.7	36.3
Rubber goods, other	223,611	126,112	97,499	43,966	987,088	525,686	461,402	231,756	43.5	46.7	19.7	23.5	23.8	23.2
Shipbuilding, iron and steel	66,217	29,270	36,947	28,752	1,456,490	643,753	812,737	595,634	55.8	55.8	43.4	40.9	12.4	14.9
Shipbuilding, wooden	22,465	9,327	13,138	8,938	165,872	66,770	99,102	66,027	58.4	59.7	39.9	40.4	18.5	10.3
Silk goods	254,011	144,442	109,569	57,615	688,470	388,469	300,001	134,597	43.1	43.6	22.7	19.6	20.4	24.0
Slaughtering and meat packing	1,651,965	1,441,663	210,303	89,697	4,246,291	3,782,930	463,361	269,175	12.7	10.9	5.4	6.3	7.3	4.6
Smelting and refining—copper	444,022	379,157	64,865	19,707	651,102	584,410	66,692	31,620	14.6	10.3	4.5	4.9	10.1	5.4
Smelting and refining—lead	171,579	154,515	17,064	7,930	196,705	179,374	17,421	11,241	10.2	8.0	4.4	5.7	5.8	3.2
Soap	127,942	88,867	39,076	14,780	318,540	235,519	78,321	33,400	30.5	24.7	11.6	11.2	18.9	13.5
Sugar refining	280,399	204,085	25,313	10,326	730,087	662,144	66,602	28,163	8.7	9.4	3.6	3.8	5.1	5.6
Tobacco, cigars and cigarettes	314,484	130,630	184,335	82,676	773,602	353,297	420,305	133,706	58.6	54.4	26.2	17.3	32.4	37.1
Woolen and worsted goods	379,484	246,497	132,888	86,500	1,065,434	665,595	399,839	199,090	35.0	37.6	22.7	18.7	12.3	18.9

TABLE 2. SHOWS FIGURES FOR ALL MANUFACTURING INDUSTRIES COVERED BY THE CENSUS STATISTICS

	Amount (000 Omitted)		Per Cent on Value of Products	
	1914	1919	1914	1919
Value of products......	$24,246,436	$62,418,079	100.0	100.0
Cost of materials......	14,368,089	37,376,380	59.3	59.9
Spread or margin......	9,878,346	35,042,689	40.7	40.1
Wages and salaries....	5,366,249	13,423,972	22.1	21.5
Balance to cover all other costs and profits......	$4,512,095	$11,617,727	18.6	18.6

rate industry show remarkably similar percentages for the value added by manufacture in 1914 and 1919. This indicated advances in costs, wages, and gross margin, quite in proportion to the increase in value of their products.

The gross spread or margin for all industries was 40.7 per cent on the value of products in 1914, and declined only to 40.1 per cent in 1919. Wages and salaries advanced a little more slowly than prices, which was to be expected, but in almost the same proportion. In 1914 they were 22.1 per cent. Deducting this from the gross margin above leaves a balance to cover all other costs and profits which was the same for both years—18.6 per cent on the value of products. With the tremendous increase in the amount of business done as measured in dollars, naturally this balance for expenses and profits increased more than 2½ times in money or from 4.5 billions to 11.6 billions.

As general and overhead expenses do not ordinarily increase or decrease in proportion with sales it follows that the margin of net profits realized on sales in the later years was somewhat larger, and considering the tremendous increase in the amount of business done, the profits remaining for investors were very much larger sums of money. The larger profits of later war years are to be noted from the reports of practically all industrial concerns.

Changed Relationships in Readjustment Period

It is now realized that the relationships, ratios, and turnovers of pre-war and war times changed greatly during the readjustment period. That is always the effect of periods of readjustment. The losses sustained by businesses in such periods are caused by these relationships between costs and values of products being out of normal proportions. Wholesale prices fell abruptly on an average of about 40 per cent. Industrial activities slackened and the volume of production became less. Wages and salaries reacted more slowly. Overhead expenses increased out of all normal proportions to the volume of business done. Competitive conditions were very unsatisfactory. All of these things are evidences of the period of reaction. They are incident to such periods and are reflected in changed relationships, ratios, turnovers, etc.

The last two years, 1922 and 1923, have seen a substantial recovery of business and more normal conditions and relationships established. These are, in many cases, substantially different from the standards of earlier years and it is apparent that the normal relationships of individual industries in the future may be quite different from those considered normal in pre-war times.

It is unfortunate that statistics such as the foregoing are not available annually to enable a more complete analysis of the trends of business affairs. They would be of vital interest and of material assistance in the conduct of business. The trends from 1919 to 1921 and the changed ratios and relationships in various industries may be noted from published statistical compilations.[1]

Characteristic Margins and Expense Ratios

Table 2 shows some striking contrasts in the characteristic margins and expense ratios prevailing in different industries. Some have wide margins to work on between buying and selling prices, while other industries customarily operate on a narrow margin. In industries a very large portion of the value of products is absorbed by wages; in others only a relatively small portion. Some of the outstanding contracts may be noted from Table 3:

TABLE 3. SHOWS SOME OUTSTANDING CONTRASTS IN CHARACTERISTIC MARGINS AND EXPENSE RATIOS IN DIFFERENT INDUSTRIES

	Per Cent Margin Added by Mfg.		Wages Per Cent to Value of Products		Per Cent Other Expenses and Profits to Value of Product	
	1914	1919	1914	1919	1914	1919
Businesses With Wide Margin Added by Manufacturing:						
Agricultural implements....	55.2	52.6	29.0	29.1	26.2	23.5
Brick and tile............	68.6	67.7	48.2	45.2	20.4	22.5
Cash registers...........	87.0	87.0	38.0	31.7	49.0	55.3
Chemicals...............	48.4	50.6	19.7	22.1	23.7	28.7
Electrical machinery.....	54.9	57.4	32.6	33.7	22.3	23.7
Foundry and machine shops	58.6	58.6	37.9	35.1	20.7	23.5
Glass...................	62.6	65.3	44.9	38.7	17.7	26.6
Lumber and timber products	60.6	66.1	38.0	29.3	22.6	26.8
Businesses With Narrow Margin Added by Manufacturing:						
Butter..................	12.7	11.8	5.8	4.9	6.9	6.9
Iron, steel and blast furnace.	16.7	21.8	9.1	11.0	7.6	10.8
Flour and grist mills.......	14.2	12.4	4.7	4.0	9.6	8.4
Oil, cottonseed and cake....	14.7	14.8	6.8	5.3	7.9	9.5
Slaughtering and meat pkg...	12.7	10.9	5.4	6.3	7.3	4.6
Copper smelting and refg....	14.6	10.3	4.5	4.9	10.1	5.4
Petroleum refining.........	18.0	23.6	6.9	7.1	11.1	16.5
Sugar refining............	8.7	9.4	3.6	3.8	5.1	5.6

It is interesting to note from the foregoing statistics that from the point of view of the cost of materials and the value of products the slaughtering and meat-packing industry is the largest in the country. The gross value of their products for 1919 was $4,246,000,000, which was 6.8 per cent of the value of all products turned out by all manufacturing industries in the country. It is also noteworthy that this industry operates on a very narrow margin between cost of materials and sales value of product; in 1914 it was 12.7 per cent and in 1919, 10.9 per cent of the value of the products.

In passing it should be mentioned that the more

---

[1] See "Financial and Operating Ratios in Management," by J. H. Bliss.

important industries operating on narrow margins between costs of materials and value of product are those which produce major products and by-products or produce joint products. This should be borne in mind as affecting the methods of cost finding and the type of income statements which should be most appropriate.

Reference is made particularly to the following industries:

- Flour and grist-mills
- Cotton-oil crushing and refining
- Slaughtering and meat-packing
- Copper smelting and refining
- Sugar refining
- Petroleum refining

In each of these industries the operations produce joint products of major products and by-products. The processes are a breaking up of materials into several parts as distinguished from the usual type of manufacturing operation, which is the building up of materials into a finished product. The operations in these industries are in this manner the reverse of ordinary manufacturing operations.

The Census reports also show statistics on the amount of capital employed in various industries. These figures considered in connection with the value of the products of the various industries give some indication of the wide differences in the turnover of various industries.

Table 4 shows for the same industries reported in the previous table, the value of the products and the amount of capital used. The turnover is also stated as the dollars of sales per year, per dollar of total capital employed. The capital here stated includes both current and fixed investments, that is, all funds employed in the business.

There may be some weaknesses in the compilation of these statistics as pointed out in the Census report. Obviously it would be quite impossible to get accurate figures for all of the various industries. However, as the purpose is only to illustrate the wide differences in turnover between them this element of error may be overlooked with propriety. The comparisons are very interesting and sufficiently sound to illustrate the point.

The average turnover and the trend as indicated by the totals for all industries are noteworthy. They are:

	1914	1919
	Billions	Billions
Value of products	$24.2	$62.4
Capital used	22.8	44.7
Dollars of product per dollar of capital	1.06	1.40

That is to say, all manufacturing industries in 1914 had on the average, sales of $1.06 for each dollar of total capital used in the business, and in 1919 had sales of $1.40 for each dollar of capital used. This improvement in turnover is significant and was to be expected with the conditions prevailing during those years. It does not necessarily indicate a better turnover of inventories or accounts receivable or other current investments, but probably is largely the result of the greater money volume of business done on the fixed investment in plants and facilities.

Considering the conditions prevailing between 1914 and 1919 industries naturally averaged somewhat better turnovers of accounts receivable and inventories, but as both of

TABLE 4. STATEMENT COMPARING, FOR DIFFERENT INDUSTRIES, THE VALUE OF PRODUCTS AND CAPITAL USED

Data from Abstract of Census of Manufacturers, 1914 and 1919 (000 omitted)

INDUSTRIES	VALUE OF PRODUCTS	CAPITAL USED	VALUE OF PRODUCTS	CAPITAL USED	DOLLARS OF PRODUCT PER DOLLAR OF CAPITAL USED	
	1914	1914	1919	1919	1914	1919
All Industries	$24,246,435M	$22,790,979M	$62,418,079M	$44,688,093M	$1.06	$1.40
Agricultural implements	$164,086M	$338,532M	$304,961M	$366,962M	$0.48	$0.83
Auto bodies and parts	129,601	94,854	692,171	470,498	1.36	1.47
Automobiles	503,230	312,876	2,387,903	1,310,451	1.61	1.82
Boots and shoes	501,760	254,591	1,155,041	612,625	1.97	1.88
Bread and other bakery products	491,893	271,262	1,151,896	529,266	1.82	2.18
Brick and tile, terra-cotta, etc.	135,921	279,860	208,423	355,848	0.49	0.59
Butter	243,379	59,625	583,163	162,302	4.08	3.59
Canning fruits and vegetables	149,175	98,738	402,243	223,692	1.51	1.80
Cars and shop cons. & rep. steam railroad	514,041	354,092	1,279,235	694,286	1.45	1.84
Cash registers	30,520	41,075	83,539	82,798	0.74	1.01
Cement	101,756	243,485	175,265	271,269	0.42	0.65
Chemicals	158,054	224,346	438,659	484,488	0.71	0.91
Clothing, men's	458,211	224,050	1,162,986	554,147	2.05	2.10
Clothing, women's	473,888	153,549	1,208,543	390,527	3.09	3.09
Cotton goods	676,569	867,044	2,125,272	1,853,100	0.78	1.15
Electrical machinery	335,170	355,725	997,968	857,855	0.94	1.16
Fertilizers	153,196	217,065	281,144	311,633	0.71	0.90
Flour and grist-mill products	877,680	380,257	2,052,434	801,625	2.31	2.56
Foundry and machine-shop products	866,545	1,246,043	2,289,251	2,104,981	0.70	1.09
Glass	123,085	153,926	261,884	215,680	0.80	1.21
Knit-goods and hosiery	258,913	215,826	713,140	516,458	1.20	1.38
Iron and steel, blast furnace	317,654	462,282	794,467	802,417	0.69	0.99
Iron and steel wk's. & roll'g mills	918,665	1,258,371	2,828,902	2,656,518	0.73	1.06
Leather	367,202	332,180	928,592	671,342	1.11	1.38
Lumber and timber products	715,310	916,574	1,387,471	1,357,992	0.78	1.02
Lumber, planing mills products	307,672	266,805	500,438	361,848	1.15	1.38
Oil, cottonseed and cake	212,127	118,073	581,245	203,457	1.80	2.86
Paper and wood pulp	332,147	534,625	788,069	905,795	0.62	0.87
Petroleum, refining	396,361	325,646	1,632,533	1,170,278	1.22	1.40
Printing and publ., book and job	367,331	247,282	597,663	446,555	1.24	1.34
Printing and publ., newspaper	495,906	384,745	924,153	614,045	1.29	1.50
Rubber goods, other	223,611	199,183	987,088	782,638	1.12	1.26
Shipbuilding, iron and steel	66,217	132,712	1,456,490	1,208,640	0.50	1.15
Shipbuilding, wooden	22,465	23,348	165,872	120,808	0.96	1.37
Silk goods	254,011	210,072	688,470	532,732	1.21	1.29
Slaughtering and meat-packing	1,651,965	534,274	4,246,291	1,176,484	3.09	3.61
Smelting and refining Copper	444,022	171,420	651,102	308,680	2.59	2.11
Lead	171,579	143,249	196,795	115,677	1.20	1.70
Soap	127,942	92,872	316,740	212,417	1.38	1.49
Sugar—refining	289,399	140,500	730,987	193,541	2.06	3.78
Tobacco, cigars and cigarettes	314,884	171,982	773,662	416,395	1.83	1.86
Woolen and worsted goods	379,484	389,653	1,065,434	831,695	0.97	1.28

these classes of investments would increase or decrease as price levels advanced or declined the improvement in turnover would not be as large as in the case of the turnover on fixed property investment. This is so because higher price levels for products would show a higher turnover figure on property investments, without a proportionate increase in physical volume.

The increase in the amount of capital used is very significant, 1919 being practically double that of 1914. Note also that it is distributed over practically every important industry represented. It is unfortunate that we are unable to determine from available statistics how much of this increase is in current investments which were expected to contract as prices fell and how much of it is due to increased investments in plant and equipment which are permanent and will add fixed expense burdens to business.

More recent reports of representative companies indicate very substantial reductions in the amount of capital tied up in inventories and accounts receivable. As these investments are current they naturally respond to price movements and in addition may be controlled —must be controlled—if proper turnovers are to be maintained. Fixed property investments, on the other hand, are permanent and cannot be reduced as volume of business drops off. These conditions have brought about very substantial changes in the ratios, relationships, and turnovers apparent in financial reports, and indicate the establishment of new normal standards and relationships.

Contrast in Turnovers

The foregoing table (Table 4) presents some very interesting contrasts in turnovers, characteristic of different types of industries.

Table 5 shows some of the outstanding comparisons:

The significance of these differences of turnover must not be overlooked. If a business turns over its total investment once a year and desires to make a return of 6 per cent on its total investment, obviously it must average an operating profit of 6 per cent on its sales. If, on the other hand, the sales of a business for a year are three times the total amount of capital used, a margin of operating profits of only 2 per cent would yield the same 6 per cent return on the total investment used.

From the foregoing comparison it will be observed that the turnover in sugar refining and meat-packing industries is three to four times as fast as the turnover in iron and steel and fertilizer industries. This indicates that the two latter industries would require a margin of profit on sales three to four times larger than the sugar and meat-packing industries in order to yield the same return on the investment used.

To emphasize further the point that financial and operating ratios are characteristic of various industries, the following Table 6 is given

TABLE 5. SHOWS SOME OUTSTANDING COMPARISONS IN TURNOVERS CHARACTERISTIC OF DIFFERENT TYPES OF BUSINESS

	Dollars of Sales per Year Per Dollar of Total Capital Employed.	
Business with Rapid Turnovers:	1914	1919
Sugar Refining	$2.06	$3.78
Slaughtering and Meat-Packing	3.09	3.61
Butter	4.08	3.59
Women's Clothing	3.09	3.09
Bread and Bakery	1.82	2.18
Businesses with Slow Turnovers:		
Cement	$0.42	$0.65
Brick and Tile	0.49	0.59
Paper and Wood Pulp	0.62	0.87
Fertilizer	0.71	0.90
Iron and Steel and Blast Furn.	0.69	0.99

showing, for several of the more important industries, the ratios of profits earned on sales and net worth, and the turnovers, for the year 1920.[2]

A review of the statistics of other years shows the same characteristic differences in these financial ratios between various industries. Of course the trends from year to year may differ somewhat, due to difference in business conditions, but this only emphasizes further the point that these measures and ratios are characteristic of various industries and are to be noted in the analysis of financial statements.

It should be borne in mind whenever considering these ratios and relationships that the effect of any unfavorable ratio may be to reduce the surplus net profits earned on stockholders' investments. That is, a poorer turnover of inventories than average, or a subnormal turnover on fixed property investment is a handicap to a business in meeting competition and earning the average competitive return on its investment, and the effect of such subnormal turnover may be translated directly into terms of forfeited profits.

[2] From "Financial and Operating Ratios in Management," by J. H. Bliss.

TABLE 6. STATEMENT SHOWING RATIOS OF PROFITS AND TURNOVERS REALIZED BY REPRESENTATIVE COMPANIES IN VARIOUS INDUSTRIES FOR THE YEAR 1920

Industries	Surplus Net Profits		Days Sales in Accts. Receivable	Dollar Sales per Dollar Inventory	Dollar Sales per Dollar Plant Investment	Dollar Sales per Dollar All Assets
	Per Cent on Sales	Per Cent on Net Worth				
Auto and truck manufacturers	7.2	11.7	$0.30	$3.10	$2.78	$0.99
Auto accessory manufacturers	5.3	4.0	0.21	4.01	4.09	1.26
Bituminous coal	18.9	7.5	0.93	13.52	0.35	0.27
Copper mining—smelting and refining	3.9	3.1	0.12	2.68	1.21	0.64
Cotton goods manufacturers	6.6	11.5	0.70	3.39	3.26	1.04
Electrical machinery manufacturers	6.2	10.7	0.95	2.51	4.85	0.85
General merchandising	5.0	7.2	0.11	5.84	13.45	2.10
Iron and steel manufacturers	5.8	7.5	0.50	4.71	0.76	0.52
Leather manufacturers	20.0	15.5	0.36	1.35	1.54	0.60
Machinery manufacturers	11.0	7.5	0.85	1.82	2.36	0.58
Mail order merchandising	1.3	2.6	0.61	2.48	7.88	1.15
Petroleum oil companies	19.5	15.3	0.42	2.23	0.92	0.50
Railway equipment manufacturers	8.2	9.2	1.07	4.06	1.77	0.73
Retail chain stores	4.7	7.9	0.2	6.87	9.03	1.40
Rubber and tire manufacturers	3.1	3.9	0.50	2.55	2.34	0.83
Slaughtering and meat-packing	0.3	1.5	0.48	7.59	10.03	2.26
Sugar production and refinery	17.0	27.3	0.18	5.55	2.12	1.07

Statistics taken from "Financial and Operating Ratios in Management."

EARLY CRITICS OF
FINANCIAL RATIOS

LIMITATIONS OF FINANCIAL AND OPERATING RATIOS

W. A. Paton

LIMITATIONS OF FINANCIAL AND OPERATING RATIOS

By W. A. Paton, *University of Michigan*

In recent years much attention has been given to the form of financial statements and reports and to the development of devices to facilitate the interpretation of statements and, through such interpretation, their effective use by business managements. It has come to be widely appreciated that the work of the accountant is not confined to recording business transactions in systematic technical form and does not end with closing entries and balancing operations, however perfectly carried out, but comes to real fruition in periodic statements and reports distinctly purposive in character and so constructed and presented as to yield the utmost in significant information to the management. Thus we find accountants on all sides laying great stress upon the arrangement of items in statements and reports (along with a general recognition of the need for discarding archaic arrangements and the development of elasticity of reports, with a view to the use of the most effective set-up from the standpoint of the particular audience for which a report is intended), and we find them experimenting with such supplementary devices as written explanations, comparative statements, graphs and charts, analyses such as statements of funds and their application, and ratios or percentages drawn primarily from income sheet and balance sheet figures. It is this last mentioned development which it is desired to discuss here.

No doubt the use of financial and operating ratios as a means of rendering accounting statements more intelligible and significant is a matter which deserves the consideration it has been receiving of late. This device certainly represents an important angle from which the problem of statement presentation and analysis can be approached, and is worthy of every encouragement. And it is a thoroughly natural and appropriate device for the accountant to emphasize. Relationships are meat and drink to him; his entire task is characterized by analysis, systematic arrangement, comparison. In fact any system of accounts may be conceived as a set-up of business data in terms of their underlying relations. It is clear, accordingly, that in presenting final statements and reports the accountant must not be satisfied that his work is complete with the compilation of masses of debits and credits. Through classification and arrangement, charts and graphs, comparisons, oral and written explanations, or other means he must see to it that all important relationships are disclosed; and this means of course that all significant financial and operating percentages must be calculated and exhibited.

On the other hand, the enthusiasm for ratios as such seems at times to go beyond reasonable bounds. What we have here after all is a very commonplace feature of accounting work, long recognized and used, and no great good can come from exaggerating its significance and scope. The calculation and exhibition of numerous income-sheet or balance-sheet ratios (or percentages drawn from both statements) is no royal road to the effective utilization of statements. At best this is merely a supplementary device, really useful and worth while only as its limitations are clearly perceived. Above all it should be emphasized that such calculations can never be a substitute for judgment. The interpretation and effective use of statements is at bottom a matter of clear-cut analysis and discriminating judgment, or common sense, if you will, and it is to be doubted if any arrangements of data, charts, percentages, or other special devices—mechanical, statistical, or otherwise—can do more than facilitate judgment. Perhaps no one has ever thought otherwise. But when one hears his friends in the bookkeeping machine game talk about their contrivances in a tone which suggests that they feel they have reduced the whole process of accounting to a purely mechanical basis—that all that is now necessary is to lead transactions to the machine by the halter as it were and press a button or pull a handle—and when one hears of statistical or other business services which are able to reduce the whole question of business standing, degree of success or efficiency, to a single arithmetical percentage on the scale of 100, it would seem appropriate to throw on a dash of cold water. It is bad enough to mark students in this way; it seems out of the question that complex business enterprises can reasonably so be graded. Let us hope that accountants will always have something to do that will require the exercise of intelligence and that the day will never come when business management will be reduced to periodic inspections of a statistical barometer.

What are the limitations of financial and operating ratios, some of which, at least, seem to be in danger of being overlooked in some quarters? In the first place we need occasionally to remind ourselves of the fact that such percentages are of different orders of importance. Obviously there is almost no end to the arithmetic ratios which may be calculated and compiled from a balance sheet and income sheet composed of a considerable number of items. But as a matter of fact, and fortunately for our peace of mind, there are only a relatively few ratios which have any considerable significance, or even any significance whatsoever, to the business management. To illustrate, there is one ratio, or group of ratios, involving both balance sheet and income sheet data, which seems to me to rank far above any and all other percentages in general significance. That is rate of return (per year or other period) realized by the enterprise to the capital investment. The principal variations or subdivisions are: (1) the rate of total operating net to total assets employed; (2) rate of return to stockholders as a body to actual book investment; (3) rate of common stock earnings to common stock equity; (4) dividend rate or rates; (5) rate of addition of surplus to investment. It seems fair to say that there is no other ratio, involving both statements, of comparable importance. This is the outstanding business fact, *earning power*. In the case of the balance sheet alone, likewise, there is only one outstanding ratio, the percentage of proprietary or residual investment to total assets. (This may be put in several other ways, all meaning substantially the same thing: (1) liabilities to assets; (2) liabilities to proprietorship; (3) assets to proprietorship; (4) assets to liabilities; (5) proprietorship to liabilities.) Assuming that it were possible to call for just one balance sheet relationship, any one, most of us without hesitation would ask for this ratio, in the form most acceptable. That is, the outstanding financial fact about a business—aside from earning power—is the relative proprietary investment. This fact alone, without other data, gives a fairly good general picture of financial structure. And in the case of the income sheet alone, also, there happens to be a single outstanding relation, the operating ratio, the percentage of expenses to total revenues. (This likewise may be put in several alternative forms, net revenue to total sales, sales to net revenue, sales to expenses, etc.) Clearly, there is no second percentage to be derived from the income sheet of equal importance.

Thus we have three ratios of the first order of significance: (1) net return to investment; (2) proprietary equity to total assets; (3)

expenses to gross earnings or volume of business. And in any discussion of ratios this fact should be indicated. Instead, we usually find, in textbooks and elsewhere, from twenty to fifty or more percentages listed, indiscriminately, for the unwary reader. Further, the reader is often given the impression that the accountant has fulfilled his obligation when he has calculated these score or more of ratios and has handed the resulting mass of figures to the executive. As a matter of fact any executive would be justified in firing, out of hand, any accountant or statistician who turned in a report of the character indicated. For to make head or tail of the mass of ratios reported would probably be a much greater task than to interpret the original statements themselves without any special statistical aids whatsoever.

Some doubtless would hold that the ratio of current assets to current liabilities is a fourth relationship of the first order, and no doubt this percentage is of considerable importance in certain connections. However, it would seem to be more reasonable to list this as a dominant example of what may be called second-class ratios. Other examples of this class, from the balance sheet, are: (1) current assets to fixed assets; (2) fixed assets to long-term liabilities; (3) current assets to unappropriated surplus; (4) surplus to total proprietorship, and so on. Examples from the income sheet are: (1) cost of sales (in terms of assigned costs) to total sales; (2) unassigned or general and administrative expenses to total sales. Examples of ratios of this type from both statements are: (1) accounts receivable to sales; (2) inventories to sales or cost of sales.

There is still a third class of ratios which have some slight significance. Examples from the balance sheet are: (1) cash to accounts payable; (2) sinking fund to bonds payable; (3) land to buildings and equipment; (4) common stock equity to total stock equity. The relation of any particular expense or narrow class of expense to sales or gross revenue, gives an example of this order drawn from the income sheet alone. The ratio of the particular item of expense or revenue to the particular asset or liability, a relation involving both fundamental statements, also falls in this group. An example is periodic depreciation expense to gross book value of depreciable assets; i. e., the rate of depreciation. It is contended, however, that as a rule little constructive information can be added to that directly evidenced by the statements through the calculation and study of such ratios.

Beyond this group come the great mass of ratios which are quite meaningless and useless as a basis for rendering accounting information more effective. What is the significance, for example, of advertising expense to reserve for additions and betterments, of prepaid insurance to bonds outstanding, and so on? Clearly, the great majority of ratios to be derived from the statements are not worth calculating.

In the second place, in dealing with financial and operating ratios, we should always remember the more or less obvious proposition that a ratio per se has little real significance. Sound managerial conclusions and policies cannot be formulated simply by scrutinizing ratios, however carefully calculated and exhibited. At best a ratio is nothing more than a clue, a starting point for study and investigation. Further, without standards most ratios do not even point the way to promising lines of investigation. In other words, the effective use of this tool in any case awaits the construction of sound standards of measurement. And adequate standards are not always easy to establish and once set up are subject to continuous revision. Past performance in the particular business, of course, gives some basis for the creation of norms, and should be studied. Of perhaps greater importance are the records of other concerns in the same line of business and more or less similarly situated, although these data are hard to obtain and harder to interpret and use wisely. Then into the construction of any proper standard must go a trace of the ideal, the hoped-for, as standards should be goals, not merely norms. Still further, ranges and trends are as important here as elsewhere and wherever possible standards should be so constructed as to include these elements.

Given adequate standards, particular ratios can be referred thereto, and if a considerable discrepancy or deviation is disclosed, a line of investigation is opened—nothing more. It is still too early to draw any conclusions, but if possible the explanation should be discovered and then, if necessary, some action may be taken by the management. Needless to say, in the great majority of cases the investigation will show that no change of policy is warranted, even if possible.

In the use of ratios, then, the procedure should be somewhat as follows:

1. Select the relatively few relationships of this character which can have any real significance, which hold forth any promise.

2. Calculate these percentages, preferably for several past periods as well as for the current period.

3. Exhibit the results in the most effective manner, perhaps in graphic form, in each case in comparison with the standard.

4. Point out all considerable variations from standard.

5. Investigate the causes of these variations wherever possible.

6. In the one or two cases, if any, where action is possible or feasible, revamp managerial policy appropriately.

To illustrate somewhat definitely the need for care and discrimination in this phase of statement analysis and interpretation, let me refer to a few ratios with respect to which we have widely accepted impressions as to standards, and endeavor to show that even these general and commonplace standards must not be taken too seriously in the particular case if errors are to be avoided, that seldom if ever can the bare statistical evidence be converted into managerial policy.

Take, for a first example, that fundamental ratio, proprietary or residual equity to total assets. In the minds of many people, I am sure, the ideal ratio here is one, and the more nearly this ideal is approached the more favorable and to be commended the situation. And certainly many of us have the instinctive feeling, in studying a balance sheet, that where this ratio falls below sixty to seventy per cent all is not well. Still, when the matter is called to our attention, we all admit that this ratio varies widely between fields of enterprise, that it may fall as low as forty per cent in the case of the railroad, to ten per cent in banking, and to zero or thereabout in governmental enterprise. Further, from the standpoint of the best interest of the proprietor, so-called, which most accountants emphasize, is not the general impression on this point quite questionable to say the least? I recall the case of a dean of a school of pharmacy who was anxious to have his students take a course in accounting, and who, in telling the accounting instructor what he wanted emphasized, stated that after talking with the boys in the fraternity house he felt that what they needed most of all was to be told how to keep out of debt, and that surely a course in accounting would do this. The instructor might have said in reply that if his course had any bearing on this question at all it was because it indicated to some extent how one might get in debt, and stay there. Undoubtedly the system of the division of capital furnishing between stockholders or proprietors and bondholders and other creditors, which has been carried so far by the modern corporation, is one of the most important sources of profit in business. By taking a residual position, and thus assuming the major element of risk, the proprietor is enabled to secure considerable capital at a contractual rate from others, and, by trading on this capital, increase the rate of return on his own equity considerably. I am not advocating doing business on a shoestring. The proprietor should invest at least a sufficient amount to carry the business during the period of depression and stringency. But I am raising a question as to whether a high proprietary ratio or an increase in this ratio from year to year (except as such increase indicates profit accumulation temporarily) demonstrates the utmost of managerial capacity from the financial standpoint. If it is feasible to use borrowed capital to the extent of fifty per cent of the total assets, for example, is it not good management to maintain this proportion continuously?

For a second example, take another very important ratio, current assets to current liabilities. Here, likewise, the general impression is that the higher this ratio the better. Perhaps this impression is reasonable as far as the position of the particular short-term creditor is concerned, especially the creditor who is interested only in the payment of the now outstanding debt and who never expects to make another advance and hence is not interested in long-run managerial policy. But is this view justified from the standpoint of the best interest of the proprietor or owner? Does a high current ratio, in itself, constitute a favorable index of present condition and managerial policy? Is an increase in this ratio from one period to the next an infallible sign of increasing success and improved management? Certainly there are enough exceptions to prove the rule if not to disprove it. Cash as such in the drawer or in the non-interest bearing bank account is in a sense a dead or useless asset. The ideal of cash administration would be a scheme of expenditures and collections which swept the cash account bare every day, which permitted the accumulation of no reserve whatever. Obviously this is not feasible under present conditions. To maintain its credit position and be able to meet all proper obligations in a situation in which the supply of cash and the legitimate demands therefor cannot be affected to coincide from day to day (and particularly in view of the fact that it is not feasible to make dividend and interest disbursements daily) any commercial enterprise must maintain some cash reserve, just as must any banking institution. But it should be the goal of the management to maintain as small an average cash balance as the essential requirements of the business permit; and as a matter of fact the development of devices and arrangements in connection with payroll, branch office cash, etc., which will reduce working capital requirements now occupies the serious attention of many progressive managements. In many instances a declining current ratio over a period of years would actually evidence improving financial administration.

A special case where a high and increasing current ratio need not be considered as implying especially favorable or improved conditions is found in the languishing business which, although making satisfactory current sales, is gradually contracting the scope of its operations, is making few if any replacements, is holding repairs at a minimum, and hence is in a strong cash position. Likewise a concern going through the process of actual liquidation may for a time show an increasing current ratio. The wasting enterprise, such as a mine, also, is likely to show an increasing current ratio over a period of years, even if its operating statements disclose a series of deficits.

Further, an increase in the current ratio may result from undue piling up of accounts receivable or merchandise or from too strenuous efforts to reduce floating debt.

For another example, turnover may be mentioned. It is not my intention to discuss the importance of this ratio to business managements, but we all know that great stress is laid upon it in many quarters and that there is a widespread feeling that increasing turnover is a desirable thing, without any qualification. As a matter of fact an increase in turnover, at least temporarily, may be due to distinctly unsatisfactory conditions. High pressure salesmanship and the use of exceptional terms and prices may result in a busines growth which is unwholesome and cannot be maintained. Turnover may likewise be increased through reduction of stocks below a proper level, with resulting unfavorable reactions.

A final illustration, less important, may be cited. Uncollectible accounts are the bane of many credit managers, and much effort is naturally directed toward the reduction of the percentage of bad debts loss. Nevertheless even in this case a reduction in the loss ratio may indicate an unfavorable rather than a favorable condition. For example, a metropolitan bank engaged a credit manager who proved to be so effective in this direction that credit losses almost disappeared under his administration. But the board of directors fired him at the end of the year, very appropriately, because his method of procedure had resulted in the loss to competitors of much promising business. The manager had cut losses to the bone, it was true, but the really significant result was the loss of a large volume of legitimate business.

To repeat, the foregoing is not intended as an argument against the calculation and use of ratios; the importance of this approach to the analysis and use of business statistics is conceded. But it is well occasionally to call attention to the fact that individual ratios mean little in themselves, must always be referred to adequate standards, and at best are nothing more than a clue to conditions which may require investigation. Further, generalizations as to the significance of even the more important ratios are dangerous; each case needs independent study.

BIBLIOGRAPHY AND ACKNOWLEDGMENTS FOR CHAPTERS IV AND V

Myron M. Strain

Chapters IV and V

There are a large number of texts dealing with ratio analysis, but few of them seem to bring a critical, scientific or even realistic spirit to their treatment of the subject. Gilman and Bliss have written excellent books which include expositions of it, and they will be referred to hereinafter in other connections. The leading exponent of pure ratio analysis is Alexander Wall, whose newest book is *Ratio Analysis of Financial Statements*, written in collaboration with R. W. Duning and published by Harper Brothers. This tome, if subjected to the same frank critical analysis as is accorded to ventures in other fields of intellectual endeavor, would be promptly labeled as the *reductio ad absurdum* of the theory that ratio analysis is a final criterion of financial adequacy; as the ultimate revelation of the incurably optimistic theorist futilely and absurdly chasing the ratio absolute. He brings every known device of higher mathematics and statistical science to his aid. It becomes mysterious, abstruse, imposing, and appalling—but it lacks the underpinning of sound or even credible premises, and the merit of essential relevance of method to subject.

EARLY EMPIRICAL STUDIES
OF FINANCIAL RATIOS

CHANGES IN THE FINANCIAL STRUCTURE OF UNSUCCESSFUL INDUSTRIAL CORPORATIONS

Raymond F. Smith and Arthur H. Winakor

BUREAU OF BUSINESS RESEARCH

Chas. M. Thompson, Ph.D., LL.D., *Director*

A. C. Littleton, Ph.D., C.P.A., *Assistant Director*

Bulletin No. 51

CHANGES IN THE FINANCIAL STRUCTURE OF UNSUCCESSFUL INDUSTRIAL CORPORATIONS

BY

RAYMOND F. SMITH
Bureau of Business Research

AND

ARTHUR H. WINAKOR
Bureau of Business Research

Published by the University of Illinois, Urbana
1935

PREFACE

This Bulletin is the second study published by the Bureau of Business Research dealing with the financial structure of failed enterprises. In Bulletin No. 31, *A Test Analysis of Unsuccessful Industrial Companies* (1930), the financial statements of 29 companies were analyzed, in an attempt to discover characteristics which would assist in anticipating probable failure.[1] The present study, based upon the financial statements of 183 companies, was undertaken in order to obtain more conclusive indications of the symptoms of approaching failure, in more detailed classifications of data than were possible in the earlier study, and to show the value of observing changes in the financial structure of companies in an effort to detect those which were likely subsequently to fail.

For the main part of the investigation the ratio analysis method is employed, but supplementary material on the capital structure and dividend policies of the companies studied is also presented.

Analysis of the financial structure of business failures is a comparatively untouched field of inquiry. Although many reservations must be made in drawing conclusions from this type of study, the factual material alone is believed to warrant presentation because of its unusual nature. The analysis also reveals that there are definite danger signals in the changing financial structures of unsuccessful concerns. By comparing specific cases with the background here presented, companies may be warned against detrimental practices and perhaps be diverted from courses which might ultimately lead to failure.

Acknowledgment is made to Dr. Rexford C. Parmelee, formerly of the Bureau staff, for his work in assembling data for this study.

May, 1935

RAYMOND F. SMITH
ARTHUR H. WINAKOR

---

[1] A subsequent study of somewhat similar nature is *Symptoms of Industrial Failures,* by Paul J. Fitzpatrick (Catholic University of America, Washington, D. C., 1931).

I. INTRODUCTION

This study presents the results of an analysis of the financial statements of a group of 183 companies which failed in recent years.[2] For the present purpose, a company to be classified as a failure must have

(a) entered into a receivership, or

(b) defaulted on its bonds, or

(c) undergone a financial readjustment which, although it did not involve receivership, resulted in material changes in the rights or equities of the owners and creditors.

Most of the 183 companies had experienced either receivership or bond default. Companies classified as failures according to these three criteria were included if balance sheets, at least, were available for three or more accounting periods prior to failure. Both balance sheets and income statements for the last ten years before failure were analyzed if available. Practically all the companies studied failed after 1926, as shown in the following tabulation:

Year of Failure	Number of Companies	Year of Failure	Number of Companies
1923	1	1928	13
1924	1	1929	18
1925	7	1930	57
1926	4	1931	69
1927	13	Total	183

The aggregate of total assets, after depreciation, of the 183 companies three years before they failed amounted to $2,232,511,000, an average of $12,200,000 per company.[3] Twenty-eight of the 183

---

[2] A few companies included in the study were Canadian concerns.

[3] The significance of the size of these enterprises is emphasized when compared with the total assets of $94,226,000,000 reported by Manufacturing, Mining and Quarrying, Construction, and Trading Corporations which submitted balance sheet data to the Bureau of Internal Revenue for 1931. *(Statistics of Income for 1931,* United States Treasury Department, Table 15, pp. 148-153, and Table 17, pp. 160-177.) Although only 83 per cent of the corporations which filed returns also submitted balance sheet data, this 83 per cent reported about 98 per cent of the gross sales. The percentage of total assets which they owned was probably only slightly less than the percentage of gross sales.

These same groups comprised 218,918 companies which submitted balance sheets in 1931. Of this number an estimated 7,208 had total assets of $2,000,000 or more each, and only 993 of these had total assets of $10,000,000 or more each. In comparison, this study contains only 28 companies with total assets of less than $2,000,000 and 155 with total assets of $2,000,000 or more, 58 of which had total assets of $10,000,000 or more.

companies had total operating assets of less than $2,000,000, 70 had less than $4,000,000 of assets, and 125 had less than $10,000,000 of assets. Thirty-four companies had operating assets ranging from $10,000,000 to $25,000,000, and an additional 24 companies had assets of $25,000,000 or more.

Although a great variety of industries was represented in the study, 157 of the 183 companies, or 86 per cent, were manufacturing concerns. The remaining 26 were retail, commercial service, and wholesale enterprises.

In contrast to the predominance of manufacturing companies in the data, it should be noted that only 9 per cent of all 1931 failures in the United States were manufacturing concerns, and that they accounted for only 8 per cent of the total liabilities.[4]

The fact that this study is concerned with large corporations made it desirable to appraise the proportion of failures in this limited field to all failures. It appears that failures as large as those here studied constitute only a small fraction of the number of all failures, but that a significant percentage of large enterprises fail, many of which are manufacturing concerns. The 183 failures analyzed had capital of $250,000 or more, whereas the total number of failures having capital of $100,000 or more as reported by Bradstreet for the same approximate period was 723.[5] The inference seems justifiable that the data presented here represent approximately 25 per cent of large industrial failures in the years covered.

The principal source of the financial statements upon which this study is based was *Moody's Industrial Manuals*.

In order to make the financial statements of the failed companies readily comparable, they were classified according to the number of

---

[4] Bradstreet's *Failure Statistics for 1931*.

[5] In the eight years, 1924 to 1931, inclusive, 187,026 business enterprises in the United States and Canada failed, according to the yearly summaries of Bradstreet's. The large majority of these were small concerns employing capital of $5,000 or less, and having liabilities of less than $20,000. More significant is the fact that in this eight-year period only 723 failures of the 187,026 had capital of $100,000 or more, and only 9,217 had liabilities of $100,000 or more—approximately 0.4 per cent and 4.9 per cent, respectively.

One reason for the preponderance of manufacturing companies in the data is the fact that apparently fewer large concerns were found in the other groups. The Bureau of the Census, Department of Commerce, reported for 1929, 11,763 manufacturing establishments ("establishment" in most cases signifies a single plant or factory) turning out products valued at $1,000,000 or more. This group constituted only 5.6 per cent of all manufacturing establishments, but its output accounted for 69.2 per cent of the total value of manufactured products. In comparison it is pointed out that the failures analyzed in this study were enterprises with sales per year of $1,000,000 or more.

TABLE I
NUMBER OF FINANCIAL STATEMENTS AVAILABLE CLASSIFIED ACCORDING TO YEAR BEFORE FAILURE*

Year Before Failure	Balance Sheets	Income Statements†
10th	54	28
9th	68	37
8th	83	47
7th	92	57
6th	113	71
5th	139	87
4th	165	104
3rd	182	115
2nd	175	111
1st	114	69

*Financial statements were not always available for the last year prior to failure, nor for consecutive years.
†In some cases, the income statements were incomplete.

years before failure. Assume that Company A failed in 1928. For it the first year before failure would therefore be 1927, and the second year before failure 1926. If Company B failed in 1931, 1930 would be called the first, and 1929 the second year before failure, respectively. The numbers of balance sheets and income statements found to be available are set forth in Table I, according to this basis of classification.

The next step involved the standardization of the financial statements,[6] and the computation of financial ratios. A complete list of the ratios computed and analyzed is contained in Table 1 of the Appendix, page 41.

By trial it was found that the mean of the middle half of the cases satisfactorily portrayed the composite changes. As a rule this fell between the values of the median and of the arithmetic mean. Averages were also computed for four groups of companies in specific industries, and for two size groups, classified according to amount of total operating assets. The ordinary mean was used in these cases. Adjustments were made in those ratios showing the relative proportions of each asset, liability, and net worth item to total assets, making the sums of assets and of liabilities and net worth, respectively, equal to total assets.

The major classifications of the data were: the entire group; four selected industries; and two size groups of enterprise. The entire group of companies gives a more reliable picture of conditions than the subgroupings of data, which were based on less adequate samples.

---

[6] See Bulletin No. 31, pages 8 and 9, for details of account classification and statement standardization.

The four industries for which sufficient cases were at hand to show trends were machinery, steel-iron, sugar, and textile manufacturing. In the final regrouping of data, companies with operating assets below $3,000,000 and those with operating assets of $20,000,000 or more were contrasted. For each of these groupings of data, a supporting table is to be found in the Appendix.

II. CURRENT POSITION

A weak current position, particularly if the cash account is depleted, is frequently an indirect, and occasionally a direct, cause of failure. The current position is exceedingly sensitive; it is quickly affected by sudden, short-time fluctuations in price levels, production schedules, etc. It is therefore likely to reveal defects in companies whose condition is problematical.

Three important measures of current position are the Cash to Total Assets ratio, the Working Capital to Total Assets ratio,[7] and the Current Assets to Current Liabilities ratio (Current Ratio). These are discussed at this point. Some other ratios equally important to an understanding of debt-paying ability, such as those dealing with inventories, notes and accounts receivable, and notes and accounts payable, are discussed later.

The Cash to Total Assets ratio indicates the proportion of total assets in the form of cash and marketable securities. Another phase of current position is revealed by the Current Assets to Current Liabilities ratio, which indicates the amount of assets which may be realized currently to meet maturing liabilities. This ratio shows the relation of all current assets—i.e., those consisting of cash, and those that may shortly be turned into cash—to current liabilities. The Working Capital to Total Assets ratio measures the proportion of net current assets (that is, the excess of current assets over current liabilities) to total assets. It shows the proportion of total assets in the form of current assets which have been provided from long-term sources or securities.

Although the Current Ratio shows the relation of current assets to current liabilities and is one test of the security of the short-term creditor, it does not necessarily throw any light on the working-capital needs of an enterprise. The Working Capital to Total Assets ratio, on the other hand, does not indicate the proportion of current assets that can be applied to meet maturing current obligations, but rather the net current assets that are free (i. e., over and above the amount of short-term obligations). The trend of this ratio reveals the ability to maintain working capital adequate to the needs of the enterprise.

---

[7] In this bulletin the term "working capital" denotes what is sometimes called "net working capital"—i.e., current assets less current liabilities. The relationship of working capital to total assets is referred to as the Working Capital Ratio.

TABLE II

CURRENT POSITION OF 183 COMPANIES FOR TEN YEARS PRIOR TO FAILURE AS SHOWN BY AVERAGE RATIOS AND RELATIVE NUMBERS

Year Before Failure	Current Ratio		Working Capital Ratio		Cash to Total Assets Ratio	
	Average Ratio	Relative (10th yr. = 100)	Average Ratio	Relative (10th yr. = 100)	Average Ratio	Relative (10th yr. = 100)
10th	2.718	100	.225	100	.046	100
9th	2.782	102	.206	92	.045	98
8th	2.590	95	.212	94	.047	102
7th	2.719	100	.203	90	.043	93
6th	3.134	115	.196	87	.045	98
5th	2.784	102	.184	82	.044	96
4th	2.922	108	.169	75	.039	85
3rd	2.473	91	.157	70	.032	70
2nd	2.057	76	.129	57	.028	61
1st	1.488	55	.062	28	.018	39

Analysis of the current position of the 183 companies showed that although cash and marketable securities had begun to decline, the Current Ratio of these companies was slightly higher in the 6th, 5th, and 4th years before failure than in the preceding years (Table II) From the 3rd year on, however, it declined sharply, but did not fall below 2.00 (commonly referred to as a "two to one" ratio) until the final year before failure. Thus in every year until the year prior to failure these companies reported in their financial statements, on the average, current assets equal to more than twice the amount of their current liabilities. Clearly this fact indicates either that these balance-sheet values were inadequate, that the current assets were of such a nature as to preclude their realization to pay maturing obligations, that unusual losses were sustained in the year prior to failure which drastically changed the situation, or else that the ratio of Current Assets to Current Liabilities was misleading. All these conditions seem to have been present, but the deceptive Current Ratio was especially important. This last shortcoming is largely disclosed by the working-capital analysis.

The Working Capital to Total Assets ratio indicates a gradual decline in the proportion of working capital for these companies even in the earlier years but becoming increasingly more acute after the sixth year. Furthermore, it should be mentioned that even in the earlier years the working capital seems to have been meager in view of the needs of most enterprises. Because of unsuccessful business operations in the following years, net working capital, which had previously amounted to .20 or more of total assets, declined to only .062 in the final year before failure.

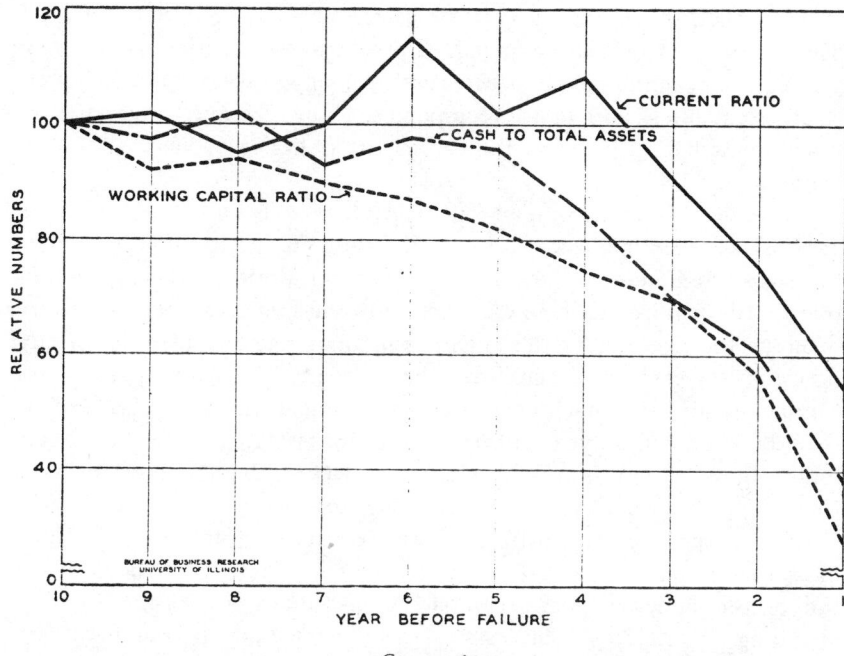

CHART 1

Trends of Current Assets to Current Liabilities, Working Capital to Total Assets, and Cash to Total Assets Ratios of 183 Unsuccessful Industrial Corporations from the tenth to the first year before failure.

(Base: 10th year before failure = 100)

The trends of all three of these ratios, which are portrayed in Chart 1, show decidedly unfavorable symptoms in the years immediately preceding failure. It is apparent that the representative failure was greatly pressed for immediately available funds in the last two or three years of its operations. It should be noticed, however, that the Working Capital to Total Assets ratio shows both a more definite and a more regular downward trend than the other two ratios and discloses more fully the extent of the difficulties faced. This ratio declined 72 per cent in the ten-year period, whereas the Current Ratio declined only 45 per cent, and the Cash to Total Assets ratio, 61 per cent. The Working Capital to Total Assets ratio, moreover, recorded a weakening in the current position of the failures much earlier than either of the other two.

Four specific types of industry were next analyzed in an effort to distinguish characteristic symptoms of failure in individual industries.

It was hoped that in this way some of the peculiar conditions of types of enterprises would be isolated. Three current-position ratios were studied for machinery manufacturing companies, steel-iron companies, sugar companies, and textile companies. The averages cover the six years immediately prior to failure, as the data for earlier years were inadequate.

It is seen from a comparison of Appendix Tables 2 to 5 that the greatest declines in the Current Ratio occurred for the textile and for the sugar companies. However, the Current Ratio of the representative textile failure fell below 2.00 in only the final year before failure, whereas the average of the sugar companies had dropped below that figure a year earlier. In contrast, the Current Ratios for the steel-iron companies and the machinery manufacturing companies were greater than 2.00 in the final year before failure, that of the former being even higher than in the 6th and 5th years. However, the averages for these two groups also declined in each of the last two years.

The proportion of working capital relative to total assets declined most for the textile and the sugar companies. The current positions of the textile and the sugar companies, as indicated by the ratio of Working Capital to Total Assets, were very poor in the final year before failure as compared with former years. For the steel-iron failures the proportion of working capital in relation to total assets seems to be less significant as an indicator of a weakened condition, as its course was very irregular. For the machinery manufacturing companies the Working Capital to Total Assets ratio shows a gradual decline from the fifth to the second year before failure and a decided drop in the final year.

The Cash to Total Assets ratio indicates a more serious drain of liquid resources for the sugar companies than for the others. Although the Working Capital Ratio of the steel-iron concerns does not show any marked decline, their Cash to Total Assets ratio reveals a consistent weakening in their liquid position from the fifth to the last year. Thus it would seem that the steel-iron companies were also pressed for ready cash in the period immediately preceding failure.

Although the ratio of Cash to Total Assets for the textile companies and for the machinery manufacturing companies indicates some degree of weakness as the year of failure approached, the decline was less marked for these concerns.

The course of these three ratios presents a rather definite picture of the current position of the failures. Apparently the textile, sugar, and machinery manufacturing companies suffered from a general lack of net working capital; the sugar companies were further handicapped by insufficient cash and other current assets. The chief difficulty in the case of the steel-iron companies was a noticeable drain of cash, but their net working capital did not fall off as was the case with the other groups.

Two groups of failures, selected according to the amount of their total operating assets, were analyzed in order to ascertain the trends of the Current Ratio and the Working Capital to Total Assets ratio for companies of different size. Such an analysis should indicate the relationship of the size of the enterprise to the current position of the failures.[8] Tables 6 and 7 of the Appendix show the averages of the three current-position ratios for those companies having total assets of less than $3,000,000, and for those with total assets of $20,000,000 or more.

Cash and marketable securities, as indicated by the ratios of both groups of companies, declined in each of the last four years of operations. It is apparent that a distinctly weakened liquid position was common to the average company of both size groups by the final year before failure. This is particularly evident when it is found that in the last few years before failure the obligations awaiting payment showed no reduction which could warrant a smaller cash balance.[9] On the whole, cash and marketable securities were greater in relation to total assets for the small companies than for the large ones. This seems to conform with the relationships between their current assets and current liabilities and their total assets as will be pointed out.

A survey of the Current Ratio reveals for both large and small companies a fluctuating and highly irregular trend from the eighth to the last year before failure. The trends do not appear significant in denoting approaching financial difficulties. Even in the last two years before failure, with probably the poorest showing, the ratios of Current Assets to Current Liabilities were not indicative of serious financial conditions, and it may be doubted whether the average ratio of itself could be said to reflect embarrassment of any kind for companies of either size group. The lowest average ratio recorded for the entire ten years for these companies was 2.73 for the small companies two years prior to failure. In the final year before failure their ratio stood at 3.31. These figures are, of course, well above the

---
[8] When the failures were grouped according to the amount of their total operating assets, a tendency for certain types of enterprises to be found in one group rather than in the other was noticed. As a result, differences in the data for these size groups may be partially due to the type of enterprise.
[9] See page 28.

so-called minimum two-to-one ratio wherein current assets are twice the size of current obligations. For the large companies, the lowest average ratio occurred in the last year before failure, at which time their current assets averaged 2.93 times their current liabilities. According to all usual standards, these ratios were neither alarming nor indicative of trouble. Perhaps the only unusual thing about them was their erratic fluctuation, suggesting that some companies had very small current liabilities, and that any change therein greatly influenced the ratio of Current Assets to Current Liabilities.

In six of the ten years the Current Ratios of the large companies were larger than those of the small companies. In most industries it is a normal situation to find the Current Ratio of large companies making a better showing than the same ratio for small companies. One writer makes the statement that "the current condition of the large companies is vastly superior to that of small companies of the same industrial group"[10] because of the larger Current Ratios of the large companies. A somewhat similar statement, although less emphatic, is found in another recent study.[11] It would appear that such conclusions are subject to some rather serious qualifications. They do not take into account variations in the nature of small and large enterprises, the greater degree of integration in large companies than in small, the volume and velocity of current-asset and current-liability turnover, and a number of other equally important financial interrelationships.

For example, the amount of the working capital which has been provided from long term securities or stocks is just as important as the Current Ratio, if not more important. Although large companies have larger Current Ratios than small companies, both current assets and current liabilities are relatively smaller in large than in small companies.[12] Consequently even though the Current Ratio may be

---

[10] Clark, Evans, *The Internal Debts of the United States,* The Macmillan Company, New York, 1933, p. 191.

[11] Crum, W. L., *The Effect of Size on Corporate Earnings and Condition,* Business Research Studies No. 8, Bureau of Business Research, Harvard University, Soldiers Field, Boston, Mass., p. 32.

[12] See Tables 6 and 7 of the Appendix for the relation of Current Assets to Total Assets for small and large companies and for their ratios of Current Liabilities to Total Assets. This situation of the relationship of current assets and current liabilities and working capital appears to hold good not only for companies approaching failure, but also for normal sound enterprises. It is to be found in many industries normally. Studies being pursued by the Bureau of Business Research, based on the Statistics of Income of the Bureau of Internal Revenue, and also published reports of selected corporations show these differences.

relatively smaller for the small companies, the net difference between their current assets and liabilities is occasionally greater for the small companies and commonly so for the moderate-sized enterprises as compared with the large.

The residual between the current assets and current liabilities—that is, the working capital—when measured in relation to the total assets of the large and the small companies, is distinctly more favorable for the latter. In general, throughout the ten years analyzed the Working Capital to Total Assets ratio of the small companies was (roughly) 50 per cent larger than the comparable ratio of large companies. For example, in the eighth year before failure the average working capital of small companies was equal to .276 of their total assets as compared with .177 for large companies. In the final year before failure, the ratio of Working Capital to Total Assets was .126 for small concerns and .071 for large enterprises.

A comparison of the trends of this ratio for large and small companies shows that, except for some slight temporary improvement, there has been a consistent decline for both. This ratio therefore appears to be a rather dependable indicator of financial difficulties—far more accurate in its implications of the future than the Current Ratio. Particularly from the fifth year on there was a constantly declining movement in the Working Capital Ratios for both large and small companies. In general, the trends of the ratios for these two size-groups are substantially alike.

It should be noticed, however, that a more serious condition is evident for the large than for the small companies. The large companies, which had relatively smaller working capital (as compared with small companies), recorded a more severe decline in their Working Capital to Total Assets ratios. This is apparent, whether measured from the eighth to the first, the fifth to the first, or the second to the first year before failure. The percentages of decline from these three years for large companies were 59.9, 61.0, and 38.3, respectively. For the small companies, they were 54.3, 49.2, and 26.7, respectively. It should be noted that the discrepancy between the large and the small companies became greater as the year of failure approached, indicating the cumulative effect of losses upon the working capital. Since the large companies had relatively less working capital than the small companies, the losses of the former evidently proved more serious and dangerous for their financial welfare than those of the latter.

It is true that large companies may maintain relatively satisfactory

Current Ratios in face of sharp working-capital losses, but financial condition, and more particularly, debt-paying ability, cannot be measured by a single ratio, nor can it be appraised adequately without considering capitalization, fixed capital, earning power, and a number of other interrelated financial determinants.

III. COMPOSITION OF ASSETS, LIABILITIES, AND NET WORTH

In this section of the bulletin the distribution of each of the asset and the liability items is shown in its relation to the total assets. These data afford a convenient picture of the relative proportions of total assets which have been invested in each major group of assets. They also measure the relative amounts of assets which have been contributed by various classes of creditors and stockholders, and, conversely, indicate some of their claims and rights to participate in the assets and their earnings.

Assets

In order to present a clear picture of the composition of the assets of the 183 failures in the period covered, the average ratios depicting the asset side of the balance sheet were plotted in Chart 2 (based upon Table 1 in the Appendix). The height of the bars represents unity of total assets in each of the ten years prior to failure.

In the tenth year before failure fixed assets accounted for .593 of total assets; current assets—composed of cash and marketable securities, receivables, and inventories—accounted for .430 of total assets; and other assets equalled approximately .017. The course of the averages thereafter denoted a gradual decline in the stability of the failures, with the most pronounced change occurring in the final year before failure, when fixed assets constituted 76 per cent of total assets, current assets only 22 per cent, and other assets 3 per cent. In general the chart shows that inventories and other current assets of the failures gradually accounted for smaller proportions of total assets as the final year approached. Consequently the proportion of total assets represented by fixed assets gradually increased.

Ordinarily a concern which suffers from operating losses and is apparently on the road to failure will have shrinking current assets in relation to total assets. The proportion of fixed assets to total assets in such a case increases, indicating drains of working capital and often the inability of the business unit to utilize its plant adequately.

Two additional ratios, Inventory to Current Assets and the sum of Cash and Receivables, or Quick Assets, to Current Assets (see Appendix, Table 1) assist materially in visualizing changing conditions.

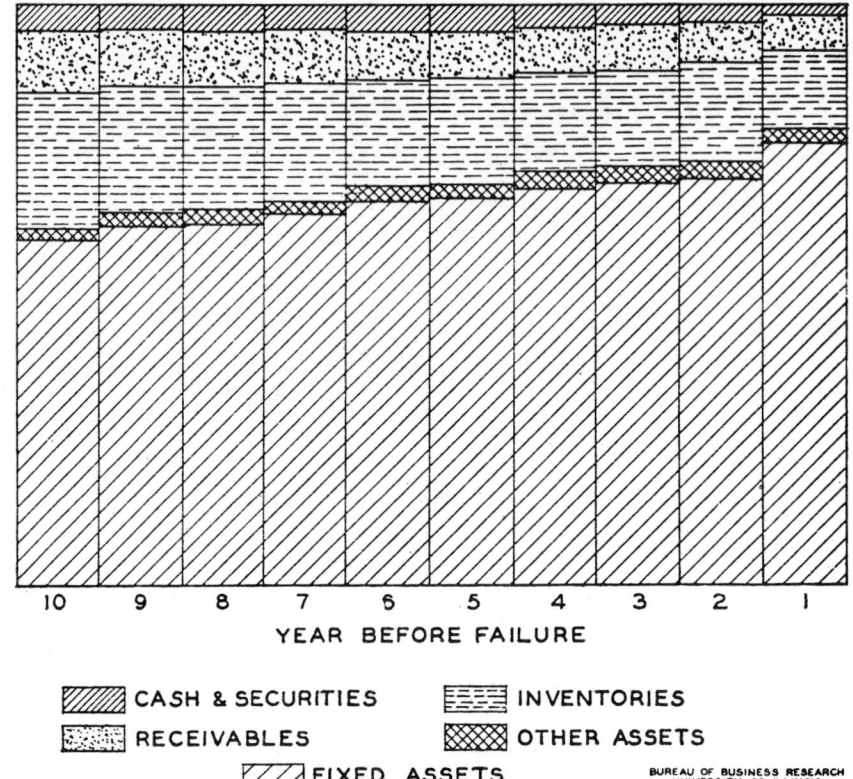

CHART 2

Changes in the Proportions of Assets Relative to Total Assets of 183 Unsuccessful Industrial Corporations from the tenth to the first year before failure.

Not only did the current assets shrink from .430 of total assets in the 10th year to .220 of total assets in the final year before failure, but their liquidity was materially reduced. The less liquid part of current assets—namely, inventories—increased from .515 to .564 of current assets in the ten-year period, and, conversely, the more liquid cash and receivables declined in relative size.

Tables 2 to 5 in the Appendix present the ratios computed for the four specific industries selected, including data on the composition of the assets and liabilities of each group. These data are for a six-year period prior to failure.

Failed companies which had been engaged in the manufacturing of machinery were first analyzed. For the period as a whole no clear-cut trends were discernible, either for current assets or for their composition. The trend of cash in relation to total assets for this industry reveals the most noticeable symptom of weakness, the ratios showing a marked decline in the last four years, from 10.8 to 5 per cent of total assets. From the fourth to the final year before failure the ratio of receivables and inventories combined showed a moderate decline from .482 to .448. In the last three years before failure there was an increase in the proportion of fixed assets.

Not until the last two years before failure was there any general indication of weakness for the steel-iron concerns, although the item of cash and securities declined in the last four years from 5.6 per cent to 1.7 per cent of total assets. It is quite probable that this shrinkage of cash and its equivalent handicapped the steel-iron companies. The last two years before failure show a moderate decline in receivables from 10 per cent to 7 per cent, but an increase of more than 1 per cent in inventories, which in the last year constituted 17 per cent of total assets. With the possible exception of the course of cash and marketable securities in relation to total assets, the changes in the distribution of the various assets are not sufficiently pronounced to be taken as significant indications of coming failure. There were indications, however, that the current assets were becoming less liquid.

Fixed assets customarily constituted a large proportion of total assets for the sugar companies: six years before failure they were equal to 75 per cent of total assets. Moreover, the course of events leading up to the year of failure resulted in a gradual increase in the proportion of fixed assets so that a year before failure they stood at 80 per cent of the total. Declines in cash and receivables, accompanied by only small changes in inventories, accounted for a decrease in current assets in relation to total assets. Cash and its equivalent, however, were quite low in the last four years before failure—less than 2 per cent of total assets. The sugar companies were doubtless handicapped because of this lack of ready cash. The more liquid parts of current assets—namely, cash and receivables—diminished in importance relative to current assets and inventories. These facts, when considered together with the sharp reduction in accounts receivable and the material increase in current obligations, reflect pressing financial difficulties.

For the textile companies a weakened financial structure is noticed after the fifth year prior to failure. Decreases in current assets occurred in each of the last four years prior to failure, showing an increasing lack of current capital. The decline in the final year was quite pronounced. Four years prior to failure current assets composed 39.8 per cent of total assets, but by the last year before failure they had declined to 21.1 per cent. Although current assets had declined markedly when compared with total assets, inventories were reduced even more quickly. Quick assets increased from .289 to .379 of current assets from the sixth to the final year prior to failure. Offsetting the decline in current assets there was a marked increase in fixed assets and a slight but irregular increase in other assets.

The analysis of the ratios of Fixed Assets to Total Assets for the two size groups indicated interesting variations in the proportions that may have been due partly to size. Appendix Tables 6 and 7 show the changes which took place in the ratios of Fixed Assets to Total Assets of these groups. The ratios point to variations in the proportion of total capital invested in fixed assets for the two groups of failures such as are normally found in companies so different in size. For the larger failures the proportion of total assets in the form of fixed assets was greater. For both groups, increased fixed assets in relation to total assets were recorded as the year of failure approached.

More significant is the relative rate or speed of increase of fixed assets in relation to total assets for each of the size-groups. As the companies approached failure, the greatest increase in the proportion of fixed assets to total assets was recorded for the small companies, indicating a more rapid shrinkage of current assets for them. The fact that current liabilities did not decline commensurately was less favorable for the small companies, which had relatively large current debts.

In spite of this shrinkage, however, the current assets of small companies were consistently larger in relation to total assets than those of large companies.[13] In the tenth year before failure the current assets of small companies were 59.1 per cent of total assets. For the large companies current assets constituted 31.2 per cent of total assets. Thus the ratio of Current Assets to Total Assets for small companies was 1.9 as large as that for large companies. By the final year before failure the ratio of small companies was 1.8 times as large as the ratio of large companies.

Although the changes which took place in the various items con-

---

[13]As shown in the Appendix tables the working capital of large companies was smaller relative to total assets than that of small companies. Not only do current assets hold a similar relationship as to size, but likewise current liabilities when compared with total assets.

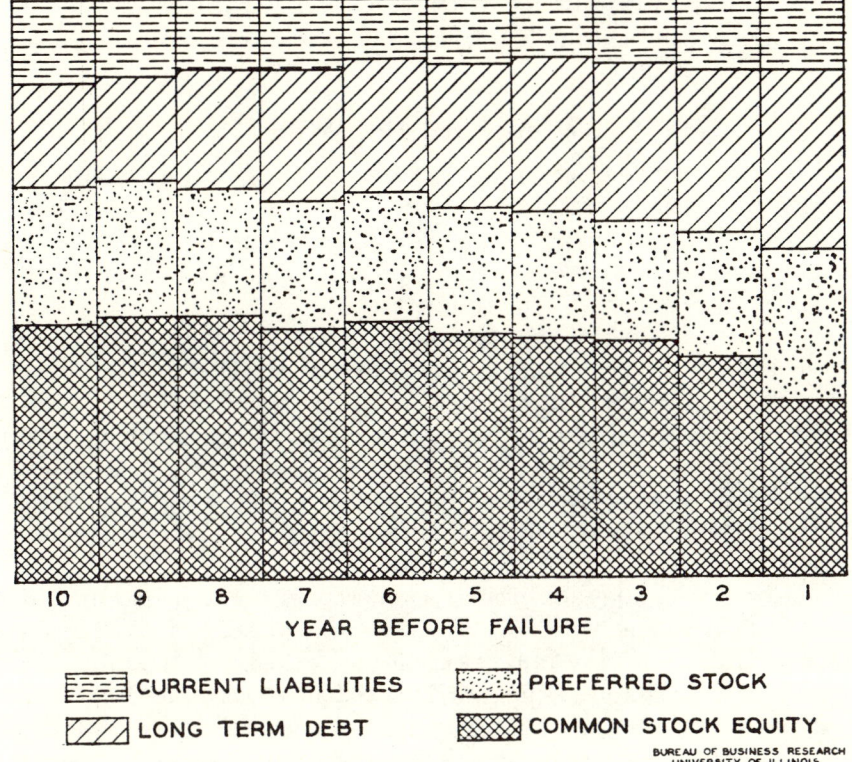

CHART 3

Changes in the Proportions of Liabilities and Net Worth Relative to Total Assets of 183 Unsuccessful Industrial Corporations from the tenth to the first year before failure.

stituting current assets were not clearly defined throughout the entire period, certain trends manifested themselves. For the large companies, which had less shrinkage in current assets, inventories declined less rapidly than current assets. Consequently, as measured by the quick assets—that is, the sum of cash and receivables—the liquidity of current assets diminished as failure approached. This was particularly evident during the last six years. The small companies, which had a greater shrinkage of current assets, actually maintained or slightly improved their liquidity. The inventories of small companies were much larger relative to total assets and also to current assets than those of large companies. The more rapid decline in inventories of small companies seems to have been due partly to inventory losses and shrinkage rather than to liquidation and realization; in so far as this condition actually existed, the apparently favorable showing of small companies was illusory.

Liabilities and Net Worth

Of equal importance with the analysis of the assets of failures is that of their liabilities and net worth. The causes underlying failure not only result in changes in the total assets and in the proportion of investments in each type of asset, but also bring about related and divergent changes in the equity interests.

An enterprise which continues to operate at a loss usually finds a shrinkage in its current assets and consequently in its total assets. When this is the case, it follows that the claims of creditors, unless commensurately reduced, increase in relation to the declining total assets. As the margin between the creditors' claims and total assets decreases, and the proportion of current assets to total assets declines, the ability of a concern to meet both current and long time obligations is reduced.

Chart 3 gives a graphic picture of the change in the composition of the liabilities and net worth of the entire group of failures. The ratios plotted in this chart are to be found in Table 1 in the Appendix. In the tenth year before failure current liabilities constituted .147 of total assets. Up to the fifth year before failure a trend toward lower ratios prevailed; thus in the sixth year before failure current liabilities were equal to only .104 of total assets. After the sixth year the proportion of current liabilities to total assets moved irregularly upward to .129 in the final year before failure.

Long term debt in relation to total assets increased steadily throughout the ten-year period leading up to failure, from .176 of total assets in the ninth year to .234 in the sixth year, and .274 and .308 in the second and first years before failure, respectively. The combined ratios of Current Liabilities to Total Assets and Long Term Debt to Total Assets clearly indicate increased claims of creditors in relation to total assets.

A consideration of the dollar amounts of long term debt and current liabilities, as well as the proportion of these items to total assets and other bases, is of special significance in the analysis of an individual enterprise. As a rule, the dollar amounts of long term debt of the failures declined in the period immediately preceding failure, especially in the last six years. This decrease probably reflected the reduction of long-term-debt obligations through sinking-fund provisions, serial-issue retirements, deferment as unpaid short term debt, etc. Only a few concerns materially increased their long term obligations outstanding in the last three or four years before failure.

No significant change can be discerned in the proportion of preferred stock to total assets from the eighth year to the second year before failure, when preferred stock accounted for .216 of total assets. In the final year, however, preferred stock increased to .261 of the total assets.

The equity of the common stockholders decreased gradually after the sixth year before failure, and declined rapidly in the two final years. If increased earning power (net income in relation to common stock equity or net worth) had accompanied this decreasing common stock equity, greater and more profitable use of borrowed capital would have been indicated. Such was not the case, however. Net income on net worth—a decreasing net worth—also declined, showing a progressive inability to earn a profit on the stockholders' shrinking capital.[14]

The liabilities and net worth of the failures were next analyzed according to the various types of industry selected for special investigation. The material supporting these analyses is to be found in Appendix Tables 2 to 5.

The average ratios of the liabilities and net worth of the machinery companies are presented in Table 2 of the Appendix. A larger proportion of the capital of the companies in the group making various types of machinery was obtained from short term creditors than for any of the other groups here analyzed. This condition, however, is consistent with the large current assets of these companies. Current obligations relative to total assets tended to increase during the period preceding failure. This is especially noticeable in the final two years prior to failure, when the ratio rose from .214 to .277. No significant trend is observed in the proportion of long term debt to total capital. Combined obligations to creditors of the machinery-manufacturing companies rose from .348 of total assets in the sixth year before failure to .491 of total assets in the final year.

From the fifth to the last year, preferred stock increased from .252 to .403 of total assets, the greatest rise occurring in the last year. From the fifth to the second year before failure there was evidence of a moderate decline in the common stockholders' equity, the ratio of Common Stock Equity to Total Assets standing at .302 in the second year as contrasted with .363 in the fifth year. In the final year

---

[14] See page 31.

prior to failure a sharp decline in the equity of the common stockholders occurred, dropping the ratio to .106. The changes in the distribution of the liabilities and net worth of the machinery manufacturing companies did not offer a very early indication of the severe financial difficulties which were to follow.

The average ratios of the steel-iron companies show that current liabilities decreased from .157 in the sixth to .102 of total assets in the third year before failure, a distinctly favorable sign. Some increases in current obligations of less than .02 occurred in the last two years preceding failure. It appears, however, that this relatively favorable showing was obscured by, or compensated by, the funding of current obligations into long term obligations, or in some cases into preferred stock. Long term debt, which constituted .239 of total assets in the sixth year before failure, increased continuously during the period, amounting to .352 of total assets in the last year before failure. Combined current and long term obligations increased from .396 in the sixth to .464 of total assets in the final year before failure.

Except for a slight drop in the third year before failure, preferred stock increased consistently from 9.9 to 23.3 per cent of total assets in the six years prior to failure. The residual equity, that of the common stockholders, reveals a general decline as the year of failure approached. As the equities of current and long term creditors and that of preferred stockholders increased, the margin of protection behind these claims—represented by the common stockholders' equity—declined from .505 of total assets in the sixth year before failure to .303 of total assets in the final year.

The ratios for the sugar companies (See Appendix, Table 4) show a distinct tendency for current liabilities to increase in relation to total assets during the six-year period prior to failure. Thus current obligations, which had equalled .111 of total assets in the sixth year before failure, increased to .194 of total assets in the final year. Long term obligations, on the other hand, after a moderate decline in the fifth year, gradually increased from .272 of total assets in that year to .295 in the second year, and then jumped to .361 of total assets in the final year. Combined obligations to creditors increased throughout the period. Whereas the creditors' equity in the total assets amounted to .418 of the total in the sixth year prior to failure, it had increased to .555 of the total in the final year before failure.

The proportion of preferred stock to total assets remained almost constant during the six-year period preceding failure, fluctuating between .16 and .18. The proportion of common stock equity to total assets, on the other hand, shows a general decline during the period from .426 in the fifth year to .272 in the first year before failure, indicating a shrinking equity of the residual risk-takers. The analysis of the liabilities and net worth of the sugar companies thus shows clear indications of approaching failure.

Current liabilities of the textile companies showed a tendency to increase during the period. In the sixth year before failure they equalled .154 of total assets, compared with .172 in the final year. Long term obligations remained fairly constant in relation to total assets until the second year before failure, after which notable increases occurred in the ratio of Long Term Debt to Total Assets, which rose from .246 to .268 and finally to .332 in the last three years. Combined current liabilities and long term debt show that obligations to creditors constantly and regularly increased from .393 to .504 of total assets from the sixth to the first years before failure.

The proportion of the preferred stockholders' equity to total capital more than doubled in the six-year period, increases occurring in the last three years prior to failure. Whereas preferred stock amounted to .168 of total assets in the sixth year before failure, it accounted for .346 of the total in the final year. The decline in the common stock equity, which decreased from .439 to .150 of total assets between the sixth and the last years before failure, is quite significant as a symptom of financial weakness, particularly in the last two years before failure. It reveals a shrinkage of the common stockholders' equity in the assets of the textile companies. Conversely, it discloses increases of the relatively fixed items, such as preferred stock and long term debt, in comparison with declining total assets. These changes indicate a more rapid decline in total assets than occurred in the combined equities of the long and short term creditors and the preferred stockholders. On the other hand the residual equity—that of the common stockholder—declined more rapidly than did total assets, reflecting both the asset losses and the relatively increased senior claims in these assets.

The analysis of the liabilities and net worth of the failures according to the size of the companies did not produce evidence which would point to materially different degrees of change in the equities of the creditors and owners attributable solely to the difference in size of the failures. Nevertheless changes which disclose approaching difficulty are discerned from an examination of the ratios presented in Appendix Tables 6 and 7.

The ratios of Current Liabilities to Total Assets point to distinct differences in the use of short-term credit as a source of capital for the two sizes of companies, but these differences are not directly referable to their failure. In part at least they represent variations inherent in the nature and size of enterprises, as pointed out on page 32. Current liabilities were much greater relative to total assets for the small failures than for the large ones. For the large enterprises the ratio of Current Liabilities to Total Assets tended to decline in the first part of the period and afterward to increase; no trend was discerned for the small companies.

Long term debt relative to total assets tended to increase for both size groups as the year of failure approached. The large companies consistently had the greater proportion of long term debt. The sum of the Current Liabilities to Total Assets ratio and the Long Term Debt to Total Assets ratio for the small companies was less than the sum of these two ratios for the large companies in seven out of ten years. The large companies relied more upon long term debt and less upon short term obligations than did the small ones.

The ratios of Net Worth to Total Assets from the tenth year to the first year before failure indicate a tendency for net worth relative to total assets to be slightly but consistently higher for the small failures than for the larger ones. Except for irregularities in one or two years, the general trend was for the Net Worth to Total Assets ratios of both groups to decline as the year of failure approached.

Perhaps equally as significant as the trends of the Net Worth to Total Assets ratios and their relative positions in large and small companies is the size of net worth relative to total assets. In the tenth year prior to failure net worth constituted approximately 70 per cent of the total for small companies and somewhat less than this proportion for large companies. In the final year before failure, however, net worth still accounted for distinctly more than half of the total assets in both groups of companies. The inferences are that assets and net worth were materially over-valued, and/or that the Net Worth to Total Assets ratio is not a satisfactory indicator of approaching difficulties.

IV. REVENUE AND OTHER RELATIONSHIPS

An analysis of such ratios as Operating Expenses to Sales (Operating Ratio) and Sales to Total Assets often points, at least indirectly, to the immediate causes of failure. These two ratios give a fair indication of the progress of the dollar volume and the cost of the operations of an enterprise, which constitute the basis for profits or losses. On the other hand, an examination of the Net Earnings to Total Assets and the Net Income to Net Worth ratios clearly reveals the earning power of an enterprise and its ability to use borrowed money to advantage. The factual data for these ratios of the 183 companies are to be found in Table 1 of the Appendix, and are also portrayed in Chart 4.

The Sales to Total Assets ratio measures the annual volume of business relative to the total assets employed. For the 183 companies this ratio was .802 in the 10th year before failure and .628 in the 5th year. It declined to .409 in the final year before failure. In other words, at the rate of sales found ten years prior to failure, it would have taken 1¼ years for sales to equal the total assets employed. Similarly, it would have taken 1⅗ years at the rate of the 5th year prior to failure, and 2⅖ years at the rate of the final year preceding failure for sales to equal assets. A falling-off in the productive use of total assets, as measured by the volume of sales, for the failures is clearly indicated.

The Operating Ratio, next discussed, indicates what portion of each sales dollar is required to pay expenses of production and operation. The average ratio of Operating Expenses to Sales for the entire group of failures was above .90 in each of the ten years preceding failure. In other words, operating costs consumed more than 90 cents of each sales dollar for the average company. In the sixth year before failure, .924 of gross revenues was required to pay for the operating expenses. Thereafter, increasingly larger proportions of gross revenues were needed to meet the operating expenses, until in the final year before failure these expenses exceeded gross revenues by 4.8 per cent.

The difference between 1.000 and the ratio of Operating Expenses to Sales is the Net Earnings to Sales Ratio. This margin of gross revenues remaining available to meet contingencies, fixed charges, and dividends, was small when considered in conjunction with the low volume of business throughout the ten-year period.

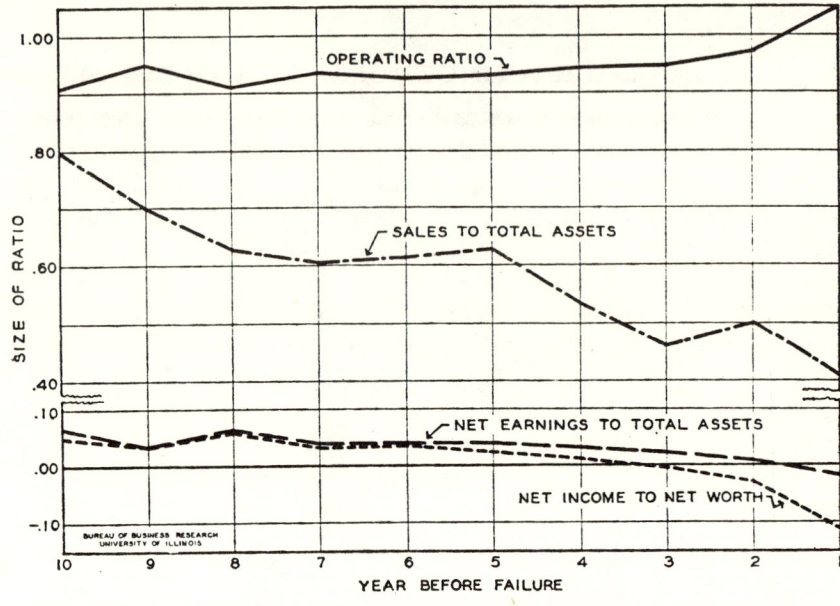

CHART 4

Changes in the Operating and Earning Power Ratios of 183 Unsuccessful Industrial Corporations from the tenth to the first year before failure.

Two ratios which are closely related to the foregoing are next presented. These are Net Earnings to Total Assets and Net Income to Net Worth, the former measuring the earning power of the total capital of the enterprise, and the latter showing the rate of return to the stockholder equity, after making provision for prior claims such as interest.

The earnings of the failed companies were modest even ten years prior to their failure, at which time an average of 6.3 per cent was earned on the total assets. After a decline in the following year, the rate again touched this figure. From the seventh year before failure, a downward trend is evident, and in the third and second years before failure only 2.4 per cent and 1.1 per cent. respectively, was earned on total assets. In the last year before failure a loss averaging 1.4 per cent of the total assets was suffered.

Quite obviously, at no time during the period were these companies earning a sufficient return, as measured by book values, to compensate the capital adequately in the way of interest payments, dividends, and risk. If the interest payments are deducted from the earnings, the remainder, when compared with stockholders' equities, shows the earnings for their investments. Since the Net Earnings to Total Assets ratio seldom, if ever, exceeded a reasonable interest cost of borrowed money, it is evident that attempted trading on the equity by the use of borrowed capital was unprofitable, and that the income of stockholders' investments was less than the rate which total assets could earn.[15] No doubt some of the companies did not seek to gain by trading on the equity, but borrowed to obtain needed capital when no other alternative could be found.

Ten years prior to failure, the ratio of Net Income to Net Worth was .051, a modest but not unsatisfactory result. The following year it dropped sharply to .029 and then recovered to .061 a year later. In the next three years the average reflected relatively stable but low returns to net worth, the ratio varying from .033 to .035. Sharp declines, indicating reduced earnings and the fixity of interest payments, brought the ratio to .001 in the third year before failure, and losses on net worth equal to .025 and .109, respectively, occurred in the last two years.

A review of these aspects of earning power leads to several tentative conclusions. Although the average earnings were modest, even in the best years shown, it was not until the last two or three years that losses encroaching on the invested capital were indicated by the average. The trends of these ratios were downward and unfavorable, and yet in every year except the last two there was some accretion to the stockholders' equity. Nor does it seem that losses of 2.5 per cent and 10.9 per cent of net worth would have hindered operations if other conditions of weakness had not been present. Doubtless the entire burden did not fall directly upon the working capital, but these were probably in part losses of excessive fixed-asset investments.[16]

Other explanations, equally as important as reduced earning power, must be sought for the causes of failure. It would appear that failure of current assets fully to realize anticipated values—i.e., shrinkage in current assets, maturity of non-refundable debts, unjustified payments of dividends, and the like—which impaired working capital and hampered operations, must be given due consideration in the determination of causes of failure.

[15] Cf. Jamison, Charles L., *Trading on the Equity by Industrial Companies*, Chapter 3, Michigan Business Studies, Vol. VI, No. 3, Bureau of Business Research, University of Michigan, Ann Arbor, 1934.

[16] See *Maintenance of Working Capital of Industrial Corporations by Conversion of Fixed Assets*, Arthur H. Winakor, Bulletin No. 49, Bureau of Business Research, University of Illinois, 1934, pp. 15 and 16; also *Analysis of Financial Statements*, H. G. Guthman, Prentice-Hall, Inc., N. Y. 1926, p. 60.

Because of inadequate operating statements, no classification of these ratios is presented for the types of industries. On the whole they pointed to conditions in substantial harmony with those already discussed.

The picture of the trends and relationships of the Operating Expenses to Sales, Sales to Total Assets, and Net Earnings to Total Assets ratios for companies with operating assets of less than $3,000,000 and those with operating assets of $20,000,000 or more is contained in Appendix Tables 6 and 7. It is found that in each year for which there were comparable data the relative volume of sales for small companies was several times that of large companies. In other words, the dollar volume of business was greater relatively for the capital of small companies than for large. This might be interpreted in part as showing a more intensive use of capital by the small than by the large companies.

An explanation of the differences in capital turnover is to be found in part in the essential characteristics of large- as contrasted with small-scale operations.[17] In general, and especially within specific industries, small enterprises tend to employ relatively less machinery than large companies. Small companies rent their buildings and other equipment more frequently than large ones. The large company tends to rely more on fixed capital for its operations—i.e., its production requires complex large-scale machinery. These characteristics of themselves largely determine many of the other financial differences between large and small companies which can be noted.

Since the large companies use relatively more machinery, their fixed assets measure the amounts of such outlays. On the other hand, the small companies rely more on simpler machine processes. But, by way of compensation, these small companies need more current assets to pay for their relatively greater supplies and materials; in comparison with their fixed assets, such items as inventories and supplies will loom much larger relatively than in the large companies.

To return now to the specific discussion of the Sales to Total Assets ratio, the preceding discussion has shed some light on the relative rate of total-asset turnover or volume of business. Even though a large company and a small company should sell the same number of units of product, and at the same price, the small enterprise would probably report a more rapid capital turnover or a larger volume of business in proportion to total-asset investment. Also its turnover of fixed-capital investment would be notably more rapid,

---
[17]See page 22.

because the total-asset and fixed-asset investment employed to turn out a unit of product are less for the small company than for the large. On this basis, it seems justifiable to conclude that the small company's success of operations is more likely to be closely linked to short-time economic, and especially price and wage changes, since these are more important to small-scale operations. Contrariwise, the success of large-scale enterprises is likely to be much more dependent upon long-term movements of prices, considering the changing values of their large fixed investments, and current wage changes and material prices may influence their operations less noticeably than those of small-scale operations.

Sales were equal to 1.78 times the total assets for small companies and only .55 of total assets for large companies, five years prior to failure. The ratio of Sales to Total Assets of small companies was thus more than three times as large as that of large companies. Although the data for these ratios were more or less irregular, definite reductions in volume of sales are evident in subsequent years for both size groups. By the first year before their failure, the ratio for small companies stood at 1.14, more than five times that for large companies, which was .22. The decline in sales volume for large companies was much more drastic than for small companies, the percentage decreases from the fifth to the first year being 61 and 36, respectively. The slow rate of turnover of capital, especially for large companies, together with the pronounced downward trends of sales, could have but one consequence—ultimate failure.

Since sales, or volume of business, measures the current assets processed and sold, and since sales are merely the measure of the flow of funds through current assets, current liabilities, and working capital, a small volume of sales, or a slowing-down in the circular flow of this capital must necessarily mean a slowing-down in the rate of current-, as well as fixed-asset turnover, and a consequent increasing lag between the values of all assets of the business as reflected on the balance sheet, and their real market values. This condition will be present unless equally as rapid a decline should occur in current assets, current liabilities, working capital, and fixed assets as in sales volume.

The Operating Expenses to Sales ratios for both large and small companies increased during the last few years before failure. For the large enterprises, the Operating Ratio was .874 eight years prior to failure, a not unreasonable figure. By the fifth year before failure the ratio stood at .934. From the eighth through the sixth year, operating expenses consumed a smaller portion of each sales dollar for the large than for the small companies. This seems reasonable in view of the relatively smaller volume of business conducted by large than small companies. But from the fifth year on (with the exception of one year) the Operating Ratio of large companies was higher than that of the small companies. In view of the slower total-asset turnover (or sales volume), the result was that large companies were in a much less favorable condition as far as operating results were concerned. In the year just prior to failure the operating expenses had increased so greatly that they exceeded revenues, the ratios averaging 1.008 for small companies, and 1.065 for large companies. Obviously, the larger the volume of business with operations at a loss, the greater would such a loss be relative to the total investment.

The ratios of Net Earnings to Total Assets, (also given in Appendix Tables 6 and 7) reflect the results of the factors analyzed in the two ratios previously analyzed—namely, Sales to Total Assets and Operating Expenses to Sales. When sales increase and operating expenses decline (relative to one another and to total assets), earnings on total assets rise. The opposite picture is the one found in the failed enterprises with sales declining, operating expenses rising, and a consequent decline in the Net Earnings to Total Assets ratio.

With a distinctly more rapid turnover of total assets, it is not surprising to find the small enterprises reporting a greater rate of earnings on total assets from the tenth to the sixth year before failure than the large companies, even though the Operating Ratios of the former were higher. Although the Operating Ratio of the small enterprises was lower as a rule from the fifth to the second year before failure than in the five earlier years, the relatively greater decline in sales volume of the small enterprises was sufficient to reduce their rate of earnings below that of the large companies in the third and following years.

With the possible exception of the tenth and eighth years before failure, the earnings of these companies were modest. In these years the small companies earned above their operating expenses 22.2 and 15.7 cents, respectively, for each dollar of total assets compared with 3.8 and 6.5 cents for the large enterprises. With one or two exceptions the trends were clearly downward.

The same general conclusions may be reached in regard to these ratios for the size groups as for the 183 companies. The volume of sales as measured by the Sales to Total Assets ratio and the trend of operating efficiency as measured by the Operating Ratio could indicate only ultimate failure if long continued. As pointed out, however, the average ratios did not reveal operating deficits until the final year before failure. Doubtless, heavier losses were incurred in the year of failure, for which data were generally unavailable. Although earnings for the entire period were rather low, losses, as compared with total assets, were not unduly severe except for small companies in the final year before failure. It does not seem likely that the full force of these losses fell on the working capital; possibly not more than half of the loss was thus absorbed.[18]

Although figures have not been presented as to the amount of loss incurred by the common stock equities, evidently it must have loomed large on such a comparative basis. Nevertheless the operating results, and the consequent small gains or even losses accruing to capital, would not have been so serious if there had not been fixed-interest burdens and perhaps dividend payments which were unwise in view of trends and subsequent events. Even then, it seems necessary to look to other items of financial policy and capitalization to obtain an adequate view of the internal financial factors contributing to and causing failure.

Dividend Policies

The records of the 183 companies prior to their failure were carefully examined in order to discover the nature of their dividend policies in the period immediately preceding their financial collapse.

The available data showed that 118, or 64 per cent of the companies, paid dividends on common or preferred stock, or both, at some time in the ten-year period before failure. For 5 additional companies, there were records of dividend payments earlier than the tenth year prior to failure. Either no dividends had been paid by the other 60 companies or no information regarding such payments was available. It is possible that some of them also paid dividends in the ten-year period.

An analysis of the 118 companies showed that even in the final year before failure dividends were paid by 19 of them, or 16 per cent; within the last three years, by 68, or 58 per cent; and within the last five years, by 97, or 82 per cent. Thus more than half of the entire group studied (97 of the 183) paid dividends five years before their failure.

---

[18] See page 31.

This record of continued dividend payments, in the face of increasing financial difficulties, may be partially explained by the fact that many companies prefer to refrain from reducing dividends if possible and are extremely reluctant to omit them altogether. They are not willing to interrupt a record of regular dividends, fearing the effect of such a step upon the market status of their stock. The directors may believe that they will incur the ill will of stockholders, whom they think of as eager for dividends. In some cases, it is feared that the general credit of the business will suffer if dividends are omitted. Although these considerations are likely to deter directors from changing their dividend policy, it would be more prudent for an enterprise which is regressing, and is not financially sound enough to withstand the continued drain of cash dividends, to retrench along the most conservative lines possible.

The problem of dividend continuance or omission is especially critical in the case of preferred stock. If dividends on some preferred stocks are not paid, the holders thereof become entitled to equal voting privileges with the common stockholders, or even sole voting power. Thus a decision to omit preferred dividends may mean that the holders of the common stock may lose control of the enterprise either partially or entirely. And yet the continuance of preferred dividends in a period of serious financial difficulties may prove detrimental to the best interests of all parties concerned. In the present study it was found that because of the omission of preferred dividends, for periods ranging from two consecutive quarters to three years, partial or sole voting power had passed to the preferred stockholders in 36 companies of the 183 analyzed.

The 68 companies which paid dividends within the three-year period to their failure were found to equal 37 per cent of the 183 companies studied. A classification of these 68 companies and the 183 companies into four size groups brought out some variations in dividend policy in companies of different size. Of the 68 companies paying dividends in the last three years before failure, 30 had total assets of less than $5,000,000, and these were 35 per cent of all the companies of similar size. Similarly it was found that 33, 40, and 48 per cent of the companies with total assets of $5,000,000 to $10,000,000, $10,000,000 to $25,000,000, and $25,000,000 or more, respectively, had paid dividends in the last three years prior to failure. There is an evident tendency for more of the larger companies to continue dividend payments into the final years of operations, suggesting that the larger concerns were more reluctant to omit dividends, and/or better able to continue them.

A further analysis was made of the companies in order to ascertain the methods by which they financed themselves—i.e., to find out whether they used capital borrowed on long term or only owners' (stockholders') capital. Concerns which continue dividend payments as they did in spite of a marked decline in earnings and the resulting drain upon liquid assets are inevitably approaching a time when the liquid funds will not suffice to meet fixed charges. A conservative dividend policy would therefore involve the discontinuance of payments at an earlier stage by a company with bonded indebtedness than by a concern financed solely by owners capital.

Of the 183 companies studied, 151, or 83 per cent, had long term obligations outstanding in the final three years before failure. Of the 151 using long term debt, 105 also had preferred stock outstanding in the same period. Thus a majority of the companies which failed were burdened both by fixed interest-bearing obligations and contingent-dividend obligations.

Reverting now to the 68 companies which paid dividends in the last three years before failure, it is found that 47 of them used long-term borrowed capital. These 47 companies constituted 31 per cent of the 151 companies with long term debt outstanding in the final three years before failure. The remaining 21 companies of the 68 were financed by stockholders capital only (in addition to current obligations), and they constituted 66 per cent of the 32 companies thus financed. A comparison of these percentages seems to show a difference in dividend policies which might reasonably be expected between concerns with and without borrowed capital.

Evidently a considerable number of the companies which subsequently failed pursued in their final years dividend policies which must have accentuated their strained financial condition. Enterprises would probably benefit if before paying dividends they built up more adequate reserves, backed by liquid funds, as a protection against any decline in net profits, and if they were less reluctant to interrupt their record of payments.

SUMMARY

As a whole, the results of this study substantiate the findings of the somewhat similar but less adequate investigation published five years ago as *A Test Analysis of Unsuccessful Industrial Companies*.

Because of the prominence usually attached to current debt-paying ability, this feature was first analyzed. A comparison of Current Ratios, Working Capital to Total Asset ratios, and Cash to Total Assets ratios revealed that, for the 183 companies studied, the ratio of Working Capital to Total Assets was a far more steady and accurate, as well as an earlier, indicator of unfavorable trends in financial health than the Cash to Total Assets or the Current Assets to Current Liabilities ratio. The weakness of the latter ratio is shown by the fact that only in the final year before failure did current assets fail to exceed current debt by the presumably safe margin of 100 per cent, as indicated by a 2 to 1 ratio.

Classification of part of the data among machinery, steel-iron, sugar, and textile companies showed that the Working Capital to Total Assets ratio was more dependable as an indicator of difficulty in three of these industries than the Current Ratio. In the fourth group—namely, textiles—there was less to choose as between these two ratios, although the Working Capital to Total Assets ratio seemed more sensitive.

In the analysis by size of enterprise the data disclosed that even for failing enterprises the usual variations in financial structure normally present between large and small companies were likewise to be found. Here again, however, the forces of unsuccessful operations were most clearly indicated by changes in the Working Capital to Total Assets ratio. Furthermore, the losses of the large enterprises disclosed a more severe decline in working capital than those of small companies. A comparison of current assets and current liabilities at no time revealed a definitely weak condition, nor did the trend of the Current Ratios appear helpful in anticipating difficulties. The Cash to Total Assets ratios were fairly definite in their downward trend and indicated lack of funds immediately available to pay debts.

In connection with the analysis of the distribution of assets in relation to total assets, and the relative claims of liabilities and net worth in the total assets, it was possible to notice also the liquidity of the current assets. In addition to analyzing each current asset in relation to total assets, the quick assets, or cash plus receivables, were compared with current assets. Although each item of the current assets—namely, cash, notes and accounts receivable, and inventories—declined relative to total assets from the tenth to the final year before failure, inventories declined less rapidly than cash and receivables. With the exception of one or two interruptions, the tendency was therefore for the current assets of the 183 companies to become less liquid. Thus both the Current Ratio and the Working Capital to Total Assets ratios were becoming poorer indicators of failure in these later years, since they failed to indicate this progressive liquidation or shrinkage of the better assets.

Among the four industries for which the data were available in sufficient quantity to show trends, the sugar companies showed a pronounced decline in current assets relative to total assets and also a sharp decline in current asset liquidity, as inventory increased from half to two-thirds of current assets in the six years preceding failure. In the machinery and the steel-iron groups current assets did not show a significant shrinkage in relation to total assets.

One of the four industries, textiles, showed a peculiar condition. Current assets dropped from .42 of total assets six years prior to failure to .21 one year before failure. Liquidity of the current assets increased, however, primarily because of the maintenance of a satisfactory cash balance and more rapid reductions in inventories than in other current assets.

As was the case for the preceding classifications of data, current assets of both large and small companies were a declining percentage of total assets as failure approached, the decline of small companies being fairly regular. No pronounced change in liquidity of current assets was noted for small companies as failure approached.

Because of the losses of working capital, which were largely reflected in reduced current assets, total assets also declined. On the other hand, fixed assets declined only slightly, and relative to shrinking total assets they actually increased. This situation manifested itself in most of the classifications of the data. Since other assets were small, fixed assets relative to total assets were usually the obverse of Current Assets to Total Assets ratios.

Current liabilities appeared to be fairly large for all classes of data throughout the period studied. The usual trend was a decline in the early years and increases in the last three or four years preceding failure. This early decline was consonant with the declines in current assets; the later increases in ratios of Current Liabilities to

Total Assets, however, occurred when the liquidity of current assets was impaired, and, in view of further current-asset shrinkage, were decidedly unfavorable omens. Certain groups, such as machinery companies, which had relatively large current assets also had large current obligations. Likewise the smaller companies, with larger Current Assets to Total Assets ratios, also had larger Current Liabilities to Total Assets ratios than the large enterprises.

When current obligations and long term obligations were combined, every classification of data portrayed a steady increase of total debt as claims in total assets. For the 183 companies total debt was .32 of total assets ten years prior to failure and .44 one year before failure. In the final year before failure Total Debt to Total Assets ratios were between .45 and .56 for all groups of data except the small companies, which had a ratio of .37. Trends of net worth were, of course, just the opposite of those of total debt.

Partly because of sharp reductions in sales volume by about half, operating expenses of the 183 companies moved upward, especially in the last five years before failure, so that there were no earnings, but instead a deficit of 4.8 per cent of sales, in the year just preceding failure. Since this was the only year in which the averages showed a deficit from operations, difficulties which caused failures were probably partly due to factors other than sales and operating expenses.

Another aspect of the material reduction in sales volume is its effect on "currentness" of current assets. With a reduced volume of business, there was a general decline in inventory and current-asset turnover. There was thus a gradually lengthening period between the purchase of goods and their sale and collection for them. Thus book values of receivables tended to lag further behind realizable market values as the year of failure approached. In other words, the velocity of current-asset circulation diminished.

Dividend policies also suggested that some of the companies had been short-sighted in their distributions to stockholders; payments were made which contributed to working capital shortages. Of the 183 companies, 118, or 64 per cent, were found to have paid dividends at some time during the ten years studied. Within the last three years preceding failure, dividends were paid by 68, or 58 per cent of the 118 concerns.

These facts seem to indicate the reluctance of directors to interrupt a dividend record. Particularly is this likely to be the case when control is at stake. In this study it was found that partial or sole voting power had passed to preferred stockholders in 36 companies because of the failure to pay dividends.

APPENDIX

TABLE 1
AVERAGE RATIOS (AVERAGES OF MIDDLE HALF) OF 183 COMPANIES FOR TEN YEARS PRIOR TO FAILURE

Average Ratio	Year Before Failure									
	10th	9th	8th	7th	6th	5th	4th	3rd	2nd	1st
Cash (including Marketable Securities) to Total Assets	.046	.045	.047	.043	.045	.044	.039	.032	.028	.018
Receivables to Total Assets	.105	.095	.095	.093	.086	.083	.078	.084	.077	.060
Inventory to Total Assets	.239	.222	.211	.205	.181	.182	.173	.166	.171	.138
Fixed Assets to Total Assets	.593	.616	.622	.637	.661	.665	.680	.689	.695	.757
Other Assets to Total Assets	.017	.022	.025	.022	.027	.026	.030	.029	.029	.027
Current Liabilities to Total Assets	.147	.138	.124	.125	.104	.115	.106	.116	.130	.129
Long Term Debt to Total Assets	.177	.176	.201	.226	.234	.246	.263	.269	.274	.308
Preferred Stock to Total Assets	.234	.232	.216	.217	.219	.216	.217	.207	.216	.261
Common Stock Equity to Total Assets	.442	.454	.459	.432	.443	.423	.414	.408	.380	.302
Current Ratio	2.718	2.782	2.590	2.719	3.134	2.784	2.922	2.473	2.057	1.488
Working Capital Ratio	.225	.206	.212	.203	.196	.184	.169	.157	.129	.062
Current Assets to Total Assets	.430	.389	.373	.358	.329	.330	.306	.298	.293	.220
Inventory to Current Assets	.515	.527	.528	.536	.533	.538	.535	.520	.552	.564
Quick Assets to Current Assets	.485	.473	.472	.464	.467	.462	.465	.480	.448	.436
Long Term Debt to Fixed Assets	.282	.307	.383	.406	.410	.416	.434	.431	.435	.457
Net Worth to Fixed Assets	1.345	1.202	1.169	1.081	1.054	1.019	.974	.922	.879	.752
Net Worth to Total Assets	.715	.683	.668	.641	.664	.642	.635	.612	.591	.552
Sales to Total Assets	.802	.701	.624	.602	.614	.628	.532	.459	.499	.409
Operating Expenses to Sales	.909	.951	.916	.937	.924	.932	.946	.952	.974	1.048
Net Earnings to Total Assets	.063	.034	.063	.039	.041	.038	.033	.024	.011	−.014
Net Income to Net Worth	.051	.029	.061	.033	.034	.035	.014	.001	−.025	−.109

TABLE 2
AVERAGE RATIOS (ARITHMETIC MEANS) OF 16 MACHINERY MANUFACTURING COMPANIES FOR SIX YEARS PRIOR TO FAILURE

Average Ratio	Year Before Failure					
	6th	5th	4th	3rd	2nd	1st
Cash (including Marketable Securities) to Total Assets	.053	.108	.071	.048	.042	.050
Receivables to Total Assets	.161	.185	.213	.190	.172	.185
Inventory to Total Assets	.296	.240	.269	.286	.298	.263
Fixed Assets to Total Assets	.467	.445	.410	.444	.459	.477
Other Assets to Total Assets	.023	.022	.037	.032	.029	.025
Current Liabilities to Total Assets	.166	.157	.201	.202	.214	.277
Long Term Debt to Total Assets	.182	.228	.207	.196	.201	.214
Preferred Stock to Total Assets	.331	.252	.272	.271	.283	.403
Common Stock Equity to Total Assets	.321	.363	.320	.331	.302	.106
Current Ratio	2.403	3.633	2.955	3.152	3.017	2.429
Working Capital Ratio	.330	.349	.314	.289	.260	.158
Current Assets to Total Assets	.513	.535	.555	.538	.513	.498
Inventory to Current Assets	.581	.478	.508	.559	.596	.532
Quick Assets to Current Assets	.419	.522	.492	.441	.404	.468
Long Term Debt to Fixed Assets	.534	.620	.588	.514	.517	.553
Net Worth to Fixed Assets	1.560	1.495	1.577	1.463	1.330	.954
Net Worth to Total Assets	.668	.606	.577	.578	.555	.444

TABLE 3
AVERAGE RATIOS (ARITHMETIC MEANS) OF 14 STEEL-IRON COMPANIES FOR SIX YEARS PRIOR TO FAILURE

Average Ratio	Year Before Failure					
	6th	5th	4th	3rd	2nd	1st
Cash (including Marketable Securities) to Total Assets	.035	.056	.042	.037	.033	.017
Receivables to Total Assets	.077	.079	.056	.101	.082	.072
Inventory to Total Assets	.168	.174	.163	.157	.164	.173
Fixed Assets to Total Assets	.698	.667	.707	.680	.692	.695
Other Assets to Total Assets	.022	.024	.032	.025	.029	.043
Current Liabilities to Total Assets	.157	.134	.103	.102	.118	.112
Long Term Debt to Total Assets	.239	.252	.319	.328	.336	.352
Preferred Stock to Total Assets	.099	.137	.158	.152	.173	.233
Common Stock Equity to Total Assets	.505	.477	.420	.418	.373	.303
Current Ratio	2.240	2.399	3.361	3.658	2.861	2.591
Working Capital Ratio	.107	.164	.152	.184	.148	.134
Current Assets to Total Assets	.281	.309	.264	.293	.275	.259
Inventory to Current Assets	.594	.608	.614	.536	.579	.679
Quick Assets to Current Assets	.406	.392	.386	.464	.421	.321
Long Term Debt to Fixed Assets	.361	.474	.473	.509	.537	.599
Net Worth to Fixed Assets	.926	1.051	.888	.873	.782	.733
Net Worth to Total Assets	.628	.636	.603	.567	.540	.517

TABLE 4
AVERAGE RATIOS (ARITHMETIC MEANS) OF 18 SUGAR COMPANIES FOR SIX YEARS PRIOR TO FAILURE

Average Ratio	Year Before Failure					
	6th	5th	4th	3rd	2nd	1st
Cash (including Marketable Securities) to Total Assets	.039	.022	.013	.014	.011	.010
Receivables to Total Assets	.071	.071	.068	.065	.057	.046
Inventory to Total Assets	.100	.126	.125	.125	.140	.112
Fixed Assets to Total Assets	.748	.750	.759	.764	.764	.802
Other Assets to Total Assets	.042	.031	.035	.032	.028	.030
Current Liabilities to Total Assets	.111	.142	.136	.142	.161	.194
Long Term Debt to Total Assets	.307	.272	.289	.292	.295	.361
Preferred Stock to Total Assets	.168	.160	.162	.167	.167	.173
Common Stock Equity to Total Assets	.414	.426	.413	.399	.377	.272
Current Ratio	7.521	3.372	3.029	3.528	1.978	1.215
Working Capital Ratio	.093	.071	.064	.056	.040	−.033
Current Assets to Total Assets	.211	.219	.205	.204	.208	.167
Inventory to Current Assets	.505	.569	.601	.590	.669	.657
Quick Assets to Current Assets	.495	.431	.399	.410	.331	.343
Long Term Debt to Fixed Assets	.441	.380	.396	.399	.399	.460
Net Worth to Fixed Assets	.776	.765	.738	.726	.697	.542
Net Worth to Total Assets	.576	.570	.558	.550	.527	.428

TABLE 5
AVERAGE RATIOS (ARITHMETIC MEANS) OF 17 TEXTILE COMPANIES FOR SIX YEARS PRIOR TO FAILURE

Average Ratio	Year Before Failure					
	6th	5th	4th	3rd	2nd	1st
Cash (including Marketable Securities) to Total Assets	.054	.067	.041	.038	.045	.042
Receivables to Total Assets	.082	.071	.084	.086	.073	.031
Inventory to Total Assets	.288	.292	.276	.250	.237	.146
Fixed Assets to Total Assets	.560	.550	.580	.607	.621	.764
Other Assets to Total Assets	.016	.020	.019	.019	.024	.017
Current Liabilities to Total Assets	.154	.153	.160	.173	.186	.172
Long Term Debt to Total Assets	.239	.250	.245	.246	.268	.332
Preferred Stock to Total Assets	.168	.180	.178	.185	.215	.346
Common Stock Equity to Total Assets	.439	.417	.417	.396	.331	.150
Current Ratio	3.309	4.025	3.620	2.974	2.456	1.636
Working Capital Ratio	.237	.253	.222	.184	.145	.013
Current Assets to Total Assets	.419	.428	.398	.373	.353	.211
Inventory to Current Assets	.711	.698	.700	.687	.668	.621
Quick Assets to Current Assets	.289	.302	.300	.313	.332	.379
Long Term Debt to Fixed Assets	.503	.526	.482	.458	.486	.499
Net Worth to Fixed Assets	1.178	1.159	1.068	.965	.861	.595
Net Worth to Total Assets	.640	.615	.606	.575	.532	.455

TABLE 6
AVERAGE RATIOS (ARITHMETIC MEANS) OF 52 COMPANIES HAVING ASSETS OF LESS THAN $3,000,000 (IN THIRD YEAR BEFORE FAILURE) FOR TEN YEARS PRIOR TO FAILURE

Average Ratio	Year Before Failure									
	10th	9th	8th	7th	6th	5th	4th	3rd	2nd	1st
Cash (including Marketable Securities) to Total Assets	.096	.056	.047	.056	.071	.064	.058	.052	.047	.029
Receivables to Total Assets	.164	.165	.152	.181	.153	.139	.131	.138	.129	.129
Inventory to Total Assets	.350	.316	.299	.294	.269	.257	.240	.225	.224	.208
Fixed Assets to Total Assets	.368	.437	.461	.437	.465	.499	.533	.546	.558	.608
Other Assets to Total Assets	.022	.026	.041	.032	.042	.041	.038	.039	.042	.026
Current Liabilities to Total Assets	.173	.194	.177	.208	.152	.170	.164	.166	.185	.167
Long Term Debt to Total Assets	.177	.156	.179	.161	.167	.190	.229	.231	.220	.206
Preferred Stock to Total Assets	.261	.273	.238	.251	.247	.250	.236	.232	.250	.313
Common Stock Equity to Total Assets	.389	.377	.406	.380	.434	.390	.371	.371	.345	.314
Current Ratio	7.098	3.214	3.919	4.348	3.896	2.955	3.259	8.981	2.731	3.310
Working Capital Ratio	.370	.264	.276	.269	.299	.248	.235	.206	.172	.126
Current Assets to Total Assets	.591	.512	.494	.517	.488	.450	.426	.405	.396	.344
Inventory to Current Assets	.581	.554	.555	.560	.556	.560	.519	.537	.536	.542
Quick Assets to Current Assets	.419	.446	.445	.440	.444	.440	.481	.463	.464	.458
Long Term Debt to Fixed Assets	.525	.403	.448	.376	.437	.461	.613	.552	.479	.402
Net Worth to Fixed Assets	2.218	1.996	1.843	1.808	2.292	1.577	1.473	1.386	1.304	1.107
Net Worth to Total Assets	.717	.681	.671	.650	.692	.660	.626	.606	.588	.616
Sales to Total Assets	2.232	2.302	3.355	2.944	2.321	1.776	1.523	1.308	1.351	1.139
Operating Expenses to Sales	1.057	.957	.953	.978	.946	.898	.917	.934	.947	1.008
Net Earnings to Total Assets	.222	.090	.157	.073	.085	.059	.049	.008	.000	−.072

TABLE 7
AVERAGE RATIOS (ARITHMETIC MEANS) OF 35 COMPANIES HAVING ASSETS OF $20,000,000 OR MORE (IN THIRD YEAR BEFORE FAILURE) FOR TEN YEARS PRIOR TO FAILURE

Average Ratio	Year Before Failure									
	10th	9th	8th	7th	6th	5th	4th	3rd	2nd	1st
Cash (including Marketable Securities) to Total Assets	.048	.038	.056	.043	.047	.056	.043	.034	.028	.020
Receivables to Total Assets	.127	.127	.114	.104	.102	.094	.087	.093	.073	.063
Inventory to Total Assets	.144	.132	.135	.129	.117	.131	.123	.126	.118	.120
Fixed Assets to Total Assets	.660	.681	.668	.696	.702	.691	.719	.719	.742	.754
Other Assets to Total Assets	.021	.022	.027	.028	.032	.028	.028	.028	.039	.043
Current Liabilities to Total Assets	.139	.146	.116	.096	.089	.091	.081	.095	.093	.114
Long Term Debt to Total Assets	.188	.193	.244	.281	.280	.281	.308	.314	.326	.336
Preferred Stock to Total Assets	.197	.188	.193	.200	.195	.189	.182	.190	.200	.259
Common Stock Equity to Total Assets	.476	.473	.447	.423	.436	.439	.429	.401	.381	.291
Current Ratio	3.584	3.244	3.376	4.706	6.566	4.189	7.335	3.942	3.345	2.927
Working Capital Ratio	.161	.132	.177	.168	.168	.182	.164	.148	.115	.071
Current Assets to Total Assets	.312	.288	.301	.272	.264	.278	.250	.250	.215	.193
Inventory to Current Assets	.430	.426	.421	.459	.452	.486	.484	.477	.510	.582
Quick Assets to Current Assets	.570	.574	.579	.541	.548	.514	.516	.523	.490	.418
Long Term Debt to Fixed Assets	.287	.290	.404	.453	.486	.486	.471	.515	.477	.487
Net Worth to Fixed Assets	1.175	1.088	1.070	1.002	.980	1.042	.916	.942	.783	.736
Net Worth to Total Assets	.681	.657	.626	.603	.614	.616	.603	.589	.571	.541
Sales to Total Assets	1.176	.517	.570	.532	.520	.547	.501	.351	.361	.216
Operating Expenses to Sales	.989	.947	.874	.933	.921	.934	.941	.970	.941	1.065
Net Earnings to Total Assets	.038	.042	.065	.042	.038	.041	.040	.022	.012	—.007

A COMPARISON OF THE RATIOS OF SUCCESSFUL INDUSTRIAL ENTERPRISES WITH THOSE OF FAILED COMPANIES

Paul J. Fitzpatrick

A Comparison of the Ratios of Successful Industrial Enterprises With Those of Failed Companies

By Paul J. FitzPatrick, Ph.D., Washington, D. C.

Introduction

THE purpose of this article is to compare the ratios of nineteen representative, successful industrial enterprises in various industries with the ratios of nineteen representative, industrial failures in the corresponding industries and for the same period. In this way, one will be able to tell whether or not the ratios of successful companies were satisfactory when the ratios of failed concerns were unfavorable. Furthermore, one will be able to tell whether the majority of the ratios of successful companies were favorable or unfavorable, and to what extent. As it is, the literature relative to comparison of successful industrial enterprises with unsuccessful companies is, indeed, meager.

In a recent investigation,† the author had analyzed the published financial statements of twenty representative industrial enterprises, in sixteen lines of business, which failed during the period of 1920-1929, for the purpose of ascertaining the condition of several well-known and widely used accounting ratios during the years immediately preceding failure. Since then, he has analyzed the published financial statements of nineteen representative, successful industrial enterprises which are in the corresponding industries and for the same period as the unsuccessful companies. In one case, a successful concern could not be found to compare with the failed one. The three competitors had encountered financial difficulties as a result of conditions existing in that particular industry.

At this stage, it is desirable to state the requirements governing the selection of a successful company in each industry to compare with the failed one. They are as follows:

a. The successful company must be financially sound.

†Symptoms of Industrial Failures.

b. It should have about the same amount of assets.

c. It should have about the same volume of sales.

d. It should handle the same product or line of products.

e. It should operate in the same section of the country.

f. The financial statements are of, or approximately, the same dates as those of the failed companies.

The foregoing requirements are some of the conditions that analysts advocate in the construction of standard ratios. In five cases, it was necessary to depart from one or two of the foregoing requirements, as will be pointed out in the interpretation of the tables. The reason for setting up these requirements was to make the selection of the successful company objective and not subjective. In other words, the successful companies were not "handpicked." The twenty failed industrials were selected at random.

One objection, perhaps, which might be raised concerning an investigation of this kind, is the lack of uniformity of financial statements and the lack of standardization of accounting terminology. This is valid, to a certain extent, in the case of industrial concerns. It may be pointed out, however, that the forty companies in this investigation are nationally known so that this objection may not be as serious as would be the case if they were local in character or engaged in a smaller scale of operations. Besides, nearly all the companies were listed on the New York Stock Exchange. Finally, the published statements, after an analysis of the items therein were reduced to a standard form before the computation of the ratios. The principle sources of the data were the Moody and the Poor Industrial Manuals.

How to Interpret Ratios

In general, we may say that there are two methods or views concerning the interpretation of accounting ratios. First, what is the position or value of the ratio and is it above the customary and minimum "standard"? And secondly, what is the trend or tendency of the ratio?

There are, in the first place, several customary and minimum "standards."

For the current ratio, which is the relationship between the current assets and the current liabilities, it is 200 per cent or 2 to 1. This margin of safety is a precaution based on the practical knowledge that the assets of a business are subject to possible shrinkage or loss, while the liabilities are not. Like taxes, liabilities always come due for payment. Moreover, ample working capital is essential to the profitable development and the permanency of an enterprise. By working capital, is meant the excess or margin of the current assets over the current liabilities. If the current liabilities are larger than the current assets, the difference is called floating debt. Working capital itself does not appear on the balance sheet. The current ratio, then, measures the working capital position of a business and indicates the amount of current assets available for the payment of current obligations in the ordinary course of operations. Therefore working capital is the lifeblood of an enterprise. The lack of working capital may seriously hinder business operations — as a condition of anemia exists which, if not corrected, may lead to pernicious anemia with its serious consequences.

It should, furthermore, be kept in mind that this 200 per cent standard varies from one industry to another; and it also varies for each individual company. Thus in one instance, a current ratio of 200 per cent may suffice; in another, a ratio of 250 per cent or more may be needed to keep an enterprise solvent, depending upon the size and the character of the business, the regularity or the seasonal nature of the business, the period of the business cycle, and other factors.

As for the quick ratio, sometimes termed the "acid-test" ratio, it should be 100 per cent. Quick assets are current assets minus inventories. This ratio states more definitely and directly the debt-paying capacity of the concern. The value of this ratio may be seen when we consider that inventories cannot be used to pay bills. Inventories must be sold before a company may be able to obtain cash or rights to cash. Thus this ratio measures the ability of an enterprise to discharge quickly its obligations, especially in time of need. This ratio, moreover, is becoming of increasing importance because of the weakness of the current ratio, since the latter ratio is generally quantitative rather than qualitative; it treats all the current assets alike and assumes that all are of the same liquid condition.

The net worth to all liabilities or debt ratio measures to what extent an enterprise is operating on its own capital and to what extent it is relying on outside assistance. The real import of this ratio may be definitely and fully realized when we consider that liabilities, both short-term and long-term, represent funds temporarily loaned by creditors while, on the other hand, net worth represent funds permanently invested in the business by stockholders or owners. It is a credit maxim that owners of an industrial enterprise should have, at least, an equal investment with creditors. In other words, this relationship should be, at least, 100 per cent or 1 to 1. Therefore, 100 per cent may be taken as a minimum standard. The higher the percentage is, the better.

Furthermore, when this important ratio is declining it is an indication that a concern is increasing its borrowings or decreasing its net worth investment — in either case, this is an unfavorable sign.

The net worth to fixed assets ratio measures to what extent the stockholders' investments are being used to provide the funds to finance all the fixed assets and a part of the current assets. It is a financial axiom that fixed assets should be financed by stockholders and not by short-term creditors. This fact, indeed, is recognized in the Federal Reserve Act which specifically states that commercial paper is only rediscountable when the proceeds from its issue have been used for commercial purposes and not for plant investment. Therefore, this ratio should be above 100 per cent. As an example, let us say that it should be 120 per cent; 100 per cent for the fixed assets and 20 per cent for the current assets. In other words, the margin above 100 per cent is the amount of funds that the stockholders have provided for use in the business as current assets.

When the net profits to net worth ratio is

reporting a loss, this obviously indicates an unsatisfactory condition. Furthermore, an enterprise should normally earn, at least, from six to ten per cent on its net worth investment. Concerns with greater risks should earn fifteen to twenty or more per cent.

The current assets to total assets ratio should be, at least, 40 per cent for industrial enterprises. Current assets are the circulating capital of a business. It is the principal means of earning profits. Cash is spent by a manufacturing concern to procure raw materials; raw materials are transformed or fabricated into finished products ready for sale; finished goods are sold and accounts receivable are created or cash is received; accounts receivable are collected and cash takes its place; cash is then spent for more raw materials and the cycle begins again. Consequently, it can be seen why ample working or circulating capital is so essential to the profitable development of an industrial enterprise. Moreover, the real significance may be appreciated when we consider that fixed assets are very difficult assets to sell to another concern. They are not liquid. Further, they are subject to depreciation and obsolescence.

The second method of interpretation of ratios is by means of their trends or tendencies. One group of ratios is presented in such a way that a downward tendency is interpreted by credit and financial analysts as an unfavorable condition. This is because factors or conditions underlying the ratio are becoming unsatisfactory. The trend, then, becomes the subject for further investigation and analysis. On the other hand, an upward tendency is obviously an improvement. A continued upward trend, which is generally to be desired, is a favorable sign. Ratios belonging to this group are: the current assets to current liabilities; the quick assets to current liabilities; the sales to fixed assets; the sales to inventories; the sales to receivables; the sales to net worth; the net worth to debt; the net worth to fixed assets; the net profits to net worth; and the current assets to total assets.

Of course, the foregoing ratios may be inverted although it is not customary. As an example, the current assets to current liabilities ratio may be inverted by stating it as the ratio of current liabilities to current assets. In that case, then, a downward trend is a favorable indication and an upward trend is an unfavorable sign.

The other group of ratios is presented in such a way that an upward swing is unfavorable while a downward tendency is a satisfactory indication. Some of the ratios belonging to this group are: the operating ratio; the inventories to receivables; the fixed assets to total assets; and the other assets to total assets.

Finally, it should be pointed out that there are times when the trend of the ratios is far more important and significant than the actual position indicated at a particular date. The following illustration is suggestive:

Ratio	1925	1926	1927	1928
The current ratio	400%	350%	310%	220%
The net worth to debt ratio	175%	160%	135%	115%

While both ratios are above the conventional standards, nevertheless, the trend is unfavorable and this is, indeed, an important indication. In such a case, the credit man should make a further investigation to ascertain what unfavorable factors are developing.

TABLE No. 1

\	Failed Concern	\	\	\	Successful Concern	\	\
Oct. 31	Oct. 29	Sept. 8		Type of Ratios	Oct. 30	Oct. 29	Oct. 27
1926	1927	1928			1926	1927	1928
203	734	875	1.	Current assets to current liabilities	386	426	503
103	302	252	2.	Quick assets to current liabilities	202	221	254
Not	Available		3.	Sales to fixed assets	936	906	1041
Not	Available		4.	Sales to inventories	1457	1500	1496
Not	Available		5.	Sales to receivables	2429	2432	2440
Not	Available		6.	Sales to net worth	768	746	763
111	114	112	7.	Net worth to debt	102	107	121
113	111	109	8.	Net worth to fixed assets	124	121	137
134	213	290	9.	Inventories to receivables	167	163	163
—01.0	—13.0	*	10.	Net profits to net worth	11.2	02.1	12.5
34.8	26.6	23.5	11.	Current assets to total assets	55.7	53.5	56.2
46.6	47.7	48.5	12.	Fixed assets to total assets	40.5	42.5	40.0
18.5	23.6	23.9	13.	Other assets to total assets	03.7	04.0	03.7

*Not available.

INTERPRETATION OF TABLE NO. 1
The two companies are in the meat-packing industry

Both concerns show their current ratio and quick ratio to be favorable for each year. But in the failed concern's case, this favorable condition is only apparent and not real because the balance sheets disclosed that about $900,-000 of acceptances had been sold and guaranteed as of October 29, 1927, and $1,400,000 a year later.

The several sales ratios of the successful company are satisfactory. Sales data for the failed concern are unfortunately not available.

The net worth to debt ratio of the failed company is somewhat low, being 112 per cent. It indicates that the stockholders are only supplying $12 of capital more per $100 than the creditors. Besides, this ratio has been practically constant for three years. The successful concern's ratio of net worth to debt has improved and is satisfactory.

The net worth to fixed assets ratio for the failed company is declining and is not satisfactory. It suggests that plant capacity is not fully utilized. Furthermore, th s figure of 109 per cent shows that there are only $109 of net worth for every $100 of fixed assets, or $9 margin of its own capital to be employed as current assets for every $100 of fixed assets—a small margin. The successful concern's ratio is good.

The inventories to receivables ratio for the failed concern is poor because it reveals a decided trend toward over-investment in inventories. The successful company's ratio is satisfactory.

The net profits to net worth ratio shows that the failed company is losing money while the successful concern is earning profits.

The current assets to total assets ratio suggests very clearly the urgent need of more working capital on the part of the failed concern. Too much capital is tied up in fixed assets and other assets. The successful company has a favorable ratio condition.

In conclusion, it can be seen that the ratios for the failed concern pointed out the approaching financial difficulties. The ratios of the successful company were generally very good.

TABLE No. 2

December 31 — FAILED CONCERN				December 31 — SUCCESSFUL CONCERN		
1919	1920	1921	TYPE OF RATIOS	1919	1920	1921
349	211	119	1. Current assets to current liabilities	509	629	475
111	70	50	2. Quick assets to current liabilities	282	312	267
Not	Available		3. Sales to fixed assets	492	322	*
Not	Available		4. Sales to inventories	472	458	*
Not	Available		5. Sales to receivables	896	1165	*
Not	Available		6. Sales to net worth	120	111	*
200	188	151	7. Net worth to debt	800	1197	966
345	244	209	8. Net worth to fixed assets	410	298	248
222	271	689	9. Inventories to receivables	190	255	329
12.5	05.0	—09.0	10. Net profits to net worth	*	18.5	19.3
39.0	35.0	20.7	11. Current assets to total assets	51.9	44.2	41.5
19.3	27.1	28.7	12. Fixed assets to total assets	21.7	31.7	36.5
41.7	37.8	50.5	13. Other assets to total assets	26.4	24.0	21.9

*Not available.

INTERPRETATION OF TABLE NO. 2
The companies are engaged in the manufacture and sale of confections

The conspicuous feature of this table is the strong and favorable condition of the ratios of the successful concern, whether compared with the unsuccessful company or not.

The unsuccessful company has a poor current ratio the last year and a poor quick ratio for the past two years. Besides, these ratios are revealing a strong downward tendency — another bad sign. This unfavorable condition is due partly to over-investment in inventories with the attendant inventory losses of approximately $5,000,000 and partly to over-expansion in plants. Thus this concern needs more working capital.

The inventories to receivables ratio strongly suggests over-investment in the last year. The trend of the ratio of net worth to fixed assets and the ratio of fixed assets to total assets indicate over-investment in plants.

At this place, it may be pointed out that the successful company also has a tendency to over-investment in inventories—attributed to the suddenness of the business depression of 1920-1921. Moreover, there is a tendency toward over-investment in fixed assets as the net worth to fixed assets and the fixed assets to total assets ratios reveal. These tendencies, however, are not serious enough to embarrass the successful company.

The net worth to debt ratio is declining for the failed concern. It drops to 151 per cent. The successful company's ratio, on the other hand, is 966 per cent. The balance sheets reveal that the former concern has a funded debt of $4,000,000 while the latter company has only $200,000.

As to the ability to earn profits, the depression did not affect the successful company, but it did affect the failed concern as the ratio of net profits to net worth shows.

The ratio of fixed assets to total assets and the other assets to total assets ratio reveal that the failed concern had an average of 68 per cent of its assets tied up in fixed and other assets for the three years. The successful company had an average of 54 per cent.

Sales data for the unsuccessful company are unavailable and so the four sales ratios cannot be computed.

TABLE No. 3

June 30	May 29	July 1		December 31		
Failed Concern				Successful Concern		
1921	1922	1923	Type of Ratios	1921	1922	1923
99	85	76	1. Current assets to current liabilities	299	493	477
36	42	38	2. Quick assets to current liabilities	166	261	256
Not	Available		3. Sales to fixed assets	Not	Available	
Not	Available		4. Sales to inventories	Not	Available	
Not	Available		5. Sales to receivables	Not	Available	
Not	Available		6. Sales to net worth	Not	Available	
64	56	57	7. Net worth to debt	523	919	853
55	47	50	8. Net worth to fixed assets	161	177	181
441	257	265	9. Inventories to receivables	237	258	292
Not	Available		10. Net profits to net worth	07.9	13.4	12.3
26.0	23.8	20.8	11. Current assets to total assets	48.0	48.4	50.0
70.9	75.1	72.2	12. Fixed assets to total assets	51.9	50.9	49.4
03.0	00.9	06.9	13. Other assets to total assets	00.0	00.6	00.5

Interpretation of Table No. 3
Both concerns are engaged in the manufacture and sale of cereals and related products

At the outset, it should be mentioned that the successful company has assets of $43,000,000 while the failed company has $7,000,000. No other competitor could be procured for comparison.

This table, like the previous one, reveals the strong and favorable position of the successful company, whether compared with the failed company or not. Moreover, the failed concern's weaknesses are emphasized.

The failed company's current ratio and its quick ratio are decidedly poor every year, being below the customary and minimum standard of 200 per cent and 100 per cent, respectively. Thus the working capital condition is very anemic.

The net worth to debt ratio is also very poor. Not in any year is it a 50-50 proposition, as creditors are supplying more capital than the owners—an unwholesome sign. This condition of under-capitalization is a serious one and there is the urgent need of additional capital to be supplied by the stockholders. Furthermore, this ratio means that there are only $56 to $64 of net worth to every $100 of debt. In other words, there are $56 to $64 of capital contributed by the stockholders to every $100 of capital advanced by the creditors—an unwise financial policy. The balance sheets, moreover, show that the failed company has a funded debt of $2,500,000 while the successful concern has none.

The ratio of net worth to fixed assets is also very poor and suggests that plant capacity is not being properly utilized. It further points out that the owners are not supplying any working capital and only a part of the fixed capital.

The inventories to receivables ratio is becoming satisfactory.

No exact data are available as to how much the failed company has been losing the past two years. The balance sheet reports a deficit of approximately $125,000 the last year. How,

then, can this company pay its bond interest?

The ratio of fixed assets to total assets, just as the net worth to fixed assets ratio indicated, shows too much capital tied up in fixed assets. The low condition, moreover, of the current assets to total assets ratio points out the urgent need of more working capital.

TABLE No. 4

Dec. 31	Mar. 31	Mar. 31		December 31		
†Failed Concern				Successful Concern		
1926	1928	1929	Type of Ratios	1926	1927	1928
306	203	277	1. Current assets to current liabilities	887	793	1039
148	91	125	2. Quick assets to current liabilities	614	544	725
301	290	243	3. Sales to fixed assets	842	761	696
238	287	321	4. Sales to inventories	385	326	311
309	483	521	5. Sales to receivables	174	153	140
82	103	88	6. Sales to net worth	140	123	108
458	296	525	7. Net worth to debt	288	282	326
390	287	285	8. Net worth to fixed assets	603	621	642
130	168	162	9. Inventories to receivables	45	46	45
12.0	03.5	—01.7	10. Net profits to net worth	08.0	05.1	03.6
54.8	48.4	41.9	11. Current assets to total assets	87.7	88.1	88.1
21.1	26.0	29.4	12. Fixed assets to total assets	12.3	11.8	11.9
24.0	25.5	28.6	13. Other assets to total assets	None	None	None

†No statement published December 31, 1927 and 1928.

Interpretation of Table No. 4
The two companies are engaged in the manufacture and sale of pianos

This table reveals that the successful company, in most instances, makes a far better showing than the failed concern.

For the last year, the failed company's current ratio and its quick ratio are satisfactory, although they were somewhat poor the previous year.

The declining tendency of the sales to fixed assets ratio and the ratio of net worth to fixed assets indicates over-investment in fixed assets. The fixed assets to total assets ratio confirms this fact. The sales to fixed assets means that the failed company is only obtaining $2.43 of sales to each dollar invested in fixed assets while the successful concern shows $6.96 of sales to each dollar invested in fixed assets.

The sales to receivables ratio is high and increasing for the failed concern. This condition is satisfactory if the company is not hypothecating its receivables or maintaining too strict a credit policy.

Furthermore, there is the important fact that sales have dropped from the high mark of $14,300,000 in 1924 to $11,400,000 for the year ending March 31, 1929, as the financial statements reveal.

The net worth to debt ratio is very good for both companies, although the failed concern's ratio is higher. Incidentally, this is one of the few unsuccessful companies, in this investigation, reporting a favorable position.

The ratio of net profits to net worth indicates that the successful company is more profitable in its operations; also that the failed concern lost money the last year, and that its profits were smaller in 1928 than for the previous period.

All in all, we may conclude that the failed company was revealing some weaknesses, as reflected by its ratios. Further, when compared with the successful concern the ratios of the failed company do not look so good.

Interpretation of Table No. 5
Both companies are engaged in the manufacture and sale of writing paper

The successful company does not publish any data for 1920. Neither is it possible to procure sales and profits data for each year. Nor is it possible to procure statements of another successful competitor to compare with the failed concern. Further, the assets of the successful company are $9,000,000 while the failed concern has about $22,000,000, if the item of goodwill is excluded. Consequently, the two companies will not be as comparable as one would desire. Nevertheless, the comparison will be helpful and interesting.

TABLE No. 5

\<-- December 31 --\> FAILED CONCERN			TYPE OF RATIOS	\<-- December 31 --\> SUCCESSFUL CONCERN		
1920	1921	1922		1920	1921	1922
266	468	267	1. Current assets to current liabilities	*	286	708
115	197	101	2. Quick assets to current liabilities	*	144	380
220	83	100	3. Sales to fixed assets	Not	Avai	lable
491	317	323	4. Sales to inventories	Not	Avai	lable
1417	852	902	5. Sales to receivables	Not	Avai	lable
112	44	54	6. Sales to net worth	Not	Avai	lable
192	231	208	7. Net worth to debt	*	264	523
195	187	186	8. Net worth to fixed assets	*	133	178
288	268	286	9. Inventories to receivables	*	229	177
05.8	—06.4	—02.0	10. Net profits to net worth	Not	Avai	lable
26.4	17.0	18.2	11. Current assets to total assets	*	44.1	39.9
33.6	37.4	36.3	12. Fixed assets to total assets	*	54.5	41.6
40.0	45.6	45.5	13. Other assets to total assets	*	01.3	18.5

*Not available.

An inspection of the ratios of the successful company reveals that they are satisfactory. But a number of the failed concern's ratios are unfavorable.

The failed concern's current ratio is satisfactory the last year, but its quick ratio is barely favorable, being 101 per cent.

The four sales ratios point out that in 1921 and 1922, they have not recovered lost ground in spite of the upward swing of the ratios and business conditions. The best showing was in 1920—the time when the depression began.

The low position of the sales to fixed assets ratio and the trend of the fixed assets to total assets ratio indicate some over-investment in plants. During reorganization "ten mills were set aside for sale, and of these six have been sold."

The net worth to debt ratio is satisfactory, being 208 per cent. The net worth to fixed assets ratio is also favorable, although there is a slight trend downward.

The inventories to receivables ratio of the failed concern is higher than the successful company's ratio and suggests some over-investment in inventories.

The net profits to net worth ratio reveals that the failed concern has been losing money the past two years. While no definite data are available, an examination revealed that the successful company was earning profits these years.

The current assets to total assets ratio is too low, being only 18 per cent. The successful company's ratio is 40 per cent. Moreover, the high figure of the ratio of other assets to total assets of the failed concern reflects the overdose of goodwill, amounting to $18,000,000.

TABLE No. 6

\<-- December 31 --\> FAILED CONCERN			TYPE OF RATIOS	\<-- December 31 --\> SUCCESSFUL CONCERN		
1920	1921	1922		1920	1921	1922
59	26	21	1. Current assets to current liabilities	146	139	158
40	11	12	2. Quick assets to current liabilities	136	133	147
Not	Avai	lable	3. Sales to fixed assets	Not	Avai	lable
Not	Avai	lable	4. Sales to inventories	Not	Avai	lable
Not	Avai	lable	5. Sales to receivables	Not	Avai	lable
Not	Avai	lable	6. Sales to net worth	Not	Avai	lable
100	52	40	7. Net worth to debt	441	729	665
60	38	32	8. Net worth to fixed assets	115	110	114
62	205	171	9. Inventories to receivables	41	23	63
06.4	—10.5	—15.7	10. Net profits to net worth	35.8	15.5	16.0
11.4	07.4	07.0	11. Current assets to total assets	26.9	16.8	20.7
86.7	89.2	89.0	12. Fixed assets to total assets	70.8	80.0	76.2
01.8	03.2	04.0	13. Other assets to total assets	02.2	03.2	03.1

INTERPRETATION OF TABLE No. 6

The companies are engaged in the production and sale of cane sugar and bananas

The failed concern has assets of $41,000,000, while the successful company's assets are $170,000,000. The successful company is much larger than the failed concern. But there is no other concern in the industry to compare with the failed concern. Consequently, it is the only comparison that may be made.

The current ratio of both companies is below the conventional two-to-one rule, although the successful company reports a better showing with a three-year average of about 148 per cent—a good showing for this type of industry. The three-year average, however, of the failed concern is only 35 per cent—a very low figure.

The failed concern's quick ratio averages only 21 per cent for the three-year period—too low a figure. The successful company's ratio, on the other hand, is never below 133 per cent and thus is very good.

The net worth to debt ratio of the failed concern is exceedingly poor. In the last year, there are only $40 of net worth to every $100 of capital supplied by creditors. Thus the business is relying too much on borrowed capital. There is, then, the urgent need of additional capital to be furnished by the owners. Furthermore, the balance sheets show that the failed company has a funded debt of $16,000,000, while the successful concern has none. The successful concern's ratio is excellent, being 665 per cent.

The low condition of the net worth to fixed assets ratio of the failed company clearly indicates that creditors are supplying working capital and a part of fixed capital. There is, indeed, too much investment in fixed assets. In fact, the fixed assets investment increased almost 100 per cent during the past three years.

The inventories to receivables ratio suggests some over-investment. It partly explains the low condition of the failed concern's quick ratio.

The net profits to net worth ratio shows that the successful company is earning profits each year. The failed concern, however, has suffered heavy losses the past two years. This in turn suggests the difficulty of meeting the interest charges on its funded debt of $16,000,000. The income accounts report that heavy fixed charges are more than $1,100,000 per annum the past two years. A striking contrast to $233,000 in 1919.

The low ratio of current assets to total assets and the high ratio of fixed assets to total assets point out the over-expansion in fixed assets at the expense of the current assets.

In conclusion, there can be no doubt that the foregoing ratios very definitely and clearly emphasized the weaknesses of the failed concern. The successful company's ratios, with one exception, were very good.

TABLE No. 7

November 30 FAILED CONCERN			TYPE OF RATIOS	December 31 SUCCESSFUL CONCERN		
1921	1922	1923		1921	1922	1923
215	156	194	1. Current assets to current liabilities	323	325	346
56	46	67	2. Quick assets to current liabilities	107	126	145
Not	Available		3. Sales to fixed assets	Not	Available	
Not	Available		4. Sales to inventories	Not	Available	
Not	Available		5. Sales to receivables	Not	Available	
Not	Available		6. Sales to net worth	Not	Available	
102	80	52	7. Net worth to debt	445	445	479
113	91	66	8. Net worth to fixed assets	222	225	230
335	274	240	9. Inventories to receivables	218	172	155
—21.4	—18.0	—30.5	10. Net profits to net worth	03.4	02.4	03.6
52.5	47.3	44.6	11. Current assets to total assets	59.3	59.8	59.8
44.5	49.0	51.2	12. Fixed assets to total assets	36.7	36.2	35.9
03.0	03.7	04.0	13. Other assets to total assets	03.9	04.0	04.2

INTERPRETATION OF TABLE No. 7

The two concerns are agricultural implement manufacturers

This is another example where the successful company makes a very good showing, as reflected by its ratios, while the failed company is in poor shape.

The failed concern has a current ratio of 194 per cent the last year and 156 per cent the previous year. The current ratio is "window-dressed" to show 200 per cent or more in 1921 and 1923 by increases in the long-term liabilities. This in turn weakens the net worth to debt ratio which falls to the low figure of 52 per cent. Moreover, the quick ratio is poor for three years, ranging from 46 to 67 per cent.

The net worth to debt ratio of 52 per cent the last year indicates that creditors are supplying $100 of capital when the owners are supplying $52. Only in one year is this ratio a 50-50 proposition, that is, the owners are furnishing as much capital as the creditors. This is a fact of considerable import. It is, indeed, an unwise financial policy when the funds advanced by creditors to an industrial enterprise exceed the capital contributed by stockholders. In this case, furthermore, the balance sheets reveal that the failed concern has a funded debt of approximately $4,000,000 while the successful company has none. These borrowings have created heavy interest charges which in turn eat up the profits.

The net worth to fixed assets ratio suggests very definitely over-investment in fixed assets, being only 66 per cent. This is confirmed by the trend of the fixed assets to total assets ratio. Further, it indicates that the stockholders are supplying no working capital and only a part of the funds for the fixed assets. This is an unwise policy in more ways than one.

The inventories to receivables ratio is becoming satisfactory.

The net profits to net worth ratio reports heavy losses for each year. This in turn points out the difficulty of meeting bond interest payments.

There is no doubt, therefore, that the ratios correctly reported the poor condition of the failed concern. It was clearly emphasized by the condition of the ratios. Moreover, the downward tendency of several ratios was another good indication.

Finally, it should be mentioned that the successful company has assets of $34,000,000 and the failed concern has $10,000,000. No other competitor could be procured for comparison.

INTERPRETATION OF TABLE NO. 8
Both concerns are engaged in the manufacture of rubber footwear

The financial difficulties of the unsuccessful concern were not serious and so its affairs were handled by a creditors' committee. Such a voluntary readjustment saves the cost of a receivership. The formation of a creditors' committee for the purpose of dealing with embarrassed businesses of considerable size, was somewhat general during the period of the depression of 1920-1921. As Dewing points out: ". . . The creditors' committee, formed for the purpose of carrying and eventually liquidating the costly inventories, was the bankers' well nigh universal response. Had they not made this response, business mortality in the autumn and winter of 1920 would have been simply stupendous . . ."*

At the outset, it is important to point out the sudden and unfavorable downward tendencies of the ratios of the failed concern in the last year. This in itself should be sufficient warning to put the credit man and the banker on their guard. It is, furthermore, a good reason why analysts must observe not only the position or value of the ratios, but also their trends. The successful company, on the other hand, does not reveal a similar condition. While it is true that some of its ratios show a slight downward tendency, nevertheless a number of its ratios are somewhat steady and consistent.

Until the last year, both the current ratio and the quick ratio of the unsuccessful company were favorable. Likewise, the net worth to debt ratio and the net worth to fixed assets ratio were satisfactory. But the sharp drop in the last year is a warning signal. The current ratio is dropping from 287 to 120 per cent; the quick ratio from 196 to 71 per cent; and

*A. S. Dewing. Financial Policy of Corporations. Revised edition, p. 1139.

TABLE No. 8

February 28 FAILED CONCERN			TYPE OF RATIOS	March 31 SUCCESSFUL CONCERN		
1919	1920	1921		1919	1920	1921
259	287	120	1. Current assets to current liabilities	201	223	186
160	196	71	2. Quick assets to current liabilities	80	132	92
Not	Available		3. Sales to fixed assets	Not	Available	
Not	Available		4. Sales to inventories	Not	Available	
Not	Available		5. Sales to receivables	Not	Available	
Not	Available		6. Sales to net worth	Not	Available	
396	369	88	7. Net worth to debt	134	84	75
173	210	138	8. Net worth to fixed assets	288	260	220
79	60	99	9. Inventories to receivables	219	95	141
Not	Available		10. Net profits to net worth	Not	Available	
52.3	61.2	63.7	11. Current assets to total assets	70.4	72.0	71.5
46.1	37.3	34.1	12. Fixed assets to total assets	20.0	17.5	19.5
01.6	01.4	02.2	13. Other assets to total assets	09.7	10.5	08.9

the net worth to debt ratio from 369 to 88 per cent.

Sales and profits data are not available for either concern. This is unfortunate because it would be interesting and worthwhile to observe whether the four sales ratios and the net profits to net worth ratio were likewise developing unfavorable tendencies. Besides, it would help to determine the effectiveness of ratios as indicators in this particular case.

The sharp drop of the net worth to debt ratio of the failed company is due to heavy short-term borrowings amounting to $4,000,000. There is no funded debt. The net worth to fixed assets ratio reveals an unfavorable trend. The inventories to receivables ratio is not bad. The fixed assets to total assets ratio, while improving, is not as good as the successful concern's ratio.

For the successful company, we note that the current ratio and the quick ratio are slightly below the 200 per cent and the 100 per cent standards, respectively, in the last year. They are, however, better than the unsuccessful concern's ratios.

The net worth to debt ratio is really the only bad indication. It is below the 100 per cent standard the past two years because of an issue of funded debt in 1920 amounting to one million dollars. The net worth to fixed assets ratio is very good.

The current assets to total assets and the fixed assets to total assets ratios are also very good.

In conclusion, it can be seen again that the successful company reports the better condition, in spite of the low net worth to debt ratio. The unsuccessful concern's ratios reported some sharp and unfavorable tendencies—too pronounced to pass by unnoticed by the credit man and the banker.

TABLE No. 9

December 31 FAILED CONCERN			TYPE OF RATIOS	December 31 SUCCESSFUL CONCERN		
1920	1921	1922		1920	1921	1922
213	138	84	1. Current assets to current liabilities	316	414	423
71	54	41	2. Quick assets to current liabilities .	139	226	306
476	211	159	3. Sales to fixed assets	390	368	261
200	139	197	4. Sales to inventories	322	392	514
758	333	288	5. Sales to receivables	620	632	663
195	184	1320	6. Sales to net worth	153	141	107
105	46	04	7. Net worth to debt	369	514	561
243	114	12	8. Net worth to fixed assets	253	261	243
379	240	146	9. Inventories to receivables	192	161	129
12.4	—19.6	—31.7	10. Net profits to net worth	N o t	A v a i l a b l e	
75.1	69.1	58.3	11. Current assets to total assets	67.3	66.9	64.0
21.0	27.5	37.0	12. Fixed assets to total assets	31.1	32.0	35.0
03.8	03.3	04.6	13. Other assets to total assets	01.5	01.1	01.0

INTERPRETATION OF TABLE No. 9
The two companies are engaged in the manufacture of phonographs and records

After an inspection of this table, there can be no doubt that the ratios of the successful company present a far better showing than the failed concern. All the ratios of the successful company are very good with the possible exception of the sales to net worth ratio which is barely satisfactory in the last year. The drop of this ratio is attributed to a decline in sales of some $10,000,000—possibly to radio competition.

Not only are the ratios of the failed concern below the conventional standards, but even the trends are downward, in some cases sharply. The current ratio and the quick ratio of the failed concern are very poor each year with one exception when the current ratio is 213 per cent in 1920.

The four sales ratios are registering unfavorable tendencies. The sales to net worth ratio with the high figure of 1320 per cent in the last year indicates overtrading. It is the result of sharp decreases in the net worth item itself due to heavy losses amounting to more than $35,000,000 in two years. Therefore, this ratio pointed out a bad condition.

The net worth to debt ratio is particularly poor. In the last year, there are only $4 of net worth to every $100 of debt—a most unfavorable condition. In other words, the stockholders are supplying $4 of capital to every $100 contributed by the creditors. In addition, the balance sheets show that the failed concern has more than $6,000,000 in long-term liabilities while the successful company has none. The increases in liabilities, both short-term and long-term, as reflected by this ratio had created heavy fixed charges which in turn ate into the profits. These interest charges amounted to about $1,500,000 per annum. It is a financial axiom that industrial enterprises generally should not have long-term liabilities because of the irregularity of earnings.

The net worth to fixed assets ratio as well as the ratio of sales to fixed assets strongly indicated over-expansion in plants. The low figure of 12 per cent for the net worth to fixed assets ratio, furthermore, pointed out that creditors were supplying the working capital and a good part of the fixed capital or assets.

The net profits to net worth ratio reports very clearly the unprofitable nature of the company's operations. The losses are very heavy the past two years. This in turn suggests the difficulty of meeting interest charges. While the successful company does not report any exact data concerning profits, an examination revealed that large profits were earned each year.

The ratio of current assets to total assets when compared with the ratio of fixed assets to total assets reflected the over-expansion in plants at the expense of working capital.

This interpretation points out another lesson in ratio analysis which is that unusually high ratios such as the figure of 1320 per cent of the ratio of sales to net worth must be investigated in order to ascertain if there are any unfavorable factor or factors existing.

TABLE No. 10

October 31 FAILED CONCERN			TYPE OF RATIOS	October 31 SUCCESSFUL CONCERN		
1918	1919	1920		1918	1919	1920
636	328	131	1. Current assets to current liabilities	198	347	194
258	165	31	2. Quick assets to current liabilities	88	160	56
405	469	200	3. Sales to fixed assets	404	387	402
402	445	458	4. Sales to inventories	341	377	254
934	676	1698	5. Sales to receivables	851	582	882
153	174	168	6. Sales to net worth	173	150	172
988	416	273	7. Net worth to debt	217	471	204
263	270	119	8. Net worth to fixed assets	233	258	233
232	152	370	9. Inventories to receivables	249	154	346
26.8	29.1	11.4	10. Net profits to net worth	21.1	21.3	15.4
58.5	63.7	35.2	11. Current assets to total assets	62.6	60.7	63.8
34.4	30.0	61.5	12. Fixed assets to total assets	29.3	31.9	28.8
07.0	06.3	03.2	13. Other assets to total assets	08.3	07.3	07.3

INTERPRETATION OF TABLE NO. 10

Both concerns are in the rubber tire industry

This table is another example where the analyst must watch the trends of the ratios as well as their position or value.

The current ratio of the successful company was slightly below the 200 per cent standard for two of the three years, being 194 and 198 per cent. The quick ratio is weaker and is below the conventional one-to-one rule for two of the three years. The inventories to receivables ratio shows over-investment in the last year due to the depression of 1920-1921. All the other ratios are very good so that, all in all, it can be said that the company is occupying a satisfactory credit and financial position.

We find, on the other hand, that a number of the ratios of the unsuccessful concern are not only below the conventional standards in the last year, but the trends of the ratios are sharply downward for the past two years. Thus there are two important warning signals.

The current ratio and the quick ratio of the unsuccessful company are very poor the last year. Besides, the trends are sharply downward for the past two years. The upward swing of the inventories to receivables ratio in the last year partly accounts for the poor showing of the quick ratio that year. There is over-investment in inventories with the attendant heavy inventory losses.

The sales to fixed assets ratio and the net worth to fixed assets ratio indicate over-expansion in fixed assets. This is further confirmed by the fixed assets to total assets ratio which jumps from 30 to 61½ per cent in one year. The current assets to total assets ratio drops sharply from 63¾ to 35 per cent in the same period. There was, indeed, an expansion in fixed assets to the extent of approximately 300 per cent in the last year. Such a policy resulted in a serious impairment of working capital. Furthermore, the net worth to fixed assets ratio of 119 per cent reveals that there are $119 of net worth for every $100 of fixed assets or a $19 margin of its own capital employed as current assets for every $100 of fixed assets—a small margin.

The net worth to debt ratio shows a very sharp drop from 988 per cent in 1918 to 273 per cent in 1920 indicating that creditors are supplying more capital each year.

A striking contrast, in conclusion, is that the unsuccessful company earned profits each year. Incidentally, this is the only failed industrial concern of the twenty companies in this investigation which reported profits in the last year instead of losses.

INTERPRETATION OF TABLE NO. 11

These companies are engaged in the production and sale of fish products

This table, unlike the other tables in this article, gives the ratios of two unsuccessful concerns. The author was unable to find a successful company in the industry to compare with the original failed concern. In his search for a successful company, the second concern was discovered. The second concern, in the hands of a reorganization committee, underwent a readjustment whereby there was a "complete and permanent refinancing of the company, for the funding of a material part of its bank loans, for restoring its credits and providing it with adequate working capital."

There were, moreover, two other concerns in the industry that met with financial difficulties; one concern went into receivership and the other effected a voluntary reorganization.

The underlying factor that hit this industry so hard was the decreased consumption of fish products. During the World War it was regarded as a patriotic duty among the people of the United States to eat fish instead of meat. These companies endeavored, by an expansion of fixed assets, to provide the facilities for increasing the production of fish products and meet this demand. It was expected that, stimulated by its use during the war, the people would become more accustomed to fish as a food. However, sales greatly declined in the year 1920-1922. The companies were unable to dispose of their stocks of inventories and so heavy inventory losses were incurred when prices fell.

This situation, then, is a good reason why reputable analysts do not place sole reliance upon financial statements when investigating credit and financial risks. Three factors—financial, personal, and cyclical should be studied.* Among the financial factors are earning power of the business, sources of capital, adequacy of capital, and other financial considerations. Personal factors are business ability, character or integrity af the management and other personal elements. The cyclical factor is the state of business activity. Business conditions are dynamic and not static. Furthermore, there are *the conditions within the industry itself* which must be given consideration. This brief discussion of the three factors, however, does not impair the value and

*A. Wall and R. W. Duning. Ratio Analysis of Financial Statements, p. 14.

TABLE No. 11

\- March 31 \-					\- December 31 \-			
ORIGINAL FAILED CONCERN			TYPE OF RATIOS		SECOND COMPANY			
1919	1920	1921			1918	1919	1920	1921
180	160	89	1.	Current assets to current liabilities	122	135	111	88
47	49	39	2.	Quick assets to current liabilities	57	47	26	21
397	318	238	3.	Sales to fixed assets	Not	Available		
290	296	492	4.	Sales to inventories	Not	Available		
951	908	957	5.	Sales to receivables	Not	Available		
155	136	139	6.	Sales to net worth	Not	Available		
248	241	176	7.	Net worth to debt	75	106	87	90
256	232	171	8.	Net worth to fixed assets	90	100	89	76
329	306	194	9.	Inventories to receivables	183	385	520	573
+ 12.1	− 01.4	− 03.5	10.	Net profits to net worth	15.5	09.8	−00.3	−12.5
51.6	46.8	32.3	11.	Current assets to total assets	51.4	44.0	43.2	33.9
27.9	30.3	37.2	12.	Fixed assets to total assets	47.7	51.7	52.2	62.1
20.5	22.8	30.5	13.	Other assets to total assets	00.9	04.3	04.5	03.9

the usefulness of ratios as important and significant indicators of weaknesses in industrial enterprises.

An inspection of the table reveals both companies having a very poor current ratio and quick ratio for each year. Besides, they are meeting with losses the past two years as the net profits to net worth ratio reveals. Moreover, the current assets to total assets and the fixed assets to total assets ratios as well as the net worth to fixed assets ratio indicate over-investment in plants at the expense of the current assets.

For the original company, we find the net worth to debt ratio, while declining from 248 to 176 per cent, is still favorable. The inventories to receivables ratio is improving.

For the other unsuccessful company, we discover a poor net worth to debt ratio and an equally poor net worth to fixed assets ratio. The upward swing of the inventories to receivables ratio shows a strong tendency toward over-investment in inventories with the subsequent losses.

INTERPRETATION OF TABLE NO. 12

The two concerns are in the cotton textile industry of New England

Inasmuch as there are three failed textile companies in this investigation, the question may arise as to how the successful and the failed companies were paired. For this table, the two companies were paired on the following basis: They have the same amount of assets—2½ millions dollars; they are located in the same city; and they manufacture the same type of product.

An inspection of this table reveals that the ratios of the successful company report the stronger credit and financial position. Its current ratio is much above the 200 per cent standard and is much better than the failed concern's. The failed concern's ratio, while above the 200 per cent standard, is not so good because of the poor condition of the net worth to debt ratio which is only 83 per cent. Only in one year is the net worth to debt ratio a 50-50 proposition, that is, the owners are furnishing as much capital as the creditors. This is an important point to consider. The successful company, on the other hand, reports a good net worth to debt position.

As for the quick ratio, the failed concern is very poor each year. The successful company's ratio, while somewhat weak, is much better than the failed concern's.

The net worth to fixed assets ratio is satisfactory for both companies.

The current assets to total assets ratio and the fixed assets to total assets ratio are practically the same for both companies and are good.

Sales, profits, and other data are not available and so other positions and trends could not be observed.

INTERPRETATION OF TABLE NO. 13

These companies are in the cotton textile industry of New England

The failed and the successful concerns are paired on the following basis: They have approximately the same amount of assets, being 27½ and 23½ million dollars, respectively; they manufacture the same type of goods; and,

TABLE No. 12

October 31 FAILED CONCERN			TYPE OF RATIOS	September 30 SUCCESSFUL CONCERN		
1918	1919	1920		1918	1919	1920
215	282	226	1. Current assets to current liabilities	232	392	356
43	66	34	2. Quick assets to current liabilities .	42	133	89
Not	Availa	ble	3. Sales to fixed assets	Not	Availa	ble
Not	Availa	ble	4. Sales to inventories	Not	Availa	ble
Not	Availa	ble	5. Sales to receivables	Not	Availa	ble
Not	Availa	ble	6. Sales to net worth	Not	Availa	ble
85	100	83	7. Net worth to debt	105	140	135
116	124	170	8. Net worth to fixed assets	116	134	177
Not	Availa	ble	9. Inventories to receivables	Not	Availa	ble
Not	Availa	ble	10. Net profits to net worth	Not	Availa	ble
60.7	59.6	73.4	11. Current assets to total assets	55.0	56.3	66.9
39.3	40.4	26.6	12. Fixed assets to total assets	44.0	43.7	32.5
None	None	None	13. Other assets to total assets	00.9	None	00.6

TABLE No. 13

December 31 Failed Concern				October 31 Successful Concern		
1922	1923	1924	Type of Ratios	1922	1923	1924
105	99	39	1. Current assets to current liabilities	170	160	160
74	71	20	2. Quick assets to current liabilities	72	65	58
33	55	17	3. Sales to fixed assets	68	147	126
178	378	360	4. Sales to inventories	179	232	238
82	157	532	5. Sales to receivables	340	400	567
42	73	30	6. Sales to net worth	53	103	95
88	90	103	7. Net worth to debt	334	216	257
80	75	58	8. Net worth to fixed assets	130	142	133
46	41	147	9. Inventories to receivables	190	172	238
—13.0	—05.7	—18.2	10. Net profits to net worth	—06.5	+10.8	—04.3
36.4	32.7	08.8	11. Current assets to total assets	39.1	50.7	44.8
59.4	63.1	86.1	12. Fixed assets to total assets	59.4	48.2	54.1
04.1	04.1	05.1	13. Other assets to total assets	01.5	01.0	01.1

for a time, they had about the same volume of sales.

The failed concern has a very poor current ratio and a poor quick ratio. They are below the 200 per cent and the 100 per cent standard, respectively, each year. The successful company is also below these standards, but its ratios are much better than those of the failed concern.

As to the four sales ratios, the failed company does not report as satisfactory condition as the successful company. Its sales to fixed assets ratio as well as the sales to net worth ratio are particularly poor. The very low figure of 17 per cent for the sales to fixed assets ratio and the low figure of 58 per cent for the net worth to fixed assets ratio strongly indicate that the plant investment of the failed company is not being utilized; that there is an over-investment in fixed assets.

The net worth to debt ratio of the unsuccessful company is poor, in spite of its upward swing. Only in the last year, is it a 50-50 proposition. For two years the creditors supplied more capital than the owners. Furthermore, the balance sheets show that there is a funded debt of more than $7,000,000 while the successful company has none.

The successful concern's ratio is very good.

The net worth to fixed assets ratio of the failed company is very poor while the successful company's ratio is good.

In the last year, both concerns show a tendency toward over-investment in inventories as reflected by the inventories to receivables ratio.

The failed concern suffered heavy losses each year. The successful company, while meeting with smaller losses in two of the three years, has fared better.

The current assets to total assets ratio is exceedingly poor, as is the fixed assets to total assets ratio in the case of the failed company. The successful concern's position is good.

TABLE No. 14

Sept. 30	Sept. 30	Feb. 28	Type of Ratios	December 31 Successful Concern		
†Failed Concern						
1923	1924	1926		1923	1924	1925
323	2525	204	1. Current assets to current liabilities	839	2764	527
111	1275	72	2. Quick assets to current liabilities	341	1541	225
Not	Available		3. Sales to fixed assets	Not	Available	
Not	Available		4. Sales to inventories	Not	Available	
Not	Available		5. Sales to receivables	Not	Available	
Not	Available		6. Sales to net worth	Not	Available	
141	169	91	7. Net worth to debt	935	3262	535
150	118	81	8. Net worth to fixed assets	562	591	572
226	142	246	9. Inventories to receivables	180	127	172
Not	Available		10. Net profits to net worth	*	03.0	00.1
51.7	34.3	27.6	11. Current assets to total assets	81.1	82.2	83.1
38.9	53.3	58.7	12. Fixed assets to total assets	16.1	16.4	14.7
09.3	12.4	13.6	13. Other assets to total assets	02.8	01.3	02.2

†No statement published September 30, 1925.
*Not available.

INTERPRETATION OF TABLE NO. 14
Both companies manufacture collars and shirts

The successful company's ratios are generally very good.

The failed concern's current ratio is 204 per cent and its quick ratio is 72 per cent which is poor. Besides, both ratios do not look so good when the net worth to debt ratio is declining from 169 to 91 per cent. The latter ratio indicates that creditors are furnishing more capital than owners. The balance sheets show, moreover, that the failed concern has long-term liabilities of about one million dollars while the successful company has none.

The failed concern's net worth to fixed assets ratio of 81 per cent is poor and suggests over-investment in plants. This is confirmed by the fixed assets to total assets ratio.

The failed concern reports no data relative to profits and, in this instance, its ratio of net profits to net worth cannot be compared with the successful company's ratio. An examination, however, revealed that the failed concern has suffered heavy losses as there is a deficit of $370,000. The successful company's ratio is low.

The decline of the current assets to total assets ratio and the increase of the fixed assets to total assets ratio are also important indications.

TABLE No. 15

⎯⎯ December 31 ⎯⎯ FAILED CONCERN			TYPE OF RATIOS	⎯⎯ December 31 ⎯⎯ SUCCESSFUL CONCERN		
1918	1919	1920		1918	1919	1920
228	274	207	1. Current assets to current liabilities	678	555	316
142	153	92	2. Quick assets to current liabilities	344	351	139
339	493	*	3. Sales to fixed assets	266	403	390
620	508	*	4. Sales to inventories	218	376	322
337	443	*	5. Sales to receivables	536	608	620
121	161	*	6. Sales to net worth	84	117	153
292	325	97	7. Net worth to debt	867	657	369
280	304	260	8. Net worth to fixed assets	317	345	253
54	87	131	9. Inventories to receivables	246	161	192
*	40.7	*	10. Net profits to net worth	Not	Availab	l e
45.6	55.3	68.4	11. Current assets to total assets	70.1	73.3	67.3
26.7	25.1	19.2	12. Fixed assets to total assets	28.2	25.2	31.1
27.7	19.5	12.3	13. Other assets to total assets	01.6	01.5	01.5

*Not available.

INTERPRETATION OF TABLE NO. 15
The two companies are engaged in the manufacture of phonographs and records

It should be mentioned that the failed company has assets of $9,000,000 while the successful company has $43,000,000. No other competitor could be procured for comparison.

Again we find the successful company occupying a strong credit and financial position. All its ratios are good.

The failed company's troubles developed in the last year as reflected by the unfavorable decline of several important ratios such as the net worth to debt ratio, the quick ratio, and others. Sales and profits data for the last year are not available and so the position and the trend of other ratios cannot be observed. The only information is that sales greatly declined the latter part of 1920, but no figures can be obtained.

The current ratio and the quick ratio are apparently "window-dressed" the last year as there is an issue of $1,500,000 of Sinking Fund notes which the balance sheet reports. This financial policy weakens the net worth to debt ratio which falls from 325 to 97 per cent. Moreover, the current ratio is falling from 274 to 207 per cent and the quick ratio is falling from 153 to 92 per cent—another bad indication.

The successful company does not show any long-term liabilities on its balance sheets.

The net worth to fixed assets ratio of the failed concern is declining, but it is still favorable.

Its inventories to receivables ratio is increasing and becoming unfavorable. This in turn helps to weaken the quick ratio. Besides, it is an indication of inventory losses as the last year is a period of business depression.

The net profits to net worth ratio cannot be

computed inasmuch as the data are unavailable for two of the three years.

All in all, while the ratios of the failed company did not begin to register unfavorable signs until the last year, nevertheless they were significant enough to be heeded by the credit man and the banker.

INTERPRETATION OF TABLE NO. 16
Both companies are in the cotton textile industry of New England

These concerns are paired because they have the same amount of assets, $5,000,000, and manufacture the same type of product.

After inspecting this table, it is apparent that the ratios of the successful company report a better showing than the failed company's ratios.

The failed concern shows a particularly poor current ratio for each year, ranging from 48 to 70 per cent, and an equally poor quick ratio which ranges from 20 to 22 per cent. There is, indeed, a very urgent need of working capital as this condition is one of anemia or rather pernicious anemia. The successful company, on the other hand, has a barely satisfactory current ratio in the last year, while the year before it was not so good, being 171 per cent. Moreover, its quick ratio is poor for each year, ranging from 44 to 52 per cent. Incidentally, this is the only ratio that is really unfavorable; this condition is the result of too much investment in inventories.

The net worth to debt ratio is satisfactory for both companies, although the successful company reports a very strong position. Neither concern has any long term liabilities.

The net worth to fixed assets ratio is poor, being 78 per cent and suggests that the failed company has too much plant investment. Moreover, it indicates that creditors are financing the current assets and a part of the fixed assets. The successful concern's position is good.

For the failed concern, we note that the current assets to total assets ratio is very low and the fixed assets to total assets ratio is too high. This is a fact of no little import. In this respect, the successful company's condition is satisfactory.

INTERPRETATION OF TABLE NO. 17
The two companies are in the woolen textile industry

The successful company's ratios report a favorable showing in spite of a weak quick ratio. On the other hand, the failed concern's financial difficulties suddenly developed the last year, 1920, as the several ratios very definitely and clearly pointed out. Several outstanding examples are the current ratio, the quick ratio, the net worth to debt ratio, the inventories to receivables ratio, and the net profits to net worth ratio. There can be, then, no mistake about their import.

The current ratio drops sharply from 507 to 95 per cent in the last year. The quick ratio takes a headlong drop from 103 to 7 per cent — an astoundingly low figure. In other words, there are only 7 cents in quick assets to every dollar in current liabilities.

The net worth to debt ratio has become very poor, falling from 632 to 85 per cent. In other words, there are now $85 of capital contributed by the stockholders to every $100 of capital supplied by the creditors. The balance sheets disclose, moreover, that the notes pay-

TABLE No. 16

December 31 — FAILED CONCERN			TYPE OF RATIOS	November 30 — SUCCESSFUL CONCERN		
1925	1926	1927		1925	1926	1927
70	51	48	1. Current assets to current liabilities	253	171	204
21	22	20	2. Quick assets to current liabilities	52	49	44
Not	Available		3. Sales to fixed assets	Not	Available	
Not	Available		4. Sales to inventories	Not	Available	
Not	Available		5. Sales to receivables	Not	Available	
Not	Available		6. Sales to net worth	Not	Available	
157	176	187	7. Net worth to debt	595	343	429
84	78	78	8. Net worth to fixed assets	138	129	135
Not	Available		9. Inventories to receivables	873	652	500
Not	Available		10. Net profits to net worth	Not	Available	
27.3	18.7	16.8	11. Current assets to total assets	37.0	38.6	38.5
72.3	80.8	82.8	12. Fixed assets to total assets	61.7	60.0	60.0
00.3	00.4	00.3	13. Other assets to total assets	01.3	01.4	01.5

TABLE No. 17

December 31 FAILED CONCERN			TYPE OF RATIOS	November 30 SUCCESSFUL CONCERN		
1918	1919	1920		1918	1919	1920
409	507	95	1. Current assets to current liabilities	280	226	236
117	103	07	2. Quick assets to current liabilities .	102	55	77
471	400	*	3. Sales to fixed assets	811	412	368
527	360	*	4. Sales to inventories	384	193	302
2271	1783	*	5. Sales to receivables	1066	803	850
194	146	*	6. Sales to net worth	254	158	178
409	632	85	7. Net worth to debt...........	267	208	281
242	274	163	8. Net worth to fixed assets	318	261	207
431	500	1774	9. Inventories to receivables	278	416	281
09.5	14.8	—34.3	10. Net profits to net worth	18.9	19.2	08.2
41.6	43.9	49.5	11. Current assets to total assets	76.2	73.1	61.9
33.2	31.5	28.2	12. Fixed assets to total assets	22.8	25.9	35.6
25.2	24.5	22.2	13. Other assets to total assets	00.9	00.9	02.3

*Not available.

able item increased from $900,000 in 1919 to $8,300,000 in 1920—a fact of great import.

The inventories to receivables ratio increased sharply from 500 to 1774 per cent another significant indication. It is no wonder, then, that the quick ratio has fallen to the very low mark of 7 per cent. The business depression which began in 1920 is partly responsible for this condition. The successful company's ratio is good.

The net profits to net worth ratio falls from a profit of 14.8 per cent in 1919 to a severe loss of 34.3 per cent in 1920. The successful company, however, is reporting profits each year.

The current assets to total assets ratio, while increasing, shows that the failed concern does not have as good a condition as the successful company. Too much capital is tied up in other assets. The successful company's current assets to total assets ratio, while good, is declining and its ratio of fixed assets to total assets is increasing.

INTERPRETATION OF TABLE No. 18

Both companies are fertilizer manufacturers

The successful company has a stronger credit and financial position than the failed concern because all its ratios are good with the possible exception of the low inventories to receivables ratio. Both companies, however, have a low ratio due to conditions in the industry. It is customary to grant long-term credit to their customers.

The failed concern's current ratio and quick ratio are above the conventional standards. They are, however, "window-dressed" because of an increase of $12,000,000 in its funded debt. This in turn causes the net worth to debt ratio to fall to the low figure of 88 per cent. The balance sheet shows a funded debt amounting to $37,000,000 in the last year. This clearly suggests that heavy interest charges must be met. And the net profits to net worth ratio is reporting losses each year!

The four sales ratios are showing a slight

TABLE No. 18

May 31 FAILED CONCERN			TYPE OF RATIOS	June 30 SUCCESSFUL CONCERN		
1921	1922	1923		1921	1922	1923
191	195	244	1. Current assets to current liabilities	371	761	944
138	153	177	2. Quick assets to current liabilities .	268	573	703
149	124	130	3. Sales to fixed assets	N o t	A v a i l a b l e	
560	721	658	4. Sales to inventories	N o t	A v a i l a b l e	
266	248	316	5. Sales to receivables	N o t	A v a i l a b l e	
141	124	151	6. Sales to net worth	N o t	A v a i l a b l e	
111	118	88	7. Net worth to debt...........	131	162	128
105	100	82	8. Net worth to fixed assets	127	125	110
47	34	48	9. Inventories to receivables	42	35	38
—20.0	—02.8	—04.5	10. Net profits to net worth	—05.8	02.3	04.3
47.6	44.0	41.5	11. Current assets to total assets	52.5	47.3	47.1
50.0	54.1	57.2	12. Fixed assets to total assets	44.7	49.6	50.9
02.3	01.9	01.2	13. Other assets to total assets	02.8	03.1	01.9

improvement due to the upturn of business conditions.

The net worth to fixed assets ratio is low and indicates that creditors are furnishing the funds for working capital and a part for fixed capital or assets.

The net worth to fixed assets ratio and the fixed assets to total assets ratio reveal a tendency toward over-investment in plants.

In conclusion, it can be seen that the foregoing ratios pointed out the approaching financial difficulties of the failed company.

INTERPRETATION OF TABLE NO. 19
The two companies are engaged in the manufacture of steel products

On account of the difference in the dates of the financial statements, the ratios of the successful company are shown for four years. Besides, sales data for the successful company in the last year could not be obtained.

All the ratios of the successful company are generally satisfactory with the exception of the quick ratio which is 80 per cent in the last year. The downward trend of some ratios can be traced to the expansion policy during 1926. Fixed assets investment increased 50 per cent and they were financed by both short-term and long-term liabilities totaling more than $7,000,000. However, in spite of the trends the company's position is still favorable.

The conspicuous weaknesses of the failed company are indicated by the net worth to debt ratio, the net profits to net worth ratio and the net worth to fixed assets ratio. These ratios are exceedingly poor each year. There can, then, be no mistake about their import.

The net worth to debt ratio of 28 per cent suggests a condition of undercapitalization and the urgent need of additional capital to be invested in the concern by its stockholders. There are now $28 of net worth to every $100 of debt. The balance sheet shows that the funded debt amounts to approximately $23,000,000.

The current ratio and the quick ratio have declined. Moreover, these ratios were "improved" in 1924 by an increase of $6,000,000 of long-term liabilities. So that the current ratio and the quick ratio do not look so good when the net worth to debt ratio is poor.

The net worth to fixed assets ratio suggests that too much capital is tied up in plants in proportion to the volume of business transacted.

INTERPRETATION OF TABLE NO. 20
Both concerns are engaged in the wholesale merchandise business

The current ratio of both companies is below the 2 to 1 standard each year. However, in the last year, the successful company's ratio is 173 per cent while the failed company is 143 per cent. The trend of the successful company's ratio is good, but this is not the case for the failed concern.

As for the quick ratio, the successful company alone is good. The failed concern's ratio, however, is falling from 96 to 69 per cent.

The net worth to debt ratio of the failed concern is only 73 per cent in the last year, declining from the high mark of 160 per cent. The successful company is just satisfactory.

The net worth to fixed assets ratio is good

TABLE No. 19

December 31 — FAILED CONCERN					June 30 — SUCCESSFUL CONCERN			
1924	1925	1926	TYPE OF RATIOS	1924	1925	1926	1927
764	619	370	1. Current assets to current liabilities	739	584	387	273
237	160	83	2. Quick assets to current liabilities	267	216	151	80
75	94	96	3. Sales to fixed assets	94	91	88	*
242	284	270	4. Sales to inventories	283	274	372	*
835	908	1148	5. Sales to receivables	1200	840	1143	*
172	249	291	6. Sales to net worth	65	63	76	*
41	34	28	7. Net worth to debt	1857	1524	476	411
43	38	33	8. Net worth to fixed assets	145	144	115	115
345	311	425	9. Inventories to receivables	425	305	357	390
—08.0	—03.0	—09.9	10. Net profits to net worth	05.1	03.4	09.4	06.2
31.2	30.4	30.6	11. Current assets to total assets	34.0	34.5	27.5	29.0
67.0	68.0	66.7	12. Fixed assets to total assets	65.5	65.2	71.4	70.1
01.7	01.5	02.5	13. Other assets to total assets	00.4	00.3	01.0	00.8

*Not available.

TABLE No. 20

Failed Concern			Type of Ratios	Successful Concern		
May 31 1918	May 31 1919	Oct. 31 1920		Nov 30 1918	Nov 30 1919	Nov 30 1920
185	191	143	1. Current assets to current liabilities	163	170	173
96	84	69	2. Quick assets to current liabilities	91	100	108
Not	Available		3. Sales to fixed assets	Not	Available	
Not	Available		4. Sales to inventories	Not	Available	
Not	Available		5. Sales to receivables	Not	Available	
Not	Available		6. Sales to net worth	Not	Available	
154	160	73	7. Net worth to debt	97	100	105
519	537	591	8. Net worth to fixed assets	657	655	600
96	139	114	9. Inventories to receivables	86	77	67
Not	Available		10. Net profits to net worth	37.9	50.1	09.0
65.3	66.0	79.4	11. Current assets to total assets	82.8	84.7	84.1
11.7	11.5	07.1	12. Fixed assets to total assets	07.5	07.7	08.5
23.0	22.5	13.4	13. Other assets to total assets	09.6	07.6	07.4

†Failed Concern
†No statement published May 31, 1920.

for both companies. Inasmuch as both are wholesale businesses, the better ratio to employ would be the sales to total assets ratio. But sales data are not available so as to compute this ratio.

The inventories to receivables ratio is satisfactory for both concerns.

The improvement in the current assets to total assets ratio may be due to the conduct of the business of the failed concern by the creditors' committee. This committee took over the affairs of the company a short time before the October 31st statement was published. The successful concern's ratio is better.

All in all, one comes to the conclusion that the successful company's ratios were better than those of the unsuccessful concern.

It should be mentioned that the successful company has assets of $20,000,000 while the failed concern has assets of $7,000,000. Besides, the successful company is located in the middle west and the unsuccessful one in the east. Financial statements of another competitor could not be procured.

Summary

After reviewing the data presented by the foregoing tables, one comes to the conclusion that the ratios of the successful companies made, by far, the better showing. In every case, the majority of the successful companies' ratios were satisfactory. Besides, in a number of instances, all the ratios were favorable. This, however, was not true for the failed concerns. In every case, they had a number of unfavorable ratios.

It appears, then, that ratios are important tools in ascertaining significant relationships of business facts. These relationships are worthwhile indicators to business managers, credit executives, bankers, and other interested persons. It should be remembered, moreover, that the author does not advocate that ratios are absolute indicators of impending financial difficulties. They are, indeed, helpful clues to be made the subject for further investigation. They are, also, tests of business health.

This investigation, furthermore, has revealed very significantly the increasing importance of such ratios as the net worth to debt and the net profits to net worth ratios. The value and the import of these ratios have been pointed out from time to time in the interpretation of the tables. The current ratio and the quick ratio are running a poor second; and while possessing some value, they should not be given as much weight in the credit decision as formerly when an industrial enterprise has long-term liabilities. An enterprise with a poor net worth to debt ratio and an equally poor net profits to net worth ratio is running the serious risk of receivership or creditors' committee because of the inability to meet the interest charges.

Even the net worth to fixed assets ratio seems to be developing into an important ratio.

Finally, one difficulty encountered in connection with this investigation has been the limited number of cases available for selection and analysis. This is because of the unavailability of the data of failed companies. It is, indeed, rather difficult to procure a sufficient number of failed companies which publish financial statements. Many concerns, successful and unsuccessful, do not publish financial statements.

PORTENTS OF DISCONTINUANCE

Charles Lewis Merwin

4

PORTENTS OF DISCONTINUANCE

Credit analysis theory is based on the assumption that since the success of a business enterprise is measured in pecuniary terms it is possible to distinguish between the sound and the unsound, the successful and the unsuccessful, by examining certain "credit" ratios. 1/ That is to say, the theory assumes that if a designated credit ratio falls below or rises above some empirically determined level - depending on the relationship measured by the ratio - that deviation signals financial difficulty and even, if it persists, portends discontinuance of business operations. The data available for use in this study permit an experimental testing of this primary assumption, particularly the assumption that persistent deviation from an empirical norm foretells disappearance of an enterprise from the business scene. Such a testing is subject to limitations, but it can ascertain whether in this particular group of corporations a systematic ratio pattern was exhibited by the discontinuing companies.

For a test of the type to which this chapter is devoted our data should pertain only to the experience of companies that are known to have suffered severe financial difficulties resulting in reorganization or failure. The sample with which we have to work is not, however, of this character. Strictly speaking, all we know is that these companies ceased filing federal corporate income tax returns. Some may have changed to a non-corporate form of organization, and others may have discontinued business voluntarily. But we have reason to believe that the majority were what may be termed involuntary discontinuances.

The data on which this chapter is based were developed as follows. The primary samples for our study consisted of a drawing of about 200 eligible companies in each of the five industries from the 1926 federal income tax returns, and of another, smaller drawing from the 1930 returns. These companies were then traced through

Portents of Discontinuance

the files for the succeeding ten and six years, respectively. The corporations studied in the foregoing chapters are those from the 1926 drawing that continued to file income tax returns through 1936. The remainder ceased filing returns some time before that year, as did nearly half of the companies in the 1930 drawing. Since companies involved in mergers and consolidations had been eliminated from the samples, and since federal law requires the filing of an income tax return by every active corporation, these companies that ceased filing returns may be assumed to have gone out of business as corporate entities. Presumably they were failures, although, as mentioned above, a few may have left business voluntarily or changed to a non-corporate form of ownership. 2/

The present analysis is based, therefore, on the returns of companies that discontinued after remaining in the sample six years or more. Thus it includes, from the 1926 drawing, the companies that discontinued some time during the years 1932-36, and, from the 1930 drawing, the companies that disappeared in 1936. These discontinuances number 200 in all, distributed among the five industries as follows: baking 47; men's clothing 41; furniture 38; stone-clay 43; machine tool 31. They are referred to as the identical sample of discontinuing companies. While the sample is small, it is, to our knowledge, the only one available for testing, in regard to small manufacturing concerns, the basic assumptions of credit analysis theory.

In studying the financial statements of enterprises that ultimately disappear from the business scene one of the most serious problems is the difficulty of reducing the tabulations to a basis adapted to temporal analysis. If all the disappearances occurred in a single year the problem would not arise, but in the present instance we are dealing with corporations that disappeared severally over a period of five years. A tabulation of their financial statements for a series of calendar years before discontinuance would not permit careful analysis, because the number of companies would change from year to year and in each year some would be nearer discontinuance than others. Therefore we have taken the year of disappearance as the point of reference, regardless of the particular calendar year it happens to be, and have tabulated the financial statements according to the number of years before discontinuance. 3/ Thus the statements of the 200 companies were grouped into six divisions, according to whether they covered the first, second, third, fourth, fifth or sixth calendar year 4/ before the company in question left the business scene. The statements in each of these divisions were then aggregated to yield a composite balance sheet and income account for each of the six year-before-discontinuance periods. The tabulations could not be carried beyond the sixth year before disappearance, for some of the corporations were in the sample only six years. 5/

FINANCIAL RATIOS AS INDICATORS

In the financial structure of our sample corporations there were many elements that gave advance evidence of ultimate discontinuance, but three ratios proved to be particularly sensitive indicators in this respect: current assets to current liabilities, net worth to total debt, 6/ and net working capital 7/ to total assets. These three were selected by the trial and error method, a large number of possible ratios being tested.

The first and third of these ratios reflect the "freezing" of working capital, the first by comparing the two determinants of working capital with each other, and the third by comparing the difference between these two components with the total assets of the company. The second ratio - net worth to total debt - reflects the relative positions of the owners and creditors in the enterprise. When the capital of an enterprise becomes less and less liquid, and the creditors' claims persist in increasing, in relation to the owners' equity, we have what are here called portents of discontinuance. It is significant that the profit ratio was a less sensitive and reliable indicator than any of the three ratios listed above. In the present chapter these three "indicator" ratios, computed for each year before discontinuance, are compared with the corresponding ratios for the continuing companies. 8/

In this comparison certain obvious difficulties have had to be surmounted. In the first place, the ratios for the surviving companies pertain to given calendar years, while those for the discontinuing companies cover given

Portents of Discontinuance   93

years before discontinuance, each of which represents a different assortment of calendar years. And in the second place, a change in a ratio between, say, the fifth and the third year before discontinuance cannot be wholly attributed to the fact that the time of disappearance was drawing nearer: some of the change may have been due to the dominance of generally prosperous years in the fifth, and of generally unprosperous years in the third, year before discontinuance.

A rather crude means of solving these problems is to determine, for the surviving companies, the high-low range of each ratio's variation during all the years 1926-35. When this method is followed any given ratio for the discontinuing companies is not regarded as out of line until it has passed outside that ratio's high-low range as established by the surviving companies. For some purposes of comparison, however, this method of correction is too conservative, because in relatively prosperous or relatively depressed years a ratio for the discontinuing companies may be dangerously high or low and still fall within the high-low range for the continuing corporations. Therefore a standardizing technique has been applied to the three selected ratios in order to derive, for each of them, the "estimated normal," that is, a ratio for the surviving companies which pertains to the same combination of calendar years that is contained in each year before discontinuance. 9/

Although both of these bases of comparison give consideration to the cyclical factor they serve different purposes. The high-low range indicates the maximum cyclical variation and hence is particularly useful in determining when the level of the disappearing companies' ratio is out of line. The estimated normal allows roughly for the cyclical influences operative in each given year before discontinuance, and thus can be used to test the direction of movement as well as the level of the disappearing companies' ratio.

In Charts 6 to 10 the three ratios mentioned above - current assets to current liabilities, net worth to total debt, and net working capital to total assets - are presented for the discontinuing companies in each industry, and for each year before discontinuance, and are compared with the estimated normal and with the high-low range es-

47 DISCONTINUING AND 81 CONTINUING BAKING CORPORATIONS: Three Selected Ratios, by Number of Years Before Discontinuance [a]

CHART 6

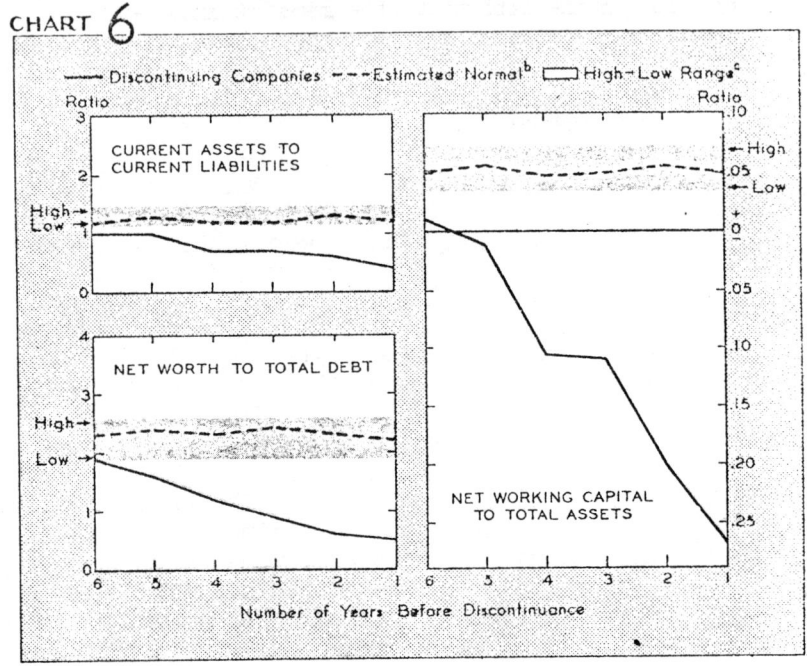

[a] Based on Table D-2 in Appendix D and Table B-22 in Data Book (see footnote 16 of Chapter I).

[b] Weighted average of the continuing companies' ratios for the various calendar years contained in each year before discontinuance; for method of estimate see Appendix D.

[c] Range of 1926-35 annual ratios for sample of continuing companies.

CHART 7

41 DISCONTINUING AND 46 CONTINUING MEN'S CLOTHING CORPORATIONS: Three Selected Ratios, by Number of Years Before Discontinuance [a]

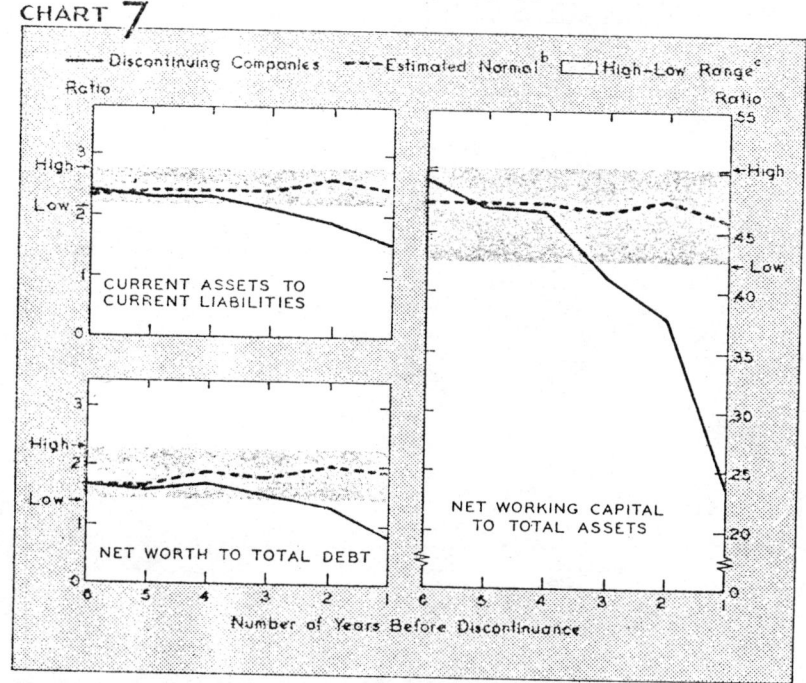

[a] Based on Table D-2 in Appendix D and Table B-23 in Data Book (see footnote 16 of Chapter I).

[b] Weighted average of the continuing companies' ratios for the various calendar years contained in each year before discontinuance; for method of estimate see Appendix D.

[c] Range of 1926–35 annual ratios for sample of continuing companies.

38 DISCONTINUING AND 66 CONTINUING FURNITURE CORPORATIONS: Three Selected Ratios, by Number of Years Before Discontinuance [a]

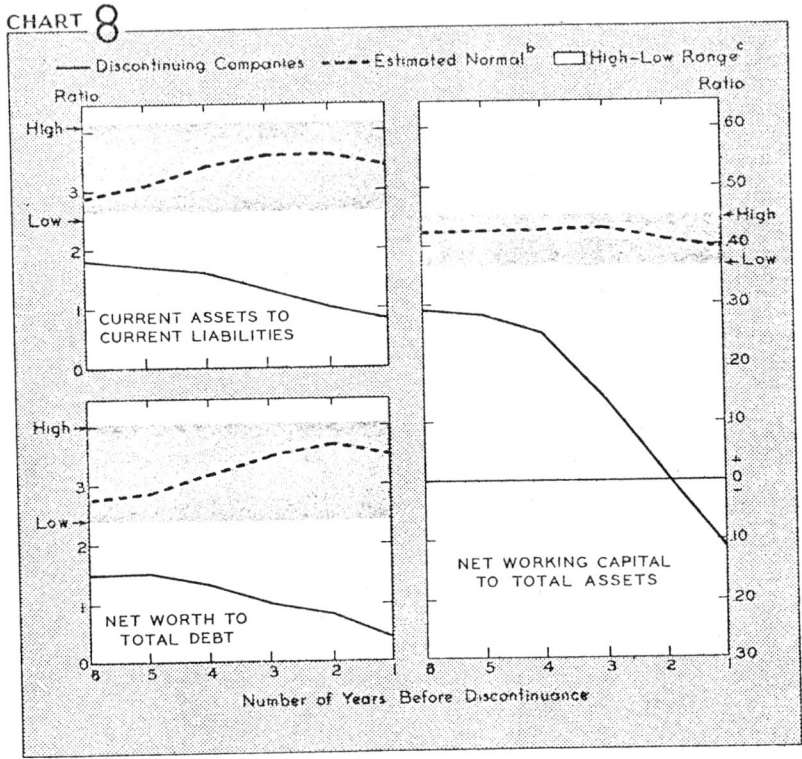

CHART 8

[a] Based on Table D-2 in Appendix D and Table B-24 in Data Book (see footnote 16 of Chapter I).

[b] Weighted average of the continuing companies' ratios for the various calendar years contained in each year before discontinuance; for method of estimate see Appendix D.

[c] Range of 1926-35 annual ratios for sample of continuing companies.

Portents of Discontinuance 97

CHART 9

43 DISCONTINUING AND 70 CONTINUING STONE AND CLAY CORPORATIONS: Three Selected Ratios, by Number of Years Before Discontinuance [a]

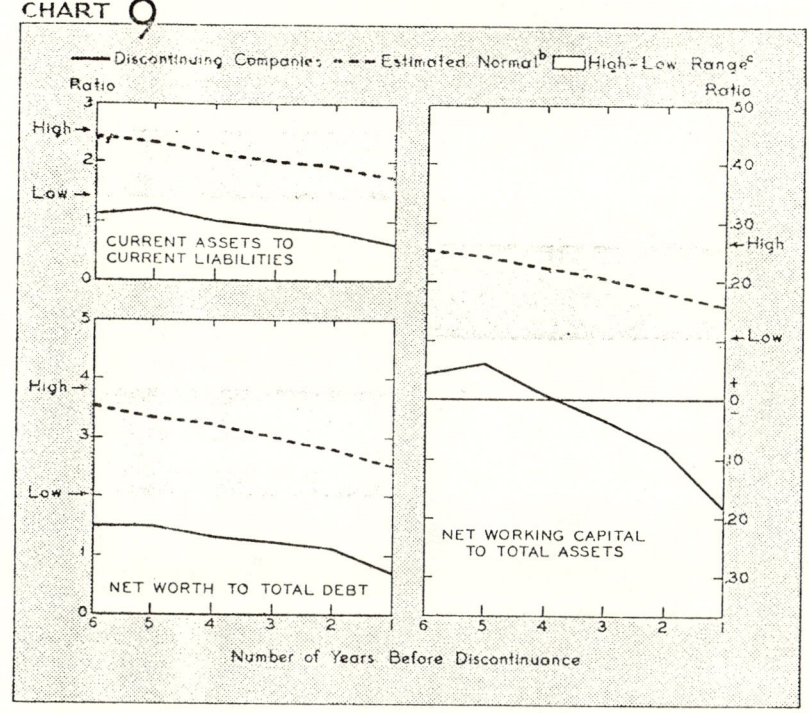

[a] Based on Table D-2 in Appendix D and Table B-25 in Data Book (see footnote 16 of Chapter I).

[b] Weighted average of the continuing companies' ratios for the various calendar years contained in each year before discontinuance; for method of estimate see Appendix D.

[c] Range of 1926-35 annual ratios for sample of continuing companies.

CHART 10. 31 DISCONTINUING AND 118 CONTINUING MACHINE TOOL CORPORATIONS: Three Selected Ratios, by Number of Years Before Discontinuance [a]

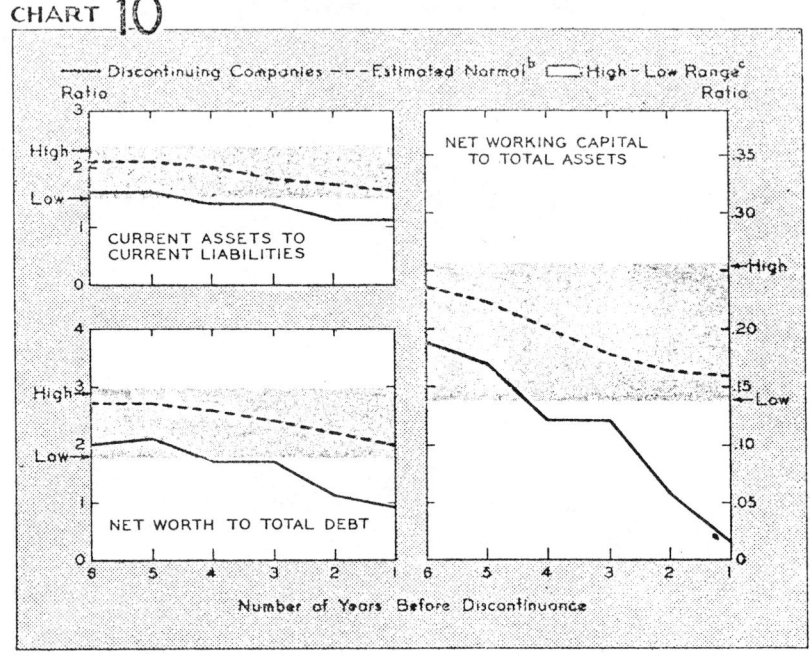

[a] Based on Table D-2 in Appendix D and Table B-26 in Data Book (see note 16 of Chapter 1).

[b] Weighted average of the continuing companies' ratios for the various calendar years contained in each year before discontinuance; for method of estimate see Appendix D.

[c] Range of 1926–35 annual ratios for sample of continuing companies.

tablished by the surviving companies over the period 1926-35. 10/ From these charts it can be observed that except in men's clothing all three ratios were below the estimated normal as early as the sixth year before discontinuance. And in three of the industries they were out of line that early even if we adopt the very conservative standard of the high-low range for the continuing companies; here machine tool and again men's clothing are the exceptions.

Equally significant is the movement of the discontinuing companies' ratios as the year of discontinuance draws near. In all five industries they declined persistently, in most instances sharply, from the sixth to the first year before discontinuance, thereby increasing their divergence from the estimated normal. For the five industries combined this increasing divergence is found to be statistically significant: in each of the three ratios the probability that chance alone would account for this persistent divergence is less than one out of a hundred. 11/

Of the three ratios shown in Charts 6 to 10, that of net working capital to total assets provides the most definite indications of ultimate discontinuance. 12/ In each industry its downward movement was sharp - more so than that of either of the other ratios - and virtually uninterrupted. It was the only one of the three to fall decisively below the high-low range in the men's clothing sample. In the stone-clay and machine tool groups its downward movement was accompanied by a decline in the estimated normal, but its decline was greater than that of the estimated normal and its level was decidedly lower.

The ratios plotted in Charts 6 to 10 are ratios of aggregates, against which it may be argued that the influence of the larger companies in the sample has more weight than that of the smaller, and that the relative influence of an individual company may vary significantly during the period. While these ratios of aggregates are, in essence, the properly weighted averages of the ratios for the individual companies, the relative weights may vary somewhat through the period. Ratios of aggregates were employed here because the open-end classes in the available frequency distributions precluded the calculation of the correct mean ratio. Medians were similarly indeterminate because of the necessity of interpolating within frequency distribution classes.

There are several reasons for believing, however, that the movements shown by the ratios plotted in these charts are representative not only of the sample companies in the aggregate, but also of the particular enterprises. In the first place, the companies in the samples are all relatively small; most had total assets between $50,000 and $150,000, with only a few over the $200,000 level. Therefore there was not the opportunity - found in some simple aggregations of financial statements - for the influence of one or a few companies to outweigh that of a great many other concerns in the group. It is this factor, incidentally, which provides the basis for the representativeness of much of the analysis in the preceding chapters of this study.

Secondly, a special tally of the ratios of the particular companies in the samples of discontinuances revealed that the great majority in each group evidenced a downward movement similar to that shown in the charts. A count was made of the number of companies in each sample for which the given ratio fell with no more than two interruptions from the sixth to the first year before discontinuance; for some of the companies there was no interruption, and the majority had only one. The results, expressed as a percentage of the number of companies in each sample, are presented herewith. It can be seen that the proportion of companies recording what may be called a persistent decline ranged from 51 percent (net worth to total debt in the men's clothing group) to 76 percent (net working capital to total assets in furniture). In most of the samples from three-fifths to three-fourths of the companies experienced the indicated decline. The comparatively small proportions for the men's clothing sample accord with our earlier observation, based on the

	Current Assets to Current Liabilities	Net Worth to Total Debt	Net Working Capital to Total Assets
Baking (47 cos.)	62%	68%	68%
Men's clothing (41 cos.)	54	51	68
Furniture (38 cos.)	66	71	76
Stone-clay (43 cos.)	70	53	72
Machine tool (31 cos.)	61	65	61

Portents of Discontinuance 101

charts, that the portents for this group were less well marked than those for the other samples.

For the companies that showed more than two interruptions the given ratio sometimes declined markedly, sometimes remained fairly stable and occasionally rose in the fifth and fourth years before discontinuance and then plunged downward. In each sample a handful of companies experienced a persistent rise in the ratio, indicating that these discontinuances were the voluntary liquidations mentioned earlier. There appear to have been four or five of these companies in each sample. If it could be established that they, and they alone, were voluntary liquidations, their elimination from these samples would further sharpen the contrasts pictured in Charts 6 to 10.

A final reason for trusting the movements shown by the ratios in these charts is provided by the fact that crudely calculated mean ratios give a similar picture. These mean ratios are characterized as "crudely calculated" because the assumed midpoint of the open-end class was held constant. Thus calculated, the mean ratios decline slightly less than the ratios of aggregates shown in the charts. But if the midpoints of the open-end and next lower classes had been moderately adjusted downward as the last year before discontinuance approached, the mean ratios would have fallen equally as sharply as the ratios of aggregates; and there is every reason to believe that the central tendencies of these upper classes in the frequency distributions actually underwent such a decline.

The fact that the mean ratios declined commensurately with the ratios of aggregates shown in the charts indicates merely that the downward movement was not brought about solely by the large companies. It would still be theoretically possible for the mean ratios to decline and the particular company ratios to fluctuate erratically over the distribution. That this did not occur is indicated by the foregoing tabulation, showing that the ratios for the majority of companies declined persistently.

Thus far we have seen that for the discontinuing companies as a group the three ratios were lower, at least from the fifth year and usually from the sixth year before discontinuance, than the estimated normals for the surviving companies as a group. But these comparisons can tell nothing about the range of variation in the ratios of the companies within each group. Such information is presented in Chart 11, which shows, for each ratio and each industry, how the discontinuing companies were distributed in the last year before discontinuance according to various ratio levels, and also the percentage distribution of the continuing companies according to the corresponding estimated normals. It is evident, as would be expected, that a greater proportion of discontinuing than of continuing companies had the more adverse ratios - those in the lowest two levels distinguished here.

But it should not be overlooked that there is a considerable area of overlap between the two groups of companies. In men's clothing, for example, about 40 percent of the discontinuing companies had a ratio of current assets to current liabilities ranging between 1 and 4, while only slightly more than 50 percent of the continuing companies had estimated normal ratios falling within this range; and two-fifths of these discontinuing companies had a ratio as high as 0.4 or more for net working capital to total assets, while as high a proportion of continuing as of discontinuing men's clothing companies had positive net working capital below the 0.4 level. In other words, there is no clearly marked dividing line between the ratios for the continuing and the discontinuing companies. Some companies in the samples survived through 1936 with relatively poor ratios, while others with relatively good ratios went out of existence before that year.

An obvious inference that might be drawn from the foregoing analysis is that these three ratios may provide an acceptable criterion for a credit analyst in evaluat-

---

FOOTNOTES FOR CHART 11

a/ Based on unpublished tables prepared by the Income Tax Study, a WPA project sponsored by the Treasury Department. The estimated normal ratio, which forms the basis for each distribution of continuing companies, is the weighted average of these companies' ratios for the various calendar years contained in the first year before discontinuance; for method of estimate see Appendix D.

b/ The stone-clay and machine tool distributions of discontinuing companies are exclusive of a few corporations that reported neither current assets nor current liabilities.

SAMPLES OF DISCONTINUING AND CONTINUING CORPORATIONS IN FIVE INDUSTRIES: Percentage Distribution in First Year Before Discontinuance, by Three Selected Ratios for Discontinuing Companies and by Corresponding Estimated Normal Ratios for Continuing Companies[a]

CHART 11

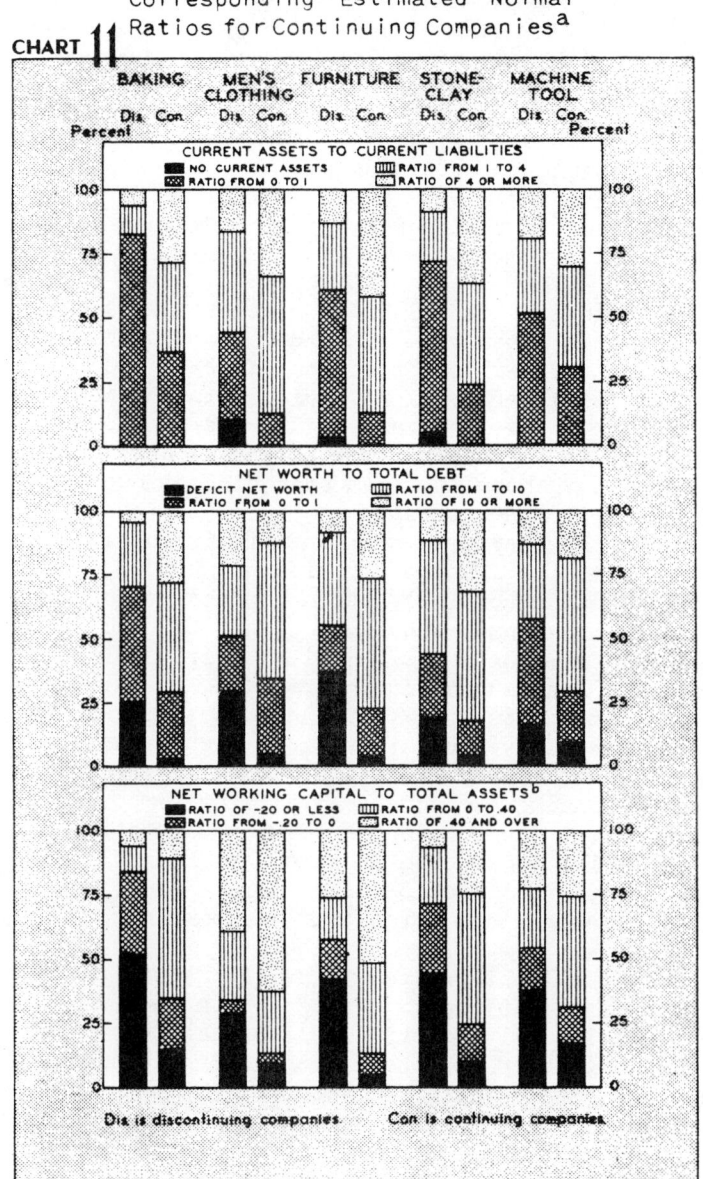

Footnotes on opposite page

ing the tendencies exhibited by an individual enterprise. Such an inference, however, cannot be fully substantiated from the data in their available form. To justify such a conclusion the material presented here should be supplemented by a more detailed study based on individual company ratios rather than on aggregates. It seems probable that values of the ratios lower than the estimated normal may be accepted as portents of discontinuance. But it has not been possible to determine whether the proportion of companies exhibiting a persistent decline differs significantly between the continuing and the discontinuing groups.

Chart 11 brings out still another point that should be stressed at this juncture to avoid misinterpretation of our analysis. It will be seen that in each industry there was some small proportion of discontinuing companies with credit ratios that are high under customary standards of credit appraisal. The companies with these high ratios may have been the ones that discontinued operations voluntarily. We stressed at the outset that for the present samples there was no means of distinguishing the voluntary from the involuntary discontinuances. Because of this absence of information on the reason for discontinuance, it seemed unduly arbitrary to eliminate these companies from the sample. While their presence in the sample calls for caution in interpreting the findings, it strengthens the contention that the adverse movements of the three "sensitive" credit ratios are significant portents of discontinuance. Chart 11 also indicates that some of the continuing companies had amazingly poor credit ratios. Whether such conditions persisted is not known, but they may well have done so in some instances. In other words, a poor credit ratio is no more a sufficient than it is a necessary condition of discontinuance.

In spite of all the necessary qualifications there are important implications in the foregoing analysis. The present samples give clear evidence that in general the financial structure of the discontinuing companies as a group began to deviate from that of the surviving companies as early as six years before actual disappearance. Moreover, most of these deviations between the two groups of companies became increasingly marked as the time of disappearance approached. The indications of disappearance were relatively definite in four of the industries, but not so marked in the remaining industry, men's clothing. This exception is probably due to the fact that the existence of small-scale men's clothing companies is generally precarious. The demand for their products is whimsical if not capricious, and style and fabric changes are introduced too suddenly for the comfort of the entrepreneur. And after one or two unsuccessful seasons a clothing company is near exhaustion, for resistance to forces of economic contraction or deflation is not so sustained as in, say, the baking industry, where the owners' equity and the investment in fixed property are comparatively large.

So far as credit analysis theory is concerned – the primary assumptions of which it has been the purpose of this chapter to test – our analysis has led to the conclusion that deviation of certain credit ratios from an empirically-determined level has definite diagnostic value. In other words, if the ratio persists in moving in an adverse direction, that movement is portentous of business discontinuance. This does not mean that a company having this financial experience will inevitably and necessarily discontinue operations. It does signify, however, that an unhealthy condition is developing which, unless corrected, will result in business discontinuance.*

The length of the period during which the financial structure of these companies gave indications of approaching discontinuance is a factor of particular importance for business cycle analysis because it reflects the ex-

---

*__Note by Oswald W. Knauth, Director__ - The sample contains companies that discontinued voluntarily as well as companies that discontinued involuntarily. Even if the voluntarily-discontinuing companies were eliminated, this analysis does not establish that any company experiencing an unfavorable movement of any or all of these three "sensitive" credit indicators is necessarily destined to discontinue operations. The author does not stress sufficiently that when unfavorable developments occur many things can happen in a company to reestablish a normally-functioning enterprise. Per contra, it happens at times that a company changes from solvency to insolvency with startling rapidity. Unrecognized weaknesses uncover each other and spiral with increasing speed.

All that can properly be deduced from the data presented is that credit ratios are an important element in forecasting the continuance or discontinuance of individual enterprises; and that weak companies frequently show signs of distress several years in advance of their formal discontinuance. These facts are already generally recognized, and the further partial corroboration offered in this chapter does not materially add to our knowledge of the subject.

tent of the resistance offered to forces of deflation. Some economists have argued that the length and severity of a crisis vary directly with the resistance to liquidation and deflation that is offered by the various groups in the economy during the downturn. Consumers have been represented as particularly slow in accepting deflation and liquidation (in the matter of owned homes, for example). Among business enterprises, too, some groups are more responsive than others to the forces of liquidation. Of the industrial samples studied here, men's clothing appears to be more flexible in this regard than the others, although all small companies, as pointed out in Chapter 1, are probably more subject to liquidation than are large companies.

ANALYSES OF THE PROBLEMS AND SHORTCOMINGS OF RATIOS

THE MULTIPLICITY
OF FINANCIAL RATIOS

Nathaniel Jackendoff

Chapter II

THE MULTIPLICITY OF FINANCIAL RATIOS

ANYONE who has read widely in the literature of accounting and business finance and who has examined the many published reports containing ratio data is faced with a confusing and frustrating array of relationships. The problem is aggravated, however, not only by the lack of uniformity in terminology, but by the redundant use of ratios which are but superficially different. Ratios are sometimes compiled with no attempt at developing some underlying rationale — a sort of doodling with the numbers in the financial statements. Less fundamental difficulties arise from technical differences in definition of accounting terms used in ratios, as well as from different statistical techniques in deriving the numerical value of the terms in the ratios.

REDUNDANCIES IN THE USE OF RATIOS

Some redundancies among ratios, such as arise from the mere switching of terms, are very obvious. Others are more subtle and require a clear understanding of the structure of the financial statement.

Reciprocal Relationships. Occasionally, the very same accounting items are related in inverse orders and counted as two separate ratios. Thus, for example, in the course of listing and defining ratios in use by trade associations, a 1946 study showed the following:[1]

1. (a) Total liabilities to net worth — shows the proportion of creditor's capital to total capital and therefore is informative for credit purposes.
   (b) Net worth to total liabilities — furnishes a complete separation of creditor's capital from investor's capital and of course is more comprehensive than net worth to fixed liabilities.
2. (a) Fixed assets to net worth — shows the amount of investor's capital permanently devoted to such items as plant and equipment.
   (b) Net worth to fixed assets — shows what proportion of investor's money is permanently allocated to plant and equipment, and therefore is not likely to be available for creditors.

It is unusual for the same analyst to use both a given ratio and its reciprocal. In the literature of ratios, however, the same statement items are very commonly to be found paired in opposite ways, and sometimes given different shades of meaning, as suggested by the preceding illustration.

Other Redundancies. Another type of redundancy arises from the use of ratios which are easily derived from one another, although the components are not identical as is true in inversions. The derivations are most apparent if one keeps in mind the basic accounting equation for the balance sheet and the interrelationships within the income statement.

One of the most obvious sets of such related ratios includes:

1. **Worth to total debt** (or its inverse, **total debt to worth**)
2. **Worth to total assets**
3. **Total debt to total assets**

These are simply variants of the equation: Total Assets = Total Debt + Net Worth. Assuming the following balance sheet figures:

Total assets 100   Total liabilities 25
                    Total net worth 75

it would seem that the most useful analytical statement that can be made is that assets can deteriorate in value by 75 percent before the creditors suffer a loss on their contribution to the assets of the business. This would therefore imply the use of the ratio of net worth to total assets.

---

[1] American Trade Association Executives, op. cit., pp. 8-9.

Another form of statement would say that the owners have three times as much invested in the business as the creditors, thus utilizing the ratio of worth to debt (or its inverse). The ratio of total debt to total assets is the complement of net worth to total assets and is hardly susceptible to any further refinements of interpretation. All three ratios have, in effect, exactly the same significance. One must, therefore, allow for personal preference in choosing one as against the others.

Just as obvious a redundancy exists with regard to the so-called "**operating ratio,**" which is the ratio of operating expenses plus cost of goods sold to sales and the "**net operating profit margin,**" which is the relationship of net operating profits to sales. The latter is derivable by subtracting the operating ratio from 100 per cent, thus being its complement, as shown by the following illustrative statement:

Net sales 100
Less: Operating expenses plus cost
  of goods sold 95
Equals: Net operating profit 5

Another set of ratios which are less directly related and certainly less obvious in their relationship includes the **acid-test** (sometimes known as the **quick** ratio or the **liquid** ratio) and the ratio of **inventory to net working capital.** The former relates cash, marketable securities, and current receivables to current liabilities. In effect, it is often calculated by taking current assets minus inventory to current liabilities.

Both ratios are refinements of the ratio of current assets to current liabilities and are intended to test the quality of the current assets in the ratio by segregating the inventory. Given the current ratio and either of the ratios mentioned, the other ratio is easily derivable. Thus, "net working capital" is equal to current assets minus current liabilities, the two terms in the current ratio. Inventory is equal to the difference between current assets and the quick assets included in the acid-test ratio. (See Figure 1.)

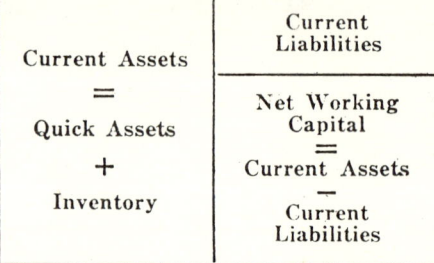

FIGURE 1

If inventory is less than net working capital, then quick assets must exceed current liabilities. If inventory is equal to net working capital, then quick assets must equal current liabilities. Finally, if inventory exceeds net working capital, then quick assets must be less than current liabilities. Worked in ratio terms, an inventory to net working capital ratio of 1:1 must mean an acid-test ratio of 1:1. An inventory to net working capital ratio exceeding 1:1 means an acid test of less than 1:1. And an inventory to net working capital ratio of less than 1:1 necessarily means an acid-test ratio exceeding 1:1.[2] (See Figure 2.)

The acid-test ratio is probably the more direct and easily understood relationship of the two. It uses directly

FIGURE 2

Quick Assets	Current Liabilities
....	
....	Net Working Capital
Inventory	

[2]This inherent relationship between the two ratios has not been clearly recognized by all analysts. One commentator on ratios, who suggests the use of both the acid-test ratio and the inventory-to-net-working-capital ratio falls into the logical inconsistency of calling for a minimum of 1:1 on the former and a maximum ⅔:1 on the latter, despite the fact that he has defined the quick assets as used in the acid-test ratio as, "Assets which are easily converted into cash along with all cash both deposited and undeposited usually can be considered current assets less inventories." John E. Graf, "How Ratios Help Control Operations," Non-Ferrous Founders' Society, Inc., 1959 Annual Meeting Papers, Special Report No. 59, Part 1, January, 1960, pp. 27, 31.

identifiable terms: cash, marketable, securities, receivables and current liabilities. "Net working capital," on the other hand, is an abstraction derived from the difference between current assets and current liabilities. In reality, one can no more logically assign inventory as a component of net working capital than one can assign to it any other single component of the current assets. In this respect, the inventory to net working capital ratio may be quite confusing. The analytical significance of the two ratios is essentially the same, however. There are those who prefer to use the net working capital as a base for various computations because of its relative seasonal constancy and to whom, therefore, inventory to net working capital is only one of a series of net working capital ratios.[3]

A ratio related to the acid-test and inventory to net working capital ratios is that of **current debt to inventory**. This is published among Dun and Bradstreet's "Fourteen Important Ratios." Given the current ratio and the inventory to net working capital ratio, current debt to inventory is derivable. Thus, for example, a firm with a 3:1 current ratio and a 1:1 inventory to net working capital ratio, must have a 1:2 current debt to inventory ratio. Actually, by inverting this ratio and subtracting from the current ratio, the acid-test ratio may be derived.[4]

It is difficult to see what the current debt to inventory contributes beyond what can be learned from the acid-test or inventory to net working capital ratios. It is an alternative to these and has been used by trade associations in several special industry studies. It is interesting to note that Roy A. Foulke completely disregards discussion of this ratio in his textbook, although he is responsible for the Dun and Bradstreet publication of the "Fourteen Important Ratios" which includes both the inventory to net working capital and the current debt to inventory ratios.

FIGURE 3

Current Assets Including Net Working Capital	Current Liabilities
	Noncurrent Liabilities + Net Worth
Noncurrent Assets	

Another group of relationships centers among net working capital, non-current (mostly fixed) assets, non-current (mostly long-term or funded debt) liabilities, and net worth. By definition:

Net working capital + noncurrent assets = Noncurrent liabilities + Net worth. (See Figure 3.)

Among the Dun & Bradstreet "Fourteen Important Ratios" are to be found both **Funded debt to net working capital** and **Fixed assets to tangible net worth**. Assuming that funded debt tends to account for practically all of the non-current liabilities and that fixed assets account for most of the noncurrent assets, there is a direct relationship between these two ratios which is derivable from the basic equation above. A 1:1 funded debt to net working capital must mean a 1:1 ratio of fixed assets to net worth. A funded debt to net working capital ratio exceeding 1:1 must mean a greater than 1:1 ratio of fixed assets to net worth. Finally, a ratio of funded debt to net working capital of less than 1:1 must mean that the fixed

FIGURE 4

Net Working Capital	Noncurrent Debt
Noncurrent Assets	Net Worth

---

[3] Dun & Bradstreet and its subsidiary, the National Credit Office have been among the proponents of net working capital ratios.
[4] 3:1 − 2:1 = 1:1.

assets to net worth ratio is less than 1:1.[5] (See Figure 4.)

The relationships among the ratios are recognized by Roy A. Foulke when he points out that a high fixed asset to net worth relationship will be associated with either: (1) low net working capital for the size of the business which would be revealed by an excessive net sales to net working capital ratio, or (2) reliance upon funded debt to furnish adequate net working capital, that is, a high funded debt to net working capital ratio.[6] As pointed out earlier(the second condition is almost necessarily true, depending upon the role of miscellaneous assets and noncurrent debts other than funded debts. The first condition would, in all probability, be accompanied by a poor current ratio and, if inventory were adequate to support the particular level of sales (as shown by inventory turnover), by a low acid-test ratio or a high inventory to net working capital ratio.

The purpose of the fixed asset to net worth ratio is primarily to measure two things: (1) the solvency of the business in case of liquidation — in this respect being a refinement of the net worth to total assets ratio by highlighting the assets most likely to dissolve in value in case of liquidation; and (2) the competitive disadvantage imposed upon the business. The latter would probably be evidenced more explicitly by a heavy depreciation charge against current income. High interest charges would also be incurred to the extent that funds were borrowed in order to support the fixed capital. A third possibility which would adversely affect the firm's competitive position would be the inability to take discounts on purchases should the high fixed capital have been acquired at the expense of net working capital.[7]

In view of the close relationship between the fixed asset to net worth ratio and the funded debt to net working capital ratio, there seems to be little point to using both. The former appears to be more direct and easy to interpret. To the extent that it is desirable to measure the adequacy of the current position and to measure the adequacy of net worth relative to long-term or total debt, other ratios are available to perform this function more directly and adequately than either of these two ratios.[8]

TURNOVER AND AGE OF CONVERSION RELATIONSHIPS

Among the important interstatement ratios are those which appear to measure the turnover of asset items through sales. Certain of these are reasonably susceptible of being converted in form so as to become "age of conversion into cash" ratios, thus becoming especially

---

[5]The difference between noncurrent assets and fixed assets is accounted for primarily by miscellaneous assets such as cash surrender value of life insurance, amounts due from officers, directors, and employees, investments in and advances to subsidiaries and affiliates, and deferred charges and prepaid expense according to the classification in Foulke's **Practical Financial Statement Analysis.** He would account for any difference between noncurrent debt and funded debt by the presence of certain reserves for contingencies and possibly unearned income. It is by allowing for these differences that we can explain the following rules of thumb to be found in Foulke's book, (pp. 272 and 294): (1) "Rarely, if ever, should the aggregate of funded liabilities exceed the net working capital." Thus, we have a maximum of 1:1. (2) "A ratio of 66⅔ to 75 percent of the tangible net worth is more than a fair leeway as a reasonable business guide for the percentage of funds to be invested in fixed assets. Smaller percentages are proportionately more favorable." Here we have a suggested maximum of ⅔ to ¾ :1 as the ratio of fixed assets to net worth.

[6]Foulke, op. cit., p. 280.

[7]Foulke suggests that all these competitive disadvantages occur simultaneously with a high fixed asset to worth ratio. Theoretically, the net working capital could be maintained at adequate levels by the assumption of long-term debt and the concomitant interest charges. Foulke, **op. cit.**, p. 291.

[8]One trade association uses the relationship of working capital to total debt among the key relationships recommended to its members. It also uses the worth to fixed asset ratio and the worth to debt ratio. Although no particular rules of thumb are recommended other than by comparison with industry aggregates, it is obvious that if worth exceeds fixed assets (noncurrent assets), net working capital probably exceeds the long-term debt. The current ratio and the acid-test or inventory to net working capital ratio adequately cover the problem of current debt relationships. The worth to debt ratio takes care of the question of overall debt financing of assets. It is difficult to see what information is added by a total debt to net working capital relationship.

useful for a crude but quick analysis of cash flows. These are the turnovers of inventory and receivables. A wide variety of other turnover relationships are used by financial analysts, the most important of which include: (1) sales to net worth, (2) sales to net working capital, (3) sales to plant and equipment, and (4) sales to total assets.

Age of Conversion of Receivables and Inventory. The turnover and aging of accounts are alternative methods of presenting the same relationships. Turnover of receivables, for example, may be determined by dividing annual sales by receivables outstanding. If turnover occurs twelve times, by dividing twelve into the number of days in the year, the average number of days to convert receivables into cash works out as 30 days. This is known as the "average collection period," the "average age of conversion" of receivables into cash, or the "average days receivables outstanding." Similarly, the turnover of inventory and average days of inventory in stock can be computed. It is also possible to compute average days in accounts payable by this technique. Purchases are used, rather than sales, in order to get the turnover of payables. The turnover is divided into 360 (or 365) to determine the average age of payables. This ratio provides a quick, though crude, measure of paying habits of the firm to suppliers. It is not as frequently used as the receivables and inventory ratios.

This type of computation into "average age" may be especially useful for the purpose of projection into budgets. As a measure of liquidity it becomes especially convenient to combine the average days in receivables and in inventory to obtain an "average age of conversion" of non-cash current assets into cash. In this case, it is probably preferable to measure turnover of inventory by using cost of goods sold rather than net sales, since inventory is usually valued at cost. Even so, it remains only a crude indicator which should not be accepted too literally.[9]

Other Turnover Relationships. Granting certain imperfections in the turnover relationships of sales to receivables and to inventory, there is at least a superficially direct interpretation possible with these, since inventory and receivables do go through an actual cycle of conversion from cash to inventory to receivables and back to cash. It is questionable whether the other turnover ratios are amenable to such interpretation, although there may be other explanations to warrant their use.

Turnover of Net Worth and of Net Working Capital. These two ratios are recommended by Roy A. Foulke and are included among the "Fourteen Important Ratios" of Dun and Bradstreet. In both cases, the major rationale for their use concerns the discovery of under-or overtrading by the firm in relation to its resources. There are no obvious rules of thumb for these ratios. They show very wide disparity from one industry to another. There is no intrinsic logic such as might be superficially derived from the current ratio, the acid-test, or the age of conversion of receivables and inventories. "Net worth" is, in essence, a residual figure, and being a form of claim against the business, is not actually turned over or converted into cash. "Net working capital" is also a derived figure, representing the excess of current assets over current liabilities. It does not turn over in any superficially real sense as does inventory.

Foulke makes the point that a firm

---

[9]Additional complications include the use of "average monthly" versus year-end inventory and receivables figures, and the distribution of inventory between that portion sold on credit rather than cash on delivery basis. The "age of conversion" concept was encountered in an article by F. E. Lunt, "Ratios—What They Tell us," **Credit and Financial Management,** February, 1942, pp. 8 ff., Lunt uses "net sales to inventory" in arriving at average age of inventory.

with too low a turnover of worth or working capital must be using its resources inefficiently with a consequent adverse effect upon the level of profits. Too high a turnover makes the firm vulnerable to minor reductions in sales, as purchase commitments may continue and current payables accumulate without sufficient cash generation to liquidate them.

A review of Foulke's discussion of these two ratios suggests that the sales to net worth relationship is superfluous since the sales to net working capital, by itself, adequately reveals trends toward under- or over-trading. Foulke points out that the turnover of working capital is a necessary supplement to the turnover of net worth since the latter is influenced by methods of financing. A reasonable level of operations may appear as excessive, using the criterion of turnover of net worth, if net worth is inadequate. Or, on the contrary, under-trading may be suggested when the real reason is an unusually high net worth relative to debt. Analysis of the illustrative cases used by Foulke for the sales to worth relationship revealed that direct answers to the problems posed were available from a combination of the sales to net working capital ratio and the net worth to total assets ratio.[10]

It might be thought that the inventory turnover relationship would serve just as well as working capital turnover to indicate either an excessive or inadequate level of sales. It is quite possible, however, for rises or declines in sales to be accompanied by corresponding movements of inventory so that the turnover of inventory may remain unchanged. The inventory changes are usually accompanied by equivalent changes in current liabilities, thus maintaining net working capital stable. The sales to net working capital is, therefore, a sensitive indicator of overtrading or undertrading — that is, of the adequacy of net working capital for the scale of operations of the firm.[11]

Plant Turnover. Plant turnover, as measured by the relationship of net sales to fixed assets, is recommended by some analysts as a useful measure and is currently in use by some trade associations. It must be recognized that this is not a true turnover in the sense that fixed assets do not generate cash through sales except in a very indirect sense. Plant turnover is a crude measure of the efficiency with which plant is being used. It tends to indicate the extent to which the fixed burden of depreciation (and, perhaps, maintenance charges and financing costs) is spread over sales. The higher the turnover, the less is the burden of fixed charges per dollar of sales, and the higher is the operating profit margin. From the point of view of management, such figures are more directly available from the profit and loss statement. As a crude indicator of competitive position, where detailed cost data are unavailable, this ratio can be useful.[12]

Turnover of Total Assets. The turnover of total operating assets, as measured by the relationship of sales to total operating assets focuses attention upon turnover of total assets as one of the factors determining the return upon

---

[10] Foulke, op. cit., Chapter XIV.

[11] For adverse criticism concerning this ratio see Harry G. Guthmann, **Analysis of Financial Statements,** fourth edition, pp. 121-122.

[12] There is some question as to whether plant should be measured at gross values before rather than after depreciation. The former is probably the more common. To the extent that this ratio is intended to evaluate the burden of fixed charges from depreciation per unit of sales, the gross against which depreciation is determined is the proper figure. Varying ages of plant would result in different dollar figures on a net basis for plants which may be imposing the same depreciation burden upon sales. It is quite true, on the other hand, that the lower net plant resulting from larger depreciation reserves has released funds for investment in other assets and so reduced the financial burden upon the business. More detailed and technical discussion of problems relating to plant turnover and related ratios may be found in Harry G. Guthmann, **Analysis of Financial Statements,** fourth edition, Prentice-Hall, N. Y., pp. 162 ff., and in Finney and Miller, **Principles of Accounting—Intermediate,** pp. 190-191.

investment. This is developed more thoroughly in the next chapter.

CURRENT DEBT TO WORTH RATIO OF QUESTIONABLE VALUE

A ratio which seems to be among the more widely used of the balance sheet ratios is that of current debt to net worth. It is included among the "Fourteen Important Ratios" published by Dun & Bradstreet and is among the more frequently used ratios in special industry studies.

It may be looked upon as a refinement of the total debt to worth (and related) ratios, which it accompanies in the Dun & Bradstreet publication. Roy A. Foulke points out that the debt to net worth and the current ratios are the oldest types of ratios used by analysts, but that the term "liabilities" formerly carried with it the connotation defined explicitly today as "current liabilities." This could be explained by the fact that until at least the last quarter of the nineteenth century, other than for the railroads, relatively few enterprises had long-term liabilities in the form of funded debt. The growth of a variety of long-term obligations made it possible for a firm with only modest current liabilities to appear to be a far better risk for current creditors than might have been indicated by the relationship of total liabilities to net worth. Hence, the ratio of total liabilities to net worth was also introduced.[13] One also encounters the ratio of long-term liabilities (or funded debt) to net worth in a number of ratio discussions and studies.

If one's concern is to measure the ultimate protection to short-term creditors in case of liquidation, with certain exceptions, as specified in the bankruptcy laws (taxes, wages, rent), current creditors cannot be singled out from the long-term creditors. Should losses from the realization of assets in liquidation wipe out the net worth of the business, all creditors must share the losses in proportion to their claims unless they have a secured position or where they have received a specific subordination of other creditors' claims. Consequently, the separate measure of current debt to net worth has no operational significance and may even be misleading to the extent that it suggests any special protection for short-term creditors. The same criticism would apply equally to a separate ratio of funded debt to net worth.[14]

NET WORKING CAPITAL TO TOTAL ASSETS AS AN INDICATOR

The ratio of net working capital to total assets has not been encountered in any textbooks on financial analysis or in any special industry analyses. It has appeared in certain research studies at the University of Illinois and has been used in studies done for the National Bureau of Economic Research.[15]

This ratio has proven itself to these authors to be the most sensitive indicator of future business discontinuance among all the ratios tested. It is described by Charles L. Merwin as, along with the current ratio, reflecting the "freezing of working capital." Nowhere does one find, however, other than for the discussion of the statistical testing, a clear discussion of the ratio.

---

[13]Foulke, op. cit., pp. 204-205. All of Chapter VII is devoted to the subject of current liabilities to net worth. It is interesting to note that every illustrative case used by Foulke for the ratio of current debt to worth shows no long-term debt, so that his analysis would have been just as effective had he used the total debt to worth ratio. In all the cases where he attempts to demonstrate the deterioration of the current position through the use of this ratio, the condition is effectively brought out by the current ratio.

[14]This point is made by Harry G. Guthmann, Analysis of Financial Statements, fourth edition, p. 166.

[15]Charles L. Merwin, Financing Small Corporations, National Bureau of Economic Research, 1942, Chapter 4, especially p. 92. At least one other study is currently in progress by Mr. Martin Seiden at the National Bureau. Merwin's study was preceded on a much smaller scale by studies of unsuccessful corporations by the Bureau of Business Research of the University of Illinois: "A Test Analysis of Unsuccessful Industrial Companies," Bulletin No. 31, July, 1930; "Changes In The Financial Structure of Unsuccessful Industrial Corporations" by Raymond F. Smith and Arthur H. Winaker, Bulletin No. 51, July, 1935; "Capacity To Pay Current Debts" by Arthur H. Winaker, Bulletin No. 53, October, 1936.

In contrast with the very common practice of relying upon the absolute dollar value of net working capital as a measure of liquidity, the ratio of net working capital to total assets suggests that the adequacy of net working capital is properly related to the size of the business as measured by total assets. It would appear to the present writer, however, that the scale of the firm's operation as indicated by net sales would provide a more meaningful base for measuring the adequacy of net working capital.

The basic intent of this ratio appears, therefore, to be served by the ratio of net sales to net working capital (turnover of net working capital.)

COMMON-SIZE BALANCE SHEETS

Summary techniques for analyzing the condition of the firm are found in so-called "common-size" balance sheets where the individual balance sheet items are related to a common base such as total assets, net working capital, or net sales.

Based on Total Assets. The most complete picture of balance sheet structure is to be found in the common-size balance sheet. This is usually presented in complete balance sheet form, expressing each of the assets, liabilities and net worth items as percentages of total assets. Sub-totals such as current assets and current liabilities are usually included. This permits the analyst to develop any intra-balance sheet relationships he deems significant. The statement can be reviewed historically within the firm, as well as compared with industry composites.

The usefulness of the common-size balance sheet is limited by the fact that the size of the base, total assets, may be affected by the inclusion of substantial non-operating assets such as investments in real estate or securities. On the other hand, total assets may be reduced considerably when a business leases the bulk of its fixed assets. Thus, changes in any one item which affect total assets substantially bring distortions in the percentages assigned to all other individual items in the statement. These can be very misleading in trend analyses when the structure of the business is being altered and result in confusion when one business firm is compared with another or to some industry composites.

The illustration, shown in Figures 5a and 5b, points out the effect of such differences between two hypothetical situations which are alike in every respect except for the items "other assets;" and "long-term liabilities" and "net worth."

One way to minimize this weakness of the common-size balance sheet based upon total assets is to work out separate subtotals for current assets and current liabilities or for any other meaningful grouping of items within the balance sheet and provide supplementary percentage breakouts for each subgroup. (See Figure 6.) Thus, in the above two hypothetical companies, the subgroup distributions of both would be the same.

This type of analysis of current items might be used to suggest some average distribution of accounts within each of the subgroups. However, it remains subject to the criticism that an unusual change in any one of the items would distort all of the apparent relationships.

The dangers of using common-size data from the balance sheet are, of course, minimized to the extent that the user does not rely exclusively upon this technique for judging financial position. The sources of difficulties may be isolated by the use of supplementary ratio analysis.

Based on Net Working Capital. Other forms of common-size balance sheets are sometimes used where the base is independent of the totals of the individual items. This has the effect of minimizing the possibility of distortions in all items arising from unusual movements in any one of them. The National Credit

THE MULTIPLICITY OF FINANCIAL RATIOS

FIGURE 5A
Balance Sheets of Two Hypothetical Companies
(Thousands of Dollars)

	Company A	Company B		Company A	Company B
Cash	5	5	Accounts Payable	20	20
Receivables	20	20	Other Current Liabilities	5	5
Inventory	25	25	Current Liabilities	25	25
Current Assets	50	50	Long-Term Liabilities	15	30
Plant and Equipment	40	40	Net Worth	60	95
Other Assets	10	60	Total Liabilities and Net Worth	100	150
Total	100	150			

FIGURE 5B
Common-Size Balance Sheets of Same Two Companies
(Percentages of Total Assets)

	Company A	Company B		Company A	Company B
Cash	5	3.33	Accounts Payable	20	13.33
Receivables	20	13.33	Other Current Liabilities	5	3.34
Inventory	25	16.67	Current Liabilities	25	16.67
Current Assets	50	33.33	Long-Term Liabilities	15	20.00
Plant and Equipment	40	26.67	Net Worth	60	63.33
Other Assets	10	40.00	Total Liabilities and Net Worth	100	100.00
Total	100	100.00			

FIGURE 6
Percentage Distribution of Current Assets and Current Liabilities, Same Two Companies

Current Assets	A	B	Current Liabilities	A	B
Cash	10	10	Accounts Payable	80	80
Receivables	40	40	Other Current Liabilities	20	20
Inventory	50	50	Total Current Liabilities	100	100
Total Current Assets	100	100			

TABLE 1
PATTERN STATEMENTS FOR MANUFACTURERS OF WOMEN'S DRESSES, 1952
SELECTED WORKING CAPITAL TURNOVER GROUPS

	Six Times and Under		Twenty-One Times and Up	
	Actual (00 Omitted)	Percent of Working Capital	Actual (00 Omitted)	Percent of Working Capital
Cash and Securities	$334	56	$ 226	49
Receivables	277	47	805	174
Merchandise	187	32	600	130
Current Assets	$798	135	$1,631	353
Fixed Assets	39	7	122	26
Other Assets	42	7	78	17
Total Assets	$679	149	$1,831	394
Trade Debt	117	20	817	177
Loans Payable	8	1	160	35
Other Current Liabilities	81	14	192	41
Current Liabilities	$266	35	$1,169	253
Funded Debt	0	0	2	0
Net Worth	673	114	660	143
Liabilities and Net Worth	$879	149	$1,831	396
Working Capital	$592	100	$ 462	100

Source: National Credit Office, Inc.

TABLE 2
SUMMARY OF DRUGS AND DRUG SUNDRIES ASSETS AND CURRENT LIABILITIES OF
SERVICE WHOLESALER DRUGGISTS AS A PERCENT OF NET SALES,
SELECTED VOLUME GROUPS, 1958

	Total U.S.	Volume Groups	
		Under $2 million	$10 million and Over
Cash on Hand and in Banks	1.69%	2.73%	1.82%
Marketable Securities Held Temporarily	0.16	0.19	0.15
	1.85	2.92	1.97
Net Receivables	10.27	9.96	9.26
Inventories	14.73	17.55	13.51
Other Current Assets	0.27	0.42	0.32
Total Current Assets	27.13	30.87	25.08
Fixed Assets (Real Estate and Other)	3.14	2.78	3.13
Deferred Charges	0.24	0.17	0.19
Total Assets Used in Business	30.53	33.85	28.42
Total Assets Exclusive of Real Estate	28.62	32.42	26.76
Accounts Payable	5.04	5.33	4.86
Notes Payable	1.48	1.24	0.89
Accrued Liabilities	1.15	1.19	0.91
Federal Income Tax Payable	1.79	1.52	1.63
Total Current Liabilities	9.48	9.30	8.30
Net Working Capital	17.65	21.57	16.78

Source: National Wholesale Druggists Association, NWDA, 1958, Operating Survey, 27th Edition, p. 46.

Office, a subsidiary of Dun & Bradstreet, at one time produced what it called "pattern statements," in which all individual balance sheet items were related to net working capital. The principal reasons given for the use of this base were:

Net Working Capital of a concern fluctuates less frequently and less widely than Total Assets, which change materially with the daily ebb and flow of business.

Net Working Capital, therefore, is more constant as a base and should cause proportionate differences in items to register more sensitively and significantly than is possible with a less stationary base when inter-statement comparisons are being made.

Further, if credit appraisal of a balance sheet centers on the ability of a debtor to meet his obligations, as they mature, out of Current Assets, then the relationship of every item in the current position to Working Capital is involved in the analysis.[16]

The pattern statements classified firms by various groupings such as working capital turnover groups, net worth groups, and price range groups. Table 1 illustrates composite pattern statements for manufacturers of women's dresses for two working capital turnover classifications. Each of these was determined by dividing net working capital into net sales. Thus, a firm with net sales of $600,000 and $150,000 of net working capital would be included in the "Six times and under" turnover grouping. A firm with the same sales volume and $25,000 of net working capital would be grouped with those showing a turnover of "Twenty-one times and up."

Based on Sales. Another approach to a common-size balance sheet is to relate individual items in the balance sheet to a sales base. Again, as with the net working capital base, the weakness of total assets is avoided — that is, the danger of distortion of all items as a percentage of the base resulting from a substantial change in only one of them. The sales base has been used by some as the most relevant, since it is assumed that the distribution of assets, liabilities, and net worth should be related to the scale of operations.[17] Thus, the shifting sales base is not, in itself, a disadvantage. On the contrary, it may be considered desirable in view of the fact that it highlights the changing financial requirements of the business as the scale of operations changes.

As used by the National Wholesale Druggists' Association, this form of statement is interpreted to suggest operating asset requirements per dollar of sales. Primary emphasis is placed upon working capital items and non-current assets used in the business. Non-current debt and net worth are excluded. Table 2 illustrates such an analysis in abbreviated form.

SUMMARY

The financial ratios discussed in this chapter are all most directly concerned with the measurement of short-term liquidity and long-term solvency. They do not deal in any clear-cut manner with the question of profitability, the subject of the next chapter. As will be apparent, however, they may contribute to an understanding of profitability as they directly influence certain of the profitability measures.

Ratios should be selected in such a way as to minimize duplicative measurements. The ratios in use should each make an independent and meaningful contribution to the analysis. For example, the ratio of total debt to net worth has no meaning different from the worth to total assets or the worth to debt ratios. It is questionable whether the ratio of inventory to net working capital tells a story any different from that of quick assets to current liabilities or current liabilities to inventory. It is doubtful that the ratio of

---

[16] Special statement issued in mimeographed form by the Research Division of the National Credit Office entitled, "Pattern Statement Items as Percentages of Working Capital, A Note of Explanation."

[17] An article by J. Fred Weston develops the use of sales as a base for projecting balance sheet requirements. See "Forecasting Financial Requirements," **The Accounting Review**, July, 1958, pp. 427-440.

net worth to noncurrent assets can offer any significantly different contribution than the ratio of funded debt to net working capital. These are all redundant sets of ratios.

The turnover ratios appear interesting and useful. Both the turnover of receivables and turnover of inventory contribute to a better understanding of the quality of current assets than is provided by either the current ratio or the acid test ratio. These are also interesting when expressed in "age of conversion" form by suggesting the average time necessary to convert these assets into cash.

The plant turnover and total asset turnover ratios appear to have less immediate significance except as arbitrary indicators of the effectiveness with which assets are being utilized. Here, one may question their usefulness other than to the extent that they contribute to an understanding of profitability. The gross plant turnover ratio indirectly suggests the burden of depreciation and associated fixed costs on the sales dollar. Such cost details are, of course, more directly measured by depreciation expense to net sales data which are to be found in a detailed income statement analysis. For external analysis, however, where the details of depreciation are often unavailable, the plant turnover ratio may be of interest. As is shown in Chapter III, the turnover of total assets is important as one of the contributors, along with the net profit margin, in determining the return on total asset investment.

The relationship of net working capital to net sales has been suggested as an important ratio in analyzing the adequacy of the capitalization of the firm relative to its scale of operations. The ratio of sales to net worth and that of net working capital to total assets appear to be superfluous, although the latter has been put to interesting uses in several scholarly studies. The relationship of net working capital to sales, although not tested in the same way, should serve better than net working capital to total assets as a sensitive indicator of over- or undertrading. The adequacy of net worth is already being tested by the worth to total assets or worth to total debt relationship and the sales to net worth ratio appears superfluous alongside the net working capital to sales relationship as a measure of the adequacy of capitalization.

Common-size balance sheets, whether based on total assets, net working capital, or sales, are an interesting supplement to the preceding ratios, although often duplicating them. They do provide an organized appraisal of the relative distribution of all the individual assets, liabilities, and net worth detailed in the financial statement. The sales base is preferred by the present writer.

CAPITALIZING LEASES—
THE EFFECT ON FINANCIAL RATIOS

A. Tom Nelson

By A. Tom Nelson

Capitalizing Leases—The Effect on Financial Ratios

The case for capitalization of long-term leases is supported by specific illustrations of the effect of capitalization on ratios used by security analysts.

THE great upsurge of leasing in the last two decades has presented a number of important financial and accounting problems. Outstanding among these is the method of recording and the reporting of these long-term leases in the financial statements. Because traditional footnote disclosure has been subject to attack from both inside and outside the accounting profession, a number of alternative proposals have been presented. The importance of the topic is underlined by the action of the Accounting Principles Board of the American Institute of Certified Public Accountants in selecting this as one of the initial topics to be studied by the Accounting Research Division. The lease study has recently been released by the Director of Accounting Research of the Institute. The summary of its results appeared in the June issue of THE JOURNAL OF ACCOUNTANCY.

The foreword to the first research study indicated that the "accounting research studies are designed to provide professional accountants and others interested in the development of accounting with a discussion and documentation of accounting problems. The studies are intended to be informative, but not conclusive. They furnish a vehicle for the exposure of matters for consideration and experimentation prior to the issuance of pronouncements by the Accounting Principles Board."

The lease study should promote further discussion and serious consideration of the capitalization proposal. A review of the literature on the subject, however, makes it apparent that capitalization has not yet received unanimous approval. In presenting a case for capitalization, one writer stated that "the inclusion of lease obligations and the related property rights in the balance sheets would produce statements that were fair to all segments of the business community; and, conversely, the present practice of omitting such obligations and assets from the balance sheet does not produce statements that fairly present the facts from the standpoint of any segment."[1]

Another writer views capitalization in quite a different light. He states that capitalization ". . . strikes at the very foundation of accounting, a foundation based on a fundamental concept of cost. Once this concept is breached, there are no reaches of the wild blue yonder into which accounting improprieties may not trespass—to the disadvantage of all segments of the public."[2]

Another charge against capitalization states that if this proposal were adopted "the standard wording of the auditor's certificate could become a mockery, and the task of the financial analyst almost impossible. Balance sheet ratios of the kind

[1] John L. Hennessy, "Recording of Lease Obligations and Related Property Rights," THE JOURNAL OF ACCOUNTANCY, March 1961, p. 46.
[2] Alvin Zises, letter to the editor, "Recording Lease Obligations," THE JOURNAL OF ACCOUNTANCY, June 1961, p. 28.

used in credit analysis for decades would become valueless and comparative figures would have no meaning."[3]

A study of the literature leaves one with the definite impression that much of the capitalization controversy is centered in emotion and vested interests—neither of which is a proper criterion for evaluating the true merits of the proposal. The test of whether any proposed change to current reporting should be adopted by the profession is whether or not the proposal will improve the end product—the financial statements.

One of the important uses of published financial statements is as a basis for calculating ratios which are used in financial analysis. There are two purposes to this article: (1) to determine whether capitalization makes financial ratios more meaningful, and (2) to see whether decision-making would be improved by capitalization. The article summarizes the results of extensive research on published financial statements of forty-four actual companies.

Limitations of ratios

A word of caution about ratios in general seems in order at this point. Ratios must be used for what they are—financial tools. Too often they are looked upon as ends in themselves, rather than as the means to the end. No ratio may be regarded as good or bad per se. Ratios may be likened to railroad signals. They tell the analyst to stop, look, and listen.

If the limitations of ratios are properly understood, they can be useful tools in the hands of the skilled analyst. The extent to which they should be relied upon is a debatable point and is not within the scope of this study. The fact is that financial ratios are widely used in financial analysis. The

---

[3] Alvin Zises, "Full Disclosure of all Contractual Commitments Including Long-Term Leases—The Question of Capitalization," reprint of an address delivered to Robert Morris Associates, Chapter 10 (New England), November 28, 1960, p. 9.

A. TOM NELSON, *CPA, is assistant professor of accounting at the University of Utah, Salt Lake City. He received his Ph.D. degree from Michigan State University last June. Dr. Nelson is a member of the American Institute and the Utah Association of CPAs. He is the author of "Forecasting Securities Prices" which appeared in the spring 1961 issue of Business Topics.*

question then, is not whether or not ratios should be used, but rather, what impact would capitalization have in those instances where ratios are used.

How capitalization works

The mechanics of capitalization may be understood by an illustration which is based upon the following assumed facts:

A plant was built by the XYZ Company to its specifications at a cost of $5,600,000. The building had an estimated useful life of forty years. Upon completion, the building was sold at cost to an insurance company under a sale-and-lease-back agreement. The lease had an original noncancellable term of twenty years during which it called for annual rentals of $420,000. The XYZ Company had options to renew the lease for an additional twenty years at the following reduced rentals: first five-year renewal at $196,000 per year; second five-year renewal at $168,000 per year; next two renewals of five years each at $112,000 per year.

The total payments required to have use of the building during its entire useful life will amount to $11,340,000. These payments will include $5,600,000 return of principal and $5,740,000 interest. The interest rate implied by these calculations is 5.61 per cent. This rate represents the true interest rate implied in the above lease agreement.

The lease would be placed on the XYZ Company's books at the discounted value of the lease rentals payable during the expected useful life of the building ($5,600,000) by debiting the lease asset account and crediting the lease liability account. The asset would then be amortized over its forty-year life in some systematic manner. Rental payments would be applied first to interest (5.61 per cent of the outstanding balance of the liability) and the balance toward the amortization of the lease liability. The journal entries required under the capitalized XYZ Company lease for the entire forty-year period are summarized in Exhibit 1, page 51.

Techniques

The first step in comparing capitalization with current reporting was to reconstruct some financial statements with capitalized amounts included therein. This proved to be a difficult task because the reporting in published financial statements was almost always confined to very brief footnotes. The rentals were usually shown for only one year or else covered a period too broad to be meaningful. Expiration dates were rarely shown and in no case was the implied interest or the original cost indicated. Few contained sufficient information to enable the writer to estimate, even reasonably, the present value of the firm's lease rentals. An examination of the Forms 10K in the files of the Securities and Exchange Commission revealed a similar situation in regard to reports that had been filed with that agency. A letter from the chief accountant of the SEC indicated that such disclosure was "satisfactory" to the Commission. However, the information generally was not sufficient to capitalize the leases

Exhibit 1

Journal Entries Required Under Capitalized XYZ Company Lease for Forty-Year Term

End of Year	Rent (Depr.) Exp.	Lease Asset	Interest Chgs.	Lease Liability	Cash	Remaining Balance in Lease Liability Acct.
0		$5,600,000		<$5,600,000>		
1	$140,000	<140,000>	$314,142	105,858	<$420,000>	$5,494,142
2	140,000	<140,000>	308,204	111,796	<420,000>	5,382,346
3	140,000	<140,000>	301,932	118,068	<420,000>	5,264,278
4	140,000	<140,000>	295,309	124,691	<420,000>	5,139,587
5	140,000	<140,000>	288,314	131,686	<420,000>	5,007,901
6	140,000	<140,000>	280,927	139,073	<420,000>	4,868,828
7	140,000	<140,000>	273,125	146,875	<420,000>	4,721,953
8	140,000	<140,000>	264,886	155,114	<420,000>	4,566,839
9	140,000	<140,000>	256,185	163,815	<420,000>	4,403,024
10	140,000	<140,000>	246,995	173,005	<420,000>	4,230,019
11	140,000	<140,000>	237,290	182,710	<420,000>	4,047,309
12	140,000	<140,000>	227,041	192,959	<420,000>	3,854,350
13	140,000	<140,000>	216,217	203,783	<420,000>	3,650,567
14	140,000	<140,000>	204,785	215,215	<420,000>	3,435,352
15	140,000	<140,000>	192,712	227,288	<420,000>	3,208,064
16	140,000	<140,000>	179,962	240,038	<420,000>	2,968,026
17	140,000	<140,000>	166,497	253,503	<420,000>	2,714,523
18	140,000	<140,000>	152,276	267,724	<420,000>	2,446,799
19	140,000	<140,000>	137,257	282,743	<420,000>	2,164,056
20	140,000	<140,000>	121,397	298,603	<420,000>	1,865,453
21	140,000	<140,000>	104,646	91,354	<196,000>	1,774,099
22	140,000	<140,000>	99,521	96,479	<196,000>	1,677,620
23	140,000	<140,000>	94,109	101,891	<196,000>	1,575,729
24	140,000	<140,000>	88,393	107,607	<196,000>	1,468,122
25	140,000	<140,000>	82,357	113,643	<196,000>	1,354,479
26	140,000	<140,000>	75,982	92,038	<168,000>	1,262,441
27	140,000	<140,000>	70,819	97,181	<168,000>	1,165,260
28	140,000	<140,000>	65,367	102,633	<168,000>	1,062,627
29	140,000	<140,000>	59,610	108,390	<168,000>	954,237
30	140,000	<140,000>	53,530	114,470	<168,000>	839,767
31	140,000	<140,000>	47,108	64,892	<112,000>	774,875
32	140,000	<140,000>	43,468	68,532	<112,000>	706,343
33	140,000	<140,000>	39,624	72,376	<112,000>	633,967
34	140,000	<140,000>	35,563	76,437	<112,000>	557,530
35	140,000	<140,000>	31,276	80,724	<112,000>	476,806
36	140,000	<140,000>	26,747	85,253	<112,000>	391,553
37	140,000	<140,000>	21,965	90,035	<112,000>	301,518
38	140,000	<140,000>	16,914	95,086	<112,000>	206,432
39	140,000	<140,000>	11,580	100,420	<112,000>	106,012
40	140,000	<140,000>	5,947	106,053	<112,000>	-41

Credits shown in brackets < >.
This illustration assumes straight-line amortization of the lease asset.

and this lack of data limited the scope of this study and served to emphasize the inadequacy of current reporting.

In eleven instances, sufficient information was obtained to estimate the capitalized value of the lease rentals. The balance sheets of these eleven companies were then adjusted as follows: The present value of the lease rentals was included among the firm's fixed assets under the caption "rights to use of leased property." The rentals due within one year of the balance sheet date were included among the firm's current liabilities under the caption "current lease rentals." The discounted value of the lease rentals (less the amounts due within one year) were included under the caption "rental obligations under long-term leases (discounted at implicit interest rates)" among the firm's long-term liabilities. The only adjustment made to the income statement was for the implicit interest which was computed by multiplying the implied interest rate by the total lease liability. The amount so calculated was merely shifted from the operating to the nonoperating section of the income statement. This treatment assumed that the sum of the depreciation and interest charges during any one year was equal to the lease rentals for that same year.

Selection of ratios

The number of financial ratios possible is almost limitless. The only ones which are applicable to this study, however, are those which would be affected by capitalization. In the previous section, it was noted the "fixed assets," "current liabilities," "long-term liabilities," and "interest charges" were all increased, while "operating expenses" were decreased by capitalizing long-term leases. All ratios which utilize any of these items will consequently be affected. The following ratios are among the most important:

Current ratio (current assets to current debt)°†
Debt to equity°†
Debt to total capital
Return on total capital
Times interest charges earned
Net profits on net working capital°
Net sales to net working capital (working capital turnover)°†
Fixed assets to tangible net worth°†
Current debt to tangible net worth
Inventory to net working capital°
Current debt to inventory°
Funded debt to net working capital°
Funded debt to net plant
Net working capital to net plant
Net plant to sales (plant turnover)

These ratios were selected from those discussed in literature in the field of financial analysis. Obviously, not all of them are of equal value and space limitations will not permit a detailed discussion of each one here. The reader is referred to texts on the subject for a detailed discussion of the purposes of each ratio.[4]

The impact of capitalization

All of the ratios listed above were calculated from the financial statements of the eleven lessee firms. Separate computations were made from the figures "as reported" and the amounts "as adjusted" in order to isolate the effect of capitalization. The ratios "before capitalization" and "after capitalization" for the eleven selected companies are summarized in Exhibit 2, page 53. The names of the companies have been omitted.

An analysis of the data in Exhibit 2 soon makes it apparent that some of these ratios are quite substantially affected. This fact immediately raises several questions. First of all, what causes the ratios to be so affected, i.e., what happens to the components from which the ratios are computed? This is answered in the first two columns of Exhibit 3, page 55. The first column indicates that ten of the numerators used in computing the ratios increased, four remained unchanged, and only one decreased, as a result of capitalization. In the case of the denominators (column 2), six were greater, four were smaller, and five remained unchanged after capitalization.

A second question raised by the fact that ratios are substantially changed by capitalization is "in what direction?" i.e., do the ratios after capitalization appear to present an "improved" financial position over that presented prior to capitalization? This question is answered in column three of Exhibit 3, where it is noted that in all but two instances capitalization presents a *less* favorable financial position than does conventional reporting.

A final question which might be raised is related to the ratio objectives. Do the ratios measure what

---

°This ratio is included in *14 Important Ratios in 72 Lines of Business* (Dun and Bradstreet, Inc., New York, 1961).
†This ratio is included in the list of nine ratios suggested as key ones for small business purposes by Richard Sanzo, *Ratio Analysis for Small Business* (Small Business Administration, Washington, D. C., 1960).

[4] See for example: Roy A. Foulke, *Practical Financial Statement Analysis* (5th ed.; New York: McGraw-Hill Book Company, Inc., 1961) and Harry G. Guthmann, *Analysis of Financial Statements* (Englewood Cliffs, N.J.: Prentice-Hall, Inc., 1953).

they are trying to measure more or less accurately after capitalization? This question is answered in column 4 of Exhibit 3, where it is noted that in *all* instances (where the ratios themselves are meaningful) the ratios are made *more meaningful by capitalization*.

Exhibit 3 and the discussion which follows imply that the ratios considered in this article meet their

Exhibit 2

Ratios Affected by Capitalization for Eleven Selected Companies

	Favorable Direction	Ratio Expressed as	Company A BC	Company A AC	Company B BC	Company B AC	Company C BC	Company C AC	Company D BC	Company D AC
Major Ratios:										
Current ratio	H	times	2.78	1.85	1.77	1.37	3.42	2.80	3.43	2.13
Debt to equity	L	%	55.0	219.7	70.8	239.9	51.9	152.6	41.4	128.2
Debt to total capital	L	%	35.5	68.7	41.5	70.6	34.2	60.4	29.3	56.2
Return on total capital	H	%	4.8	5.4	8.3	7.1	4.1	4.6	7.7	7.0
Times interest charges earned	H	times	6.3	1.6	20.1	2.2	12.5	2.0	8.4	2.5
Fixed assets to tangible net worth	L	%	59.8	224.5	73.7	242.7	32.9	144.7	67.6	154.4
Funded debt to net plant	L	%	37.2	76.9	18.3	68.6	63.2	79.5	39.4	67.6
Minor Ratios:										
Net profits on net working capital	H	%	12.2	17.1	32.3	52.3	7.6	8.5	26.7	35.7
Net sales to net working capital	H	times	14.3	20.0	22.9	37.1	4.8	5.2	5.9	7.9
Current debt to tangible net worth	L	%	28.7	43.1	54.1	70.1	31.1	37.7	14.8	23.8
Inventory to net working capital	L	%	107.6	149.9	158.3	256.8	66.9	73.5	99.6	133.2
Current debt to inventory	L	%	52.4	78.6	82.0	106.2	61.3	75.6	41.3	66.5
Funded debt to net working capital	L	%	43.7	472.4	32.4	648.3	27.5	169.5	74.3	388.7
Net working capital to net plant	H	%	85.2	16.3	56.6	10.6	230.2	46.9	53.1	17.4
Net plant to sales	L	%	8.2	30.8	7.7	25.4	9.1	40.8	32.0	73.1
Other Ratios:										
Leased assets to total assets		%		51.5		49.7		44.5		38.0
Leased assets to net plant		%		73.2		69.7		77.6		56.2

			Company E BC	Company E AC	Company F BC	Company F AC	Company G BC	Company G AC	Company H BC	Company H AC
Major Ratios:										
Current ratio	H	times	2.56	1.95	7.50	6.16	2.25	2.01	3.40	3.35
Debt to equity	L	%	34.5	111.9	15.8	65.8	71.6	111.2	128.1	153.0
Debt to total capital	L	%	25.6	52.8	13.7	39.7	41.7	52.6	56.2	60.5
Return on total capital	H	%	4.3	4.9	4.0	4.6	7.0	6.8	7.1	6.9
Times interest charges earned	H	times	27.2	2.1	320.6	2.5	6.1	3.3	3.8	3.1
Fixed assets to tangible net worth	L	%	47.6	125.0	23.1	73.0	52.9	92.4	68.1	93.0
Funded debt to net plant	L	%	--	53.6	17.1	66.4	47.9	64.2	106.8	100.8
Minor Ratios:										
Net profits on net working capital	H	%	10.5	13.2	6.0	6.5	17.2	19.0	15.0	15.8
Net sales to net working capital	H	times	7.5	9.4	2.0	2.2	10.8	12.0	4.1	4.3
Current debt to tangible net worth	L	%	33.6	44.0	11.9	17.3	46.3	51.8	54.6	58.4
Inventory to net working capital	L	%	109.8	137.2	49.5	53.2	117.0	129.2	88.1	92.6
Current debt to inventory	L	%	58.5	76.7	31.1	45.2	68.5	76.6	78.2	83.8
Funded debt to net working capital	L	%	--	106.4	5.1	67.5	43.8	113.4	91.9	124.5
Net working capital to net plant	H	%	109.8	33.4	334.6	98.4	109.3	56.6	116.2	81.0
Net plant to sales	L	%	12.2	32.0	14.9	47.2	8.4	14.7	21.2	28.9
Other Ratios:										
Leased assets to total assets		%		36.6		30.2		18.7		9.9
Leased assets to net plant		%		62.1		68.4		42.7		26.8

BC = Before Capitalization
AC = After Capitalization
H = High Ratio Generally Desirable
L = Low Ratio Generally Desirable

Exhibit 2 (continued)

	Favorable Direction	Ratio Expressed as	Company I BC	Company I AC	Company J BC	Company J AC	Company K BC	Company K AC
Major Ratios:								
Current ratio	H	times	2.04	1.99	1.15	1.14	3.40	3.35
Debt to equity	L	%	73.0	90.1	417.1	441.8	75.7	82.0
Debt to total capital	L	%	42.2	47.4	80.7	81.5	43.1	45.0
Return on total capital	H	%	11.5	11.0	(6.8)	(6.2)	8.5	8.4
Times interest charges earned	H	times	7.7	5.8	(5.5)	(4.3)	7.7	6.6
Fixed assets to tangible net worth	L	%	53.4	70.6	71.5	96.1	45.0	51.3
Funded debt to net plant	L	%	33.4	47.5	54.0	62.1	85.3	86.0
Minor Ratios:								
Net profits on net working capital	H	%	30.2	31.0	(74.5)	(79.6)	14.5	14.6
Net sales to net working capital	H	times	5.3	5.5	23.1	24.7	3.7	3.7
Current debt to tangible net worth	L	%	55.1	56.5	375.5	379.1	37.3	37.9
Inventory to net working capital	L	%	111.3	114.2	305.6	326.6	76.7	77.2
Current debt to inventory	L	%	86.3	88.6	220.2	222.3	54.4	55.2
Funded debt to net working capital	L	%	31.1	60.0	69.2	114.3	43.0	49.6
Net working capital to net plant	H	%	107.3	79.2	78.0	54.3	198.5	173.2
Net plant to sales	L	%	17.5	23.1	5.5	7.5	13.7	15.6
Other Ratios:								
Leased assets to total assets		%		9.0		4.6		3.4
Leased assets to net plant		%		24.3		25.7		12.1

BC = Before Capitalization
AC = After Capitalization
H = High Ratio Generally Desirable
L = Low Ratio Generally Desirable

---

objectives better after capitalization than they do before capitalization. This conclusion raises another question of importance: Do the changes have a significant effect on financial analysis? i.e., would the decisions which the financial analyst would make based upon the analysis of these ratios be any different if leases were capitalized than if they were not?

This question is answered in part by Exhibit 4 where the eleven companies are ranked both before and after capitalization for each ratio. In each case the company with the most favorable ratio is given the highest ranking. "Favorable" is used here to mean the general direction which financial analysts consider as being desirable for any given ratio. In Exhibit 2 this direction is indicated for each ratio under the heading "favorable direction." For example, it is generally considered desirable to have a high current ratio but a low debt to equity ratio. Therefore, the company with the *highest* current ratio (Company F) is given the highest ranking in regard to that ratio while the company with the *lowest* debt to equity ratio (also Company F) is ranked first in regard to the latter ratio.

In order to isolate the effect of capitalization on any particular ratio, each one was considered independently of the others. For example, the ranking of the current ratios indicates how each company stood in relation to each of the others in regard to the *current ratio only*. Reading on Exhibit 4 across the lines, we find how each of the companies listed at the top ranked in regard to each of the ratios listed at the left; first, before capitalization (shown as BC), and then, after capitalization (AC).

This exhibit emphasizes several important points. First of all, in all but one of the cases (the return on total capital) the ranking changes after capitalization. This means that, other things remaining equal, the financial analyst could easily have made faulty decisions (except in regard to the return on total capital) if he had based his analysis on ratios which were computed from conventional financial statements.

The number of firms which were given a different ranking as a result of capitalization is also of significance. Of the eleven companies, the following number were given a different ranking after capitalization from that which they had before:

Current ratio	7
Debt to equity	9
Debt to total capital	9
Return on total capital	0

(Continued on page 56)

Exhibit 3
The Impact of Capitalization on Selected Financial Ratios

	Effect on		Does capitalization "improve" the firm's financial position?	Does capitalization help the ratio meet its objectives?	Notes
	Numerator	Denominator			
Current ratio	NC	+	No	Yes	(1)
Debt to equity	+	NC	No	Yes	(2)
Debt to total capital	+	+	No	Yes	(3)
Return on total capital	+	+	*	Yes	(4)
Times interest charges earned	+	+	No	Yes	(5)
Net profits on net working capital	NC	—	Yes	NA	(6)
Net sales to net working capital	NC	—	Yes	NA	(7)
Fixed assets to tangible net worth	+	NC	No	Yes	(8)
Current debt to tangible net worth	+	NC	No	Yes	(9)
Inventory to net working capital	NC	—	No	Yes	(10)
Current debt to inventory	+	NC	No	Yes	(11)
Funded debt to net working capital	+	—	No	Yes	(12)
Funded debt to net plant	+	+	No	Yes	(13)
Net working capital to net plant	—	+	No	Yes	(14)
Net plant to sales	+	NC	No	Yes	(15)

*Return on total capital may or may not improve depending on the lease terms. In five of the eleven companies studied, capitalization improved the return on investment.
NC = No Change.
NA = Not Applicable. See note indicated.

Notes to Exhibit 3

1. The inclusion of current lease rentals makes the ratio a better measure of the current debt paying ability.
2. By including all assets used in the business the ratio reflects more completely the relative proportion of the assets that have been furnished by owners and by creditors (outsiders).
3. By including all assets used in the business the ratio reflects more completely the relative proportion of the assets that have been furnished by owners and by creditors (outsiders).
4. The ratio is improved because the "return" reflects income before implied interest and "capital" includes assets furnished from all sources.
5. The ratio better meets its objectives because all interest charges are reflected, including "hidden" interest on financial leases.
6. The ratio of net profits on net working capital has been subject to wide misuse. It implies that profits are earned on working capital only and that all other assets are nonproductive parasites. While the importance of working capital cannot be denied, it is nevertheless only one of the factors which contribute to profit. All of the resources of a firm, from whatever source supplied, jointly generate profits; and a relationship which implies otherwise is faulty and actually may be misleading. Because of the limitations of this ratio, it was not possible to determine whether or not capitalization would help it meet its objectives.
7. The ratio of net sales to net working capital has similar limitations to those of the ratio of net profits on net working capital. Because of these limitations, it was not possible to determine whether or not capitalization would help the ratio meets its objectives.
8. All fixed assets used in the business from whatever source obtained are included in the computation of the ratio only after capitalization.
9. Current lease rentals are included as an obligation that must be paid during the year only after capitalization.
10. Current lease rentals are included as obligations that must be met out of net working capital only if leases are capitalized.
11. Current lease rentals are included as an obligation that must be paid during the year only after capitalization.
12. All current liabilities and all long-term liabilities are considered in the computation including those arising from leases.
13. All assets used in the business are included as well as all "funds" supplied by outsiders.
14. Since all assets are included in the computation when leases are capitalized, the ratio better reflects the proportion of capital that is tied-up in fixed assets.
15. When leases are capitalized, this ratio reflects the fact that management should be held accountable for all assets which are used in the business.

(Continued from page 54)

Times interest charges earned	10
Fixed assets to tangible net worth	10
Funded debt to net plant	7
Net profits on net working capital	5
Net sales to net working capital	2
Current debt to tangible net worth	7
Inventory to net working capital	5
Current debt to inventory	8
Funded debt to net working capital	11
Net working capital to net plant	11
Net plant to sales	9

In 56 per cent of the cases (92 out of 165 observations), there was a spread of two or more places between the firms' positions before and after capitalization. In 7 per cent of the cases (11 out of 165 observations), the spread was *six or more places*. For example, Company I ranked eighth in regard to the ratio of debt to equity prior to capitalization, but actually ranked second after giving consideration to the capitalized leases.

Exhibit 4 illustrates further that the companies which lease a high percentage of their assets are the ones whose ratios are changed most by capitalization. The firm making the greatest use of leases, Company A, fell in the rankings twelve times, remained the same twice, and improved only once. At the other extreme, Company K, the firm which

Exhibit 4
Ranking of Lessee Companies by Ratio Before and After Capitalization

		Company A	Company B	Company C	Company D	Company E	Company F	Company G	Company H	Company I	Company J	Company K
Leased assets to total assets	BC											
	AC	11	10	9	8	7	6	5	4	3	2	1
Leased assets to net plant	BC											
	AC	11	9	10	8	7	6	5	4	3	2	1
Current ratio	BC	5	10	3	2	6	1	8	7	9	11	4
	AC	9	10	3	5	8	1	6	4	7	11	2
Debt to equity	BC	5	6	4	3	2	1	7	10	8	11	9
	AC	9	10	7	6	5	1	4	8	2	11	3
Debt to total capital	BC	5	6	4	3	2	1	7	10	8	11	9
	AC	9	10	7	6	5	1	4	8	2	11	9
Return on total capital	BC	7	3	9	4	8	10	6	5	1	11	2
	AC	7	3	9	4	8	10	6	5	1	11	2
Times interest charges earned	BC	8	3	4	5	2	1	9	10	6	11	7
	AC	10	7	9	6	8	5	3	4	2	11	1
Fixed assets to tangible net worth	BC	7	11	2	8	4	1	5	9	6	10	3
	AC	10	11	8	9	7	3	4	5	2	6	1
Funded debt to net plant	BC	5	3	9	6	1	2	7	11	4	8	10
	AC	8	7	9	6	2	5	4	11	1	3	10
Net profits on net working capital	BC	7	1	9	3	8	10	4	5	2	11	6
	AC	5	1	9	2	8	10	4	6	3	11	7
Net sales to net working capital	BC	3	2	8	6	5	11	4	9	7	1	10
	AC	3	1	8	6	5	11	4	9	7	2	10
Current debt to tangible net worth	BC	3	8	4	2	5	1	7	9	10	11	6
	AC	5	10	3	2	6	1	7	8	9	11	4
Inventory to net working capital	BC	6	10	2	5	7	1	9	4	8	11	3
	AC	9	10	2	6	8	1	7	4	5	11	3
Current debt to inventory	BC	3	9	6	2	5	1	7	8	10	11	4
	AC	7	10	4	3	6	1	5	8	9	11	2
Funded debt to net working capital	BC	7	5	3	10	1	2	8	11	4	9	6
	AC	10	11	8	9	7	3	4	6	2	5	1
Net working capital to net plant	BC	8	10	2	11	5	1	6	4	7	9	3
	AC	10	11	7	9	8	2	5	3	4	6	1
Net plant to sales	BC	3	2	5	11	6	8	4	10	9	1	7
	AC	7	5	9	11	8	10	2	6	4	1	3

BC = Before Capitalization
AC = After Capitalization

used leasing to the smallest degree, improved in the rankings ten times, remained unchanged four times, and dropped only once. The four firms making the greatest use of leasing fell in the rankings thirty-five times, remained unchanged fourteen times, and improved only eleven times. On the other hand, the four firms that made relatively little use of the lease as a means of financing were higher in the rankings thirty-five times, unchanged twenty-one times, and lower only five times.

Dangers of current reporting

The dangers of current techniques for reporting long-term leases are made more apparent by this pilot study. For example, an analysis of the published financial statements of Company B and Company G reveals that they have almost identical ratios of *debt to total capital* (Company B, 41.5 per cent and Company G, 41.7 per cent). Since these companies are both members of the same industry, one might conclude that from the standpoint of relative proportion of assets supplied by "outsiders" the two companies are comparable; and, other things being equal, that the degree of "risk" would be the same. An investor contemplating the purchase of some stock or the banker considering a loan application would tend to consider the companies a "standoff."

Consider now this same ratio calculated for the same two companies from financial statements *in which leases have been capitalized*. Instead of the almost identical ratios which were noted above, it is found that Company B has a substantially higher ratio (70.6 per cent) than does Company G (52.6 per cent). Neither the proportion of funds supplied by outsiders nor the relative "risk" is comparable for the two firms as implied by the preceding calculations. The truth of the matter is that the ratios which were computed from the published financial statements were based upon incomplete data and, accordingly, are inaccurate and misleading. The investor or banker acting on this information could easily have been misled because a very significant portion of the assets supplied by "outsiders" were omitted from the calculations.

Similar comparisons may be made with other ratios. For example, the *current ratio* of Company D is 3.43 times before capitalization and is comparable to the 3.40 times of Company K. Based on this comparison one might conclude that the two firms should meet their current obligations with equal ease. Comparison of the two companies after capitalization reveals that Company K with a *current ratio* of 3.35 times appears to be in a much stronger current position than does Company D with a current ratio of 2.13 times.

Other significant comparisons include *times interest charges earned* of Company A and Company G of 6.3 times and 6.1 times, respectively, before capitalization and 1.6 times and 3.3 times respectively, after capitalization. The ratio of *fixed assets to tangible net worth* before capitalization of Company D at 67.6 per cent is comparable to that of Company H, at 68.1 per cent. After capitalization these same ratios are 154.4 per cent and 93.0 per cent, respectively.

The usefulness of many important financial ratios is limited by current reporting practices. These limitations do not stem so much from weaknesses in the ratios themselves, as they do from faulty procedures for reporting leases which are primarily financial in nature.

Capitalization is here proposed as the soundest process for overcoming the current weaknesses in financial lease reporting inasmuch as it reflects the financial impact of leasing in the financial statements. It is a process which is compatible with generally accepted accounting principles and only an extension of the long-recognized concept of looking through legal details to the financial and economic facts. Because capitalization recognizes leasing for what it really is, a means of financing, the financial ratios which are computed from statements containing capitalized leases *are meaningful*. These ratios are, of course, subject to the general limitations of ratio analysis; however, they seem much more valid than ratios computed from conventional financial statements and therefore seem to make intercompany comparisons more meaningful.

Although financial statements are basically representations of management, the accounting profession must assume the responsibility for the inadequacies in current reporting. The financial statements are based upon generally accepted accounting and auditing standards and these are determined not by management but by the accounting profession. Business managements have tended to lean on minimum standards of reporting and accordingly have not capitalized leases in their financial statements because no requirement to do so has existed.

The difficulty encountered in obtaining the information upon which this study is based underscores the inadequacy of this reporting. It is important that in those instances where leases are not capitalized, the footnotes be expanded to reflect sufficient lease details to enable the reader to adequately appraise the financial impact of these transactions.

Although no organization has the power to decree accounting and reporting standards, the American Institute of Certified Public Accountants and the Securities and Exchange Commission do have a profound influence on their development. These organizations must take the initiative if any widespread change is to be adopted. Some day the truth about leasing will be out and the "illusions" will vanish. If the accounting profession takes the initiative in bringing this about, the prestige of the profession will be enhanced. On the other hand, if no action is taken by the accounting profession until the financial analysts have perfected techniques for revising the published financial statements so that they do reflect the financial facts, then it is this latter group who will be considered the professionals.

Accounting is a profession, and as such must assume the responsibility for adopting new reporting techniques to reflect properly the changing nature of the business world. Leasing has been developed by the financial world as a new means of financing, and the accounting profession must quickly respond by adopting a new device which will properly reflect this new transaction. The results of this study would tend to support the position that capitalization may be the needed device.

The Art of Poor Speaking

Many students of speech have found it surprisingly easy to acquire the usual tricks of poor speaking. However, to do a consistently substandard job, one must grasp a few main principles.

1. Ignore the audience
2. Be wordy, vague and pompous
3. Do not prepare your speech

Unfortunately, the above principles are too easily grasped. How can members of the accounting profession avoid them?

Examples of common speech faults are not hard to find. At a meeting a few years ago one of the speakers was getting his message over well during the early part of his speech. But suddenly he apparently became nervous and from there on nearly every sentence was prefaced by the word "now." Soon his listeners were leaning forward, waiting eagerly in anticipation, reaching mentally out, for the next "now." Needless, to say, the remainder of his speech was a passed ball, too far outside the plate for his catchers to reach. The speaker probably never even knew he was using that "awful" word.

In another case, illustrating the way in which a nervous tendency reared its ugly head, a speaker developed an itchy nose. Most of his message never got past the nose to which all eyes were attracted.

Monotony of voice is another common failing. For example, it is not unusual to look around at a meeting and find that the speaker's voice is so monotonous that some of the audience actually have fallen asleep.

From "The Art of Poor Speaking" by JOHN W. EMERSON, CPA
Pennsylvania CPA Spokesman, October 1962

LIFO AND RATIO ANALYSIS

George C. Holdren

LIFO AND RATIO ANALYSIS

GEORGE C. HOLDREN[*]

INVESTORS, creditors, and managers are all interested in financial analysis. While they may have different goals in mind and may utilize a number of different methods, the most important methods used have one element in common. This is comparison. The actual data for the firm under analysis are compared to some standard in an attempt to measure the desirability of the results for this company. These standards may be from internal sources, such as a budget or past data concerning operations, or external sources, such as results of other companies in the same industry.

One of the most common forms of comparative financial analysis involves the use of various ratios drawn from the financial statements. If such ratios were used only by an occasional analyst, any vagaries found in the make-up of information would be of minor importance. The fact is that these ratios are used almost universally by analysts. Virtually all textbooks in the area of financial analysis stress the importance of such ratios and devote a major part of their coverage to the composition and application of ratios.

Many accountants discount the value of ratios used in comparative financial analysis. However, the fact remains that a great number of analysts do utilize such ratios. In addition, any factor which disturbs the comparability of ratios will most probably also disturb any other form of comparison as well. Since comparability of data is essential if ratio analysis is to have validity, any variance in asset valuation which has a significant effect on ratios becomes a matter of considerable importance. To whatever extent ratios might be affected by differing inventory valuation methods, it becomes important to know just what the effect might be and also what steps may be taken by the analyst to adjust for any variations which may occur.

It is not the purpose here to attempt to either prove or disprove the validity of ratio analysis in general. Since ratio analysis does have wide acceptability in publications and reports, the only purpose will be to examine the effect which the last-in, first-out method of inventory valuation may have on the uniformity of financial statements and thus the comparability of the ratios which may be drawn from these statements.

The ratios to be examined have been selected primarily because (1) they are in common usage and (2) they are affected, either directly or indirectly, by inventory valuation. One of the selected ratios is a balance sheet ratio, one an income statement ratio, and the third combines information from both statements. The first ratio selected, the current ratio, was included because it is undoubtedly the most widely used of all ratios. The other two ratios are net profit to net sales, which is an income statement ratio, and inventory turnover (net sales to inventory) which utilizes both income statement and balance sheet accounts.

In order to discover what effect the last-in, first-out method of inventory valuation may have on financial ratios, two items of information are essential. These are, first, the results recorded through the use of this

---

[*] George C. Holdren is Assistant Professor in the College of Business Administration of the University of Nebraska, Lincoln. He has contributed to the periodical literature in accounting previously.

method, and second, the results which would have been obtained had this method not been used. With this information it should be possible, by comparison, to determine what effect this method of inventory valuation has on the various financial ratios.

The first source examined in an attempt to gain this information was the published annual reports of 405 manufacturing and commercial firms. Utilities and service businesses were excluded because it was felt that the small inventories in such businesses would minimize the effects of LIFO and would also be of less concern to analysts. It was found that these reports commonly reveal the year in which LIFO was adopted. Many firms indicate the portion of inventories valued through use of the last-in, first-out method by stating the dollar amount, the percentage, or the classes of inventory items so valued. In the year of the change to LIFO it is also the usual practice to report the effect of the change on inventory valuation and on profits for this one year. For years subsequent to adoption of LIFO the difference between inventory valuation under LIFO and the method previously used is rarely available. The annual reports of only five of the companies examined included all the necessary information. Prospectuses of companies issuing new securities were also found to be of no assistance. Such information is required by neither the Securities and Exchange Commission nor the Internal Revenue Service.

Correspondence with business firms using LIFO proved to be only partially successful. Only twelve of seventy-one companies contacted supplied all the necessary information. Several firms indicated that they do not maintain records which will furnish such information. An even greater number indicated that they do have the information but decline to disclose it for a variety of reasons. Several firms stated that the reason was merely "company policy". A number of replies indicated that their refusal to disclose the information was due to fear of violating requirements of the Internal Revenue Service. However, only two replies stated outright that this was the reason. One of these referred specifically to Section 472(c) of the 1954 Internal Revenue Code. This section of the Code reads as follows:

"Condition—Subsection (a) (authorization to use last-in, first-out method of inventory valuation) shall apply only if the taxpayer establishes to the satisfaction of the Secretary or his delegate that the taxpayer has used no procedure other than that specified in paragraphs (1) and (3) of subsection (b) (method applied in arriving at last-in, first-out valuation) in inventorying such goods to ascertain the income, profit, or loss of the first taxable year for which the method described in subsection (b) is to be used, for the purpose of a report or statement covering such taxable year—
  (1) to shareholders, partners, or other proprietors, to to beneficiaries, or
  (2) for credit purposes.[1]

This concern appears somewhat questionable in view of the fact that some companies do make this information available even to the extent of publishing it in their annual reports. The important fact, as far as the financial analyst is concerned, is that, regardless of the reason given, the information necessary to analyze the effects of differing inventory valuation methods is rarely available.

Five of the companies for which sufficient information for analysis was available were the only ones from their industrial groupings and have therefore been eliminated for purposes of this study. The remaining twelve companies may be classified as steel manufacturers, paper manufacturers, and department stores. While it would no doubt be helpful to have a larger sample, the information gained here should be sufficient to give some indication of the effects which may be expected. Since the

---

[1] Sec. 472(c) I.R.C., 83d Cong. 2d Sess. (1954).

majority of the firms which did respond requested that the information be kept confidential, none of the firms included will be identified.

It should be noted that last-in, first-out inventory valuation refers, not to one precise method, but rather to a group of methods. Nearly all methods of LIFO involve incremental "layers" of inventory costs. Under some applications, the quantity of goods on hand forms the basis for the valuation of these increments while others, such as "dollar-value" LIFO, use dollars rather than units of goods. However, all LIFO methods are based on the assumption that the costs of the latest purchases are those first applied to the cost of sales, while costs remaining in inventory are those from an earlier point in time. Because of this common basis for all methods, it is felt that any differences in the effects on the ratios by the variation in methods will be insignificant.

The analyst can seldom be certain of the exact method of application of LIFO since this information is rarely stated in annual reports or other published statements. The method of application for the companies included in this examination is known with certainty only for the department stores which use the "retail LIFO" method. Those companies adopting LIFO subsequent to 1948 probably use "dollar-value LIFO", but no positive assertion may be made to this effect.

A problem arises concerning how much variation can occur in any one ratio before the difference may be regarded as distorting the interpretation of the results. Use of the standard deviation was found to be unsatisfactory as a means of measurement in this respect since differences of much less than one standard deviation often appear quite significant. It is probably not possible to select any absolute variance which may be regarded as significant with any ratio. For example, a variation of one half point in a current ratio might be very significant in a ratio of two to one but of much less importance in a ratio of seven to one. It would appear that a percentage variation could be used to better advantage.

It is impossible to state with precision how much of a percentage variation in any ratio may be tolerated as unimportant. No information regarding this question has been found in any textbooks or articles dealing with ratio analysis. Experimentation with various ratios revealed that variations of less than 5 per cent may be viewed as relatively insignificant and those of 10 per cent or larger appear to have definite significance. The assumptions made in this study will utilize these limits, and no attempt will be made to arrive at any exact line of demarcation between significant and insignificant variations in ratios.

THE CURRENT RATIO

The first ratio to be examined is the current ratio. In comparing this ratio drawn from the figures as reported under the use of the last-in, first-out method of inventory valuation with that which would have resulted had this method not been in use, several factors will have to be taken into account. The valuation of the inventory which is included in current assets is, of course, the most obvious of these. Since the period covered by this study has been one of generally increasing prices, one can expect the inventory valuations reported on the balance sheet to be somewhat lower than those which would have resulted if the inventory had been valued at current cost or by application of the first-in, first-out method of inventory valuation. This is due to the fact that LIFO inventories will reflect prices of an earlier point in time than will the other two methods. This lowering of total inventory values will have the effect of lowering the current ratio to some extent.

There are also other, less immediately

apparent, effects to be recorded due to the influence of using the last-in, first-out method of valuation for inventories. Use of this method will result in a different cost of goods sold, and hence, net profits at a different level than would otherwise have been the case. During a period of generally rising prices, such as that covered by the period examined, the cost of goods sold will be greater and profits thus lower if the last-in, first-out method is utilized.

The effect of last-in, first-out inventories on profits will also mean that in the following year, the amount paid in income tax will be altered. For purposes of this study, the change in the amount of income tax paid on earnings will be treated as an adjustment to current assets. The reason for this is that the immediate effect of the change in the amount of income tax would be reflected in the cash account. Any effect on current assets beyond this one year will be ignored. It is felt that there is too much uncertainty to permit any other method. While a portion of this change might well remain reflected in current assets, or even in current liabilities, it could just as well be found in permanent investments, in the amount of dividends paid, or in other areas. There is no reason to believe that it would be permanently reflected in the current ratio. Therefore no cumulative effect of this tax saving is carried into the calculation.

Comparability of information. Since the entire idea of ratio analysis is based upon comparability, every effort should be made to make the information used as comparable as possible. For example, some companies include prepaid expense items in current assets while others treat them as non-current assets. Some of the companies used in this study included prepaid expenses in current assets during the period under examination while others did not.

In order to provide comparability, the figures for all companies were converted to the same basis. This was done by removing prepaid expense items from current assets in those cases where they were so included. While current accounting theory favors including prepaid expenses as current assets, it was decided here to eliminate them since the companies which did not include these items in current assets often included such items as bond discount and expense with prepaid expenses, and it was impossible to segregate the amount allocable to prepaid expenses alone.

The inventory of supplies may be considered as a prepaid expense. This item, however, was left as an element of current assets for all the firms here included except for the department stores. The reason for this is, again, ease in handling the information. Several of the companies included supplies with their raw materials inventories and no separation was possible using reported figures.

The three department stores, on the other hand, included supplies as a part of their prepaid expenses. Therefore, for the department stores, supplies have been omitted from current assets while for all the remaining firms they have been included. This aids comparability within each of the groups, and, since supplies make up such a minor portion of the total current assets of department stores, should do little to destroy what comparability there may be between that group and other groups.

Procedure to be followed. In attempting to examine the effect of last-in, first-out inventory valuation on the comparability of current ratios, the first step will be to investigate the extent of such influences for each of the various classes of industries included in this study. If any potentially important variations in this ratio do appear, attempts will be made to (1) explain the reasons for such variations and (2) discover any possible methods which may be used to adjust ratios drawn from reported figures to what they would have been had current cost or first-in, first-out inventory valuation been used.

It is to be expected that current cost valuation of inventory may not be identical with first-in, first-out valuation of the same inventory. The first-in, first-out method assumes that the goods on hand are those most recently purchased, and the costs assigned are those of these purchases.

The exact meaning of current cost is somewhat less definite. It is probably most often considered as replacement or reproduction cost at prices prevailing at the balance sheet date. The Research Department of the American Institute of CPAs, however, considers this too narrow and contends that current cost should also include amounts determined by other methods, such as latest cost if near the balance sheet date, or an amount obtained by pricing the inventory in accordance with a method different from the one employed but which substantially approximates prices current at the balance sheet date.[2] Thus, in many instances, current cost may be synonymous with first-in, first-out valuation. It is believed that the results in all cases will be sufficiently similar to satisfy the requirements of this examination.

Effect on the current ratio. An examination of the influence of last-in, first-out inventory valuation on current ratios reveals that, for the most part, the effect is comparatively small. A great majority of the comparisons result in variations of less than 10 per cent. Only five comparisons yield differences in excess of 15 per cent with a high of 18 per cent. Three of these five larger differences are found with one company (D-2). There does seem to be some indication that the magnitude of the variation to be expected varies from one industry to another. All differences found in companies from the paper industry were quite small while two of the department stores had no variation as low as 5 per cent.

For the most part, the percentage of inventory valued through application of the last-in, first-out method seems to have had little influence on the differences found in the ratios. Only in the department store area would this appear as a possible important factor. It is unfortunate that the necessary information for such comparisons is not available for more firms in this area. The possibility that the percentage of inventory valued by the LIFO method may have a significant influence on the current ratio makes it desirable to find some method of adjusting for this factor, if possible. It would, no doubt, be informative to adjust the information for all companies to record what the result would have been if the entire inventory were valued by use of the last-in, first-out method in each case. This, unfortunately, is not possible as will be demonstrated.

At first glance, it might seem possible to multiply the difference between inventory valuation found by the last-in, first-out method and the valuation at current cost or first-in, first-out by some figure to arrive at the total difference which would have been its value had the entire inventory been valued by the last-in, first-out method. For example, if 50 per cent of the inventory is valued by the last-in, first-out method, and a difference of $5,000 is found between value of the total inventory by this method and that which would have resulted if the entire inventory had been valued at current cost, it might appear logical that if this difference were to be multiplied by two, in this case making a figure of $10,000, one would get the adjustment which would have been necessary

---

[2] Research Department of the American Institute of Accountants, "Should Estimated Current Value of Inventories be Disclosed?," *The Journal of Accountancy*, September, 1949, p. 218.

TABLE I. COMPARISON OF CURRENT RATIOS FOUND UNDER VARYING INVENTORY VALUATION METHODS

Year	With LIFO	With FIFO or Curr. Cost	% Differ- ence	Inv. ÷ by Curr. Assets	% of Inv. on LIFO	With LIFO	With FIFO or Curr. Cost	% Differ- ence	Inv. ÷ by Curr. Assets	% of Inv. on LIFO	With LIFO	With FIFO or Curr. Cost	% Differ- ence	Inv. ÷ by Curr. Assets	% of Inv. on LIFO	With LIFO	With FIFO or Curr. Cost	% Differ- ence	Inv. ÷ by Curr. Assets	% of Inv. on LIFO
	Company P-1 (LIFO adopted 1951)					Company P-2 (LIFO adopted 1950)					Company P-3 (LIFO adopted 1941)					Company P-4 (LIFO adopted 1953)				
1950	—	—				5.08	4.99	1.8[a]	33%	24%	2.04	2.07[d]	1.5	30%	35%	—	—			
1951	2.25	2.24	0.4[a]	34%	84%	5.12	5.05	1.4[a]	39	50	1.69	1.71	1.2	40	29	—	—			
1952	2.06	2.07	0.5	37	86	5.71	5.84	2.3	27	51	2.82	2.85	1.1	32	29	—	—			
1953	2.24	2.29	2.2	29	80	6.60	6.65	0.1	35	52	2.10	2.14	1.9	35	34	3.07	3.01	2.0[a]	62%	107%
1954	2.14	2.21	3.3	33	88	3.16	3.24	2.5	35	54	1.74	1.78	2.3	54	21	2.50	2.55	2.0	62	9
1955	2.25	2.30	2.2	37	81	5.75	5.83	1.4	40	48	1.92	1.97	2.6	61	15	2.35	2.41	2.6	60	9
1956	2.17	2.23	3.0	34	83	5.24	5.29	1.0	38	49	1.94	1.98	1.0	52	13	2.59	2.64	1.9	63	9
1957	2.72	2.78	2.2	32	83	3.38	3.44	1.8	42	56	2.95	2.00	1.7	67	15	2.67	2.71	1.5	64	9[a]
1958	2.76	2.85	3.3	36	87	3.59	3.71	2.3	43	55	2.44	2.51	2.9	58	20	n.a.	n.a.		66	
	Company S-1 (LIFO adopted 1950)					Company S-2 (LIFO adopted 1940)					Company S-3 (LIFO adopted 1950)					Company S-4 (LIFO adopted 1950)				
1950	2.15	2.15		48%	100%	1.50	1.55	3.3	28%	approx. 88%	2.83	2.82	0.4[a]	34%	approx. 85%	1.90	1.91	0.5	62%	80%
1951	2.14	2.18	1.9	50	100	1.35	1.38	2.3	25		2.38	2.39	0.4[a]	40		1.51	1.56	3.3	56	75
1952	2.06	2.15	4.4	55	100	1.84	1.91	3.5	25		4.28	4.24	0.9[a]	45		1.91	2.03	6.3	54	80
1953	2.23	2.38	6.7	60	100	1.65	1.70	3.0	36		3.22	3.36	4.3	55		2.13	2.32	8.9	49	80
1954	2.76	3.07	11.2	61	100	2.12	2.13	0.5	64		3.30	3.54	7.3	44		2.10	2.44	15.2	63	85
1955	2.28	2.36	3.6	50	100	1.84	1.84	0.0	46	87	2.84	3.00	5.6	42		2.24	2.44	8.9	58	80
1956	2.53	2.60	2.8	54	100	1.90	1.90	0.0	48	90	4.03	4.13	2.5	44		1.80	1.96	8.9	61	80
1957	3.10	3.49	12.6	62	100	2.49	2.70	8.4	55	87	3.56	3.78	6.2	50		1.81	2.07	14.4	57	70
1958	3.65	4.12	12.9	61	100	2.23	2.37	6.3	44		2.98	3.50	17.4	60		1.56	1.76	12.8	65	80
	Company S-5 (LIFO adopted 1951)					Company D-1 (LIFO adopted 1948)					Company D-2 (LIFO adopted 1941)					Company D-3 (LIFO adopted 1941)				
1950	—	—				2.71	2.94	8.5	38%	100%	2.53	n.a.	n.a.	38%	100%	3.06	3.14[b]	2.6	45%	d
1951	2.11	2.12	0.5	38%	75%	2.64	2.89	9.5	35	100	2.89	3.47[d]	8.7	49	100	3.44	3.51	2.0	44	d
1952	3.07	3.07	0.0	37	75	2.62	2.90	10.7	35	100	3.10	3.60	16.1	38	100	3.29	3.42	4.0	41	45
1953	4.15	4.20	1.2	43	74	3.03	3.34	10.2	32	100	2.94	3.47	18.0	44	100	3.38	3.53	4.4	41	d
1954	2.80	2.83	1.1	49	76	2.79	3.08	10.4	34	100	2.91	3.37	12.5	38	100	3.38	3.51	4.2	43	d
1955	2.07	2.09	1.0	50	79	2.71	2.94	8.5	35	100	2.71	3.05	11.7	37	100	3.38	3.48	3.0	43	d
1956	2.63	2.66	1.1	54	77	2.63	2.84	8.0	33	100	2.23	2.49	11.7	42	100	3.41	3.49	2.3	43	d
1957	2.06	2.12	2.9	47	79	2.54	2.75	8.3	34	100	2.74	3.05	11.3	47	100	3.37	3.46	2.7	47	40
1958	1.67	1.79	7.2	60	82	2.64	2.87	8.7	34	100	2.72	3.07	12.9	51	100	3.30	3.42	3.6	47	d

[a] Ratio resulting from the use of LIFO is larger than with alternate method.
[b] The exact percentage is unknown, but information given by this firm indicates that it probably averages about forty-five per cent.
[c] Estimated.
[d] Does not include the effect of LIFO on the prior year's profits.

had the entire inventory been valued by LIFO.

Insufficient information is available to test this method of adjustment for any one company. For this reason, one is forced to use separate companies. Of the firms included in this study, the department stores most probably have inventories showing the greatest similarity in make-up, and these will, therefore, be used to try this procedure.

For the year 1957, one of the companies having all of its inventory valued by the last-in, first-out method shows a difference between LIFO and FIFO valuations of approximately 27 per cent while another discloses a difference of approximately 24 per cent. The third company, with 40 per cent of its inventory valued by LIFO, shows a variation of only $7\frac{1}{2}$ per cent. Multiplying this by $2\frac{1}{2}$ (since the percentage of inventory valued by LIFO is $2\frac{1}{2}$ times, 100/40, as great for the other two companies) gives a result of only approximately 19 per cent.

The percentage of inventory valued by the last-in, first-out method by Company D-3 is known for only one other year, 1952. For this year the two companies with all their inventories valued by LIFO show less similarity than in 1957. The inventory as valued under LIFO would need to be increased by nearly 36 per cent in one case in order to arrive at the first-in, first-out valuation while the other would require an increase of slightly over 29 per cent. The third company, with 45 per cent of its inventory on LIFO would need an increase of slightly more than 9 per cent. Multiplication of this figure by 100/45 would result in a figure just in excess of 20 per cent, still considerably less than the other two firms. Thus, a large factor of correction is necessary in each case, but the extent of the needed correction is unpredictable. If such a procedure proves unsuccessful in businesses having such similar inventory situations as would department stores, it is evident that it could not be expected to be successful elsewhere.

There are undoubtedly many reasons why this method does not prove workable. Perhaps the most important of these is that the difference between last-in, first-out valuation and first-in, first-out or current cost would vary to a greater extent with some items than it would with others. While the prices of most items tended to increase over the period of this study, some increased much more rapidly than others, and the prices of some items even declined.[3] Because of this, an adjustment which would apply to some items would be far out of line when applied to others. This factor alone would make the method unworkable. It is also possible that the LIFO method would be first applied to those components of inventory in which a price increase seems most likely, thus contributing to the distortion.

Influence of the portion of inventory valued by LIFO. Since there is a significant difference, in some cases, between the current ratios found using the varying inventory valuation methods, it would be desirable to discover some method of adjusting such ratios to a common basis, or at least of estimating to what extent differences

---

[3] For example, wholesale price indexes (1947–1949 = 100) for various commodities which would influence inventory values in the department store group are as follows:

Commodity	1950 Index	1958 Index	Increase (Decrease)
Furniture and other household durables	105.3	123.2	17.9
Textile products and apparel	99.2	93.5	(5.7)
Metals and metal products	110.3	150.4	40.1
Hides, skins, and leather products	104.6	100.6	(4.0)
All commodities	103.1	119.2	16.1

Sources: *Federal Reserve Bulletin*, February, 1959, and later issues.

might be expected to exist so that allowances could be made in conducting a financial analysis. One might logically expect that the greater the proportion of inventory valued by the last-in, first-out method, the greater the change to be recorded in the current ratio as a result. This anticipated result cannot be checked for all companies since the percentage of inventory valued by LIFO is not known for all years for some of the firms here included.

For the companies in the paper industry there is only one company for which the greatest percentage of change in the current ratio is found in the year with the largest proportion of its inventory on LIFO valuation. In the group of steel companies, however, for the three companies where the necessary information is available, the greatest degree of change in the current ratio is found in the year having the highest proportion of inventory valued by the last-in, first-out method.

Since the steel companies initially appear to provide a sound relationship between the percentage of inventory valued by LIFO and the change in current ratio at this level, it would be well to follow this through. If this theory is to prove workable, the year with the second highest percentage of inventory on LIFO should show the second highest change in the current ratio, and so on, until the year with the smallest percentage should show the least change.

At this point the theory disintegrates. The information necessary to follow through on this is available for only two of the companies. For one of the companies (S-5) there are two years tied for second place. One year does show the second highest degree of change in the current ratio. The other year, however, falls much further down the list on the percentage change in this ratio. For the second company, one finds the second highest percentage change in the ratio not in the year with the second highest portion of the inventory on LIFO but in the year with the lowest portion of its inventory so valued. In neither company does the year with the smallest portion of inventory result in the smallest degree of change in the current ratio. Thus it would seem that this method of estimating the degree of change in the current ratio is much too undependable to use.

Importance of the Relationship of Inventory to Total Current Assets. Another possibility which exists is that, since inventory is only a part of the current asset figure entering into the computation of the current ratio, the size of inventory relative to total current assets might play an important part. This theory proves even more unworkable than the former one, however. For only three of the twelve companies included in this examination does the year showing the greatest degree of adjustment necessary to the current ratio prove to be the one in which inventory made up the highest percentage of current assets. The steel industry includes two companies (S-3 and S-5) where this situation exists, both in 1958, and one paper company (P-1) shows a similar result in 1954. For the paper company this degree of change was also reached in one other year. Following through on this, other years fail to yield a similar relationship. Again there seems to be no basis for estimating the differences to be found in the current ratios resulting from the use of LIFO rather than some other method of inventory valuation by examining the proportion of current assets which is to be found in inventories.

Effect of the Time of Adoption of LIFO. Another factor which would account for differences is the time at which various elements of inventory were placed on the last-in, first-out basis of valuation. In most instances, the longer the period of time, the more change one could expect to find in prices. Under the last-in, first-out valuation method, the items remaining in stock are considered as having been purchased first, and thus, in periods of rising prices, the longer the period of time since adoption of LIFO, and the greater the number of inventory turns, the larger the gulf between the inventory cost and the current replacement cost.

Even if a firm's inventory consisted of only one type of item, application of a percentage based on the price index of this item would prove satisfactory only if the number of items in inventory remained absolutely constant year after year. This is so because any increase in inventory would be at a price different from the price of the items already in inventory, and hence, to make an adjustment of this kind, it would be necessary to know not only how many items were included in inventory and at what price, but also exactly when each was added. The firms included in this examination, as in the case with virtually all firms, have many different elements making up their total inventory, and the complications involved become too complex for any such simple adjustment.

In only seven of the 101 comparisons examined in this study did the current ratio, found by using figures resulting from the use of LIFO, exceed the ratio resulting from the use of the more traditional inventory valuation methods. In each of these seven exceptions the resulting difference proved to be of minor importance. The greatest difference found in this group reached only 2 per cent (P-4, 1953). Seventeen of the current ratios drawn from reported figures included in this study were less than the traditionally desired two to one. Of these ratios, three of them would have exceeded the two to one level if current cost or first-in, first-out inventory valuation had been used.

The financial analyst will rarely have available the information necessary to determine the extent of the influence of varying inventory valuation methods on the current ratio. In addition, without more information concerning the effect of last-in, first-out valuation than is generally available, the analyst will find himself unable to make dependable adjustments for any potential differences. Since the necessary information is so difficult, or even impossible, to obtain, it is fortunate that there are redeeming factors; the impact of the inventory valuation method on this ratio is generally small, and the current ratios resulting from use of LIFO inventory valuation are commonly lower, and thus, more conservative, than those resulting from utilization of other methods. From the information here examined, it would appear that analysts can continue to use the current ratio without correction for the method of inventory valuation.

INVENTORY TURNOVER

The second ratio to be examined is the inventory turnover ratio. There are several different methods used to compute this ratio. The method most commonly used by financial analysts is division of net sales by ending inventory. Therefore, this will be the method used here. In each instance, net sales will be divided (1) by the ending inventory reported by each company as valued using LIFO techniques and (2) by inventory as it would have been valued had FIFO or current cost been employed. By comparing the results of these two computations it should be possible to gain an indication of what influence the different inventory valuation methods have on the inventory turnover ratio.

Since prices were generally increasing during the period under examination, it is to be expected that inventories including valuations as determined by LIFO will be somewhat less than if some other method

TABLE II. COMPARISONS OF INVENTORY TURNOVER RATIOS FOUND UNDER VARYING INVENTORY VALUATION METHODS

Year	With LIFO	With FIFO or Curr. Cost	% Difference	% of Inv. on LIFO	With LIFO	With FIFO or Curr. Cost	% Difference	% of Inv. on LIFO	With LIFO	With FIFO or Curr. Cost	% Difference	% of Inv. on LIFO
		Company P-1				Company P-2				Company P-3		
1950	—	—	—		—	Company P-2	—		8.82	8.51	3.5	35
1951	7.44	7.02	5.6	84	10.68	10.22	4.3	24	8.59	8.06	6.2	29
1952	8.43	7.70	8.7	86	10.33	9.66	6.5	50	6.87	6.52	5.1	29
1953	7.90	7.26	8.1	80	10.63	9.98	6.1	51	8.23	7.67	4.4	34
1954	7.87	7.31	7.1	88	10.06	9.24	8.2	52	7.31	6.99	4.4	21
1955	8.44	7.63	9.6	81	8.94	8.40	6.0	54	6.31	6.07	3.8	15
1956	8.68	7.73	10.9	83	12.07	11.06	8.4	48	4.86	4.69	3.5	13
1957	7.97	7.09	11.0	81	11.02	10.18	7.6	49	4.47	4.30	3.8	15
1958	7.39	6.51	11.9	87	10.77	9.70	9.9	56	5.56	5.35	3.8	20
					9.66	8.66	10.4	55				
		Company S-1				Company S-2				Company S-3		
1950	6.64	6.07	8.6	100	10.94	9.12	16.6		6.91	6.60	4.5	
1951	7.22	6.46	10.5	100	11.03	9.50	13.9		6.73	6.04	10.3	
1952	5.29	4.66	11.9	100	10.42	8.88	14.8	approx. 88%	5.26	4.51	14.3	approx. 85%
1953	6.45	5.68	11.9	100	10.15	10.00	7.9		4.97	4.31	13.3	
1954	4.88	4.52	7.4	100	3.16	3.00	5.1		5.31	4.56	14.1	
1955	5.83	5.04	13.6	100	7.18	6.54	8.9		6.19	5.18	16.3	
1956	5.28	4.37	17.2	100	6.60	5.34	19.1	87	6.12	4.87	20.4	
1957	4.91	4.24	13.6	100	5.66	5.14	9.2	90	5.91	4.53	23.4	
1958	3.82	3.34	12.6	100	5.60	4.95	11.6	87	4.98	3.93	21.1	
		Company S-5				Company D-1				Company D-2		
1950	5.05	4.95	2.0	75	7.60	5.93	22.0	100	11.14	8.32	25.3	100
1951	4.62	4.51	2.4	75	8.67	6.50	25.0	100	8.49	6.28	26.0	100
1952	4.80	4.71	1.9	74	8.40	6.85	22.6	100	10.50	7.40	29.5	100
1953	4.21	4.12	2.1	76	8.88	6.67	22.9	100	9.45	6.95	26.5	100
1954	4.44	4.15	6.5	79	8.50	6.70	21.5	100	9.32	6.97	25.2	100
1955	4.49	4.09	8.9	77	8.36	6.70	19.9	100	9.10	7.07	22.3	100
1956	3.91	3.39	13.3	79	9.22	7.18	22.1	100	8.31	6.59	20.7	100
1957	3.47	3.06	11.8	82	8.65	6.80	21.4	100	8.09	6.52	19.4	100
1958					8.70	6.83	21.5	100	8.89	7.03	20.9	100
		Company P-4				Company S-4				Company D-3		
1950	—	—	—	—	5.79	5.35	7.6	80	6.56	6.07	7.5	b
1951	—	—	—	—	7.45	6.38	14.4	75	6.95	6.28	9.6	b
1952	3.51	3.33	5.1	10	7.43	6.26	15.7	80	7.16	6.55	8.3	45 b
1953	3.83	3.68	3.9	9	7.75	6.45	16.8	85	7.44	6.82	8.3	b
1954	4.29	4.12	4.0	9	5.57	4.65	16.5	80	7.04	6.57	6.7	b
1955	3.86	3.73	3.4	9	6.96	5.79	16.8	80	6.60	6.21	5.9	b
1956	3.88	3.77	2.8	9[a]	6.94	5.50	20.7	70	6.50	6.09	6.3	b
1957	n.a.	n.a.			8.09	6.40	20.9	80	6.79	6.32	6.9	40
1958					4.37	3.68	15.8		7.11	6.61	7.0	b

[a] Estimated.
[b] The exact percentage of inventory valued by the last-in, first-out method is not known for all years. Information given by this company indicates that it probably averages about 45 per cent.

had been employed; thus, inventory turnover ratios may be expected to be somewhat higher as a result of this method. Somewhat greater differences are anticipated with this ratio than with the current ratio for two reasons. First, both factors used in computing the current ratio were affected by varying inventory valuation methods and the effects tended to offset one another. With the inventory turnover ratio, only one of the factors, inventory, is affected. Second, while inventory constituted only a portion of one of the factors used in computing the current ratio, inventory alone forms one of the factors used in determining the inventory turnover. Thus any change in inventory valuation should have a proportionately greater effect on the resulting ratio.

Extent of the effect of LIFO on inventory turnover. Examination reveals that the inventory turnover ratios resulting from the use of inventory valued, at least in part, through the use of LIFO were somewhat higher than those resulting from the use of FIFO or current cost valuation methods. In only one case (S-2, 1953) did the use of LIFO result in a lower turnover ratio than would otherwise have been found. The generally higher turnover ratios found during this period using inventories valued through the use of LIFO was anticipated. This is because the increasing level of prices would result in inventories valued by the first-in, first-out or current cost methods following the rising price level more closely than would those valued through use of the last-in, first-out method since the latter method would reflect costs incurred at an earlier point in time.

In comparing the inventory turnover ratios found with the use of inventories valued by LIFO and those determined with inventories valued by other methods, one finds that a greater degree of change is apparent in this ratio than in the current ratio. Of the 102 comparisons made in this study, only sixteen—nearly 16 per cent—showed less than a 5 per cent change between the reported turnover ratios and the ratios which would have resulted had the first-in, first-out or current cost methods of inventory valuation been utilized (Table III). On the other hand, twenty-one comparisons, over 20 per cent, show a percentage change exceeding 20 per cent.

The degree of the effect of LIFO inventory valuation on the inventory turnover ratio makes this a matter of considerable interest to the financial analyst. If the inventory turnover ratio of a company is being compared with previous ratios of the same firm, the method of inventory valuation may be of little importance. As long as the portion of inventory valued by any particular method remains fairly constant, comparability should not be lost. However, if this ratio is being compared with those of

TABLE III. PERCENTAGE BY WHICH INVENTORY TURNOVER RATIOS RESULTING FROM THE USE OF FIFO OR CURRENT COST INVENTORY VALUATION VARY FROM THOSE RESULTING FROM REPORTED FIGURES

Percentage Variation	Number of Comparisons				Per Cent of Total
	Paper	Steel	Dept. Stores	Total	
0.0– 4.9	11	5	0	16	15.7
5.0– 9.9	16	9	9	34	33.3
10.0–14.9	4	16	0	20	19.6
15.0–19.9	0	9	2	11	10.8
20.0–24.9	0	5	10	15	14.7
Over 25%	0	0	6	6	5.9
Totals	31	44	27	102	100.0

other businesses in the same general field, the variances caused by different methods of inventory valuation present a formidable problem. It appears that the inventory turnover ratio cannot be reliably used as a measure of comparability between commercial or industrial firms unless they employ similar methods of inventory valuation, and even then, the reliability of the comparison is questionable if LIFO valuation is in use.

NET PROFIT TO NET SALES

It is felt desirable to examine a purely income statement ratio influenced indirectly by inventory valuation. For this purpose, the ratio of net profit to net sales has been selected. This ratio is found by dividing the net profit figure, after deduction of income taxes and interest, by the dollar amount of net sales and is stated as a percentage. Inventory valuation will affect this ratio through influence on the cost of goods sold, and as a result of this influence, the amount of income taxes.

Factors to be considered. Only one of the components entering into computation of the ratio of net profit to net sales will be affected by varying inventory valuation methods. This is the amount of net profit. The initial effect of differences in inventory values will be reflected in the cost of goods sold. During a period of rising prices, such as that covered by this examination, one may expect that the utilization of the last-in, first-out method of inventory valuation will result in a somewhat higher cost of goods sold, and hence, lower reported net profits than would have been evident had first-in, first-out or current cost inventories been employed. This, of course, will have the effect of lowering the ratio of net profits to net sales.

A secondary effect on this ratio will be found due to influence of income taxation. The effect of a higher cost of goods sold figure will be partially offset by a somewhat lower income tax figure. In the majority of cases, during this period, it is to be expected that the net effect of LIFO inventory valuation will be to reduce somewhat the ratio of net profits to net sales.

Extent of the differences found in this ratio. One of the first facts to come to notice in this examination is the relatively small effect of the inventory valuation method on the ratio of net profit to net sales in the majority of the comparisons. 101 comparisons involving this ratio were made in this study. The ratios found using figures which would have resulted had first-in, first-out or current cost been utilized varied less than 5 per cent from the ratios found using reported figures in 68 comparisons, over 67 per cent of the total. Of these, 23 comparions, nearly 23 per cent of the total, resulted in a difference of less than 1 per cent. Only four comparisons, approximately 4 per cent of the total, revealed differences in excess of 15 per cent. In contrast to prior ratio examinations, the department store area holds no monopoly on the more extreme differences (see Table V).

While LIFO inventory valuation demonstrates a pronounced effect on the ratio of net profit to net sales in only a small minority of the comparisons, the extent of some of these differences makes this a matter of considerable importance. The differences recorded in this study ran as high as 49.5 per cent with company S-2 in 1954. The possibility of such extreme variations would certainly cause serious concern regarding the reliability of comparisons of this ratio between different companies.

Because of the occasional extreme variations found, it would be of great value if some method of adjustment could be found. Even a very cursory examination reveals that the percentage of inventory

TABLE IV. COMPARISON OF RATIOS OF NET PROFIT TO NET SALES FOUND UNDER VARYING INVENTORY VALUATION METHODS

Year	With LIFO	With FIFO or Curr. Cost	% Difference	% inc. in Rptd. Inv.[a]	% of Inv. on LIFO	With LIFO	With FIFO or Curr. Cost	% Difference	% inc. in Rptd. Inv.[a]	% of Inv. on LIFO	With LIFO	With FIFO or Curr. Cost	% Difference	% inc. in Rptd. Inv.[a]	% of Inv. on LIFO	With LIFO	With FIFO or Curr. Cost	% Difference	% inc. in Rptd. Inv.[a]	% of Inv. on LIFO
	Company P-1					Company P-2					Company P-3					Company P-4				
1950	—	—	—	—	—	13.56	13.80	1.8	19.4	24	7.36	7.37	0.1	10.1[b]	35	—	—	—	—	—
1951	9.96	10.34	3.8	18.6	84	11.70	11.87	1.5	34.4	50	7.28	7.52	3.3	57.0	29	—	—	—	—	—
1952	8.16	8.36	2.5	0.9	86	11.53	11.47	0.5	10.8[b]	51	7.29	7.29	0.0	22.9	29	5.21	5.92	13.6	0.7	10
1953	7.49	7.47	0.3	3.8	80	9.30	9.46	1.7	17.1	52	7.09	7.17	1.1	6.2[b]	34	6.36	6.15	3.3	3.7[b]	9
1954	7.46	7.43	0.4	8.5	88	10.23	10.14	0.9	11.7[b]	54	8.23	8.22	0.1	56.1	21	6.81	6.82	0.1	2.3	9
1955	7.55	7.70	2.0	1.5	81	11.60	11.67	0.6	13.7[b]	48	8.65	8.67	0.2	24.9	15	5.97	5.98	0.2	25.8	9
1956	8.50	8.64	1.5	10.9	81	13.21	13.29	0.6	45.3	49	8.27	8.35	1.0	42.2	13	4.90	4.87	0.6	1.0	9[c]
1957	8.48	8.61	1.5	18.9	81	11.28	11.42	1.2	0.8	56	7.84	7.91	0.9	10.6	15	n.a.	n.a.			
1958	6.82	6.95	1.9	8.4	87	9.98	10.04	0.6	8.9	55	7.76	7.69	0.9	16.0[b]	20					
	Company S-1					Company S-2					Company S-3					Company S-4				
1950	5.53	6.33	14.5	25.7	100	9.96	10.57	6.1	20.2		8.28	8.67	4.7	0.3[b]		6.32	7.11	12.5	23.9	80
1951	3.86	4.11	6.5	18.5	100	6.52	6.58	0.9	35.5		6.63	7.14	7.7	16.0		4.87	5.42	11.3	1.6	75
1952	3.14	3.41	8.6	13.0	100	5.34	5.44	1.9	6.2	approximately 85%	5.19	5.76	11.0	13.0	approximately 85%	3.72	3.88	4.3	3.2[b]	80
1953	3.23	3.27	1.2	4.7	100	5.44	5.38	1.1	35.6		5.88	6.13	4.3	32.9		5.38	5.40	0.4	5.4[b]	80
1954	2.50	1.88	24.8	7.2[b]	100	2.87	4.29	49.5	81.8		7.74	7.65	1.2	13.3[b]		3.45	3.11	9.9	15.9[b]	85
1955	5.87	6.61	12.6	25.9	100	5.62	5.96	6.0	7.8		7.95	8.25	3.8	6.2		4.37	4.69	7.2	29.4	80
1956	5.34	6.06	13.5	23.7	100	5.37	6.51	2.6	23.0		7.29	7.89	8.2	11.5		4.47	5.08	13.6	19.1	80
1957	4.37	3.01	10.5	0.3	100	5.24	4.53	13.5[b]	27.7	87	7.71	8.26	7.1	8.7		3.03	2.75	9.2	16.0[b]	70
1958	2.90	2.68	7.6	2.9[b]	100	5.83	6.07	3.6[d]	3.6[b]	87	7.30	6.99	4.2	1.9		3.89	3.99	2.6	47.8	80
	Company S-5					Company D-1					Company D-2					Company D-3				
1950	8.82	9.05	2.6	10.8	75	5.13	5.57	8.6	32.4	100	1.87	n.a.		43.3	100	3.40	3.54	4.1	28.7	[d]
1951	6.78	6.88	1.5	24.7	75	3.68	3.79	3.0	10.6[b]	100	1.50	2.19	46.0	23.5[b]	100	1.73	1.93	11.6	2.2	[d]
1952	6.17	6.09	1.3	8.0[b]	74	3.61	2.53	2.2	8.8	100	.84	.66	21.4	6.1	100	2.42	2.33	3.7	2.2	45[d]
1953	4.21	4.27	1.4	20.8	76	3.63	3.58	1.4	4.1[b]	100	1.47	1.38	6.1	11.3	100	2.29	2.27	0.9	1.1[b]	[d]
1954	6.15	6.86	11.5	15.1	79	3.82	3.74	2.1	2.2	100	1.40	1.36	2.9	3.7	100	2.43	2.37	2.1	11.5	[d]
1955	15.65	16.22	3.6	19.9	77	3.96	3.96	0.5	13.2[b]	100	1.49	1.44	3.4	13.3	100	2.40	2.40	0.0	14.1	[d]
1956	10.29	11.19	8.7	19.1	79	3.99	4.12	3.3	4.4[b]	100	1.59	1.67	5.0	15.8	100	2.32	2.38	2.6	7.4	40[d]
1957	2.99	2.66	11.0	1.8[b]	82	3.79	3.84	1.3	9.2	100	1.56	1.64	5.1	15.5[b]	100	1.95	1.99	2.1	1.6[b]	[d]
1958						3.43	3.45	0.6	0.7	100	1.44	1.48	2.8	7.3[b]	100	1.86	1.85	0.5	2.8[b]	[d]

[a] Increase in the total inventory over that for one year earlier.
[b] Decrease.
[c] Estimated.
[d] Exact percentage is not known, but information from this company indicates that it probably averages about 45 per cent.

TABLE V. EFFECT OF INVENTORY VALUATION ON THE RATIO OF NET PROFIT TO NET SALES

Variation between Ratio from Adjusted Figures[a] and Ratio from LIFO Figures	Number of Comparisons				Per Cent of Total
	Paper	Steel	Dept. Stores	Total	
Less than 5%	30	19	19	68	67.3
5.0–9.9	0	12	4	16	15.8
10.0–14.9	1	11	1	13	12.9
15.0–19.9	0	0	0	0	0.0
20.0–24.9	0	1	1	2	2.0
Over 25%	0	1	1	2	2.0
Totals	31	44	26	101	100.0

[a] Found by using the figures which would have resulted had first-in, first-out or current cost been used in valuing inventories.

valued by use of the last-in, first-out method offers a most inadequate explanation. In only one company where such a comparison is possible did the greatest variation occur in the year in which the greatest percentage of inventory was on LIFO valuation (P-4, 1953).

Effect of the annual change in inventory valuation. The difference in net profits found by varying inventory valuation methods is primarily a function of the change in the difference between such inventory valuations from one year to the next. For this reason, it seems plausible that the change in reported inventory from year to year might well show a close relationship to the change in the difference between inventory values found through utilization of the last-in, first-out method and the inventory values which would have resulted from use of the first-in, first-out method or current cost. For this reason, it was decided to examine the differences between the ratio of net profits to net sales as found by the different inventory valuation methods for those years showing the greatest increase in reported inventories for the companies included in this study.

The results of this examination for all increases in excess of 40 per cent in reported inventory valuation may be seen in Table VI. It is readily evident that while the two greatest differences between ratios found by the varying inventory valuations are in this group, the overall result is inconclusive. The remaining ratio differences in this group are all less than 5 per cent.

Effect of the change in the relative portion of inventories valued by LIFO. It might appear quite logical that extreme differences between a ratio of net profit to net sales resulting from use of LIFO and one which would have occurred had first-in, first-out or current cost inventories been used might be a result of a sizable change in the portion of inventories valued by the last-in, first-out method. However, this,

TABLE VI. RELATIONSHIP OF RELATIVE RATIO DIFFERENCES TO INCREASES IN REPORTED INVENTORIES IN EXCESS OF 40 PER CENT

Company	Year	Percentage Increase in Reported Inventories[a]	Percentage Difference in Ratio of Net Profit to Net Sales[b]
S-2	1954	81.8	49.5
P-3	1952	57.0	3.3
P-3	1955	56.1	0.1
S-4	1958	47.8	2.6
P-2	1956	45.3	0.6
D-2	1951	43.4	46.0
P-3	1957	42.2	1.0

[a] Increase in the total inventory over that for one year earlier.
[b] Difference between the ratio resulting from application of LIFO and that resulting from FIFO or Current Cost.

too, proves to be unworkable as a means of solution.

The three ratios in this study showing the greatest differences occur in years in which there has been little, or no, change in the portion of the inventories valued by the last-in, first-out method. The largest difference occurs in a company (S-2, 1954) which reports that approximately 88 per cent of its inventory was valued by the LIFO method in both the preceding and current years. The second two largest differences occur in companies (D-2, 1951 and S-1, 1954) consistently valuing their entire inventories through use of the last-in, first-out method.

It is, thus, obvious that neither a change in the total volume of inventory nor the relative portion of inventory valued by the last-in, first-out method alone presents a satisfactory explanation for large variations between ratios of net profit to net sales due to differing inventory valuation methods. The basic explanation must be in the relative size of the difference between inventory valuations as found by the different valuation methods.

There are several factors which could influence this. As mentioned previously, two of these factors might be changes in inventory volume or in the percentage of inventory valued through the use of LIFO. Other factors would include changes in the price levels of inventory components and addition of new categories of inventory or dropping of old ones. Without information concerning inventory valuation by both last-in, first-out and first-in, first-out or current cost methods, it is impossible to make any satisfactory adjustment. Such information is not ordinarily available to the external financial analyst.

Earlier it was stated that, during the period covered by this study, the expectations would be for the ratio of net profit to net sales to be somewhat lower under application of the last-in, first-out method of inventory valuation. It is rather surprising, then, to find that in twenty-eight comparisons, nearly 28 per cent of the total, the ratio as found using reported figures was higher than it would otherwise have been.

In most comparisons in which this situation appears, however, the extent of the difference is rather small. The three primary causes for this situation seem to be (1) a decline in total inventory valuation, (2) a decline in the relative portion of inventory valued by the LIFO method, and (3) a smaller difference between inventory values as found by the varying valuation methods even though reported inventory valuation increased.

In the great majority of cases in this study, valuation of inventories by the LIFO method has a relatively minor effect on the ratio of net profit to net sales; less than was evident with the preceding two ratios examined. In fact, most of the time, financial analysts could ignore differences in inventory valuation methods without serious consequences. There are, however, exceptions, and these are of sufficient magnitude to make this a matter of considerable importance.

The concern raised by these exceptions is magnified by the fact that there seems to be no reliable method of predicting when important variations may be expected. While the largest differences in this ratio tend to be found in instances where there has been a sizable change in the volume of reported inventories, this is not always the case, nor do all sizable changes in reported inventory have a marked effect on the ratio.

Conclusions. Extreme differences in ratios resulting from differing asset valuation methods would not be detrimental to comparative financial analysis if some means could be found either to accurately predict the magnitude of such differences or to adjust for them. If this were possible, the ratios for companies using different valuation methods could be reduced to some common basis, and the comparative value would not be impaired. Unfortunately for the financial analyst, no reliable method of adjustment has been found.

There is some indication that the percentage of inventory on LIFO valuation may bear a positive relationship to the extent of the variation found in the ratios. However, this factor was found not to bear a sufficiently positive relationship to the extent of the differences found in the ratios to be used as a reliable means of adjustment.

The exact influence of LIFO inventory valuation on financial ratios can be discerned only if one has information regarding the difference between the inventory valuation under LIFO and what it would have been under some other method. The average financial analyst does not have this information and, in nearly all cases, will be unable to obtain it. Very few companies include this information in their annual reports and those which do not will normally refuse, for various reasons, to divulge it. It is, therefore, fortunate that the effect of LIFO inventories on ratios does prove to be a rather insignificant variation in most instances. In those instances where it is significant it is not consistent from year to year, which minimizes large differences when they do appear. However, because of the differences in the effect of LIFO on financial ratios which may be expected, not only in connection with each ratio but also between industrial groups for any one ratio, it is desirable that the analyst be aware of these possibilities.

When comparing ratios between companies using varying inventory valuation methods, the analyst needs to be continually aware that sizable differences in the ratios are a possibility. Comparisons over a period of several years will be preferable to comparing the results for only one year as this will permit the discounting of occasional sizable variances which may occur.

Reliability of comparisons of some ratios in some industrial areas may be rendered invalid by differing valuation methods. Only comparisons of ratios between companies not using the LIFO method are unaffected. Since the effects of LIFO are not uniform between companies, even those in the same industry, a comparison between two companies utilizing this method may be no more reliable than would comparisons between a company using the LIFO method and another employing FIFO or current cost.

AN EXAMINATION OF THE WORKING CAPITAL RATIO

F. K. Wright

AN EXAMINATION OF THE WORKING CAPITAL RATIO

F. K. Wright

THE working capital ratio has been described as "one of the most important, if not *the* most important, structural balance sheet relationships."[1] Yet the interpretation of this ratio seems to be attended by confusion and uncertainty. It will be the object of this paper to discover the reasons for this.

Definitions[2]

Working capital is generally defined as the excess of current assets over current liabilities; the working capital ratio is defined as the ratio of current assets to current liabilities.

Current assets are taken to include cash, bank balances, temporary investments in readily marketable securities which can be converted into cash without impairing the business, book debts, stocks, and prepayments of current operating expenses.

Current liabilities include bank overdrafts (unless secured and fixed for a term of more than one year), trade creditors, accrued liabilities for operating expenses, loans maturing within one year, provision for taxation and dividends payable.

Significance of working capital

Working capital may be regarded from two points of view. On the one hand, it is the amount of funds available to finance the day-to-day operations of the business. If this amount is not adequate, settlement of creditors' accounts will have to be delayed, resulting in loss of credit standing and of cash discounts; quantity discounts will be lost through inability to buy in economical lots; stock may have to be realised at cut prices to obtain cash quickly; and in extreme circumstances the business may even be forced into liquidation.

On the other hand, working capital is also the amount of funds provided by management, out of capital or long-term loans, for the day-to-day operation of the business. For a given sales volume, there is a limit to the amount of working capital which a business can profitably employ. When the business is settling its accounts promptly, carrying an adequate range of stock, and financing its customers within the usual terms of trade, any further increase in working capital will add very little to profits unless sales can be expanded. Thus an excess of working capital means unprofitable use of funds which would be better employed elsewhere.

The amount of working capital tends to be increased by additions to paid-up capital, long-term borrowing, retention of earnings, provision for depreciation, and sale of fixed assets. It tends to be decreased by repayment of capital or loans, losses, and investment in fixed assets.

In any financial period, there will be an increase or a decrease in working capital unless the factors just listed cancel out exactly. Good financial management seeks to adjust these factors to avoid idle cash balances on the one hand, and cash shortage on the other.

---

1. A. A. Fitzgerald, *Analysis and Interpretation of Financial and Operating Statements*, 1947, p. 73.
2. The definitions in this section have been taken from A. A. Fitzgerald, *op. cit.*, pp. 62-3, 71-2.

Significance of the working capital ratio

The concept of working capital as an amount of funds which should be adequate to the requirements of the business, seems a straightforward one. By contrast, the significance of the *ratio* of current assets to current liabilities is at first sight rather obscure. Why should balance sheet analysts emphasise the ratio, rather than the difference, between these two account groupings?

Briefly, the reason seems to be that the adequacy of the amount of working capital cannot be judged except in relation to the sales which it has to finance. Unable to relate working capital to sales value, which is rarely published, balance sheet analysts have done the next best thing and related the components of working capital to one another.

The problem then becomes how to assess the adequacy of the amount of working capital from the ratio. That is a matter of some difficulty since "a ratio which is satisfactory in one industry may be quite unsatisfactory in another."[3]

This paper will be largely concerned with the problem of the interpretation of the working capital ratio. A brief critical survey of current methods of interpretation will be followed by a theoretical analysis of the working capital ratio.

Critical survey of current interpretations of the working capital ratio

Comparison with an arbitrary standard

The working capital ratio has been regarded primarily as an index of financial strength and stability, not as a measure of efficient utilisation of funds. Balance sheet analysts have therefore been more concerned at the danger of too low a working capital ratio than at the danger of too high a ratio. At times, this concern has been expressed in the form of an arbitrary requirement that the ratio shall not fall below 2 : 1. This rule-of-thumb is open to criticism on several grounds.

First, it is one-sided. It states that a working capital ratio of less than 2 : 1 is too low, but it imposes no limit in the other direction.

Second, it completely disregards all the factors influencing the working capital requirements of a business. It makes no distinction between a business which sells for cash and one which sells on credit, or between a business with a high rate of stock turnover and one with a low rate.

Third, it disregards the fact that "many successful concerns of undoubted stability in Australia operate on a lower working capital ratio than 2 : 1, [while] many could not carry on without financial strain unless their working capital ratio was maintained at a much higher level."[4]

Comparison with a flexible standard

Mr. K. C. Keown, in his paper on "Working Capital and Its Importance in Company Finance",[5] introduces a variant of the two-to-one rule which overcomes some of the criticisms just made.

He recognises that working capital can be too high, as well as too low, and that some types of business may require a higher or a lower ratio than 2 : 1. He says, however: "Any departure from this standard [the two-to-one rule], either upward or downward, should be the subject of enquiry; if upward, the management should be able to show that the increased margin is necessary and is not a wasteful use of the proprietors' capital; if downward, it should be demonstrated that, because of the rate of turnover of debtors or stock, or both, or for some other reason, an undue risk is not being incurred."[6]

The implication seems to be that a working capital ratio of 2 : 1 or less can never be too high—which is a doubtful proposition—and that a work-

---

3. A. A. Fitzgerald, *op. cit.*, p. 76.
4. A. A. Fitzgerald, *op. cit.*, p. 77.
5. *The Australian Accountant*, March 1953, p. 106.
6. *The Australian Accountant*, March 1953, p. 111.

ing capital ratio of 2 : 1 or more can never be too low—which is almost certainly wrong.

Mr. Keown might feel that this implication was not intended by him; but if he did not mean this, there was no point in his referring to the two-to-one rule at all.

Comparison with multiple standards

Sir Alexander Fitzgerald (then Mr. A. A. Fitzgerald) wrote in 1947: "Before it can be said that a ratio of a certain size is or is not indicative of financial strength, there must be some standard by reference to which the ratio may be compared. Any standard used for such a purpose must be scientifically determined. Obviously a ratio which is satisfactory in one industry may be quite unsatisfactory in another."[3]

Up to the present, however, no scientifically determined standards of working capital ratio have been published in Australia.

The study of trend

This approach is summarised in Sir Alexander Fitzgerald's statement that "the chief use of the ratio is to disclose trends over a period of years. Development towards an unsatisfactory working capital position will be indicated by a falling trend in the ratio."[3]

Unfortunately, the significance of a trend cannot be definitely interpreted unless we know the state of the working capital at the beginning of the trend period. If the working capital position at the beginning of the period under study was just right, or on the weak side, a falling ratio would seem to indicate a deterioration in the position. If, on the other hand, the working capital was originally excessive, a falling ratio might indicate an improvement.

The trouble is that an upward or downward trend in the working capital ratio can be due to a variety of causes. A rising trend might indicate that bad buying, poor production planning, weak stock control, or lax collection methods have allowed depreciation funds and retained earnings to become absorbed in excessive stock or debtors; or it might mean that prompter settlement of accounts has enabled the business to take better discounts, cut selling prices and increase sales, with a proportionate increase in book debts.

Similarly, a falling trend might indicate a steady improvement in the rate of stock turnover, as a result of clearing excessive inventories, better planning of purchases and production, reduction in the stock range, or more effective selling, the funds thus released having been invested in fixed assets. On the other hand, a falling trend might reflect increasing reliance on the forbearance of creditors, or on bank finance.

It would seem, therefore, that there is a good deal of ambiguity in the interpretation of trends in working capital ratio.

Theoretical analysis of the working capital ratio

The difficulties in the interpretation of working capital ratio, discussed in the preceding section, suggest that this ratio is not as useful an index as is often claimed. There does seem to be something wrong with an index which may rise through strengthening of the financial position or through sheer bad management, and which may fall through shortage of funds or through improved efficiency.

In this section, an attempt will be made to analyse the working capital ratio into its logical components, in order to see whether a less ambiguous index can be constructed.

Definition of circulating capital

Of the dozen or so items which enter into the definition of working capital and the working capital ratio, three items share an important characteristic which distinguishes them from the remaining current assets and liabilities.

These three items are stock, book debts, and trade creditors. The important characteristic which they share is that *each is related to sales* by a ratio which is typical of the kind of trade in which the concern is engaged. For book debts and trade creditors, that ratio is called the terms of trade. For stock, in a trading concern, it is the rate of stock turnover; in manufacturing, the ratio between sales and total stocks is more complex, but still reasonably constant in the long run and typical of the kind of manufacture undertaken.

Because of the special characteristics of these items, it seems reasonable to give them a special name; accordingly, the following definitions are offered:

Circulating capital: The circulating capital of a trading business is the value of trading stock, plus trade debtors, less trade creditors. The circulating capital of a manufacturing concern is the value of stocks of material, work-in-process and finished goods, plus trade debtors, less trade creditors.

Circulating capital ratio: The circulating capital ratio is the ratio of the value of stocks (as just defined), plus trade debtors, to the value of trade creditors.

Circulating capital of a trading concern

In this sub-section, a mathematical formula for the circulating capital of a trading concern will be derived.[7]

A few assumptions will help to keep the algebra simple. Let us assume that the concern is trading steadily, with constant sales, constant purchases and constant stock levels. Let us further assume that all merchandise is bought on credit, while all operating expenses are paid out weekly.

Let the weekly purchases be £x;
let the average mark-up be $100m\%$ on purchase price, so that weekly sales are £$x(1+m)$;
let the stock be turned over t times per annum;
let the average number of weeks credit extended to customers be s; and

---

[7]. A formula for the circulating capital of a manufacturing concern has also been derived, but on account of its complexity, it will not be reproduced here.

let the average number of weeks credit granted by suppliers be p.
Then the value of trade debtors will be £$x(1+m)s$;
the value of trade creditors will be £xp;
and the value of stock at cost will be £$52x/t$.
The circulating capital will therefore be
$$C = x(1+m)s + 52x/t - xp \quad \text{Equation (1)}$$
and the circulating capital ratio will be
$$R = \frac{(1+m)s + 52/t}{p} \quad \text{Equation (2)}$$
(the x's having cancelled out).

The meaning of equation (2) will be seen more clearly, perhaps, if some typical figures are substituted for the algebraic symbols. Suppose that the debtors take, on average, 7 weeks' credit, while the concern takes only 6 weeks from its suppliers; suppose that the stock turns over 4 times a year, and that the mark-up is 25%. That is to say,
$$s = 7$$
$$p = 6$$
$$t = 4$$
$$m = 0.25$$

Substituting these values in equation (2), we have
$$R = \frac{(1+0.25).7 + 52/4}{6} = \frac{8.75 + 13}{6}$$
$$= 3.6$$

This concern would therefore have a circulating capital ratio of 3.6 : 1.

Role of liquid assets

It may seem strange that cash has been left out of the definition of circulating capital, since no business can function without it.

It is possible, however, to imagine conditions which would enable a trading business to dispense with a cash balance: Under absolutely steady trading, the proceeds of each week's collections would pay for the invoices and expenses due in that week, the remainder being drawn out by the proprietor on account of profits.

In practice, a cash balance, or an overdraft below the overdraft limit, is required for one or more of the following purposes:

(i) To absorb fluctuations in purchases or sales. The balance of available cash increases when receipts from sales are heavy relative to payments for purchases and declines when sales receipts are relatively light.

(ii) To make intermittent payments of expense or profit. Many such payments are made monthly or annually, and money must be available when they fall due.

(iii) To finance expansion in trading or in fixed assets.

(iv) Paradoxically, cash may also be needed to finance a contraction in trading, as sales often decline faster than purchases can be cut.

Examination of these four functions reveals that there is not a very close connexion between the amount of cash required by a business and the current level of trading. Moreover, for the first two purposes an overdraft limit is just as good as ready cash. Hence the bank balances of quite similar businesses may bear no resemblance to each other.

Where there are temporary investments in readily marketable securities, these are probably held for the third purpose. Hence, there is even less connexion between sales and the value of temporary investments than there is between sales and the state of the bank account.

For these reasons, it seems preferable to leave liquid assets and overdrafts out of the definition of circulating capital.

Prepayments, accruals, and provisions for taxation and dividends

These components of working capital are, in effect, adjustments to the amount of liquid assets. For instance, a provision for dividends payable means that some of the available cash will be required shortly to pay a dividend. Accruals indicate the extent to which the cash balance represents a fund for making intermittent payments of expense, while prepayments indicate the extent to which that fund has been depleted by payments made in advance.

The reasons given for exclusion of liquid assets from circulating capital therefore apply to these items also.

(Loans maturing within a year may be placed in the same category as provisions for taxation and for dividends.)

Relationship between working capital and circulating capital

The working capital of a concern can be regarded as composed of two factors: the circulating capital of the concern, and the remainder of the current assets and liabilities.

The difference between working capital and circulating capital depends mainly on the overall financial policy of the concern. If the policy is to carry a substantial cash balance, or if the assets include "investments in readily marketable securities which can be converted into cash without impairing the business," the working capital will be larger than the circulating capital. If the concern relies to a large extent on bank finance—i.e., if it normally operates on an overdraft—the working capital will be smaller than the circulating capital. An intermediate position would be occupied by a concern which averaged a nil balance at the bank (sometimes in credit, sometimes in debit), or one which carried on its balance sheet both marketable securities and an overdraft.

Temporary cash balances may also affect the relationship between working capital and circulating capital. For instance, a company which has just made a call will show a big increase in its working capital until the call moneys are spent; similarly, a concern which is accumulating funds to pay for new plant on order will show a temporary increase in working capital. Circulating capital should remain unaffected in both cases. (Theoretically, these funds should perhaps be left out of working capital also, as they are held for non-current purposes. This fact may however not be evident from the balance sheet.)

Interpretation of the circulating capital ratio

Circulating capital ratio and the efficient employment of funds

The circulating capital ratio of a business may be compared with:
(i) a theoretical standard, computed

from the equation given above, or some variant thereof;

(ii) the circulating capital ratios of other businesses in the same trade or industry;

(iii) the circulating capital ratios of the same business in former years.

From these comparisons, an impression may be gained that the ratio is on the high side, on the low side, or about right.

Now, this ratio should be regarded primarily as an index of the efficient employment of working funds by the management of the business. If stock is slow-moving or dead, or if collection procedures are lax, the ratio will tend to be high. If stocks are turned over frequently, if credit control is tight, if favourable terms of payment have been negotiated with suppliers, the ratio will tend to be low.

At first sight, therefore, it appears that a low circulating capital ratio is a healthy sign, a high ratio an unhealthy one. While the latter conclusion is generally true, the former conclusion needs to be qualified. For a low circulating capital ratio will also result from non-payment of creditors' accounts when they fall due.

If we know the sales figures and the approximate terms of trade, this ambiguity can be easily resolved. If we do not, we can only say that a low circulating capital ratio is a good sign *provided that there is no evidence of financial stringency.*

Circulating capital ratio and financial stability

We have just seen that financial weakness may come to be reflected in the circulating capital ratio when non-payment of accounts inflates the value of trade creditors. But can the circulating capital ratio be regarded as an index of financial stability in a broader sense? For instance, does the size of the margin of circulating assets over trade creditors have any influence on the financial stability of the concern?

Let us consider a trading business which normally operates on a small cash balance, adequate for its day-to-day needs. If for some reason a shortage of cash arose, would the margin of circulating assets over trade creditors be of any assistance?

To answer this question, we must make some assumptions about the manner in which the cash shortage came about.

It could be brought about, for instance, by a sudden drop in sales, whilst purchases previously ordered continue to arrive. In these circumstances, the whole trade is likely to be in the same boat, and stocks may be quite unsalable. Book debts may fall at first, but stock will rise at the same rate, so that there is no reduction in the total of circulating assets. Later, book debts may rise again as the firm is forced to extend longer credit in order to make any sales at all.

The firm's only hope, in these circumstances, seems to be an overdraft or a loan; in trying to arrange this, the extent to which the fixed assets, particularly land and buildings, are already mortgaged may be more important than the excess of current assets over current liabilities.

Again, financial strain could arise through a general tightening of credit, which would make it difficult to collect promptly the accounts of customers whose overdrafts had been cut. In these circumstances, it would be extremely difficult to turn either stock or book debts into cash, except at a heavy loss.

It appears, from a consideration of these two cases, that circulating assets may not be of very much assistance in a financial emergency. Conversely, trade liabilities, unless they were overdue before the emergency began, do not present any danger, as they cannot be called up for payment. In other words, circulating capital might well be disregarded in an assessment of the financial strength of a business.

Interpretation of the working capital ratio

If the excess of stock and book debts over trade creditors does not make any appreciable contribution to financial stability, what becomes of the working capital ratio as an index of financial strength? It would seem that, in assessing the financial strength of an undertaking, the circulating capital should be deducted from working capital before attempting an interpretation.

If this point were conceded, we would be left with liquid assets, less overdraft, accruals and non-trading current liabilities, as the measure of financial strength. This virtually amounts to saying that a business with a large bank balance or marketable securities is financially stronger than one with an overdraft and no liquid assets.

In other words, there would be no need to compute a working capital ratio at all.

But is it true that a business with a bank balance is necessarily stronger financially than one with an overdraft? After all, many of our most successful companies rely heavily on bank finance, while some of the less successful ones might not be able to get an overdraft if they tried. It has already been suggested that a good deal depends on the value of the freehold, the extent to which it is encumbered, and the extent to which non-equity financing has been employed—none of which are reflected in the working capital figures.

It would appear, therefore, that the interpretation of the working capital ratio is so ambiguous as to be almost worthless. An increase in the working capital ratio may indicate overstocking, poor credit control, loss of sales, or repayment of overdrafts; a decrease may reflect better stock and credit management, greater use of bank finance, or overtrading and non-payment of creditors.

If anything is worth salvaging, it is probably the circulating capital ratio— the ratio of stock plus book debts to trade creditors. This ratio, while not free from ambiguity, may be capable of being checked against a scientifically determined standard, and it may prove possible to make useful comparisons of the circulating capital ratios of different firms in the same industry.

FUTURE THRUSTS:
NEW RATIOS AND SYSTEMATIC MODELS

APPRAISING THE DEFENSIVE POSITION OF A FIRM

G[eorge] H. Sorter and George Benston

APPRAISING THE DEFENSIVE POSITION OF A FIRM: THE INTERVAL MEASURE*

G. H. Sorter
Assistant Professor, University of Chicago

AND

George Benston
Assistant Professor, Georgia State College of Business

THE measurement of a firm's short run[1] ability to pay its debts as they come due is a very important aspect of financial analysis. A quantitative, formula type of measurement is required for such purposes as bond indentures, bank loans, and comparative analysis of firms, although a subjective analysis of a firm's capacity to withstand temporary delays or declines in receipts may perhaps be more appropriate. At present, the current ratio is generally used for this purpose. But is it adequate for the task? Is it reasonable to insist that a firm maintain (or have, on a certain date) a specified ratio of current assets to current liabilities? If the current ratio is a valid measure, current assets should provide a good indication of short run financial strength; current liabilities should measure the extent of the firm's requirements for current assets, and the resulting ratio of 2:1, 3:1, etc. should have operational meaning. None of these requirements is met by the ratio, as the analysis, below, will demonstrate.

The "interval measure" is proposed as an alternative to the current ratio. It measures the defensive interval (the number of day's expenditures on hand) by relating a firm's present ability to pay its debts to the debts it will have to pay in the short run. This relationship is expressed by the formula:

The necessity of this relationship is inherent in the purpose for which a firm hold defensive assets. These assets are held as a buffer against the uncertain future flow of funds.[2] There will probably be times when receipts do not come in as quickly as expected or when sales decline temporarily. Conversely, the firm might be faced with a sudden increase in expenditures caused perhaps, by an increase in production in response to an order which must be filled immediately or by the opportunity to make an especially advantageous purchase.

The firm's holdings of defensive assets will enable it to meet its requirements for funds without decreasing normal production or incurring additional liabilities.

Defensive Assets

Cash is the most obvious defensive asset. Apart from considerations of changes in

---

* A preliminary version of this paper was read at the *Ford Foundation Seminar*, "New Developments in Business Education" conducted by the University of Chicago at Williamstown, Massachusetts, August 1959. The authors acknowledge the help of their colleagues Sidney Davidson, David Green, Jr., Charles T. Horngren, Samuel Laimon, William Paton, and Ezra Solomon.

[1] The short run is taken to be the longer of a year or the accounting cycle, in conformity with general practice.

[2] This relationship has long been noted by economists. For example, see J. M. Keynes, *The General Theory of Employment, Interest and Money*, New York (1936), chapter 15.

$$\text{I.} \quad \frac{\text{defensive assets (assets available for the payment of debts)}}{\text{projected expenditures (present and future expenditures)}} \times 365 \text{ days}$$

the price level, a firm holds cash, an apparently non-earning asset, in order to avoid suffering the costs of being unprotected from the uncertainties of fund flows. Some cash is held, aside from its value as a defensive asset, for the normal transactions of a firm. However, the entire cash balance is considered a defensive asset since the amount held because of expected variations in fund flows cannot be effectively separated from the asset amount held for defensive purposes. Adjustments, then, will have to be made for firms which experience a greater expected variation in net receipts if they are to be compared with firms whose expected cash flows are very stable.

Current receivables like cash are also defensive assets. Receivables serve as a substitute for cash, although the amount held at any time is a function of sales and sales policy. If a rational allowance for uncollectibility has been set up, the net amount of receivables should be a good approximation of the future debt paying capacity of these assets. It is, of course, true that these assets are not immediately available to meet disbursements, at least not at the balance sheet amount but then, neither do current liabilities require immediate disbursement.

Similarly, marketable securities are defensive assets. Conversion to cash is usually easily accomplished, although this requires voluntary action by a second party (purchase). There is rarely a problem in evaluation if the securities are short term governments, since the face value of the bonds is, generally, very close to their market or cash conversion value. Other investments present more of a problem, especially if they are stated in the balance sheet at cost rather than at market value. However, many balance sheets disclose the market value of securities in a footnote, or this information can be obtained directly from the firm.

Prepaid expenses (more correctly titled "costs applicable to the following period") and inventories usually are not defensive assets. Prepaid expenses generally will not be converted into cash, except in the sense that the services which they represent are required for the production of revenue. Sales must be made before inventory is converted into funds available for the payment of debts. Since the sum of defensive assets is important in the event of a delay or decline in sales receipts, it is clearly incorrect to include inventories in this group. Their realization depends upon the continuation of sales. However, a firm's holdings of these assets is important to the extent that the firm can reduce its future expenditures. This point will be discussed further in the next section. The amount of current liabilities must also be considered in relation to the availability of defensive assets. If it is assumed that the firm will be able to continue to obtain normal short-term credit as it carries on operations then the average current liabilities at this level of operations will continually be renewed and will not require a disbursement of defensive assets. The actual current liabilities at any given date may of course differ from the normal or average level and in that case an adjustment of defensive assets is indicated as follows:[3]

1) Defensive assets on hand less
2) Actual liabilities plus
3) Average liabilities

and the *adjusted interval measure* reads as given in expression II on the next page.

If it is impossible or impractical to compute the average amount of liabilities, the *unadjusted interval measure* given in expression III on the next page may be used.

The two measures will be equal when-

---

[3] Research is being conducted in order to determine the feasibility and advantages of using data averaged from monthly or quarterly published reports.

$$\text{II.} \quad \frac{\text{defensive assets} - \text{actual liabilities} + \text{average liabilities}}{\text{projected expenditures}} \times 365 \text{ days}$$

$$\text{III.} \quad \frac{\text{defensive assets}}{\text{projected expenditures}} \times 365 \text{ days} = \text{unadjusted interval}$$

$$\text{IV.} \quad \frac{\text{defensive assets} - \text{actual liabilities}}{\text{projected expenditures}} \times 365 \text{ days} = \text{no credit interval}$$

ever actual current liabilities are the same as average current liabilities. It can also be assumed, alternatively, that the firm will no longer be able to obtain short term credit; this condition can be examined by the *no credit interval measure* which is defined as given in expression IV above.

Estimate of Projected Expenditures—The Future Outflow of Funds

The defensive assets of a firm, then, usually include cash, net receivables, and marketable securities. Simply computing the total defensive assets, however, is obviously not enough; they must also be related to the use for which they are required. This involves a determination of the amount of present and future obligations which will have to be met with the defensive assets, should the inflow of funds be delayed or reduced.

The firm's cash budget for the coming year would provide the best estimate of future fund flows, if it were available. However, this information cannot usually be obtained by outsiders, and many times it is not available even to the firm itself. The estimate will, therefore, have to be based on the less reliable estimate of future expenditures made by projecting past data.

The estimate of a firm's expenditures for the next year is based on the assumption that, despite a reduction in receipts, a firm will continue its operations as in the past. This is a reasonable assumption, since a firm's short term paying ability, rather than its ability to withstand a long term cyclical decline in revenues, is being measured. (The interval measure can also be used for this situation, as will be discussed below.) The basic source of data, therefore, will be the firm's revenue and expense statement.

Expenses, as given in the statement, must be adjusted to determine projected expenditures, since expenses and expenditures are not the same. Four types of adjustments have to be made. First, depreciation, bond discount, and other allocations of non-current assets must be subtracted because these expenses do not require the expenditure of funds. Second, expenses are reduced by the amount of prepaid expenses and raw materials inventory that the firm has on hand; these assets save the firm from expending funds to purchase them, for it can "live off" its inventories of raw materials, supplies, etc., while maintaining present production. If it is felt that the maintenance of certain levels of raw material and prepayment inventories is an essential part of normal operations, these amounts should not be deducted from projected expenses. Work-in-process and finished goods inventory cannot be similarly deducted because a reduction in these assets is not consistent with the assumption of continued production. The third adjustment concerns changes in operations, expenditure pattern, tax rates, etc. from the previous year about which special information is available. The fourth adjustment accounts for a reduction of income taxes resulting from the reduction in sales, and, hence, a reduction in taxable profits.

It will be noted that an adjustment for changes in year end inventory was not made, in other words the amount of expenses not expenditures was used. This omission is consistent with a projection of future expenditures based on the assumption that the same quantity of goods will be available for sale in the year to come as in the previous year. Fewer goods will be produced if the firm spends less than the same amount as its previous year's expenses, assuming that there was no change in its production function. For example, a firm might have a beginning inventory of $10,000, expenditures of $90,000 and an ending inventory of $15,000 in 1958. Expenses, then, were $85,000. If the firm plans to sell the same quantity in 1959 as in 1958, its expenditures in 1959 will be the same as its expenses in 1958, unless it builds up or reduces 1959 ending inventory from the $15,000 amount with which it began this year. However, a change in ending inventory violates the assumption of unchanged operations. Expenditures in 1959, then, must be the same as expenses (less depreciation, etc.) in 1958.

The estimate of future expenditures, the projected expenditures of a firm, can be summarized as follows:

Expenses given in the revenue and expense statements less:

1. depreciation, bond discount, and other allocations of non-current assets,
2. prepaid expenses and raw materials inventory,
3. changes about which special information is available,
4. reduction in income taxes

equals: projected expenditures

The Interval Measure

The interval measure,

$$\frac{\text{defensive assets (adjusted)}}{\text{projected expenditures}} \times 365 \text{ days},$$

shows the number of days that normal, i.e. last year's, operations can be continued despite a complete cessation of revenues without having to resort to additional financing.[4] This concept may be attacked as being unrealistic since a complete cessation of revenue is unlikely, as is the assumption that the firm either would not or could not reduce expenditures. A complete cessation of revenue however is used as a base measure; other interval measures, employing different assumptions, are discussed later. Furthermore in seasonal business it may well be desirable to equalize production despite little or no revenue. While companies would of course attempt to reduce expenditures in response to decreased revenue they cannot do so instantaneously and the interval measure proposed would measure the duration of this lag that the company can support without increased financing. Knowing the debt paying interval of a firm is not enough, however; the adequacy of the interval for a *specific* firm must be determined. As was mentioned above, a firm requires defensive assets for *expected variations*. The extent of the expected variations could be estimated from an examination of the firm's monthly statements, from general knowledge of the fund flow pattern of the firm's industry, or from other sources.[5] The number of days expenses required, as determined, should be deducted from the debt paying interval. The balance must then be evaluated against the unexpected fund flow variations faced by the firm.

[4] This is true only if expenditures are assumed to flow evenly. Further investigation of interim reports might provide sufficient information to adjust the measure for actual and uneven patterns of cost incurrence.

[5] See James E. Walter, "Liquidity and Corporate Spending," *The Journal of Finance*, Volume VIII, No. 4 (Dec. 1953), pp. 369–387.

Comparison with the Current Ratio

At the beginning of the paper it was stated that the current ratio is not an effective measure of the debt paying ability of a firm. This criticism can be made more explicit now that the operational meaning of "debt paying ability" has been analyzed. In the first place, current assets are not the same as defensive assets, since they include prepaid expenses and inventories. Hence, they do not measure the assets that a firm has on hand to pay its debts. Even if current assets were the same as defensive assets, a firm's current liability position on the balance sheet date would have to measure correctly its need for these assets, if the ratio is to be a valid standard. This relationship will be seriously affected if the amount of current liabilities on the balance sheet date is atypical of the average amount of current liabilities. This is well recognized and leads to the possibility of "window dressing." "Window dressing" is the distortion of the amount of current liabilities at balance sheet date due to the purposeful timing of exchanges of assets and liabilities. Suppose that a firm has current assets (in the form of cash) of $75,000 and accounts payable of $50,000 with no other current liabilities and, therefore, a current and quick ratio of 1.5:1. If the firm pays $25,000 of its payables it will now have cash of $50,000 and accounts payable of $25,000 with a current and quick ratio of 2.1.[6] Yet, it is generally felt that no real change in the debt paying ability of the firm has taken place.

However, the concern about willful "window dressing" has been over emphasized; more important is accidental "window dressing." This will occur any time that, through chance variations of timing, the amount of liabilities at balance sheet date is atypical. If the firm reports on the basis of the natural business year, it is probably true that the liabilities shown will, in fact, be atypical. All the following events will decrease the current ratio (if it originally is in excess of 1:1 for cases 1, 2 and 3, and greater than 1.9:1 (actually 100:52) for case (4)) if they happen to occur the day before rather than the day after closing:

(1) The purchase of inventory on credit.
(2) The borrowing of short term money.
(3) The receipt of deferred income.
(4) The sale of inventory at a profit. Although current assets would increase by an amount equal to the gross profit, current liabilities in the form of taxes payable would increase by 52%, assuming an incremental tax rate of 52% and an original ratio equal to or greater than 1.9:1 (100:52).

On the other hand, the following transactions would increase the current ratio (assuming an initial ratio in excess of 1:1 for cases 1, 2, and 3 and greater than 1.9:1 (100:52) in case (4)), if they happened to occur the day before rather than the day after the balance sheet date:

(1) The payment of the weekly payroll.
(2) The repayment of short term loans.
(3) The earning of "deferred income."
(4) The sale of inventory at a loss, assuming the existence of taxes payable equal to 52% of the loss and an original ratio greater than 1.9:1 (100:52).

The timing, by design or by chance, of these events would change the current ratio without changing the debt paying ability of the firm. The adjusted interval measure, on the other hand, is not subject to these chance variations. Suppose, for example, that on the balance sheet date a firm has quick assets of $18,000, current liabilities of $9,000, which are the same as average liabilities, and its projected expenditures are computed to be $365,000. The quick ratio then is

$$2:1 \left(\frac{18,000}{4,000} \right)$$

---
[6] Had the original ratio been less than 1:1, then the ratio would have declined rather than increased.

and the debt paying interval

$$\frac{18{,}000-9{,}000+9{,}000}{365{,}000}\times 365 = 18 \text{ days}$$

How are the measures affected if the firm pays payables of $3,000 just before its balance sheet date? The quick ratio is now

$$2.5:1 \left(\frac{15{,}000}{6{,}000}\right)$$

an increase of 25%. The interval measure is unchanged however

$$\frac{15{,}000-6{,}000+9{,}000}{365{,}000}+365 = 18 \text{ days}$$

Using the unadjusted interval because the average amount of liabilities is unknown, there will be some change but the change will be smaller than and opposite to the corresponding change in the quick ratio. The unadjusted interval will be *18 days*

$$\left(\frac{18{,}000}{365{,}000}\times 365\right)$$

before the repayment and *15 days*

$$\left(\frac{15{,}000}{365{,}000}\times 365\right)$$

after repayment. Thus the unadjusted interval has *decreased* by 1/6th while the quick ratio has *increased* by ¼th. A greater reduction of current assets and liabilities would emphasize this point even more. In general, most of the events over which the firm has complete control will decrease the unadjusted interval measure but increase the current or quick ratio. Management thus could worsen its unadjusted interval but would be hard put to better it. It bears repeating at this point that the *adjusted interval* is immune from any window dressing.

The assumption that the need for defensive assets is correctly measured by a multiple of current liabilities must still be examined even if the "window dressing" problem could be corrected by using average rather than balance sheet figures. For the above assumption to be valid, projected expenditures must be a function of current liabilities, because a firm's holdings of defensive assets has meaning only when they are measured against its requirements for these assets. A brief analysis of the factors which determine the amount of current liabilities will demonstrate that this functional relationship does not necessarily exist.

The amount of these liabilities is determined not only by the amount of expenses incurred, but also by the firm's pattern of discharging its liabilities. This may best be illustrated by an example. Assume two identical companies, except that Company "A" pays its employees weekly whereas Company "B"'s employees are paid every four weeks. If it is assumed that, for both companies, the annual wage cost is $52,000 then Company A's average wages payable are $500 (½ week) while Company B's average wages payable are $2,000 (2 weeks). In order to have the same current or quick ratio Company B would have to hold four times the defensive assets of Company A. This requirement is unrealistic. It can be asserted that if the two firms had the *same* defensive assets they would have equal defensive strength given that each firm can continue to obtain existing credit terms from their employees. At the extreme, if Company B's defensive assets exceed Company A's assets by the difference in their liabilities, B's defensive strength is at least equal to A's. In our example if B had $1,500 more defensive assets than A, it could reduce its outstanding liabilities to A's level (by reducing its assets by $1,500), after which transaction both companies would have equal assets, equal liabilities and equal expenditures. It may then be argued that after such a transaction Company B would have a stronger defensive position than Company A, because B's employees are willing to grant the company more liberal credit terms. And in fact the adjusted interval of B would then be larger than A's adjusted interval. The no credit interval (see expression IV, page 635) would have been the same for the two companies if B originally had $1,500 more defensive assets than A. While the other intervals (see expressions II and III, page 635) would have been equal for the two companies if B had held the same assets as A. This example could be carried to an unnatural extreme if it is assumed that company A pays its employees daily. It would then have an infinite quick ratio and, presumably, an infinite debt paying ability as long as it has at least one dollar in quick assets.

The operational meaning of differences in current ratios must still be determined, even if current liabilities are strict functions of expenditures (i.e., all companies always have the same disbursement pattern for all expenditures) and further, if the liabilities at the balance sheet date are always equal to average liabilities. What is the difference between a ratio of 3:1 and one of 2.8:1 or, for that matter, between 3:1 and 5:1? Proponents of the ratio method have suggested that industry averages be used as a yardstick for determining the adequacy of a particular firm's ratio. However, critics of the current ratio have correctly pointed out that an industry average ratio of, say, 2:1 does not necessarily indicate that 2:1 is "good" for any member of the industry. An average of all firms in an industry is just an average, not a yardstick for appraisal. Stating the required defensive position of a firm as a multiple of current liabilities has little relationship to measuring the needs of a particular firm.

Additional Uses for the Interval Measures

The concept of the interval measure can be expanded to appraise the ability of a firm to sustain itself under a variety of conditions. For example, one might wish to determine the interval for which a firm can operate without receipts either from additional sales or from the collection of presently outstanding receivables. Accounts receivable can then be excluded from the firm's stock of defensive assets to appraise this situation. The "cash interval," as it may be titled, is computed as:

$$\text{V.} \quad \frac{\text{cash and marketable securities}}{\text{projected expenditures}} \times 365 \text{ days}$$

One might want to compute the interval during which the firm can continue its normal operations should sales decline less than 100%. The "reduced sales interval" is determined by:

$$\text{VI.} \quad \frac{\text{defensive assets}}{\text{projected expenditures less anticipated receipts}} \times 365 \text{ days}$$

Of great interest, also, is the financial ability of a firm to weather a depression or recession. The firm could, in this situation, probably reduce its operations in response to decreased revenue, but probably could not borrow or otherwise raise outside funds. Its collections would, no doubt, also be delayed. To calculate the "reduced operations interval," predictions about the cost behavior of the firm at different levels of operations would have to be made.[7]

Assuming that these predictions could be made, the "reduced operations interval" is measured by:

---

[7] Research is now being conducted to determine whether valid predictions as to cost behavior can be made on the basis of published reports. The possibility of developing more useful information from more frequent reports or from a firm's own records is also being investigated.

$$\text{VII.} \quad \frac{\text{defensive assets}}{\text{projected expenditures less savings on expenditures because of reduced operations}} \times 365 \text{ days}$$

Conclusion

The interval measure is proposed as a method of appraising the debt paying ability of a firm. In measuring the defensive position of a firm against its projected expenditures, it focuses attention directly upon the relationship between liquidity and the need for liquidity. Although more research on such areas as the flow of receipts and expenditures, cost behavior, and average measures for industries clearly remains to be done, it is hoped that this presentation is a first step in replacing the current inadequate measure of the defensive position of a firm with an inherently more rational and useful measure.

ACCOUNTING RATIOS

What ratios between items in the accounts can be usefully compared from one concern to another? Or from one concern to a group of others? How should the ratios be arrived at? A study group answers these questions.

Accounting Ratios

AT THE INSTANCE of the British Institute of Management,* a group was formed in January, 1955, to study the use of accounting ratios for the purpose of making inter-firm comparisons. The object was to identify ratios that would help the managements of small and medium-sized firms:
 (a) to test their relative "efficiency" (in a broad sense);
 (b) to make policy decisions for the future.
The members of the group were:
Chairman: Professor F. Sewell Bray.
 (1) *Industrial Accountants*
  Mr. K. Adams,
  Mr. E. H. Davison,
  Mr. C. E. Sutton.
 (2) *Practising Accountant*
  Mr. T. Kenny.
 (3) *Applied Economists*
  Dr. T. Barna,
  Mr. R. J. Brech,
  Mr. Leo T. Little,
  Mr. A. R. Smith.
 (4) *From the British Institute of Management*
  Mr. H. Ingham,
  Mr. R. Warwick Dobson,
  Mr. L. Taylor Harrington.
In this report an attempt is made to set out the general principles governing the preparation and use of accounting ratios for inter-firm comparisons. As background to the examination of the subject, the group has had the benefit of consulting a paper prepared by the British Institute of Management on American Management Ratios and the opinions of a number of individuals and companies in this country.

GENERAL CONSIDERATIONS

An accounting ratio is an arithmetical expression of the relationship between two figures produced as a result of the normal accounting process. In view of the widely varying accounting practices in use, it is essential that, in comparing ratios, comparability of the figures and consistent definition of terms in any given trade should be established as a first step to any inter-firm comparisons.

*The British Institute of Management is carrying out a special study of methods of interfirm comparison. The study has been made possible by a grant from the Department of Scientific and Industrial Research from funds derived from United States economic aid.

Inter-firm Comparisons

As a general rule, it is only among firms† in the same industry that comparisons have any usefulness for management purposes, though an examination of ratios in different industries may illustrate (1) different methods of trading, or (2) different uses or sources of capital, or (3) different policies.

The primary purpose of inter-firm comparisons of accounting ratios, however, is to indicate to the managements of firms in the same industry significant variations between the internal accounting ratios of the firm and such ratios of other firms, or groups of firms, so that weaknesses in the financial structure or deficiencies in the profitability of the firm may be revealed. Comparisons made with such a purpose demand a higher degree of comparability than normally exists between large and small firms in the same industry; indeed completely valid comparisons can be made only between firms of similar size engaged in similar business and (particularly in large countries such as the United States) in similar localities.

In addition, therefore, to industrial grouping, consideration must be given to grouping of similar businesses within the industry, either by size of firm, or by locality, or by product groups, or by a combination of such factors.

Heterogeneous Activities

Many large firms, furthermore, consist of a number of units each engaged in a different industry. Opinions differ regarding the value of accounting ratios prepared from the aggregate figures of such firms. For inter-firm comparisons within a given industry, the total figures of such firms must be broken down so that separate figures of the firm's activities in that industry are available for comparison with those of other firms in the industry.

Presentation of Comparisons

Accounting ratios, even those produced for homogeneous groups of firms, expressed as a simple arithmetical average have serious limitations as a guide to management. They do no more than indicate an average performance, and in particular give no indication of the extent of the improvement to be achieved within the

†The word "firm" is used herein to denote any business unit, whatever its legal constitution.

firm. In addition to the average ratio there should therefore be indicated the ranges in each group.*

The extent of the elaboration of the presentation must depend on the importance attached to each aspect of the figures, but as a general rule it should be borne in mind that (particularly in the small and medium-sized business) interpretation of the ratios will often depend on individuals to whom simple figures are more likely to appeal and to prove useful.

Even in the presentation of simple ratios, however, much may be gained by presenting the figures in such a way that improvement in a position is consistently indicated by an increase in the ratio. This approach simplifies inter-firm comparisons, and also internal comparisons of ratios between one period and another. On the other hand, in some cases it is not certain in which direction "improvement" lies, and this is particularly so in considering ratios of capital employed. In the case, for instance, of the ratio of stock turnover, the average may well be the ideal, and departure from the average may indicate in the one direction that business is being lost through lack of stock, in the other direction that investment in stock is too high.

Consistency

Finally, in a general examination of the principles and purposes of accounting ratios, it must be borne in mind that they will indicate no more than the direction in which improvements within the business must be sought and a broad guide to the possible scale of improvement. Arithmetical precision is not to be expected nor is it necessary; consistency in presentation however must always be sought.

THE ESTABLISHMENT AND USE OF RATIOS
The Primary Ratio

That ratio which embraces all the investment and activities of a firm is "return on capital employed," indicating the efficiency, in the financial sense, of the use of capital. The preparation of this ratio necessitates the establishment of a consistent method of stating both capital employed and the return thereon.

Capital Employed

The statement of capital employed involves consideration of the relationship between money values at different points in time. A marked inflationary trend, for instance, will lead to the statement of assets in monetary terms which progressively become out of scale with the monetary terms in which current income and expenditure are represented. In the long run, even allowing for loss of efficiency and high repair bills, old assets will tend to be represented as producing a higher proportionate return than new, a result purely of their date of acquisition.

For management use, therefore, capital employed

---

*One commonly accepted method in a financial comparison is to show the arithmetic average, the median and the first and third quartiles, but other and simpler methods may be sufficient when the number of firms is small. In some cases it may be appropriate to calculate the mode.

should invariably be represented in current monetary terms; this will usually involve adjusting the value of fixed assets (and, if appropriate, the relevant depreciation provisions) into line with current replacement costs, for instance, by reference to current fire insurance valuations. To be strictly accurate, stock ought also to be valued in current terms, but in the short term differences in age of stock will not matter for the purpose of inter-firm comparisons.† Many firms carry on activities outside their main operations, such as investment in associated companies or other securities, housing, and retail outlets in the case of manufacturing companies. For all ratio comparisons, whether inter-firm or internal, such ancillary investments must be excluded from the capital employed, which should be restricted to the capital invested in operations. If the firm carries on more than one homogeneous business, a separate statement of capital employed should be prepared for each.

It should be understood that capital employed is here regarded in terms of a statement of net operating assets, i.e., gross assets, excluding intangible assets such as goodwill, *less* current liabilities, and this approach is necessary if further examination is to be made into the component parts of employed capital. If on the other hand comparisons are to be made indicating the rate of return to the suppliers of capital, regard must be paid to the sources of capital rather than to its employment. Sources of capital are, however, expressed either in terms of a fixed sum, not affected by monetary inflation, or by a figure of "equity" which is consequential upon the way in which assets are stated in the balance sheet. Such figure of "equity" is therefore not readily susceptible to adjustment for monetary instability without reference to any adjustment in asset values which may be necessary, and its use leads therefore to the calculation of ratios which may easily be difficult to understand, or at worst misleading unless carefully explained.

Components of Capital Employed

The essential figures in the statement of "capital employed" fall into three groups:
  (a) Fixed assets, excluding intangible assets.
  (b) Stocks, stores, and work-in-progress.
  (c) Other net current assets.

For practical purposes it will usually be found that the aggregate of fixed assets and stocks, stores, and work-in-progress can be treated as the capital employed in operations. In some industries, however, the employment of capital in other net current assets, particularly in debts, may be of importance and such assets should then be included in the comparison of capital employed. This method avoids the difficulty of defining the amount of working capital other than stocks, which is not readily ascertainable, and is frequently a matter of policy.

Current Replacement Cost

Furthermore, for purposes of comparison of operating

---

†It must be remembered that, if there is a material element of fixed assets in the valuation of stock, an adjustment must be made to the valuation of stock.

efficiency it may be found more useful to include fixed assets in "fixed capital employed in operations" at current replacement cost before deduction of provisions for depreciation.

There is a difference of opinion concerning the deduction of depreciation. On the one hand it is asserted that to deduct accumulated provisions is to prejudge the declining efficiency of fixed assets which it is the purpose of the ratios to disclose and measure, and provisions for depreciation are largely a matter of policy, in which uniformity is not to be expected: their deduction from the investment in fixed assets inevitably leads to lack of comparability in inter-firm comparisons and is a source of some misconceptions in comparisons within individual firms.

On the other hand it is felt by some that the logic of including fixed assets in operating capital employed at current cost as new is open to some doubt in those industries where an active secondhand market in used assets exists. The usefulness of approximate tests based on gross current costs where the fixed assets have long effective working lives can be seen. But the argument is perhaps not so convincing when the fixed assets have relatively short lives because of technological change.

In any event, whenever accounting ratios are published the definition and methods of valuation of fixed assets must be clearly stated.

Return on Capital

The return on capital is expressible in terms of "net profit" as usually understood for accounting purposes. As in the statement of capital employed, however, income and expenditure relating to activities ancillary to the main business must be excluded from the calculation of "operating profit," and the provision for depreciation must also be adjusted to the provision appropriate to current replacement cost.

It is for consideration whether both "profit before tax" and "profit after tax" be presented in relation to the return on capital employed by the firm, but in presenting a ratio confined to the operations of the company this may not be practicable, and the purpose of the ratio will be served by dealing only with "profit before tax."

Component Figures

The figures composing the "return on capital" therefore comprise the normal headings under which income and expenditure are recorded in the profit and loss account, and the extent of the analysis which may be necessary will depend on the type of business and the extent of the examination of the accounting ratios.

In a manufacturing business the general headings will be:

I. Income:
   (*a*) from sales.*
   (*b*) other income.

---

*The return on capital can also be looked at in terms of substituting for sales the value of output at selling prices.

II. Expenditure:
   (*a*) Materials consumed in sales.
   (*b*) Conversion cost of sales, adjusted for stocks and work-in-progress and analysed as necessary under such headings as wages (including salaries and remuneration of working proprietors), depreciation, repairs and maintenance, and administrative overheads.
   (*c*) Other expenses.

Use of the Primary Ratio

The value of the ratio of the total return on total capital employed is that it indicates the efficiency with which the latter is being used, i.e., a low return may indicate underemployment of capital, or alternatively it may indicate that capital is fully but (in the financial sense) inefficiently employed. To locate the cause of a low return the ratio must be broken down into its constituent elements of operating capital compared with operating profit, and of other capital compared with other income.

In inter-firm comparisons only "return on capital employed in operations" is of any significance, and from this point onwards "capital employed" is used in this sense, as defined on page 268 above. Should such a ratio for an industrial group indicate to the management of a firm that some internal improvement is possible, it is apparent that further help must be sought in explanatory ratios (or "Secondary Ratios"). These will be of three kinds:
   (*a*) Ratios between the constituent elements of capital employed and other balance sheet items;
   (*b*) Ratios between the constituent elements in the calculation of profit.
   (*c*) Ratios between the constituent elements in the calculation of capital employed and the constituent elements of profit.

These are referred to as "Financial Ratios," "Expense Ratios," and "Operating Ratios" respectively.

Secondary Ratios

Financial Ratios

Examination of financial ratios may be undertaken to indicate, by comparison with group ratios, possible faults in the structure of the business which may lead to unsatisfactory profitability or financial difficulty.

Some ratios are indicated below:

(*a*) *Fixed assets: stocks, stores, and work-in-progress*
A high ratio here could indicate either (i) efficient stock and stores management, or (ii) underemployment of fixed assets.

A separate statement of unused capacity would result in a clearer indication of which of these alternative explanations is appropriate. For comparability, all firms in one industry must measure capacity in the same way.

In any industry the efficiency of the use of capital employed depends heavily on a proper balance of the components of capital employed. It is probable that (in a normally efficient industry in periods of normal prosperity) the average ratio will indicate a proper balance in this case. Should an abnormal ratio in any part of the group be allied to an abnormally high "return on capital" ratio, however, this might indicate, e.g., that there is room for a general improvement in stock control in the industry as a whole.

(b) Capital employed: liquid assets
Liquid assets mean all immediate financial claims, such as bank and cash balances, and short-term marketable securities, e.g., tax reserve certificates. In assessing the cash resources of a business it will also be appropriate to include any unused overdraft facilities which may be available.

A low ratio would indicate under-employment of resources and a high ratio might indicate a lack of finance. In this case an indication of a low ratio is more positive, since a lack of finance is probably better indicated by other ratios. (See (c) below.)

(c) Current assets (excluding stocks, etc.): current liabilities
This indicates the adequacy (or otherwise) of the cash resources and money claims of the business. Again, in assessing the cash resources of the business it will be appropriate to include any unused overdraft facilities available. A downward trend coupled with a ratio of unity or less might indicate financial stringency, but may alternatively indicate current liabilities on long-credit terms compared with debtors on short-credit; the rate of money turnover will be important (liquid balances to total transactions).

(d) Fixed assets: accumulated provisions for depreciation
Fixed assets in this ratio mean gross fixed assets.

If any uniformity can be achieved within the industrial group, this ratio (in which both parts are expressed in terms of current costs) indicates the elapsed life of the fixed assets. This has special significance in relation to the return on operating capital employed, as an indication of the extent to which modernisation of plant can in practice improve the profit-earning capacity of the firm. To make the comparison as informative as possible, the firms within the industrial group should be grouped so as to show the highest, lowest and average returns on capital employed as compared with the ratios of fixed assets to accumulated depreciation provisions. If provisions for depreciation represent a high proportion of fixed asset values, a correspondingly high proportion of liquid resources to total capital employed should be revealed, otherwise further calls for money for asset replacement in the near future may be indicated.

Expense Ratios
The main purpose of the comparison of expense ratios is to reveal to the individual firm unsatisfactory relationships between income and the components of expense.

The choice of ratios will depend heavily on the type of business involved; in the case of a manufacturing business the number of possible comparisons would normally be greater than in a retail business, since in a manufacturing business the various components of costs of production are of major importance in the assessment of efficiency.

As examples the following three ratios are given:

(a) Sales income: the material component in cost of sales
A comparison of this kind may indicate the results of good or bad buying or the effective use of materials.

(b) Sales income: the conversion cost component of sales income
This, for a manufacturing business, is probably the most useful comparison as indicating the general efficiency of the production process. In an industry in which the raw material cost forms a high proportion of total cost, and especially if its price is subject to violent fluctuations, this ratio can, however, be misleading.

In current circumstances labour is often the limiting factor and an indication of the economical or wasteful use of labour is highly valuable to many businesses.

(c) Sales income: the overhead content of cost of sales
A comparison of this kind naturally presents many difficulties in the achievement of uniformity within an industry. The comparison, however, provides a valuable guide to the economy of administration.

OPERATING RATIOS
The preparation of ratios linking up the elements of capital with the various elements in the income from and expenditure on operations provides a wide and complex choice of ratios. Below are indicated a few of those which are regarded as being of most value in general use, though in certain industries certain aspects of each ratio may require special and separate treatment.

The main object is regarded as being the most efficient use of capital and the ratios that follow may reveal certain aspects of the primary ratio that lead to a purposeful investigation of special aspects of an individual business.

(a) Sales income: operating capital employed
This ratio obviously reveals the rate of turnover of the capital employed which, in most businesses, is one of the governing factors in profitability. It can be, however, no more than a broad indication of efficiency or inefficiency, after which, if there is cause for investigation, there must be an examination of ratios in sectors of the capital employed.

(b) (i) Sales income: fixed assets
  (ii) Sales income: stocks, stores, and work in progress
These comprise two fields for investigation in relation to unsatisfactory trends revealed in ratio (a) above. Both are susceptible to further analysis which may be necessary in considering the special aspects of individual industries. As already pointed out in the section devoted to financial ratios, careful consideration must be given to the way in which the investment in fixed assets must be expressed and similar considerations will in many cases apply to the statement of stocks, stores, and work in progress.

In many businesses of a seasonal character it will be necessary to average the investment in stocks, stores, and work in progress over the period of the sale income. This may be done broadly on an average of quarterly figures or more accurately on an average of monthly investment in stocks, stores, etc.

(c) Sales income: trade debtors
This is a comparatively simple and often-used ratio which indicates the general state of the credit allowed and the efficiency with which credit control is administered.

(d) Operating profit: net sales
This ratio indicates the profitability of sales. The ratio is not so significant for a business with a slow rate of turnover as for a business with a fast rate of turnover. It should be compared with the ratio of operating profit to capital employed, since a high figure of profit on sales may mask a low yield on capital employed.

If the ratio indicates the need for further analysis, it might be appropriate, where possible, to break down the total cost of production and selling into its constituent parts (adjusting each for the cost element of work-in-progress, as necessary) and to express each part as a percentage of the net sales figure.

(e) (i) *Conversion cost: stocks, stores, and work in progress*
(ii) *Conversion cost: work in progress*

If an indication of a slow rate of turnover of capital employed is given by an examination of ratio (*a*) above, an examination of either (i) or (i) and (ii) combined will narrow the field of inquiry. In a manufacturing business the rate of turnover of work in progress is usually of the highest importance.

CONCLUSION

The above suggestions provide no more than a general framework within which a system of financial ratios can be built up. It is not suggested that all the ratios will prove necessary or even informative in all cases. Careful selection must be made to ensure that the main aspects of each industry are revealed without duplication, and if this is done the use of ratios may provide a spur and a pointer to improved efficiency.

The collection of information for publication must necessarily be done by special arrangement within the industries or groups within the industries concerned. The published accounts of companies are clearly not sufficiently uniform, either in presentation or in the way in which assets are stated, to have more than a very limited value.

THE DEVELOPMENT OF
CONTEMPORARY ACCOUNTING THOUGHT

An Arno Press Collection

Baldwin, H[arry] G[len]. **Accounting for Value As Well as Original Cost** *and* Castenholz, William B. **A Solution to the Appreciation Problem.** 2 Vols. in 1. 1927/1931

Baxter, William. **Collected Papers on Accounting.** 1978

Brief, Richard P., Ed. **Selections from Encyclopaedia of Accounting, 1903.** 1978

Broaker, Frank and Richard M. Chapman. **The American Accountants' Manual.** 1897

Canning, John B. **The Economics of Accountancy.** 1929

Chatfield, Michael, Ed. **The English View of Accountant's Duties and Responsibilities.** 1978

Cole, William Morse. **The Fundamentals of Accounting.** 1921

Congress of Accountants. **Official Record of the Proceedings of the Congress of Accountants.** 1904

Cronhelm, F[rederick] W[illiam]. **Double Entry by Single.** 1818

Davidson, Sidney. **The Plant Accounting Regulations of the Federal Power Commission.** 1952

De Paula, F[rederic] R[udolf] M[ackley]. **Developments in Accounting.** 1948

Epstein, Marc Jay. **The Effect of Scientific Management on the Development of the Standard Cost System** (Doctoral Dissertation, University of Oregon, 1973). 1978

Esquerré, Paul-Joseph. **The Applied Theory of Accounts.** 1914

Fitzgerald, A[dolf] A[lexander]. **Current Accounting Trends.** 1952

Garner, S. Paul and Marilynn Hughes, Eds. **Readings on Accounting Development.** 1978

Haskins, Charles Waldo. **Business Education and Accountancy.** 1904

Hein, Leonard William. **The British Companies Acts and the Practice of Accountancy 1844-1962** (Doctoral Dissertation, University of California, Los Angeles, 1962). 1978

Hendriksen, Eldon S. **Capital Expenditures in the Steel Industry, 1900 to 1953** (Doctoral Dissertation, University of California, Berkeley, 1956). 1978

Holmes, William, Linda H. Kistler and Louis S. Corsini. **Three Centuries of Accounting in Massachusetts.** 1978

Horngren, Charles T. **Implications for Accountants of the Uses of Financial Statements by Security Analysts** (Doctoral Dissertation, University of Chicago, 1955). 1978

Horrigan, James O., Ed. **Financial Ratio Analysis—An Historical Perspective.** 1978

Jones, [Edward Thomas]. **Jones's English System of Book-keeping.** 1796

Lamden, Charles William. **The Securities and Exchange Commission** (Doctoral Dissertation, University of California, Berkeley, 1949). 1978

Langer, Russell Davis. **Accounting As A Variable in Mergers** (Doctoral Dissertation, University of California, Berkeley, 1976). 1978

Lewis, J. Slater. **The Commercial Organisation of Factories.** 1896

Littleton, A[nanias] C[harles] and B[asil] S. Yamey, Eds. **Studies in the History of Accounting.** 1956

Mair, John. **Book-keeping Moderniz'd.** 1793

Mann, Helen Scott. **Charles Ezra Sprague.** 1931

Marsh, C[hristopher] C[olumbus]. **The Theory and Practice of Bank Book-keeping.** 1856

Mitchell, William. **A New and Complete System of Book-keeping by an Improved Method of Double Entry.** 1796

Montgomery, Robert H. **Fifty Years of Accountancy.** 1939

Moonitz, Maurice. **The Entity Theory of Consolidated Statements.** 1951

Moonitz, Maurice, Ed. **Three Contributions to the Development of Accounting Thought.** 1978

Murray, David. **Chapters in the History of Bookkeeping, Accountancy & Commercial Arithmetic.** 1930

Nicholson, J[erome] Lee. **Cost Accounting.** 1913

Paton, William Andrew and Russell Alger Stevenson. **Principles of Accounting.** 1918

Pixley, Francis W[illiam]. **The Profession of a Chartered Accountant and Other Lectures.** 1897

Preinreich, Gabriel A. D. **The Nature of Dividends.** 1935

Previts, Gary John, Ed. **Early 20th Century Developments in American Accounting Thought.** 1978

Ronen, Joshua and George H. Sorter. **Relevant Financial Statements.** 1978

Shenkir, William G., Ed. **Carman G. Blough: His Professional Career and Accounting Thought.** 1978

Simpson, Kemper. **Economics for the Accountant.** 1921

Sneed, Florence R. **Parallelism in Two Disciplines.** (M.A. Thesis, University of Texas, Arlington, 1974). 1978

Sorter, George H. **The Boundaries of the Accounting Universe** (Doctoral Dissertation, University of Chicago, 1963). 1978

Storey, Reed K[arl]. **Matching Revenues with Costs** (Doctoral Dissertation, University of California, Berkeley, 1958). 1978

Sweeney, Henry W[hitcomb]. **Stabilized Accounting.** 1936

Van de Linde, Gérard. **Reminiscences.** 1917

Vatter, William J[oseph]. **The Fund Theory of Accounting and Its Implications for Financial Reports.** 1947

Walker, R. G. **Consolidated Statements.** 1978

Webster, Norman E., Comp. **The American Association of Public Accountants.** 1954

Wells, M. C., Ed. **American Engineers' Contributions to Cost Accounting.** 1978

Worthington, Beresford. **Professional Accountants.** 1895

Yamey, Basil S. **Essays on the History of Accounting.** 1978

Yamey, Basil S., Ed. **The Historical Development of Accounting.** 1978

Yang, J[u] M[ei]. **Goodwill and Other Intangibles.** 1927

Zeff, Stephen Addam. **A Critical Examination of the Orientation Postulate in Accounting, with Particular Attention to its Historical Development** (Doctoral Dissertation, University of Michigan, 1961). 1978

Zeff, Stephen A., Ed. **Selected Dickinson Lectures in Accounting.** 1978